D1565883

FINANCIALIZATION, NEW INVESTMENT FUNDS, AND LABOUR

Financialization, New Investment Funds, and Labour

An International Comparison

Edited by

HOWARD GOSPEL,

ANDREW PENDLETON,

and

SIGURT VITOLS

OXFORD

UNIVERSITY PRESS

OXFORD
UNIVERSITY PRESS

Great Clarendon Street, Oxford, OX2 6DP,
United Kingdom

Oxford University Press is a department of the University of Oxford.
It furthers the University's objective of excellence in research, scholarship,
and education by publishing worldwide. Oxford is a registered trade mark of
Oxford University Press in the UK and in certain other countries

First Edition published in 2014
Impression: 1

Published in the United States of America by Oxford University Press
198 Madison Avenue, New York, NY 10016, United States of America

British Library Cataloguing in Publication Data
Data available

Library of Congress Control Number: 2013955757

ISBN 978–0–19–965358–4

Printed and bound in Great Britain by
CPI Group (UK) Ltd, Croydon, CR0 4YY

Preface

The financing, ownership, and governance of firms have long been subjects of considerable interest, but in recent years debates on this topic have become more prominent in advanced industrial economies. This interest has been further accentuated by the impact of the global financial and economic crisis from 2007 onwards. Observers have drawn attention to the growing 'financialization' of advanced industrial economies, whereby the power of finance has become more prominent in many aspects of economic and social life. The recent crisis has highlighted and intensified concerns about the sustainability and desirability of this development. An important element of this debate has been the relationship between financiers, owners, and managers. Who has, and who should have, the greater influence in the management of production and service provision?

For the most part and in most countries, the role of labour has been less of a focus of interest. However, in recent years, with increasing financial pressures on firms and changes in labour relations and employment systems, there is a growing need to consider how finance, ownership, governance, and labour interact together, both theoretically and empirically, and to understand this interaction over time in a variety of countries.

Over the last quarter century, there have been substantial changes in the ownership of enterprises, with a shifting balance in most economies between the public and private sectors. Within the latter, there have been major shifts between family owners and institutional owners such as pension, insurance, and mutual or trust funds. A significant development has been the emergence of so-called 'new' or 'alternative' investment funds as a new type of institutional owner. These take the form of private equity funds, hedge funds, and sovereign wealth funds. The activities of these various types of funds have been the subject of considerable controversy in many countries. Private equity and hedge funds have been extensively criticized for transferring resources from companies, workforces, and taxpayers to fund managers and investors in these funds. For their part, sovereign wealth funds have raised concerns that assets will come under the *de facto* control of foreign governments who may have political as well as financial objectives.

Preface

This book focuses on these funds and their impact on labour. The contributors pose several questions. How significant have these funds become? To what extent have national frameworks regulating the activities of these funds changed? How have the activities of funds impacted on employment and the type of jobs in companies? Have these changes affected pay and conditions and the distribution of rewards within companies? How, if at all, have they affected the nature of work and skill systems? How have they fed through and affected industrial relations systems and employee voice arrangements within companies? It is not always easy to answer these questions as the linkages between fund activity and labour outcomes are often complex and indirect, and relevant data are often unavailable.

A key consideration is that there are many factors which combine to shape these changes in the labour area and their interaction with wider developments. In particular, national laws which regulate financial markets and labour markets are important variables shaping the extent and trajectory of change. In addition, national industrial relations institutions, embedded in labour law, trade unions, and other forms of employee representation, are likely to play a key part in shaping what happens to labour when these funds become involved in companies. It is likely that there will be considerable differences between countries in the impacts on labour because of these variations in institutions and regulation.

This book had its origins in research for the European Commission and for the European Foundation for the Improvement of Living and Working Conditions. This project was concerned with identifying the activities and impact of these funds in a spread of European countries to illuminate discussions during the passage of the EU Alternative Investment Fund Managers Directive. The book contains chapters on six European countries considered in these research projects: the United Kingdom, Germany, the Netherlands, Sweden, Italy, and Poland. This gives a good coverage of country types within Europe, as it includes countries which are seen to exemplify Anglo-Saxon, Rhenish, Nordic, Latin, and Central and Eastern European transition economies. To these the authors have added the USA and Australia as further examples of Anglo-Saxon systems and Japan as an example from an Asian coordinated market economy.

The chapters show that policies and regulation in three areas— the activities of the funds themselves, corporate practices, and labour and industrial relations—influence the overall level of activity by funds in the countries under review. Of these, labour market and industrial relations regulation is probably the least important in influencing the extent of fund activity but plays a critical role in shaping the character of fund interventions and the nature of labour outcomes. Resistance to changes by labour and social actors, especially employee voice institutions, can shape and nuance what happens to employees. There are, therefore, quite substantial differences in fund activity and labour effects in the countries reviewed in the book. The chapters consider the role of national norms and institutions and path dependencies in creating and sustaining these differences.

The activities of private equity and hedge funds attracted a great deal of public debate in the period before the onset of the financial and economic crisis. They seemed to exemplify one particular feature of financialization: the transfer of resources away from companies, employees, and taxpayers for the benefit of those already possessing considerable financial wealth and power. The onset of the crisis led to a reduction in fundraising and investment activity by many of these funds. But, in the last couple of years, there has been a substantial resumption of both. The questions posed in the European Foundation study are every bit as relevant now as they were in that earlier study. Some issues have become even more compelling. One area of concern is whether companies owned by funds are going to be hit by a 'wall of debt' built up in the peak years but only coming to maturity now. Another broader issue is the extent to which distinctive national patterns of economic activity and regulation can be sustained in a context of globalization and financialization.

For those interested in these questions, the book provides a most useful and stimulating review of the issues and evidence.

Donald Storrie
European Foundation for the Improvement
of Living and Working Conditions
Dublin
May 2013

Acknowledgements

This book grew out of two research projects, one for the European Commission and the other for the European Foundation for the Improvement of Living and Working Conditions. The authors are particularly appreciative of the support given by Donald Storrie of the latter organization. In connection with the earlier research we would also like to thank Mike Wright and Nick Bacon for valuable advice. The project was led by Peter Wilke, managing director of Wilke, Maack and Partner wmp consult in Hamburg, Germany, and to him we also owe a considerable debt.

This initial research was followed by two workshops at the Wissenschaftzentrum Berlin in 2011 and 2012, which enabled the authors to develop their material further. We would like to thank WZB for supporting these workshops. In addition, some of the chapters were presented as papers at the Labor and Employment Relations Association annual conference in Chicago in 2012 and the Society for the Advancement of Social Economics at the Massachusetts Institute of Technology in 2012. We would like to thank Eileen Appelbaum and Rosemary Batt in particular for organizing these events.

The authors of the chapters would like to thank their families and colleagues for their support and forbearance while the chapters were under preparation. All of us, but especially the editors, would like to thank Anne-Marie Kortas for her excellent help with the bibliography and preparation of the manuscript. Finally, we would like to acknowledge the support and encouragement of David Musson and Emma Booth of Oxford University Press.

Contents

Contents

List of Figures

List of Tables

Abbreviations

AA	Automobile Association
ABL	Aktiebolagslagen (Swedish Companies Act)
ABS	Australian Bureau of Statistics
ADI	authorized deposit-taking institution
ADIA	Abu Dhabi Investment Authority
AFSL	Australian Financial Services Licence
AFL	Aktiefondslagen (Equity Act)
AGM	Annual General Meeting
AIF	alternative investment fund
AIFI	Associazione Italiana del Private Equity e Venture Capital
ASIC	Australian Securities and Investment Commission
ASX	Australian Securities Exchange
ATC	Australian Trade Commission
AU$	Australian dollar
AUM	assets under management
AVCAL	Australian Private Equity and Venture Capital Association
BaFin	Bundesanstalt für Finanzdienstleistungsaufsicht
BLER	board level employee representation
BO	buy-out
BRIC	Brazil, Russia, India, and China
BVCA	British Private Equity & Venture Capital Association
BVK	Bundesverband Deutscher Kapitalbeteiligungsgesellschaften
CAR	cumulative abnormal return
CEIF	closed-end investment funds
CEE	Central and Eastern Europe
CEO	chief executive officer
CGIL	Confererazione Generale Italiana del Lavoro
CGT	capital gains tax
CFIUS	Committee on Foreign Investment in the US
CIC	China Investment Corporation
CISL	Confederazione Italiana Sindicati Lavoratori
CLERP	Corporate Law Economic Reform Programme
CMBOR	Centre for Management Buy-out Research
CME	coordinated market economy

COBAS	Confederazione dei Comitati di Base
DME	dependent market economy
EBITDA	earnings before interest, taxes, depreciation, and amortization
EBRD	European Bank for Reconstruction and Development
EFTA	European Free Trade Association
EC	European Commission
ES	early stage
ETUC	European Trade Union Confederation
EU	European Union
EVCA	European Private Equity and Venture Capital Association
FDI	foreign direct investment
FF	Future Fund
FII	Fondo Italiano di Investimento
FSA	Financial Service Authority
FSB	Finanicial Stability Board
FTSE	Financial Times Stock Exchange
FWA	Fair Work Act
GAO	Government Accountability Office
GDP	gross domestic product
GIC	Singapore Government Investment Corporation
GSM	General Shareholder Meeting
HCA	Hospital Corporation of America
HF	hedge fund
HR	human resource
HRM	human resource management
HVAC	heating, ventilation, and air conditioning
IFSL	International Financial Services London
ILO	International Labour Organization
IPO	initial public offering
IRCJ	Industrial Revitalization Corporation of Japan
IRR	internal rate of return
ITUC	International Trade Union Confederation
JASDAQ	Japanese Association of Securities Dealers Automated Quotation
KKR	Kohlberg, Kravis, and Roberts
LAS	Lagen om anställningsskydd (The Employment Protection Act)
LBO	leveraged buy-out
LIF	Lagen om investeringsfonder (Swedish Act on Investment Funds)

LME	liberal market economy
LO	Landsorganisationen i Sverige (Swedish Trade Union Confederation)
LTCB	Long-Term Credit Bank of Japan
M&A	mergers and acquisitions
MBI	management-buy-in
MBO	management-buy-out
MBL	Medbestämmandelagen (Employment Act)
NBN	National Broadband Network
NHP	Nursing Home Properties
NIF	new investment fund
OECD	Organisation for Economic Cooperation and Development
PE	private equity
PEP	private equity partners
PIPES	private investment in public equity
QIA	Qatar Investment Authority
R&D	research & development
RBA	Reserve Bank of Australia
RBS	Royal Bank of Scotland
REIT	real estate investment trust
ROA	return on assets
ROE	return on equity
SEC	Securities and Exchange Commission
SFSA	Swedish Financial Supervisory Authority
SGR	generalist' savings management companies
SIFA	Swedish Investment Fund Association
SME	small and medium-sized enterprises
SVCA	Swedish Private Equity & Venture Capital Association
SWF	sovereign wealth fund
TCI	The Children's Investment Fund
TUC	Trades Union Congress
TXU	Texas Utility Corporation
UGL	Unione Generale del Lavoro
UIL	Unione Italiana del Lavoro
US$	US-dollar
VC	venture capital
VoC	varieties of capitalism
VPFL	Lagen om värdepappersfonder (Swedish law on investment funds)
WRA	Work Reform Act

Notes on Contributors

EILEEN APPELBAUM is Senior Economist at the Center for Economic and Policy Research, in Washington, DC. She was formerly Professor in the School of Management and Labor Relations at Rutgers, the State University of New Jersey, USA.

ROSEMARY BATT is the Alice Hanson Cook Professor of Women and Work at the Industrial and Labor School, Cornell University, USA, and Editor of the *Industrial and Labor Relations Review*.

BRUNO CATTERO is Professor of Economic Sociology at the University of Eastern Piedmont Amedeo Avogadro, in Alessandria, Italy.

STEFAN DUNIN-WĄSOWICZ is an economist and financial controller, currently Board Member of the consulting group BPI Polska, Poland.

EWALD ENGELEN is Professor of Financial Geography at the University of Amsterdam, the Netherlands.

HOWARD GOSPEL is Professor of Management at King's College, University of London, and an Associate Fellow of the Said Business School, University of Oxford, UK.

JAKOB HAVES is a consultant working for the consulting company Wilke, Maack and Partner wmp consult in Hamburg, Germany.

TOMAS KORPI is Professor of Sociology at the Swedish Institute for Social Research, Stockholm University, Sweden.

KATSUYUKI KUBO is Professor of Business Economics, in the School of Commerce, Waseda University, Japan.

JAE EUN LEE is a doctoral student in Human Resource Management at Cornell University, USA.

JOHN MURRAY is a Lecturer in Work and Organizational Studies at the University of Sydney Business School, Australia.

ANDREW PENDLETON is Professor of Human Resource Management at the University of York Management School, UK.

PERCEVAL PRADELLE is a consultant cooperating with the consulting company BPI Polska in Warsaw, Poland.

SIGURT VITOLS is Head of Project Group, Modes of Economic Governance, at the Wissenschaftszentrum Berlin für Sozialforshung, Berlin, Germany and Associate Researcher, European Trade Union Institute, Brussels, Belgium.

MARK WESTCOTT is a Senior Lecturer in Work and Organisational Studies at the University of Sydney Business School, Australia.

PETER WILKE is Managing Director of the consulting company Wilke, Maack and Partner wmp consult in Hamburg, Germany

1

Financialization, New Investment Funds, and Labour

HOWARD GOSPEL AND
ANDREW PENDLETON

Introduction

New investment funds (NIFs), in the form of private equity (PE) funds, hedge funds (HFs), and sovereign wealth funds (SWFs), have become an important, but controversial, feature of the global economy in the last ten years.[1] In his 2012 re-election campaign US President Obama referred to PE funds as 'vampire capitalists'. Earlier, German social democrat politician Franz Müntefering had called PE and HFs 'swarms of locusts'. These critical descriptions highlight the claim that NIFs, also sometimes referred to as alternative investment funds, subjugate the interests of firms, their employees, and the wider public to the pursuit of high financial returns by a small class of speculative investors. More broadly, the development of these funds may be viewed as one important symptom of a growing 'financialization' of the world economy, whereby financial actors and instruments have acquired a steadily greater influence on the well-being of companies and natinal economies. Some critics (ETUC 2009; Lysandrou 2012) also claim that some of these funds were partially responsible for the financial crisis, due to their speculative activities and transmission of contagion across financial markets.

By contrast, others claim that NIFs make a positive and valuable contribution. Fund managers and some scholars and observers have argued that NIFs assist smaller firms and rejuvenate under-performing companies, thereby contributing to long-term enterprise success and employment growth (BVCA 2006; EVCA and PriceWaterhouseCoopers 2001; Gilligan and Wright 2010). It has been suggested that PE funds, for instance, supply expertise in governance, strategy, and operations to both private and mature, stock-market-listed firms (Klein et al. 2012). Furthermore, it is claimed that these funds improve the stability and functioning of financial markets by providing liquidity and diversifying risk (Coalition of Private Investment Companies 2009).

This book focuses on the impact of NIFs on labour and employment and evaluates the contention that these funds have secured returns at the expense of labour (PES 2007; Watt 2008). We present the results of a programme of research which brought together scholars from a range of countries to assess the effects of investment funds on employment, work, and industrial relations.[2] This programme had several objectives. The first was to compare and contrast the characteristics of these relatively new forms of investment fund. The second was to consider their effects on employment and industrial relations within their investee firms. The third was to consider the extent of variation between countries and to assess the influence of financial market and labour market regulation on the level of fund activity and labour outcomes. A fourth was to consider the effects of the global financial and economic crisis since 2007 on these funds and in turn on their impact on labour and employment.

In the following chapters, we consider the effects of funds on restructuring practices and labour outcomes in nine countries—the USA, the UK, Australia, Germany, the Netherlands, Sweden, Italy, Poland, and Japan. These countries were chosen because NIF activity has been relatively high within them. They also provide a spread of different 'varieties of capitalism' (VoC), including both liberal and coordinated market economies (LMEs and CMEs) (Hall and Soskice 2001), as well as social democratic and Mediterranean systems (Amable 2003).[3] In each country-based chapter, the contributors review the literature on investment fund activity, including that produced by governments, inter-governmental agencies, industry bodies, and the social partners (employers' associations and trade unions). Second, they discuss the research literature on the effects of these funds on employment and labour. This material includes individual case studies and larger statistical studies. Third, they weave into the analysis a number of their own case studies of companies in which funds have invested. These case studies are not presented in full in this book, but inform the analysis in each chapter.[4]

The structure of the book is as follows. In this introductory chapter we outline the ways in which PE, HFs, and SWFs work and provide an overview of their size, coverage, and operations. Their growth is

contextualized in a broader setting of financialization. We then introduce the main issues arising in relation to their effects on labour and
employment, before providing a broad picture of developments since
the financial crisis of 2007. In like manner, the subsequent chapters
focus on each country. The final chapter draws some broad conclusions on the operation of funds and their effects on labour outcomes.
It also evaluates the role of these funds in broader processes of financialization and considers how they have been affected by the present
financial and economic crisis.

New Investment Funds

New investment funds, such as PE, HFs, and SWFs, have developed since the 1970s and especially during the 2000s. They share
some common features in that they are all large sums of pooled
money which are invested in various assets, including portfolio
companies; they are run by professional investment managers
who are usually paid on a performance basis; and until recently
they have operated outside of much traditional securities regulation. They differ from other institutional investors, such as pension
and mutual funds, in that they typically take a bigger share in or
acquire whole companies (PE), become more involved in company
governance and management (PE and HFs), or mixtures of these
(SWFs). In general, these funds are seen as riskier than traditional
forms of institutional investment but claim to have correspondingly higher returns.

These new funds are smaller than pension, mutual, and insurance funds, representing just over 11 per cent of total assets under
management (AUM) worldwide in 2011, but with the exception of
the crisis year, 2008, have been growing more rapidly than other
vehicles for asset management (TheCityUK 2012a). Of the three,
SWFs are the largest, having more than quadrupled in size since
the early 2000s (Figure 1.1). However, although the NIFs remain
smaller than other forms of institutional investment, their impact
and significance has been disproportionate because of the nature of
their investment and governance strategies and the nature of their
impact on companies.

In the next sections, the main features and incidence of each type of
fund are outlined, preparatory to considering their effects on labour
outcomes.

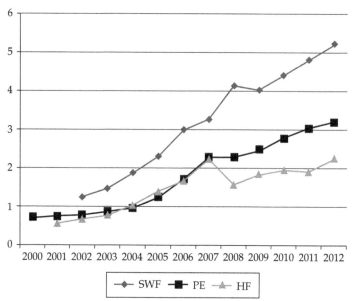

Figure 1.1 *Assets under management by new investment funds, 2000–2012 (US$ trillion)*
Source: Rivas 2013; Preqin 2013: 5; <www.TheCityUK.com>.

Private Equity

Private equity houses typically raise the largest proportion of their funds from institutional investors, banks, foundations, and wealthy individuals, for a set period of time, usually the lifetime of the fund. These investors are so-called 'limited partners'. The 'general partners', from the PE house itself, charge investors an annual management fee (typically 2 per cent) and take a percentage of the annual returns of the fund (typically 20 per cent) above a pre-agreed 'hurdle' rate of return payable to investors (so-called carried interest). The general partners direct the fund or funds, make investments in portfolio companies, and oversee the management of these companies (Folkman et al. 2009; Gilligan and Wright 2010; Treasury Select Committee 2007; Watt 2008).

Private equity funds may invest in companies at early stages of their development ('venture capital'), but they also mount buy-outs of established and mature companies. The book concentrates on this latter activity, which typically accounts for the lion's share of PE investment by volume. PE funds acquire companies with a view to managing and restructuring their operations, prior to a resale, secondary buy-out by another PE fund, or stock market flotation some years later. On average PE houses hold a company for around four to five years. In most cases, a sizeable proportion (typically over half) of the purchase price is met by debt, most of which is secured against the assets and returns of the company being acquired, with the remainder contributed by the PE fund. PE funds act either singly or in conjunction with other PE funds and usually acquire target companies in their entirety.

Unlike other institutional investors in equity markets, PE funds take a highly activist approach to the governance of their investee companies. They are able to do so because they have large ownership stakes. In addition, the highly leveraged character of most PE acquisitions limits the availability of 'free cash flow' which might be used by managers for their own benefit or that of their workforces (Jensen 1986). Instead, debt, coupled with high-powered performance incentives, is said to motivate company managers to focus on significant enhancements of company performance. These managers, often newly installed by the PE fund, are monitored closely and rewarded for the achievement of restructuring goals. Typically they are provided with equity-based incentives and may contribute a portion of the purchase price.

Several sources of gain from PE can be identified. First, there may be genuine improvements in company performance arising from new strategies and better management. Second, there may be transfers from other capitalists, that is, the PE fund acquires under-priced companies and sells them at higher prices. Third, there may be value transfers from government and taxpayers arising from 'financial engineering'—the use of debt to limit corporation tax, lower capital gains in place of higher income tax, the transfer of profits abroad, and the sale of company pension funds (Folkman *et al.* 2009). Finally, there may be value transfers from employees achieved by employment and work restructuring (Watt 2008). In principle, a PE buy-out can achieve gains via any of these routes or combinations of them. Some critics emphasize the role of financial engineering as the primary source of gain, at least when credit was more readily available (Folkman et al. 2009), whereas trade union critics argue that gains are mainly made at the expense of workers and taxpayers. The latter argue that high debt repayments coupled with high investment returns sought by PE funds has transferred value from firms and workers, and threatened the viability of some companies (PES 2007; Watt 2008). By contrast, the PE industry itself argues that the main source of gain has been real value creation.

Private equity funds have also been criticized for secrecy and lack of accountability (PES 2007). Because they do not usually seek retail investors, regulations governing the sale of retail investment products do not usually apply. The registration requirements are generally 'lighter touch' than for other investment funds, and funds have not been required to report on their investments. Moreover, when taken private, acquired companies are largely exempt from the disclosure and corporate governance requirements faced by stock market-listed firms. Other areas of controversy have been the tax treatments of PE investments and returns. Major issues have also been the capacity for general partners to subject their carried interest to capital gains rather than income tax and the ability of investee companies to secure company tax concessions on debt. In response to widespread criticism, in recent years, there have been moves towards greater voluntary disclosure. More important though are regulatory initiatives such as the European Union (EU) Alternative Investment Fund Management Directive implemented in Europe in 2013.

At the end of 2011, PE funds globally had approximately $3 trillion of AUM. The volume and importance of PE investment has grown considerably since the 1990s (though with a pause during the financial crisis). Moreover, institutional investors, along with HFs and SWFs, have increasingly invested in PE to achieve higher returns than are typically obtained from indexing strategies. The largest PE houses by volume of capital raised are shown in Table 1.1. As can be seen, the largest are based either in the USA or the UK, though the funds themselves are often registered in low tax jurisdictions such as the Cayman Islands or Bermuda.

In the buy-out boom of the late 1980s, most activity by value was in the USA, with just 10 per cent occurring in Europe (of which most was in the UK). Europe became an increasingly attractive market for PE deals in the 1990s and 2000s. During 2000–2005, nearly half of activity by value took place in the UK and Europe, with most of the growth outside the UK (Kaplan and Strömberg 2009). Bernstein et al. (2010) find that, within the Organisation for Economic Co-operation and Development (OECD), PE activity is concentrated in the USA, the UK, the Netherlands, and Sweden. Poland is also an important site of PE activity in Central and Eastern Europe (CEE). Table 1.2 shows the relative importance of PE in the European countries studied in this book.

Table 1.1 *Top twenty private equity firms by capital raised between 2006–2011*

Rank	Fund manager	Headquarter's country	Capital raised 2006–2011 (US$ million)
1	TPG Capital Fort Worth (Texas)	USA	50,553
2	Goldman Sachs	USA	47,224
3	The Carlyle Group	USA	40,541
4	Kohlberg Kravis Roberts	USA	40,216
5	The Blackstone Group	USA	36,419
6	Apollo Global Management	USA	33,813
7	Bain Capital	USA	29,403
8	CVC Capital Partners	UK	25,069
9	First Reserve Corporation	USA	19,064
10	Hellman & Friedman	USA	17,200
11	Apax Partners	UK	16,638
12	General Atlantic	USA	15,100
13	Warburg Pincus	USA	15,000
14	Cerberus Capital Management	USA	14,900
15	Advent International Boston	USA	14,520
16	Permira	UK	13,572
17	Oaktree Capital Management	USA	13,046
18	Terra Firma Capital Partners	UK	12,250
19	Providence Equity Partners	USA	12,100
20	Clayton Dubilier & Rice	USA	11,404

Source: PEI (2011).

There is considerable variety in the target companies of PE. They include the acquisition of companies in their entirety and the purchase of product divisions and subsidiaries divested by larger companies. Some of the most dramatic cases have been public-to-private transactions, whereby large listed companies have been taken into private ownership (e.g. RJR Nabisco and Health Corporation of America in the USA, Alliance Boots in the UK, or Gambro AB in Sweden). PE invests in a variety of sectors, with retail, manufacturing, and business services being especially prominent. As several chapters document, PE has also become active in social care services as these activities have been increasingly privatized, and this has been especially controversial.

Table 1.2 *Private equity investment in the selected countries as a percentage of GDP, 2011*

	Japan	Italy	Poland	Germany	Australia	Netherlands	UK	Sweden	USA
Private equity investment as% of GDP	0.08	0.14	0.18	0.24	0.28	0.48	0.59	0.88	0.97

Source: AVCAL (2012), EVCA (2012), McKinsey (2012), and Pitchbook (2012).

Hedge Funds

Hedge funds are NIFs which aim at securing high returns in both upturns and downturns of the market. The term derives from the activities of an American investment fund manager Alfred Winslow Jones. In the late 1940s he created a 'hedged' fund, by balancing the purchase of under-valued stocks using leverage and short-selling of over-valued stocks. In this way, Jones and his partners were able to generate profits independently of movements of the market as a whole. Today, the term is used more loosely to cover a variety of investment strategies, many of which do not involve hedging as such.

There are, however, several characteristics common to them: they are pooled, privately organized alternative investment vehicles which invest in all kinds of assets; they are not widely available to the public; they are run by professional investment managers who often have significant personal investments in the fund and are paid on a performance basis; and they are less subject than other kinds of institutions and funds to securities regulation and registration requirements (Brav et al. 2008). As such, they are usually exempt from the requirement typically faced by pension, mutual, and insurance funds to hold diversified portfolios and to maintain specified liquidity levels to permit fund withdrawals (Clifford 2008). The focus of HF activity may include equities, commodities, currencies, and debt instruments. Typically HFs use leverage and invest in derivatives based on these products, which allows them to multiply their returns, but correspondingly increases the risk of loss.

The number of HFs worldwide in 2011 was estimated at around 9,900, having declined somewhat from a peak of over 10,000 in 2007, and with over $1.9 trillion AUM (TheCityUK 2012a). The USA is the largest international centre for HF managers and most of the largest funds are American. Outside the USA, London is the second largest international centre. Elsewhere in Europe, Paris and Geneva have also established themselves as secondary centres for HF headquarters. However, the funds themselves are usually registered in offshore centres, with the Cayman Islands and Bermuda being especially important centres. Table 1.3 shows the twenty largest HFs by AUM.

In this book our attention focuses on HFs which invest in equity and directly buy company shares. Here the most important investment approaches are (1) 'directional', (2) 'event-driven', and (3) 'activist' strategies (Coggan 2011; Fruhan 2010; Temple 2001). HFs with directional strategies are the most common. Only a small fraction of HFs

Table 1.3 *Top twenty hedge funds by assets under management, 2012*

Rank	Firm/fund	HF country	Firm/fund capital, Jan 2012 (US$ billion)
1	Bridgewater Associates	USA	76.1
2	J. P. Morgan Asset Mgmt	USA	53.6
3	Man Group	UK	36.5
4	Brevan Howard Asset Mgmt	UK	34.2
5	Winton Capital Mgmt	UK	30.0
6	Och-Ziff Capital Mgmt Group	USA	28.8
7	BlackRock	USA	28.8
8	BlueCrest Capital Mgmt	UK	28.6
9	Baupost Group	USA	25.2
10	AQR Capital Mgmt	USA	23.2
11	Paulson & Co.	USA	22.6
12	Angelo, Gordon & Co.	USA	22.1
13	Renaissance Technologies Corp.	USA	20.0
14	D. E. Shaw & Co.	USA	19.5
15	Elliott Mgmt Corp.	USA	19.2
16	Farallon Capital Mgmt	USA	19.2
17	King Street Capital Mgmt	USA	17.6
18	Davidson Kempner Capital Mgmt	USA	17.0
19	Adage Capital Mgmt	USA	16.0
20	Goldman Sachs Asset Mgmt	USA	15.3

Source: Institutional Investor (2012).

follow activist strategies, accounting for an estimated $50 bn of AUM, that is about 2.5 per cent of total HF assets (Cusworth 2011).

In the case of directional strategies, HFs seek margins by exploiting, and even causing, market movements. The most well-known and controversial version of this is 'short-selling'. This involves the borrowing of shares from other owners, such as pension and mutual funds, with a view to selling them if the price falls. The HF then repurchases shares at a lower price and returns the shares to their owner, taking the margin between the sale and repurchase price, minus a fee for borrowing the shares. This kind of activity can drive down share prices, especially as much of the trading is computer-generated, involving 'herding' behaviour, and can lead to instability in company strategies as corporate managers are forced to respond to falls in the market valuation of the company. Shorting is thought to have played a role in the downfall of Lehmann Brothers in the USA in 2008. More controversial is 'naked short-selling', where funds do not purchase or borrow the shares or assets they are shorting. Since the financial crisis in the late 2000s, the regulation of short-selling has been tightening, initially with temporary bans, but now with more permanent measures. From November 2012 HFs short-selling within Europe have been required to disclose short-sales when they exceed certain proportions of a company's equity.

Event-driven strategies secure returns through interventions in particular situations such as mergers and acquisitions (M&As) or bankruptcies, taking advantage of the share premium and uncertainty which usually arises in such situations. Over time, event-driven activity has grown in volume. Such interventions can put pressure on firms to adapt their strategies. In our chapters, a number of cases of event-driven strategies are referred to: these include Cadbury in the UK, Yellow Roadway Worldwide in the USA, Cewe Color in Germany, and ABN Amro in the Netherlands.

Activist HFs, a major focus in this book, include Icahn Associates, Pershing Square Capital Management, Third Point Management, Cevian, and The Children's Investment Fund Managers. Their strategy is to acquire company stock and then influence company strategies to enhance the returns accruing to shareholders. In a study of 1,059 instances of HF activism in the USA over the period 2001–06, Brav et al. (2008) found that interventions were motivated by the following objectives: to correct and exploit under-valuation, modify capital structure, reform business strategy, sell the target, and achieve governance reforms. Other evidence suggests that HFs tend to focus more often on value transfers, through share buy-backs and special dividends, than on changes to business and operating strategies (Klein and Zur 2009). The evidence suggests that they frequently achieve these aims. However, unlike PE, activist HFs rarely secure controlling stakes (Brav et al. 2008) and usually focus on publicly-listed companies. Occasionally they acquire larger stakes and also bad debt ('distressed securities'), with the ultimate goal of gaining control of a company, as in the case of Schefenacker in Germany (Wilke et al. 2009).

Activist HFs are controversial because their activities can arguably transfer value from other stakeholders, such as labour, to shareholders, and they sometimes seek to restructure companies in ways which threaten jobs and employment security. They usually seek cooperation with the existing management and shareholders, but put pressure on managements when the latter are slow to respond to their claims. Whilst some of this pressure is exerted in private, HFs often release information to the media to ratchet-up pressure, typically in the run-up to a company's annual shareholder meeting (Achleitner and Lutz 2009). HFs may then sponsor or support resolutions at the meeting to achieve the desired changes. Hostile activist interventions appear to be more profitable for the HFs than cooperative ones (Becht et al. 2010). Some of the most visible cases of HF activism have been those where a HF contests the incumbent management. Examples discussed in the chapters include Ameron and Iron Mountain in the USA and KUKA in Germany (Wilke et al. 2009).[5]

Table 1.4 lists some of the most prominent activist HFs, whilst Table 1. 5 provides summary detail on the incidence of HF public activism in the countries covered in the book.

Table 1.4 *Prominent activist hedge funds*

Name	Main location	AUM on 1 Jan 2007 (US$ billion)	Strategy
ESL Investments	New York	18	Activist, distressed
Atticus Capital	New York	14	Event-driven
The Children's Investment Fund (TCI)	London	10.3	Activist
Highfields Capital	Boston	10	Activist
Elliott Associates	New York	7	Distressed, activist, multi-strategy
Icahn Partners	New York	5.5	Activist
Omega Advisors	New York	5.5	Value/activist
Third Point Partners	New York	4.7	Event-driven
Sparx Group	Tokyo	4.5	Multi-strategy
Steel Partners	New York	4	Activist
Centaurus Capital	London	4	Event-driven, equity long/short
Hermitage Capital Management	London and Moscow	3.2	Activist (in Russia)
Boussard & Gavaudan	London and Paris	2.1	Multi-strategy with a strong activist slant
Bulldog Investors	Saddle Brook, NJ	1	Activist

Source: Financial Times (2007).

Table 1.5 *Number of hedge funds activist events per country, 2000–2010*

Country	HF activist events
USA	1,059
UK	150
Japan	103
Germany	43
Netherlands	29
Australia	20
Italy	13
Poland	n/a

Note: US data for 2001–2006.
Source: Brav et al. (2008); Katelouzou (2011).

A moot point concerns the extent to which HF activism differs from 'traditional' shareholder activism by some institutional investors. Some pension funds, such as the California Public Employees' Retirement System in the USA, are notable for activist engagement with investee companies. It has been argued that HF activism differs in the extent of changes which are sought and in the *ex ante* strategic nature of the activity (Kahan and Rock 2006). Activist HFs become part-owners of companies with the prior intention of securing major changes, such as the break-up of conglomerates. They are usually able to devote more resources to these interventions than other institutional investors because their portfolios are typically much narrower. It is the extent of HF ambitions for particular companies which have made them so controversial: their activities have led in some instances to major changes in company size and operations, with labour and employment being a significant, though indirect, casualty.

Sovereign Wealth Funds

Sovereign wealth funds are investment funds owned and operated by governments or their agencies. They have been defined as funds which acquire and administer assets to achieve national financial objectives and which employ a set of investment strategies including investing in foreign financial assets (IFSL 2009). They are the largest of the three NIFs covered in this book, accounting for about half of the total assets managed by these funds. SWF are used by countries with high foreign reserves to obtain a greater rate of return on their assets than would be available from the issue of government bonds or from the purchase of domestic assets (Sethi 2008). In many countries this capital is generated by the oil industry, but in some cases also by the successful accumulation of non-commodity trade surpluses and by pension payments.

The largest SWFs are based in Norway, the United Arab Emirates, China, Saudi Arabia, and Singapore. Table 1.6 provides details of the twenty largest SWFs by AUM in 2012. Overall, AUM by SWFs increased from under $1 trillion in 1999 to $5.2 trillion in 2012. Since 2007 SWF direct investments have amounted to at least $59bn annually (IFSL 2010; TheCityUK 2012b). On top of the assets of SWFs, an additional $7.7 trillion were held by other sovereign investment vehicles, such as development funds and pension reserve funds. Taking into account a further $8.4 trillion in official foreign exchange reserves, governments with SWFs have access to over $20 trillion in funds (TheCityUK 2013).

Sovereign wealth funds take various forms and engage in different strategies.[6] Kunzel et al. (2011) identify three types of SWFs with distinct objectives and investment horizons: savings (designed for long-term objectives), stabilization (to insulate the national budget), and pension reserve funds (for unspecified pension liabilities). Dyck and Morse (2011) distinguished two objectives of SWF investment: financial portfolio versus domestic developmental agendas, with the latter particularly important for Middle Eastern and Asian SWFs. There is some debate as to whether political objectives may also influence SWF investment behaviour (Johan et al. 2011). Another distinction in the case of SWFs is between 'generalist' and 'specialist' funds (Rehman 2010). The largest are generalist funds investing in a wide variety of asset classes. Unlike PE and HFs, they are open-ended (i.e. there is no set date for winding up the fund) and are able to take a long-term perspective. They are more flexible in their investment strategies than institutional investors and make use of a large number of external fund managers. Where they take equity stakes in companies, their ownership level is usually below public disclosure requirements and they have been largely quiescent in their approach to governance. Incumbent managements are usually allowed to remain in place, and few demands for substantial changes in governance, structures, or operations are made (Rehman 2010; Sethi 2008). However, some generalist funds are starting to acquire larger stakes in companies and to take more of an activist approach.

Specialist government investment vehicles are smaller than generalist funds. These often take strategic stakes in portfolio companies and pursue more activist governance strategies, in some cases

Table 1.6 *Top twenty sovereign wealth funds by assets under management, October 2012*

Country	Sovereign wealth fund name	Assets (US$ billion)	Origin
Norway	Government Pension Fund— Global	656	Oil
UAE—Abu Dhabi	Abu Dhabi Investment Authority	627	Oil
China	SAFE Investment Company	568	Non-commodity
Saudi Arabia	SAMA Foreign Holdings	533	Oil
China	China Investment Corporation	482	Non-commodity
Kuwait	Kuwait Investment Authority	296	Oil
China—Hong Kong	Hong Kong Monetary Authority Investment Portfolio	293	Non-commodity
Singapore	Government of Singapore Investment Corporation	247	Non-commodity
Singapore	Temasek Holdings	157	Non-commodity
Russia	National Welfare Fund	150	Oil
China	National Social Security Fund	135	Non-commodity
Qatar	Qatar Investment Authority	115	Oil
Australia	Australian Future Fund	78	Non-commodity
UAE—Dubai	Investment Corporation of Dubai	70	Oil
UAE—Abu Dhabi	International Petroleum Investment Company	65	Oil

(Continued)

Table 1.6 (Continued)

Country	Sovereign wealth fund name	Assets (US$ billion)	Origin
Libya	Libyan Investment Authority	65	Oil
Kazakhstan	Kazakhstan National Fund	62	Oil
Algeria	Revenue Regulation Fund	57	Oil
UAE—Abu Dhabi	Mubadala Development Company	53	Oil
South Korea	Korea Investment Corporation	43	Non-commodity

Source: SWF Institute (2012).

acquiring full control of investee firms (Rehman 2010). In some respects, these funds might be seen as typical multinational owners. In other respects, these funds are rather more similar to PE houses. Indeed, there is some evidence that some of these smaller funds increasingly structure themselves on PE lines (Sethi 2008). Specialist funds also invest more substantially in PE, HFs, and other higher-risk asset classes than generalist SWFs (Sethi 2008).

Sovereign wealth funds are estimated to be invested in around one-fifth of listed companies around the world, but their investments are highly concentrated in a few countries, as shown in Table 1.7. As with PE and HFs, the UK and the USA are substantial recipients of SWF investments. The UK is also a significant base for SWF fund

Table 1.7 *Sovereign wealth funds investments into selected countries, 2005–2011*

Country	Investments (US$ billion)	Total investment (%)
USA	76	19
UK	68	17
China	38	10
France	28	7
Switzerland	27	7
Germany	26	7
Qatar	15	4
Others	121	30

Source: TheCityUK (2012b).

Table 1.8 *Sovereign wealth funds investments in listed companies by country, 2007*

Country	Firms with SWF investment (%)	% of firms with large SWF investment
Netherlands	41	6.6
UK	19	5.3
Sweden	27	4.3
Japan	35	3.5
Italy	46	2.7
Germany	18	2.0
USA	31	1.7
Australia	13	0.8
Poland	0	0.0

Source: Fernandes (2011: Table 5).

management. As shown in Table 1.8, substantial proportions of listed companies in most of the countries covered in this book have some SWF ownership, though only minorities have substantial ownership (above disclosure limits). A notable case is the Norwegian fund which has stakes of around 1 per cent in many companies worldwide, making it akin to a giant index fund.

Sovereign wealth funds have given rise to concern, because it is argued they enable overseas governments to acquire important stakes in companies in other countries, thereby offering the potential to exert strategic, but hidden, influence on other countries' economies (Bernstein et al. 2013). They are seen to be secretive, being concerned not to reveal too much about positions and being aware of charges of interference. Less information tends to be disclosed than by PE and HFs. Of the larger SWFs, only the Norwegian fund makes public detailed reports on its activity and returns. To counter negative perceptions, SWFs have adopted voluntary self-regulation. In the 2008 Santiago Principles, SWFs undertook to maintain a clear separation between the economic and commercial orientation of SWF investment principles and the political or strategic interests of their sponsoring governments.

Summarizing Funds and their Strategies

This review of PE, HFs, and SWFs shows several similarities and differences between them. They are similar in that they are all largely products of the latest period of financialization, with substantial growth over the last quarter century. They are large private funds which invest in equity, though many HFs and SWFs also have wider non-equity interests. They are relatively lightly regulated with limited obligations to disclose their activities. The main difference between them resides in the size of ownership stakes in companies. PE investments are usually substantial and often a majority of the ownership. By contrast, HFs typically hold smaller stakes, though in some instances these are large compared to the norm for institutional investors. SWFs traditionally held small investments to keep below legal disclosure limits, but there is some development towards larger, strategic ownership stakes, especially by specialist SWFs. Activist HFs and SWFs tend to invest in publicly-listed companies, whereas PE invests in privately-owned firms or takes publicly-listed firms into private ownership.

Other important dimensions are the extent of fund involvement in governance and management and also the time horizons of investment funds. PE is the most involved, but so are some activist HFs, whilst SWFs have traditionally been passive. PE has direct involvement in the strategic direction of portfolio companies via majority ownership, but activist HFs rely instead on a range of governance instruments such as proxy contests. Of the three, PE typically has the strongest influence on target company strategies, though activist HFs can have major one-off effects on company strategy and structure. It is arguable that the governance strategy of PE tends to focus on value creation (though, as we will see, this has been a highly contentious claim), whereas activist HFs are mainly concerned with value transfer (though the funds themselves argue that they correct market imperfections).

The time horizons for returns tend to differ between the three types of fund. On average portfolio companies are held by PE for around five years (Kaplan and Strömberg 2009; Strömberg 2007). Much of the return to investors comes from the resale of portfolio companies. Activist HFs typically have a shorter time horizon, aiming to secure returns from activism within a year or so (Brav et al. 2008). SWFs have tended to have the longest time horizons, emanating from their generally passive approach to their investments, although there is some evidence that this may be changing (The CityUK 2013).

Financialization

The development of NIFs is one aspect of the process of financialization which has taken place since at least the 1970s. Financialization refers to the increasing importance of financial markets, actors, and values in the economy and society at interconnected levels. For reasons of focus, we leave aside the question as to whether financialization involves an intensification of long-run trends or represents a paradigmatic transformation of capitalism (Dumenil and Levy 2011; Engelen and Konigs 2010; Lapavitsas 2011; van Treeck 2009). With this proviso, financialization is usually taken to refer to the share of financial services and products in world economic activity and the role of financial assets and instruments in global trade. At the national level, it highlights the increasing proportion of the finance sector in gross domestic product, company profits, and employment. More diffusely, it draws attention to the penetration of financial values into everyday life and culture, such as education, the arts, and healthcare (see Epstein 2005 and Krippner 2011 for a review of relevant literatures). The growing ascendancy of finance is key to our discussion in that we see non-financial firms as being increasingly subject to financial pressures, actors, and values. Drawing on Epstein, Dore, and others, we highlight four dimensions of financialization—markets, actors, ideologies, and regulation (Dore 2008; Engelen and Konings 2010; Epstein 2005; Krippner 2011)—all of which help to locate the growth and role of NIFs.

First, financialization refers to the increasing significance of financial markets, both in terms of the expansion in the number and types of products traded on financial markets (financial instruments) and in the growth of trading volumes on these markets. NIFs have clearly benefited from these developments, though in differing ways. Many countries have tried to promote their financial markets by, for example, easing access to stock markets for early stage companies. Besides raising funds through stock market flotations and stock issues, secondary trading of existing shares has also grown substantially in the last quarter century or so and in some countries has come to be the main function of stock markets (Kay 2012). Increased turnover of shares in secondary markets and the decline of relational investing have enlarged the market for buying and selling firms and parts of firms—the so-called market for corporate control (Manne 1965). On the one hand, this has helped companies pursue expansionary strategies through M&As, which are frequently financed through an exchange of stock (Lazonick and O'Sullivan 2000). On the other hand, in recent decades, these markets have also been a growing source of pressure on firms, since the latter need to maintain or boost their share price as a measure of corporate and managerial performance and to discourage hostile takeovers. Whilst M&A activity is highly cyclical, the duration of takeover booms has become longer through each cycle, and takeover activity has extended to countries where traditionally it has been muted, such as Japan and Germany (Jackson and Miyajima 2008). Greater change in ownership and control has provided opportunities for new financial actors to acquire companies or parts of them and to embark on corporate restructuring.

The development of NIFs and their investment activity around the world can be understood in this context. Active markets for corporate control have provided an opportunity for PE to acquire companies in two ways. In some cases PE houses have been able to buy up listed companies in their entirety. More commonly, PE has been able to acquire unwanted parts of companies which have been divested in the wake of corporate takeovers and mergers. Liquid stock markets, associated with a trend towards greater ownership dispersion, have also provided opportunities for activist HFs and SWFs to acquire ownership stakes in companies. In the case of HFs, liquidity and stock market price movements have provided opportunities to secure margin opportunities, and this has provided the basis of directional investment strategies. Well-developed stock markets have also provided an exit route for PE funds to liquidate their investments in target companies, though 'trade' sales to other PE houses,which have become more widespread than initial public offerings (IPOs).

Recently, in some countries, firms have made decreasing use of stock markets for raising funds and have bought shares back from the market. This is sometimes blamed on the high disclosure requirements and short-term demands from institutional investors on listed companies. The net effect in some countries is that the buying back of shares has exceeded new issues. Such repurchasing of shares is significant, as it can push up the price of company stock, to the benefit, at least in the shorter term, of shareholders and senior managers, but it may have adverse effects on funds available for investment (Kay 2012; Lazonick 2011; Orhangazi 2008). PE has benefited from the recent reaction against disclosure and short-termism, whilst activist HFs have promoted the use of share buy-backs as a way of transferring value to shareholders.

Second, an important aspect of financialization concerns changing or new financial actors. Here we draw attention to a number of major developments, accelerating over the last quarter century, as they have affected non-financial companies.

Ownership patterns have changed in many countries. This includes privatization of state-owned companies, increases in foreign ownership, and a shift from family to institutional ownership. Such new owners may not necessarily be less 'patient', but they are certainly more distant from companies in which they hold shares and may be said to have lower commitment to specific investments. Here also a major change is the lengthening of the ownership chain, with a shift from direct ownership by individuals to indirect ownership by institutional investors such as pension, mutual, and insurance funds. In turn, the latter increasingly outsource asset management to 'professional' asset managers, some of whom now manage hundreds of separate funds (Davis 2008). As a result, there may be many steps between the ultimate owner and the company. For example, an individual's pension savings may be held in a pension fund, which is invested via an asset manager in a fund of funds, which in turn invests in PE and in HFs holding shares in companies. This process is increasingly taking place across national boundaries as investors and asset managers try to diversify risk or seek new financial opportunities. One consequence of this lengthening of the ownership chain is that the proportion of income accruing to the finance sector increases via the payment of fees at each stage of the process (Kay 2012; Sinclair 2005).

Traditional actors have also changed due to the availability of capital and credit in conjunction with pressures for higher returns. Alongside the three kinds of NIFs, other new financial institutions have emerged, such as structured investment vehicles, special purpose entities, and money market funds. These funds are often seen as part of a so-called 'shadow banking' system (Financial Stability Board 2012). Typically they are subject to less regulation than traditional banks and institutions because they do not take deposits or interface with the general public. They also offer, though do not always deliver, higher rates of return than traditional investments or bank savings, and can be seen as a systemic response to the abundance of credit prior to the 2007 crash. The source of these higher returns has been controversial, as, according to some, these funds have secured returns at the expense of taxpayers, companies, and employees. It has been argued that changes in ownership and demands for higher returns puts pressure on companies, can encourage shorter-term horizons, and may divert funds from internal investment (Kay 2012; Orhangazi 2008; Sinclair 2005).

Third, financialization also relates to ideologies, in the sense of values and ways of thinking about markets and firms. Historically, there have always been different ways of viewing markets. Some have seen them as inherently efficient and benign, with overall benefits exceeding costs. Others have viewed markets as subject to periodic failures and in need of basic corrections and regulation. Similarly, there have always been different concepts of the business enterprise. Some have seen the firm as a private organization, answerable to owners who bear the residual risk. Others have seen the company as more of a public entity, more broadly constituted to include other participants, such as employees, communities, and customers and with a broader set of commitments (Gospel and Pendleton 2012; Mayer 2013).

From early in the final quarter of the twentieth century, the first set of views gained increasing prominence in the business and policy communities and increasingly came to pervade corporate conduct and the framing of regulation (Stedman Jones 2012). This was especially marked in the USA and the UK, but such ideas have spread to other countries as well. Several theories and ideologies comprised this new conventional wisdom. The 'efficient markets hypothesis' asserted that markets efficiently process all available information and will thus provide a reliable and self-correcting measure of value. On this basis, regulation should be kept to a minimum (Fama 1970). 'Principal–agent' theory highlighted the role of self-interest and divergence of interest between owners and managers, with the latter seen as self-serving and opportunistic (Jensen and Meckling 1976). To correct this, the interests of owners and executives needed to be 'aligned' and managers and workers needed to be incentivized by various financial instruments, linked to outcomes sought by owners. Crucially, for many, 'shareholder value' rather than 'stakeholder rights' came to be the clarion call for the purpose of the firm and the role of its managers. Ultimately, the contention is that the purpose of the firm and the aim of top management are to maximize the value of owners (Friedman 1970). These views coalesced from the 1980s to provide an ideology for liberal market capitalism and financial control of the firm. These views were also used to justify the increasing rewards in terms of wealth and income enjoyed by top managers (Bebchuk and Fried 2004; Fligstein 2004; Khurana 2007; Lazonick and O'Sullivan 2000; Zorn 2004). PE and HFs have been associated with this view of management and have taken advantage of the evolving conception of firms and managers. Thus, activist HFs put pressure on managements to deliver shareholder value, whilst PE claimed to narrow the agency gap between owners and company managers.

Fourth, financialization relates to the web of rules which regulate financial markets, actors, and instruments. General trends in regulation have varied over time and also significantly between countries, with each country having its own sets of institutions and policy-making patterns. In the decade from the 1930s to the 1950s, in response to the Great Depression and the increasing desire of many countries to use the financial sector to 'steer' industry, many restrictions were introduced on the types of activities which financial actors could undertake. Furthermore, those responsible for oversight (such as ministries, regulatory agencies, and central banks) gained increased formal rights and informal influence over financial actors (Vitols 1997 and 2001).

However, in the last three decades of the twentieth century, a complex shift in the nature of regulation took place. On the one hand, there was significant deregulation, in the sense that restrictions placed on the activities of financial actors were diluted or removed (for example, the repeal of the Glass–Steagal Act in the USA in 1999). It was suggested that the problems these had been designed to correct had been solved, and it was now preferable to allow freer economic and financial activity. Thus, deregulation freed up options and derivatives markets and reduced controls over banking and securities activities, enabling the supply of bank debt to increase considerably (MacKenzie 2006; Vitols 2003). This provided opportunities for new financial actors such as NIFs to develop, as well as for established actors, such as banks, to move into new activities.

On the other hand, there has been increased regulation of markets with the goal of making these markets function more 'efficiently'. This new regulation is also characterized by a variety of instruments, including guidelines and codes ('soft law') as well as formal legislation. There is also a growing tendency for supra-national activity, both at the global and regional (e.g. EU) levels. Examples of growing regulation include corporate governance codes and harmonization of international accounting standards (Generally Accepted Accounting Principles and International Financial Reporting Standards). These developments have provided opportunities for NIFs to extend their activities into new geographical areas by creating 'level playing fields', thereby lowering the costs of entry and monitoring. For instance, the use of 'passports' in EU securities legislation (and the Alternative Investment Fund Managers Directive) can enable investment firms to enter new European markets without undergoing further authorization once initial approval has been given in one country.

In identifying these dimensions of financialization and drawing attention to changes over the last 30 years and more, we are not claiming that it is an entirely new phenomenon. In fact, it has come in various stages. Historically, there was a first stage in the late nineteenth and early twentieth centuries, coming to a halt and being reversed with two world wars and interwar economic upheavals. Slowly, through the post-Second World War period, financial markets have become more liberal and have spread more widely. This process accelerated in the final quarter of the twentieth century because of the change in economic ideas, rapid developments in information and communications technologies, and growing international competition between companies and between countries (Krippner 2011). The global financial and economic crisis, beginning in 2007, raises the question as to whether this long era of financialization has come to an end or just a temporary halt. We revert to this question in the conclusion.

Moreover, financialization has developed at different speeds in different countries, reflecting historical inheritances, the strength of ideas, and different institutional arrangements. Broadly, and in line with the VoC approach, LMEs, such as the USA and the UK, have led, while more CMEs, such as Germany and Japan, have followed, though to varying extents (Hall and Soskice 2001; Fligstein 2001; Kogut 2012). However, the picture is varied, with some LMEs, such as Canada and Australia, incorporating neo-liberal ideas into policy to a lesser extent than the USA and the UK (Konzelmann et al. 2012). Moreover, some CMEs, as we will see with the Netherlands and Sweden, have experienced strong levels of growth in equity markets and in the activities of NIFs. One of the main objectives of this book is to consider how national institutions, both in financial and labour markets, have moderated the relationship between financialization, NIFs, and labour.

National Influences upon Fund Activity

A key aim of this book is to provide a comparative treatment of the incidence of NIFs and of their activity in portfolio companies. Most PE and HFs are to be found in the USA, followed by the UK. SWFs are different in that they are headquartered in their country of origin, though they typically manage some of their investment activities from regional offices in the UK and the USA. Most of the portfolio activities of PE and HFs are to be found in their headquartered countries but many are notable for also investing in companies elsewhere in Europe and further afield. There has been considerable controversy over the role and impact of US and UK NIFs operating in other countries, as will become clear in the following chapters.

There have been several attempts to grade the attractiveness of countries to NIFs. The European Private Equity and Venture Capital Association (EVCA) has periodically produced a benchmarking survey of European countries in terms of their attractiveness to PE funds, whilst Groh et al. (2012) produce an annual guide to the attractiveness of countries worldwide for PE. There are no equivalents for HFs or SWFs, though Preqin (2012) provides systematic annual coverage of SWF characteristics and investments.

In relation to the regulatory environment for funds and their investors, the EVCA highlights *inter alia* the following important dimensions: the presence of funded pension systems able to invest in PE, the capacity of insurance companies to invest in PE, the availability of suitable fund structures with tax transparency for limited partners, and the level of taxation on fund management fees (EVCA and KPMG 2008). The taxation of carried interest is also highly relevant: is income accruing to general partners taxed as income or capital gains, and at what marginal rate? As for investee companies, the EVCA highlights *inter alia* the level of company or corporation tax, the deductibility of net interest payments, and fiscal incentives for research and development and similar expenditure. The second is highly relevant given the practice of financing buy-outs with leverage added to the balance sheet of the target company. Other significant factors would seem to be the extent of regulation of takeovers and acquisitions, including whether there are prohibitions or constraints on takeovers by foreign companies. The size and liquidity of the stock market is also significant in that it facilitates not only acquisitions, but also exits via IPOs (Groh et al. 2012).

On this basis it can be seen why LMEs, with large liquid stock markets and a tendency towards limited regulation, have witnessed especially high levels of fund management investments. These features have also had a beneficial effect on HF and SWF investment activity. Corporate governance practices influence HF activity in so far as the rights and duties of shareholders, especially minority investors, affect the capacity of activist HFs to put pressure on incumbent management. For instance, the ease with which boards can be replaced is important given that HFs often aim to put their own nominees on company boards.

Labour regulation is also likely to influence activity by funds in portfolio companies. Bozkaya and Kerr (2009) find an inverse relationship between PE investments *per capita* by country and country employment protection scores found in the 1998 OECD Employment Protection Index. It has been argued that lower levels of employment protection and mandatory employee consultation have encouraged NIF activity in some countries by facilitating restructuring (Shertler 2003). However, there is some debate as to the extent and nature of its effects. Some studies have suggested that employment protection regulation does not prevent fund activity, but the extent of mandatory consultation affects the capacity of worker representatives to contest restructuring initiatives by funds (Gospel et al. 2011b). Other studies have shown that labour regulation influences the type of buy-out activity. Boucly et al.'s (2008) study of 830 French leveraged buy-outs (LBOs) suggests that a restrictive labour regime in France means that buy-outs tend to be confined to targets with good growth prospects. Investment funds are reluctant to invest in poorly performing firms because employment protection legislation will restrict the extent to which they can restructure firms through workforce reorganization.

Although it is difficult to evaluate the relative importance of labour regulation, our chapters aim to shed light on this question in comparative perspective.

Labour and Employment Effects of New Investment Funds?

New investment funds, especially PE and HFs, have been highly controversial in trade union and political circles because employees are said to have often suffered redundancies, work intensification, and changes in voice and representation arrangements after interventions by NIFs. The substance of these criticisms is that, in seeking high returns, NIFs transfer value from existing stakeholders, such as workers, to the funds. NIF fund managers, and managers in NIF-acquired companies, are highly incentivized to secure these value transfers by the profit distribution policies of these funds. A related argument suggests that managers in target companies are impelled to breach implicit contracts with stakeholders, such as labour, by the financial pressures arising from the PE and HF business models, such as high leverage and debt repayments (Appelbaum, Batt, and Lee in this volume). Against these arguments, some argue that significant value transfers from labour occur in a minority of cases, and that these cases tend to be ones where a 'do nothing' approach is likely to have consequences that are at least as harmful. It is thus argued that employment reductions and other innovations are necessary surgery to ensure the longer-term health of the target company (EVCA and PriceWaterhouseCoopers 2001).

Linkages

To evaluate these arguments, and the evidence for and against them, it is necessary to consider how NIF activities and 'labour outcomes' are connected. As argued elsewhere (Gospel and Pendleton 2003), new owners may introduce new constraints *and* new opportunities. On the one hand, there may be new demands on labour which have adverse effects on jobs, wages, and industrial relations. On the other, there may be new opportunities to offer greater long-term job security, higher pay, and better benefits in return for more productive work. In the case of both constraints and opportunities, there are various transmission mechanisms which may operate.

First, new ownership may affect *time horizons*. Broadly speaking, HFs tend to have short-term, PE medium-term, and SWFs long-term time horizons. These can be set against the time horizons of other owners, such as individuals and families, banks, and institutional investors. Short-term horizons, with a high propensity to sell, may lead to higher pay-back demands and a disinclination to invest in longer-term, intangible assets, such as human resources. In turn, this may affect the likelihood of investing in training and prospects of job stability. It may also mean that investors with shorter time horizons create mechanisms, such as performance-based pay, to obtain a quick return on human capital. However, there has been some debate about the time-scale of PE funds. The funds themselves claim that they are long-term compared with many stock market investors, as the average holding period of listed shares is less than one year. Against this, the taking of special dividends and 'sale and lease back' of property assets, often early in the life cycle of portfolio investments, indicate more short-termist orientations.[7]

Second, NIFs may affect corporate *strategies* in various ways. The acquisition of a sizeable proportion of shares by a new investor may induce firms to expand or contract, to acquire or divest, or to pursue greater market share or financial maximization. Some PE funds specialize in mounting turnaround buy-outs where significant changes to strategies and practices are viewed to be necessary to rescue the portfolio company. Even where NIFs, such as activist HFs, have a small minority share of ownership, pressure may be put on management to modify business strategies and to divest entire areas of company activity. In turn, the choice of such strategies may have related implications for job security, promotion prospects, and pay and benefits. In this respect, the impact of NIFs on labour is essentially indirect, mediated through the business strategies which follow from NIF ownership and interventions.

Third, new owners may shift the balance in *governance* between stakeholders. Since PE and HFs take a more active approach to governance, managers in firms owned by a NIF will likely have to re-orientate the balance of returns and voice in favour of these NIFs relative to other stakeholders, such as labour. High levels of debt on the balance sheet of portfolio companies, in the case of PE, can impel managers to break 'implicit contracts' with labour (Appelbaum, Batt, and Lee in this volume) so as to service and repay debts and deliver returns to the fund. Thus, activist HFs have pressured companies to pay special dividends to shareholders and mount share buy-backs, both of which transfer resources out of companies and away from the workforces.

Methodological Issues in Assessing Outcomes

There is considerable variation in the amount and quality of evidence and research on the effects of NIFs on labour and employment. Most of the evidence is derived from PE, with little on HFs and SWFs. This reflects the fact that the impact of the latter is essentially indirect: fund influence on governance and strategy may have a 'downstream' impact on labour, but this is not easily traceable to fund activity. By contrast, since PE funds are usually the sole owners of portfolio companies, it is more straightforward to attribute changes to the activities of the fund. A further issue with SWF in particular is that they rarely indulge in public activism or active governance. Identifying the effects of SWF activity of any sort can be very difficult indeed, especially as they are increasingly allocating funds indirectly via PE and HFs. The upshot is that identifying the labour effects of NIFs is challenging. Most of the chapters in the book inevitably focus on those NIFs for which the conceptual linkages and data are clearest.

Much of the evidence generated up to now has come from studies conducted in the USA and the UK, though increasingly evidence is available from other European countries, including some pan-European studies, and from Japan. The evidence has been quite divergent, and it has been suggested that methodology and the identities of researchers or their backers have been key influences (Hall 2007). Case studies have tended to generate more adverse portrayals of the effects on labour than large-scale statistical surveys. In turn, it has been claimed that case study evidence reflects selection biases, with more controversial cases or those where the company was likely to fail anyway being chosen for analysis. Equally, surveys may be prone to survivor bias, that is, cases where employment decline has been severe because failed companies tend not to show up in these surveys. It has also been argued that research assisted by NIF bodies tends to generate findings which are more favourable to NIFs, whereas that undertaken or supported by labour organizations tends to focus on the negative effects. Thus, debates on the labour effects of NIFs tend to be highly charged, with much hinging on the nature and rationales for the methodologies used.

Labour Outcomes

Here, as a precursor to the succeeding chapters, we briefly review the evidence to date, and the issues which have emerged, on employment, wages and benefits, work organization, and industrial relations arrangements.

Employment

The issue which has attracted most attention has been the effects of NIFs on employment. In the case of PE, it has been claimed that pressures for greater efficiency, enforced through leverage, will force portfolio companies to reduce labour costs. Much of the empirical literature has focused on this claim. In one of the best studies to date, by Davis et al. (2011), it is found that in the USA net employment change is slightly negative compared to similar non-PE-backed firms. Behind this headline finding there is greater job loss in PE-backed firms, but also greater job creation via the creation of new establishments. The researchers refer to this as 'creative destruction'. Smaller-scale studies in other countries, such as Japan (Nose and Ito 2011) and the UK

(Goergen *et al.* 2011) also find employment reductions. Similarly, a range of case studies have also highlighted employment reductions (Clark 2009a; Faber 2006; Kaserer et al. 2007; PES 2007; SEIU 2007; Wilke et al. 2009). Other studies have also found evidence of employment growth after initial employment reductions (Amess and Wright 2007; Amess et al. 2008; Cressy et al. 2007; Boucly et al. 2008).

Activist HF interventions may lead to employment reductions due to pressures to redirect resources to shareholders and to break-up conglomerate companies. But it is difficult to trace employment change to HF activity because interventions are aimed at changing management strategy and governance rather than labour utilization directly. The extant evidence on the effects of HFs is case-study derived. These are reported in Wilke et al. (2009), PES (2007), and Gospel et al. (2011a, 2011b). The latter show how, in the case of KUKA (a German robotic manufacturer), an activist US HF forced a comparatively fast restructuring process, leading to a large divestment programme but also to increased profitability. In this case, employment in the firm fell, but this was mainly due to transfer of employees to other owners. In the case of the UK confectioner, Cadbury, successive interventions by activist HFs led to a series of divestments and eventually to a plant closure in the UK and ultimately to takeover by Kraft Foods. It is difficult to quantify the net employment effects because production was transferred to other companies or plants within the group. It is also difficult to attribute these effects unambiguously to HF activity.

The same can be said of SWF. Given SWF quiescence in governance, it is difficult to determine how or whether they affect employment. Gospel et al. (2011a) consider the case of the acquisition of the UK logistics company, P&O, by Dubai Ports World, allied to the Dubai SWF. They show no negative effect on employment levels, but small changes in voice and pensions arrangements were detrimental to labour. The most important, but indirect, effect of SWFs may be via their growing tendency to invest in PE funds.

Wages and Benefits

There is much less evidence on the impact on wages and benefits, and once again nearly all of the evidence comes from PE. In the USA, Davis et al. (2009) found a relative reduction in wages in PE-backed firms which initially had higher wages. For the UK, Thornton (2007) finds that pay grows more slowly in PE-owned firms than in the wider economy. Nevertheless wages grow in the period immediately after the buy-out, though average wages tend to be lower in PE-backed firms than others, especially in buy-ins involving incumbent managers (Amess and Wright 2007; Wright et al. 2007). It is possible that cuts in employment might be traded for higher wages, or that there are compositional changes in the workforces of NIF-backed companies in favour of more highly-paid workers. Alternatively, there may be substitution by lower-paid employers for more highly-paid employees in some sectors.

Case study evidence from the USA indicates reductions in employer healthcare provision (SEIU 2007). Pensions are also an area of concern, though there has been little systematic evidence: PE firms may close existing pension schemes to new entrants to reduce employer costs and may sell-on pension schemes to secondary operators to shore up balance sheets (Clark 2009b). However, the impact on pensions is likely to differ considerably between countries because of large variations in national pension regimes and legal systems.

Work Organization

Pressures from NIFs for restructuring and value transfer may lead to changes in work organization. It is possible that whilst some PE-owned firms may reduce employment, they may create better quality jobs for surviving employees. Unfortunately, there are few studies which test this proposition. However, the balance of evidence suggests that PE has positive effects on aspects of work organization, with PE-backed firms using a variety of 'high commitment' work practices (Bacon et al. 2004; Bacon et al. 2010b; Bruining et al. 2005). Others, however, have argued that many of these new work practices take the form of 'hard' human resource management and impose greater pressures on workers (Thornton 2007). A study of management practices from around the world has found that PE-backed firms tend to have more uniformly high levels of high performance practices, focusing on performance management and targets (Bloom et al. 2009).

Once again, we lack data on the impact of other types of NIFs on work organization possibly because any effects are likely to be indirect. Where HF activism focuses on the break-up of conglomerates, there may be implications for work organization, but the indirect character of these linkages makes it difficult to attribute work reorganization to the HF. To date, there is a similar lack of empirical evidence on SWFs.

Industrial Relations

The same intuitions govern predicted consequences of NIF activity for industrial relations, which is taken to cover the institutions and practices of employee representation, joint consultation, and collective bargaining. The financial pressures on PE-backed firms and their managers may lead them to disregard consultation and withdraw from relationships with trade unions. As with the areas discussed above, there is divergent evidence on these issues. Although some case studies show withdrawal from collective bargaining and union recognition (Clark 2009a; Evans and Habbard 2008; Faber 2006; ITUC 2007), there is equally evidence of PE-backed businesses working closely with employee representatives (Beeferman 2009; Westcott 2009). In some instances, unions view PE positively because of its potential to rescue failing firms and also to generate good returns for employer-union pension funds (Beeferman 2009). Other survey evidence meanwhile indicates little change in union recognition, collective bargaining, and joint consultation in most instances. There is some evidence, albeit not conclusive, that there may be increases in employee consultation in some cases (Bacon et al. 2010b).

Evidence from HFs and SWFs is again hard to come by, and the possible linkages between NIF activity and industrial relations practices are hard to trace. Most activist HF interventions occur away from the typical industrial relations arena (i.e. in company annual meetings), but may set in motion management strategies that ultimately lead to changes in industrial relations. Equally there are cases where unions have taken advantage of HF activism to raise industrial relations issues, as in the British bus company National Express in 2011. As for SWFs, two case studies by Wilke et al. (2009) of the UK company P&O by the Dubai SWF and the French company Cegelec by the Qatari SWF indicate little consultation with employees or their representatives, but no reduction in employment or conditions greater than the industry average.

The Moderating Effect of Labour Regulation

Each country chapter reviews existing evidence on the impact of NIFs on labour and adds new evidence. A key issue is also whether national labour systems influence the nature and extent of labour changes in response to NIF activity. To date, most research studies have not engaged with the possible moderating effects of national regulation and practices. However, the role of national regulatory systems can be captured by comparative studies, and evaluation of these is a major objective of this book.

NIFs' impact upon labour occurs through the changes which companies make in response to NIF ownership and interventions. Company responses are likely to be constrained by the extent and strength of employment protection and industrial relations legislation and institutions. On this basis, the impact of NIFs is likely to vary between countries, with greater and potentially more adverse effects on labour in countries with weaker labour and union protections. This suggests that labour will suffer more from NIF activity in LMEs, such as the USA and the UK, where employment protection, statutory voice arrangements, and unions are relatively weak. It is arguable too that weaker institutional constraints encourage higher levels of NIF activity especially of the type leading to extensive restructuring. The following features of national systems are likely to play a moderating role:

- *Employment protection legislation.* This is likely to affect the costs and benefits which a fund can expect to obtain from any restructuring. Legislation on layoffs and redundancy will affect the cost of restructuring. It should be noted that in certain European countries, such as the UK, PE takeovers, as share transactions, are not viewed as a change of control which trigger employee rights under the EU Directive on Safeguarding Employee Rights in the Event of Transfer of Undertakings.[8]
- *Laws on information and consultation.* Depending on the jurisdiction, this may be relevant and may require employers to disclose details of their activities and plans and to consult employees. In some cases, such as Germany and the Netherlands, this is enshrined in extensive legislation which *inter alia* provides rights for works councils. In other countries, such as the USA, the UK, and Italy, employee rights to be informed and consulted are more limited. In some countries, such as Germany, the Netherlands, and Sweden, employees may have rights to co-determine certain matters.
- *Law on employee directors.* Once more, in some jurisdictions, again such as Germany, the Netherlands, and Sweden, employees have the right to representation on company boards in certain circumstances, and this can provide information and resources which employees may be able to mobilize in the event of a fund intervention.

- *Trade union organization.* Along with the law, employees may be able to influence what NIFs do via their trade unions and collective bargaining. Crucially, success in this respect would seem likely to depend on the effectiveness of the trade union, which in turn depends on union membership levels and information/bargaining rights.

Nathusius and Achleitner (2009) argue that the institutional context moderates the effects of PE on employment, based on their finding that studies in France, Spain, and Belgium (all relatively highly regulated countries) indicate positive employment effects. The case studies of funds reported in Wilke et al. (2009) show how well-developed information and consultation institutions and co-determination rights can modify and mitigate restructuring attempts likely to impact negatively on employment and jobs. Finally, a recent study of the effects of PE by Bacon et al. (2010a), comparing employee relations changes under different social models in Europe, found that national institutional differences persist after buy-outs and PE funds adapt to national systems. However, in a follow-up study, they find no effects of either country of origin or activity on the propensity to introduce high performance work practices (Bacon et al. 2012).

The Effect of the Global Financial and Economic Crisis since 2007

With the advent of the global financial crisis and economic recession from 2007, investment funds have been affected in various ways, with varying implications for labour outcomes.

In the case of PE, with the drying up of cheap money and persistent uncertainties, PE houses have found it more difficult to raise funds. From 2008 onwards, returns to the limited partners in most PE funds proved disappointing, which has made raising new funds difficult. As a result, some funds have closed and the amount of new capital raised has declined. Worldwide, the number of deals and deal values fell from 2007 to 2009 (Kaplan and Strömberg 2009). Countries which were most affected were the USA and the UK. However, from a low in 2009, the number of deals has risen again and has exceeded 2005 levels (Pitchbook 2011). Nevertheless, the recession has reduced the number of new opportunities for investment and PE funds have large amounts of 'dry powder'—funds committed by limited partners which must be invested or returned along with the relevant management fees (Pitchbook 2011; Preqin 2011).

The response of PE funds to the recession has been varied with differing consequences for portfolio companies and their employees. On the one hand, recession has offered turnaround opportunities for PE houses and these may have helped save jobs in the long term. The difficulty of exiting from portfolio firms (Ernst and Young 2011) has also increased the number of mature portfolio investments, and this means that PE houses are living longer with these companies and their employees. On the other hand, servicing huge debt burdens in a recession puts pressure on PE owners to reduce costs and extract more value from their portfolio companies.

An important result of the recession has been changes in PE funds' exit behaviour. The number of IPOs has fallen since 2007 to around 10 per cent of the number of exits by trade and secondary sales in Europe (EVCA 2012). Meanwhile, there has been an increase in the number of secondary buy-outs where PE-owned companies are sold to other PE funds. Secondary buy-outs allow the exiting PE firm to make distributions to its limited partners and the purchasing fund to use some of its 'dry powder'. However, such buy-outs may pose problems for employees, who face yet another owner, further uncertainty, and the possibility of being subject to new pressures for value extraction, especially if the level of debt and debt servicing is increased.

An important issue is the potential distress and bankruptcies experienced by PE-owned companies. Even before the recession, as the US chapter suggests, bankruptcy rates of LBOs in that country were higher than those of comparable publicly-traded firms (see also Strömberg 2007). Since then, many companies acquired by PE have been forced to seek bankruptcy protection, such as the US NewPage Corporation (paper products), or breakup such as UK Southern Cross (care homes), or sale to major competitors as in the case of the UK EMI (music industry). There was a big increase in write-offs by PE houses in the immediate aftermath of the financial crisis, though this has been gradually declining in Europe since 2009 (EVCA 2012). A critical issue is whether the levels of leverage added to the balance sheets of portfolio companies by PE fund managers has added to the risk of business failure during the the crisis. It should be remembered that the legal structure of PE funds limits partners' losses to the equity invested in the distressed portfolio company. If a portfolio company defaults on its loans, the PE owners lose only the equity which was initially used to buy the company at risk. However, the costs for employees can be considerable.

Overall, the evidence suggests that, despite some high profile casualties, PE funds and PE-backed firms have so far weathered the worst of the crisis. However, looking to the future, it has been argued that the maturity of debt contracts entered into during the boom years threatens a 'wall of debt' between 2012 and 2016 (Linklaters 2012). This poses serious problems of refinancing and raises the prospect of defaults, which could hit some companies and their workforces hard in the next few years.

Since the onset of the crisis, the global HF industry has experienced substantial losses. Total AUM fell from around $2 trillion in 2007 to $1.5 trillion in 2008, though this has now recovered to a figure approaching 2007 levels (TheCityUK 2012a). HFs significantly reduced their equity holdings during the financial crisis because many investors withdrew their funds where they could (Ben-David et al. 2012). At the same time, some 2,000 HFs have gone out of business, with the number of HFs in 2008 being some 3,000 lower than in 2007. As of 2012, this figure has recovered somewhat to just under 9,000 HFs today.

A key factor impacting on HFs during the financial crisis was the decision by G20 countries in 2008 to introduce temporary bans on short-selling, especially in financial stocks. As for activist HFs, there was a lull in activist interventions from the onset of the financial crisis with some major activist HFs, such as The Children's Investment Fund (TCI), renouncing activism. However, TCI has subsequently resumed activist interventions; overall, activist campaigns in 2012 returned to the level observed in 2008 and there have been new campaigns, including the involvement of the US HF Third Point in Sony in Japan (Factset Research Systems 2012).

Since the financial crisis, HF investment in distressed debt has yielded the highest returns compared to other strategies—with average overall returns of 4 per cent in 2011 (Or and Barr 2011). In this way, it might be argued that HFs are filling a gap in the supply of capital, where traditional sources, such as commercial banks, are unwilling to take risks. Small and mid-sized companies, unable to raise money from banks or compete in bond markets for credit, have turned to HFs to borrow for both on-going operations and for new strategies and innovations. However, while filling a needed role in the post-crisis period, it should be remembered that HFs charge high interest rates. Moreover, they are known for their short time horizons, raising questions about whether they will quickly foreclose on loans which fall into arrears—a strategy referred to as 'loan to own' (Ahmed 2011).

In the case of SWFs, in the first two years of the financial crisis, the size of their AUM fell. However, in 2010, AUM by SWFs increased by 11 per cent to a record $4.2 trillion, with an additional $6.8 trillion held in other sovereign investment vehicles, such as development funds and pension reserve funds (TheCityUK 2011). There is some evidence that, in recent years, SWFs have shifted from low-risk to higher-risk/higher-return strategies. A key development has been the expansion of investment in PE and HFs. This has involved both relatively greater investments and also the acquisition of minority stakes in the firms themselves. Thus, the Abu Dhabi SWF has bought a 9 per cent stake in Apollo and a 7.5 per cent stake in Carlyle; the Kuwait and the Singapore funds have gained a 5 per cent stake in the Texas Pacific Group; the Chinese fund has bought a $3 billion share of Blackstone (de Swann 2010; Zuckerman 2011). Chinese SWFs have also invested significantly in HFs (Strasburg and Carew 2009). As a result of these developments, it is becoming increasingly difficult to tell who is invested in whom. In addition, due to dissatisfaction with fund performance during the financial crisis, some SWFs have begun to take more direct and proactive roles as investors. Thus, the investments of Qatar Investment Authority, for example, earned it a seat on the board of Veolia Environment in France and director-level representation at Harrods in the UK (Monitor Group 2011; Rugaber 2008; Weiss 2008).

Nevertheless, as the US chapter shows, SWFs are still constrained in expanding their influence over firms by national legislation and political sensitivities. Because of their continued secrecy and the complexity of their investments, it remains difficult to assess what effect they might have on companies and their employees.

Overview of the Book

The first three countries studied are all classified as LMEs in the VoC literature. In Chapter 2 on the USA, Appelbaum, Batt, and Lee show how PE and HFs had their origins in that country and have been the largest in terms of AUM and interventions in large companies. Despite legal constraints, SWF activity has also been significant in the USA, with growing involvement in banking and financial services.

The financial market and labour market regulatory contexts in the USA are described as weak. Drawing on the studies by Davis et al. (2008, 2009, 2011), the authors suggest that PE has had a negative effect on employment. Using case study material, they also cite other negative effects on wages and conditions. In addition, they point to the fact that PE has for the most part tried to avoid dealing directly with trade unions. HFs have had less effect on governance and employment relations, and here the authors cite evidence of both positive and negative effects. To date, SWFs have kept a low profile, preferring not to be seen to be involved in political and social matters. Overall, the authors suggest that all three types of investment funds saw a decline in their activities as a result of the 2007 crisis, but they have recovered relatively quickly and funds have moved into new areas, such as distressed debt.

The UK (Chapter 3) has the highest levels of PE, HF, and SWF activity in Europe. This is explained primarily by the permissive nature of UK financial and securities regulation and, to a lesser extent, of labour regulation. Fund activity grew significantly up to 2007 and then declined in the case of PE and HFs; since 2010, there has been a recovery in PE and HF activity. As for labour outcomes, it is rare for NIFs to consult with labour before and during the acquisition process. Overall, the studies suggest that NIF intervention and acquisition creates some turbulence in employment, with initial job loss, though also with some evidence of later job creation. Evidence on the effect on industrial relations is limited, but suggests that NIFs do not make major changes. Since the recession there have been several high profile cases of PE having a negative effect on employment systems. However, as yet their typicality is unknown.

Chapter 4 on Australia provides a third LME country study. It highlights two contradictory trends. Successive federal governments have attempted to create a favourable regulatory environment for financial institutions, including NIFs, through a series of general (reform of the financial market regulation) and specific (tax breaks for venture capital and investment fund capital gains) regulatory initiatives. At the same time, the mix of corporate and labour law in Australia imposes significant impediments to the capacity of new owners to restructure their obligations to the workforce inherited by their purchase. The regulatory web of labour law, with its provisions for transfer of business and rights for unions to be bargaining agents, means that investors taking over Australian corporate assets have little room to reduce their labour costs in the short term. Notwithstanding these restrictions, PE in particular has become more active in the acquisition of mature businesses, though HFs investing in Australian assets seem to be relatively inactive.

The next four countries examined are classified as European CMEs. Chapter 5 examines the German case, which is seen as one of the leading examples of coordinated capitalism in comparative political economy. However, several observers argue that financialization is leading to the dissolution of the German model, as banks are retreating from an active role in corporate governance and 'relational finance' is under pressure. Prior to the financial crisis, a heated public debate took place on the role of PE and HFs as 'locusts' in Germany. This chapter shows that NIFs are only one of a number of sources contributing to this transformation. Activist HFs appear not to have been very successful in Germany and their activity there has almost completely stopped since the crisis. Furthermore, works councils and board level employee representatives play important roles in moderating the impact of NIFs on labour.

Chapter 6 discusses the Netherlands, usually seen as another example of a CME. Due to the hybrid nature of the Dutch political economy, a 'compartmentalized' mode of financialization is hypothesized. This is characterized by an intermediate level of NIF penetration but a low level of NIF impact in terms of labour outcomes. These expectations are largely born out by the evidence. First, the Netherlands is indeed hospitable to foreign NIFs and has become one of the larger European targets for Anglo-American PE funds and HFs. The crisis since 2007 does not seem to have changed this. Second, in terms of labour outcomes, buy-outs do not negatively affect industrial relations and work relations. This is because labour market regulation and economic citizenship rights are determined at the national and sector level and are hence non-negotiable at the level of the firm. Before the crisis there was a striking mis-match between the absence of negative effects on labour and a hostile public discourse over foreign PE and HFs. This discourse has quietened as large public-to-private buy-outs have disappeared and HF activism has become more restricted to smaller firms and more defensive strategies. However, the fallout from the crisis is such that an unwilling government is increasingly forced to clamp down on banks and other financial actors. The Netherlands seems to be retracing some of its steps towards an Anglo-American system.

In Chapter 7 the Swedish case is discussed. It is shown how the deregulation of financial markets in Sweden in the late 1980s changed the structure of corporate ownership and paved the way for NIFs. However, in the light of the vocal criticisms of such funds heard elsewhere, the stance of Swedish labour appears strikingly different. Much of the legislation facilitating NIFs was in fact enacted under Social Democratic governments, and trade unions have been guardedly positive in their assessment of the funds. Whether this should be described as a capital–labour accord on financialization is open to debate. Although many of the regulatory changes were backed by the major trade union confederations, other reforms were resisted by them. In particular, the major blue-collar confederation, Landsorganisationen i Sverige (LO), disagreed with the deregulation of international capital mobility that was fundamental for the ascendance of NIFs. The current stance of the trade unions might be summarized as making the best of a bad situation, arguing from a position of weakness rather than strength. Instead of actively trying to shape the market economy to further the interests of labour, trade unions are now restricted to curbing the excesses of the market. This could of course still be labelled an accord, yet one radically different from earlier compromises in Sweden.

In Chapter 8, it is shown that PE has been a significant development in Italy, but HF and SWF investments have been limited and without significant consequences for labour and industrial relations. Building on statistical data, three short case studies, and empirical evidence linked with the financial crisis, Cattero discusses the thesis that there is a specific 'Italian way' to PE. Four ideal types of PE are proposed: two types which are antithetical to each other (the 'entrepreneurial' and the 'speculative') and two hybrid forms (the 'industrial buy-out' and the 'financial expansion'). Given the weakness of trade unions in the private sector, the limited nature of collective bargaining at company level, and the absence of any form of participation in the governing body of companies, trade unions and their representatives have very little potential to bargain over the possible entry of funds into companies. They may be informed about the entry of PE as negotiations are underway but normally they receive information after the event. At best, they may be able to bargain over the restructuring which follows PE investment. However, in the case studies, unions were for the most part unable to exert any influence.

In Chapter 9, the activities of NIFs are examined in Poland. Nölke and Vliegenthart (2009) have suggested that the LME/CME typology is difficult to apply to CEE, since it was based on advanced industrialized countries. Instead, Poland should be seen as a dependent market

economy, since most dominant firms are branches of foreign multinationals or owned by foreign investors. Poland is a country where PE
is well-established, but where HF and SWF presence is sporadic. The
authors consider three detailed case studies of PE investment: in a
household appliances, a telecoms, and an IT company. Their research
shows that the impact of PE on working conditions and labour in
Poland has been neutral. They point out that the trends and practices
in the case study companies are broadly in line with those observable among competitors and in the private sector more generally.
Although the authors are cautious about generalizing, because of
the small number of observations, they highlight that changes in
employment in two of the surveyed companies are similar to what
has occurred amongst non-PE competitors. Likewise, their data on
pay levels suggest that there is little difference between PE-backed
and other companies. Union structure is not altered by PE involvement. They therefore conclude that the impact of PE on labour has
been neutral overall.

The tenth chapter focuses on a leading non-European CME,
Japan. This chapter examines the assumption that the behaviour
of investment funds is inconsistent with the traditional focus by
Japanese managers on employees' interests as much as on shareholders' wealth. In the 1990s, there were significant changes in
Japan's financial markets, including an increase in foreign shareholders and the introduction of new financial products. In response
to these changes, new legislation was introduced. One of the main
aims of these changes was to make it easier for firms to undertake
reorganizations. This has facilitated mergers, acquisitions, divestments, and other types of restructuring. It is important to note that
there is little mention of employees in these new laws which are
mainly aimed at revitalizing financial markets. Although PE, activist HFs, and SWFs have been less active in Japan than some other
countries, the number of transactions, as well as the transaction
size, increased, at least up to the late 2000s. Some statistical studies
show that PE transactions have a negative effect on employment
and a positive effect on shareholder returns. However, it is still difficult for management to make significant organizational change
without the consent of employees. The number of hostile takeovers
is still very low and this provides an important context for fund
activity.

Finally, the concluding chapter summarizes the main lessons
learned from the country chapters, draws out the implications for the

literature on financialization and comparative capitalisms, and suggests some research priorities for the future.

Conclusions

Together, the chapters bring out the important implications of NIFs and financialization for labour outcomes. We conclude with a number of general points which are derived from the country chapters and which are returned to in the concluding chapter.

First, the advent of these NIFs is to be seen as an important aspect of the growing financialization of the economy and the firm over the last three decades or so. Financialization involves other developments, such as the the growth of financial markets, changes in the nature of financial actors, the spread of neo-liberal ideologies and values concerning markets and firms, and a complex deregulation and re-regulation of finance. However, one key aspect of financialization has been the increasing number and importance of new types of ownership in the form of PE, HFs, and SWFs. Some aspects of their activities have declined since the advent of the global financial and economic crisis beginning in 2007. However, there has been some recovery and moves into new areas of activity, including different geographical areas. In the past, PE and HFs have passed through waves of expansion and contraction and, along with SWFs, they are likely to continue to be an important aspect of the financial environment in the future.

Second, the evidence suggests these new funds pose challenges for employment and labour. They raise questions as to how employees and their representatives are to communicate with these new owners. For the most part, employees have not been consulted at the acquisition stage, though equally new owners have usually not radically changed industrial relations arrangements in portfolio companies. The balance of evidence is that they also pose a threat to employment and to traditional ways of working. If they do not always destroy jobs and sometimes indeed create more jobs in the longer term, they nevertheless create employment turbulence and uncertainties for employees. In addition, they can impact wage systems, wage hierarchies, and benefit systems within firms. The effect varies, with PE, HFs, and SWFs having a differential effect in that order. The aim of the book is to elaborate and draw conclusions on the nature and extent of these challenges.

Third, the comparative evidence shows that institutions and regulation matter. This is not just in terms of capital market institutions and regulations, but also labour laws and labour institutions. Variations in employment protection regulation do not inhibit fund-invested companies from undertaking large-scale restructuring. However, national regulations relating to employee voice and worker representation affect the extent to which employee representatives are informed and consulted in restructuring. These are important considerations at the present time when all countries are searching for new ways to regulate the power of finance.

NOTES

1. It should be noted that there is no universally accepted definition of NIFs. The chapters in this book mainly use the term 'new investment funds' but sometimes 'alternative investment funds' to refer to these three types of funds.
2. This book builds on two earlier studies by some of the researchers for the European Commission (Wilke et al. 2009 and Voss et al. 2009). This particular project was for the European Foundation for the Improvement of Living and Working Conditions (Gospel et al. 2010).
3. We do not cover the fast developing and emerging economies, such as the BRIC (Brazil, Russia, India, and China) countries and countries in Latin America and Africa. This is because, as yet, the activities of NIFs within these countries are relatively small-scale, though some (China, for instance) play an important role in SWF activity
4. Full versions of most of these case studies have been published in Gospel et al. (2010).
5. For Germany, see the recent case of the German Stock Exchange as well as other examples in Voss et al. (2009) and Holler and Bessler (2008). For the UK, see the boardroom battle over the leisure company M&B.
6. For detailed asset allocations of each SWF, see Monitor Group's SWF database <http://www.monitor.com/tabid/202/L/en-US/Default.aspx>, which covers the investment activities of 33 SWFs from 1981 to the present.
7. For example, it is estimated that PE took \$188bn in dividends out of their portfolio companies between 2004 and 2011 (*Economist* 28 January 2012).
8. 2001/23/EC. This replaces Directives 77/187/EC (the Acquired Rights Directive) and 98/50/C.

BIBLIOGRAPHY

Achleitner, A.-K. and Lutz, E. (2009). 'Angels or demons? Evidence on the impact of private equity firms on employment', *Journal of Business Economics (ZfB)*, Special Issue Entrepreneurial Finance, 5: 53–81.

Ahmed, A. (2011). 'Bank said no? Hedge funds fill a void in lending', *New York Times*, 8 June, <http://dealbook.nytimes.com/2011/06/08/bank-said-no-hedge-funds-fill-a-void-in-lending/>.

Amable, B. (2003). *The Diversity of Modern Capitalism*. Oxford: Oxford University Press.

Amess, K. and Wright, M. (2007). 'The wage and employment effects of leveraged buy-outs in the U.K.', *International Journal of Economics and Business*, 14 (2): 179–95.

Amess, K., Girma, S., and Wright, M. (2008). 'What are the Wage and Employment Consequences of Leveraged Buy-Outs, Private Equity and Acquisitions in the UK?', CMBOR Occasional Paper, London: Centre for Management Buy-out Research (CMBOR).

Australian Private Equity and Venture Capital Association (AVCA) (2012). *Newsletter*, <http://www.avcal.com.au/news>

Bacon, N., Wright, M., and Demina, N. (2004). 'Management buy-outs and human resource management', *British Journal of Industrial Relations*, 42 (2): 325–47.

Bacon, N., Wright, M., Scholes, L., and Meuleman, M. (2010a). 'Assessing the impact of private equity on industrial relations in Europe', *Human Relations*, 63 (9): 1343–70.

Bacon, N., Wright, M., Scholes, L., and Meuleman, M. (2010b). 'The Impact of Private Equity on Management Practices in European Buy-outs: Short-termism and Anglo American Effects', CMBOR Occasional Paper, London: Centre for Management Buy-out Research (CMBOR).

Bacon, N., Wright, M., Scholes, L., and Meuleman, M. (2012). 'The impact of private equity on management practices in European buy-outs: Short-termism and Anglo-American effects', *Industrial Relations*, 51 (2): 605–26.

Bebchuk, L. and Fried, J. (2004). 'Pay without Performance: The Unfilled Promise of Executive Compensation', UC Berkeley Public Law Research Paper, 537783, Cambridge, MA: Harvard University Press.

Becht, M., Franks, J., and Grant, J. (2010). 'Hedge Fund Activism in Europe', ECGI Working Paper Series in Finance, 283/2010, May, <http://papers.ssrn.com/sol3/papers.cfm?abstract_id=1616340>.

Beeferman, L. (2009). 'Private equity and American labor: Pragmatic responses mirroring labor's strengths and weaknesses', *Journal of Industrial Relations*, 51: 543–56.

Ben-David, I., Franzoni, F., and Moussawi, R. (2012). 'Hedge fund stock trading in the financial crisis of 2007–2009', *Review of Financial Studies*, 25: 1–54.

Bernstein, S., Lerner, J., Sorensen, M., and Stromberg, P. (2010). 'Private equity, industry performance and cyclicality', in A. Gurung and J. Lerner (eds), *Globalization of Alternative Investments*. Working Papers, 3, The Global Economic Impact of PE Report 2010, New York: World Economic Forum USA.

Bernstein, S., Lerner, J., and Schoar, A. (2013). 'The investment strategies of sovereign wealth funds', *Journal of Economic Perspectives*, 27 (2): 219–38.

Bloom, N., Sadun, R., and van Reenen, J. (2009). 'Do Private Equity Firms have Better Management Practices?', Occasional Paper 24, London: London School of Economics, Centre for Economic Performance.

Boucly, Q., Sraer, D., and Thesmar, D. (2008). 'Leveraged Buy-Outs: Evidence from French Deals', Working Paper, The Global Economic Impact of Private Equity Report 2009, New York: World Economic Forum.

Bozkaya, A., and Kerr, R. (2009). 'Labor Regulations and European Private Equity', Harvard Business School Entrepreneurial Management Working Paper, 08-043 / MIT Sloan Research Paper, 4771-10, <http://ssrn.com/abstract=1527168>.

Brav, A., Jiang, W., Partnoy, F., and Thomas, R. (2008). 'Hedge fund activism, corporate governance, and firm performance', *Journal of Finance*, 63 (4): 1729–75.

Bruining, H., Boselie, P., Wright, M., and Bacon, N. (2005). 'The impact of business ownership change on employee relations: Buy-outs in the UK and the Netherlands', *International Journal of Human Resource Management*, 16: 345–65.

BVCA (2006). *The Economic Impact of Private Equity in the UK*. London: British Private Equity and Venture Capital Association (BVCA).

Clark, I. (2009a). 'Private equity in the UK: Job regulation and trade unions', *Journal of Industrial Relations*, 51: 489–500.

Clark, I. (2009b). 'The private equity business model and associated strategies for HRM: Evidence and implications', *International Journal of Human Resource Management*, 20 (10): 2030–48.

Clifford, C. (2008). 'Value creation or destruction? Hedge funds as shareholder activists', *Journal of Corporate Finance*, 14: 323–36.

Coalition of Private Investment Companies (2009). 'Hedge Funds: How They Serve Investors in U.S. and Global Markets', August.

Coggan, P. (2011). *Hedge Funds, What They Are, What They Do, Their Risks, Their Advantages*. Hoboken: Wiley and Sons.

Cressy, R., Munari, F., and Malipiero, A. (2007). 'Creative Destruction: Evidence that Buy-Outs Cut Jobs to Raise Returns', Working Paper, Birmingham: University of Birmingham.

Cusworth, E. (2011). 'Prospects looking better for activist hedge funds after 2011 rough ride', *Hedge Funds Review*, 31 October, <http://www.hedgefundsreview.com/hedge-funds-review/feature/2118270/prospects-looking-activist-hedge-funds-2011-rough-ride>.

Davis, G. (2008). 'A new finance capitalism? Mutual funds and ownership re-concentration in the United States', *European Management Review*, 5 (1): 11–21.

Davis, G., Haltiwanger, J., Jarmin, R., Lerner, J., and Miranda, J. (2008). 'Private equity and employment', in A. Gurung and J. Lerner (eds), *Globalization of Alternative Investments*. Working Papers, 1, The Global Economic Impact of PE 2008, New York: World Economic Forum, 43–64, <http://www.weforum.org/pdf/cgi/pe/Full_Report.pdf>.

Davis, G., Haltiwanger, J., Jarmin, R., Lerner, J., and Miranda, J. (2009). 'Private equity: Jobs and productivity', in A. Gurung and J. Lerner (eds), *Globalization of Alternative Investments*. Working Papers, 2, The Global Economic Impact of PE 2009, New York: World Economic Forum, 27–43.

Davis, G., Haltiwanger, J., Jarmin, R., Lerner, J., and Miranda, J. (2011). 'Private Equity and Employment', NBER Working Paper, 17399, Cambridge: National Bureau of Economic Research, <http://www.nber.org/papers/w17399>.

de Swann, J. (2010). 'China goes to Wall Street: Beijing's evolving U.S. investment strategy', *Foreign Affairs*, 29 April, <http://www.foreignaffairs.com/articles/66398/jc-de-swaan/china-goes-to-wall-street>.

Dore, R. (2008). 'Financialization of the global economy', *Industrial and Corporate Change*, 17: 1097–112.

Dumenil, G. and Levy, D (2011). *The Crisis of Neo-liberalism*, Cambridge, MA: Harvard University Press

Dyck, A. and Morse, A. (2011). 'Sovereign wealth fund portfolios', in AEA. *AEA Annual Meeting*. 7 January, Chicago.

The Economist (2012). 'Private equity under scrutiny: Bain or blessing? The buy-out industry is under attack for destroying jobs: Its returns to investors are the real problem', 28 January, London, New York: Economist.

Engelen, E., and Konings, M. (2010). 'Financial capitalism resurgent: Comparative institutionalism and the challenges of financialization', in G. Morgan, J. Campbell, C. Crouch, and O. Pedersen (eds), *The Oxford Handbook of Comparative Institutional Analysis*. Oxford: Oxford University Press, 601–24.

Epstein, G. (2005). *Financialization and the World Economy*. Aldershot: Edward Elgar.

Ernst and Young (2011). Return to Warmer Waters: How do Private Equity Investors Create Value? Study of 2010 North American Exits, Ernst and Young.

ETUC (2009). 'Memorandum of the European Trade Union Confederation to the UK Parliament', April, European Trade Union Confederation (ETUC).

Evans, J. and Habbard, P. (2008). 'From shareholder value to private equity: The changing face of financialisation of the economy', *Transfer*, 14 (1): 63–76.

EVCA (2012). *Pan-European Private Equity Performance Benchmarking Study*. Brussels: European Venture Capital Association (EVCA).

EVCA and KPMG (2008). 'Benchmarking European Tax and Legal Environments: Indicators of Tax and Legal Environments Favouring the Development of Private Equity and Venture Capital, and Entrepreneurship in Europe'. Zaventem: EVCA/KPMG.

EVCA and PriceWaterhouseCoopers (2001). 'Survey of the Economic and Social Impact of Management Buyouts & Buyins in Europe', Research Paper, Zaventem: EVCA.

Faber, O. (2006). 'Finanzinvestoren in Deutschland: Portraits und Investitionsbeispiele unter besonderer Berücksichtigung der Auswirkungen auf die Beschäftigung', Arbeitspapier 123, Düsseldorf: H ans-Böckler-Stiftung.

Factset Research Systems (2012). 'Hedge Fund Ownership', New York: Factset.

Fama, E. (1970). 'Efficient capital markets: A review of theory and empirical work', *Journal of Finance*, 25 (2): 383–417.

Fernandes, N. G. (2011). 'Sovereign wealth funds: Investment choices and implications around the world', <http://ssrn.com/abstract=1341692>.

Financial Stability Board (2012). *Global Shadow Banking Monitoring Report 2012*. Basel: Financial Stability Board.

Financial Times (2007). *100 Hedge Funds to Watch* <http://www.ft.com/cms/02fd5a42-f338-11db-9845-000b5df10621.pdf>.

Fligstein, N. (2001). *The Architecture of Markets: An Economic Sociology of Twenty-First-Century Capitalist Societies*. Princeton, NJ: Princeton University Press.

Folkman, P., Froud, J., Williams, K., and Johal, S. (2009). 'Private equity: Levered on capital or labour', *Journal of Industrial Relations*, 51: 517–27.

Friedman, M. (1970). 'The social responsibility of business is to increase its profits', *New York Times Magazine*, 13 September: 32–3, 122–6.

Fruhan, W. (2010). 'The Hedge Fund Industry', Background Note 208-126, April, Cambridge, MA: Harvard Business School.

Gilligan, J. and Wright, M. (2010). *Private Equity Demystified: An Explanatory Guide*. London: ICAEW.

Goergen, M., O'Sullivan, N. and Wood, G. (2011). 'Private equity takeovers and employment in the UK: some empirical evidence', *Corporate Governance*, 19 (3): 259–275.

Gospel, H. and Pendleton, A. (2003). 'Finance, corporate governance and the management of labour: A conceptual and comparative analysis', *British Journal of Industrial Relations*, 41 (3): 557–82.

Gospel, H. and Pendleton, A. (2012). 'Corporate governance and labour', in M. Wright, S. Donald, K. Keasey, and I. Filatotchev (eds), *The Oxford Handbook of Corporate Governance*, Oxford: Oxford University Press.

Gospel, H., Vitols, S., and Wilke, P. (2010). 'The Impact of Investment Funds on Restructuring Practices and Employment Levels', European Foundation for the Improvement of Living and Working Conditions, Dublin, 1–103.

Gospel, H., Haves, J., Pendleton, A., Vitols, S., Wilke, P., Catero, B., Duman, A., Dunin-Wasowicz, S., Engelen, E., Korpi, T., and Pradelle, P. (2011a). *The Impact of Investment Funds on Restructuring Practices and Employment Levels: Company Case Studies*. Dublin: Eurofound.

Gospel, H., Pendleton, P., Vitols, S., and Wilke, P. (2011b). 'Investment funds, corporate governance, and labour outcomes', *Corporate Governance International Review*, May, 19 (3).

Groh, A., Liechtenstein, H., and Lieser, K. (2012). *The Global Venture Capital and Private Equity Country Attractiveness Index*. Navarra: IESE Business School.

Hall, D. (2007). *Methodological Issues in Estimating the Effect of Private Equity on Employment*. London: University of Greenwich.

Hall, P. and Soskice, D. (2001). *Varieties of Capitalism: The Institutional Foundations of Comparative Advantage*. Oxford: Oxford University Press.

Holler, J., and Bessler, W. (2008). 'Capital Markets and Corporate Control: Empirical Evidence from Hedge Fund Activism in Germany', Discussion Paper, Giessen: University of Giessen.

IFSL (2009). 'Hedge Funds 2009', April, London: International Financial Services London (IFSL).

IFSL (2010). *Sovereign Wealth Funds 2010*. March, London, International Financial Services London (IFSL).

Institutional Investor (2012). *Hedge Funds and Alternatives* <http://www.institutionalinvestor.com/Asset-Management-Hedge-Funds-and-Alternatives.html>.

ITUC (2007). *Where the House Always Wins: Private Equity, Hedge Funds and the New Casino Capitalism*. ITUC Report, Brussels: International Trade Union Confederation (ITUC).

Jackson, G. and Miyajima, H. (2008). 'A comparison of mergers and acquisitions in Japan, Europe, and the United States', in R. Strange and G. Jackson (eds), *Corporate Governance and International Business: Strategy, Performance and Institutional Change*. Academy of International Business Series, 15, London: Palgrave Macmillan, 186–207.

Jensen, M. (1986). 'Agency costs of free cash flow, corporate finance, and takeovers', *The American Economic Review*, 76 (2): 323–9.

Jensen, M., and Meckling, W. (1976). 'The theory of the firm: Managerial behaviour, agency costs and ownership structure', *Journal of Financial Economics*, 3 (4): 305–60.

Johan, S., Knill, A., and Mauck, N. (2011). 'Determinants of sovereign wealth fund investment in PE', in AEA, *AEA Annual Conference 2012*. Chicago: AEA.

Kahan, M. and Rock, E. (2006). 'Hedge funds in corporate governance and corporate control', *University of Pennsylvania Law Review*, 155: 1021–93.

Kaplan, S. and Strömberg, P. (2009). 'Leveraged buy-outs and private equity', *Journal of Economic Perspectives*, 23: 121–46.

Kaserer, C., Achleitner, A.-K., von Einem, C., and Schiereck, D. (2007). *Private Equity in Deutschland: Rahmenbedingungen, ökonomische Bedeutung und Handlungsempfehlungen*. Norderstedt: Books on Demand.

Katelouzou, D. (2013). 'Myths and Realities of Hedge Fund Activism: Some Empirical Evidence', *Virginia Law and Business Review*, 7 (3): 459–511.

Kay, J. (2012). *The Kay Review of UK Equity Markets and Long-Term Decision Making*. London: Department of Business, Innovation, and Skills.

Khurana, R (2007). *From Higher Aims to Hired Hands*. Princeton, Princeton University Press.

Klein, A. and Zur, E. (2009). 'Entrepreneurial shareholder activism: Hedge funds and other private investors', *Journal of Finance*, 64 (1): 187–229.

Klein, P., Chapman, J., and Mondelli, M. (2012). 'Private equity and entrepreneurial governance: Time for a balanced view', *Academy of Management Perspectives*, 29 November.

Kogut, B. (2012). *The Small Worlds of Corporate Governance*. Cambridge, MA: MIT Press.

Konzelmann, S., Fovargue-Davies, M., and Schnyder, G. (2012). 'The faces of liberal capitalism: Anglo-Saxon banking systems in crisis?', *Cambridge Journal of Economics*, 36 (2): 495–524.

Krippner, G. (2011). *Capitalizing on Crisis: The Political Origins of the Rise of Finance*. Cambridge, MA: Harvard University Press.

Kunzel, P., Lu, Y., Petrova, I., and Pihlman, J. (2011). 'Investment Objectives of Sovereign Wealth Funds: A Shifting Paradigm', IMF Working Paper, WP/11/ 19, Monetary and Capital Markets Department

Lapavitsas, C. (2011). 'Theorising financialisation', *Work, Employment and Society*, 25 (4): 611–26.

Lazonick, W. (2011). 'Reforming the financialised business corporation', mimeo, Uinversity of Massachusetts.

Lazonick, W. and O'Sullivan, M. (2000). 'Maximising shareholder value: A new ideology for corporate governance', *Economy and Society*, 29 (1): 13–35.

Linklaters (2012). *Off Piste: Negotiating Europe's LBO Debt Mountain*. London: Linklaters.

Lysandrou, P. (2012). 'The primacy of hedge funds in the subprime crisis', *Journal of Post Keynesian Economics*, Winter 2011–12, 34 (2): 225.

MacKenzie, D. (2006). *An Engine Not a Camera: How Financial Models Shape the Markets*. Cambridge, MA: MIT Press.

Manne, H. (1965). 'Mergers and the market for corporate control', *Journal of Political Economy*, 73 (2): 110–20.

Mayer, C. (2013). *Firm Commitment*. Oxford: Oxford University Press.

Monitor Group (2011). *Braving the New World: Sovereign Wealth Fund Investment in the Uncertain Times of 2010*. SWF Report, <http://www.monitor.com/tabid/69/ctl/ArticleDetail/mid/705/CID/20110606072349951/CTID/1/L/en-US/Default.aspx>.

Nathusius, E. and Achleitner, A.-K. (2009). 'Angels or Demons? Evidence on the Impact of Private Equity Firms on Employment', Munich: Technical University, Center for Entrepreneurial and Financial Studies.

Nölke, A. and Vliegenthart, A. (2009). 'Enlarging the varieties of capitalism: The emergence of dependent market economies in east central Europe', *World Politics*, October, 61 (4): 670–702.

Nose, Y. and Ito, A. (2011). 'Kokai Izigata Biauto Zisshi Kigyo no Choki Pafomansu' [The Long-term Performance of PIPEs in Japan], Hitotsubashi IS-FS Working Paper Series FS-2011-J-002, Tokyo: Hitotsubashi University.

Or, A. and Barr, A. (2011). 'Hedge-fund assets reclaim pre-crisis level: Aim higher', *Wall Street Journal*, 10 March.

Orhangazi, O. (2008). 'Financialization and capital accumulation in the non-financial corporate sector', *Cambridge Journal of Economics*, 32 (6): 863–86.

PES (2007). *Hedge Funds and Private Equity-A Critical Analysis*. Report of the PSE-Group in European Parliament, Party of European Socialists (PES).

Pitchbook (2011). *The Private Equity Breakdown 4Q2011*. Report, Seattle: Pitchbook.

Preqin (2011). *Preqin Global Private Equity Report*. London, New York, Singapore, Redwood Vally: Preqin.

Preqin (2012). *The 2012 Preqin Sovereign Wealth Fund Review*. London: Preqin.

Preqin (2013). *The 2013 Preqin Global Private Equity Report*. February, 9 (2), London, New York, Singapore, Redwood Vally: Preqin.

Private Equity International (2011). *PEI 300* <http://www.peimedia.com>.

Rehman, A. (2010). *Gulf Capital and Islamic Finance: The Rise of the New Global Players*. New York: McGraw-Hill.

Rivas, T. (2013). 'Relative value now largest hedge fund strategy by AUM: JPMorgan', *Barron's*, Focus on Funds, 20 March.

Rugaber, C. (2008). 'Funds transparency woes could worsen', *AP Business*, 3 March.

SEIU (2007). *Behind the Buy-Outs: Inside the World of Private Equity*. New York: Service Employees International Union (SEIU).

Sethi, A. (2008). 'Sovereign wealth funds, private equity funds, and financial markets', *The Journal of Private Equity*, Fall 2008, 11 (4): 12–27.

Shertler, A. (2003). 'Driving Forces of Venture Capital Investments in Europe: A Dynamic Panel Data Analysis', EIFC Working Paper, 03-27, Maastricht: United Nations University.

Sinclair, T. (2005). *The New Masters of Capital: American Bond Rating Agencies and the Politics of Creditworthiness*. Ithaca, NY: Cornell University Press.

Sovereign Wealth Fund Institute (2012). *Fund Rankings* <http://www.swfinstitute.org/fund-rankings/>.

Stedman Jones, D. (2012). *Masters of the Universe: Hayek, Friedman and the Birth of Neo-Liberal Markets*. Princeton, NJ: Princeton University Press.

Strasburg, J. and Carew, R. (2009). 'Oaktree to receive $1 Billion from CIC', *Wall Street Journal*, 28 September, <http://compliancesearch.com/wallstreetjobreport/current-affairs/oaktree-to-receive-1-billion-from-cic/>.

Strömberg, P. (2007). *The New Demography of Private Equity*. Stockholm: Swedish Institute for Financial Research.

Temple, P. (2001). *Hedge Funds: The Courtesans of Capitalism*. Chichester: Wiley and Sons.

TheCityUK (2011). *Sovereign Wealth Fund*. Financial Market Series, April, <http://www.thecityuk.com/assets/Uploads/Sovereign-Wealth-Funds-2011.pdf>.

TheCityUK (2012a). *Fund Management*. November, London: TheCityUK.

TheCityUK (2012b). Sovereign Wealth Funds, February, London: The CityUK

TheCityUK (2013). *Sovereign Wealth Funds*. March, London: TheCityUK.

Thornton, P. (2007). *Inside the Dark Box: Shedding Light on Private Equity*. London: the Work Foundation.

Treasury Select Committee (2007). *Private Equity*. Tenth Report of Session 2006-07, 1, Report together with formal minutes, HC567-1, London: Treasury Select Committee, House of Commons.

Van Treeck, T. (2009). 'The political economy debate on "financialisation"—a macroeconomic perspective', *Review of International Political Economy*, 16 (5): 907–44.

Vitols, S. (1997). 'Financial systems and industrial policy in Germany and Great Britain: The limits of convergence', in D. Forsyth and T. Notermans (eds), *Regime Changes: Macroeconomic Policy and Financial Regulation in Europe from the 1930s to the 1990s*. Providence: Berghahn Books, 221–55.

Vitols, S. (2001). 'The origins of bank-based and market-based financial systems: Germany, Japan, and the United States', in W. Streeck and K. Yamamura (eds), *The Origins of Nonliberal Capitalism: Germany and Japan*. Ithaca, NY: Cornell University Press, 171–99.

Vitols, S. (2003). 'From banks to markets: The political economy of liberalization of the German and Japanese financial systems', in K. Yamamura and W. Streeck (eds), *The End of Diversity? Prospects of Germans and Japanese Capitalism*. Ithaca, NY: Cornell University Press, 240–60.

Voss, E., Vitols, S., Wilke, P., and Haves, J. (2009). *Data Collection Study on the Impact of Private Equity, Hedge and Sovereign Funds on Industrial Change in Europe*. Report prepared for the European Economic and Social Committee, Hamburg: Wilke, Maack und Partner.

Watt, A. (2008). 'The impact of private equity on European companies and workers: Key issues and a review of the evidence', *Industrial Relations Journal*, 39 (6): 548–68.

Weiss, M. (2008). *Sovereign Wealth Funds: Background and Policy Issues for Congress*. CRS Report for Congress RL34336, 03 September, Washington, DC: Congressional Research Service.

Westcott, M. (2009). 'Private equity in Australia', *Journal of Industrial Relations*, 51: 529–42.

Wilke, P., Vitols, S., Haves, J., Gospel, H., and Voss, E. (2009). *The Impacts of Private Equity Investors, Hedge Funds and Sovereign Wealth Funds on Industrial Restructuring in Europe as Illustrated by Case Studies*. Report to European Commission: Employment, Social Affairs and Equal Opportunities.

Wright, M., Burrows, A., Ball, R., Scholes, L., Meuleman, M., and Amess, K. (2007). *The Implications of Alternative Investment Vehicles for Corporate Governance: A Survey of Empirical Research*. Report prepared for the Steering Group on Corporate Governance, Paris: OECD.

Zorn, D. (2004). 'Here a chief, there a chief: The rise of the CFO in the American firm', *American Sociological Review*, 69, June: 345–64.

Zuckerman, G. (2011). 'Kuwait and Singapore acquire slice of TPG', *Wall Street Journal*, 2 April, <http://online.wsj.com/article/SB10001424052748 703806304576236424131916608.html>.

2

Financial Intermediaries in the United States: Development and Impact on Firms and Employment Relations

EILEEN APPELBAUM,
ROSEMARY BATT, AND
JAE EUN LEE

Introduction

Private equity (PE), hedge funds (HFs), sovereign wealth funds (SWFs), and other private pools of capital form part of the growing shadow banking system in the United States, where these new financial intermediaries provide an alternative investment mechanism to the traditional banking system. PE and HFs have their origins in the USA, while the first SWF was created by the Kuwaiti Government in 1953. While they have separate roots and distinct business models, these alternative investment vehicles have increasingly merged into overarching asset management funds which encompass all three alternative investments. These funds have wielded increasing power in financial and non-financial sectors—not only via direct investments but also indirectly, as their strategies—such as high use of debt to fund investments—have been increasingly adopted by investment arms of banks and by publicly-traded corporations. In this chapter we outline the changes in the US regulatory environment which have facilitated the rapid growth of alternative or new investment funds (AIFs or NIFs) and then examine the specific features of these funds, including their growth, business models, and implications for firms and employees.

The Institutional Environment

Part of the power and dramatic growth in the activities of PE and other NIFs is related to the weak regulatory environment in the USA—particularly the financial regulatory regime, and to a lesser extent, labour market laws, and institutions.

Financial Regulation

Four laws provide the regulatory framework for US public corporations and the financial services industry: the Securities Act 1933, Securities Exchange Act 1934, Investment Company Act 1940 (Company Act), and Investment Advisers Act 1940 (Advisers Act). The Securities Act prohibits fraud, requires registration and public reporting by publicly-traded firms, and gives authority to the Federal Securities and Exchange Commission (SEC) to regulate the industry. The Company Act requires investment funds to disclose their financial policies, restricts activities such as the use of leverage and short-selling, and requires a board structure with a substantial percentage of disinterested members. The Advisers Act requires the registration of fund managers, enforces compliance with fiduciary responsibilities, and limits the performance fees they may charge (Goldberg et al. 2010).

In practice, most PE and HFs have avoided these regulations by limiting their funds' size to that which is defined as exempt under law. This has allowed them, in contrast to mutual funds for example, to engage in financial practices such as selling securities short, making use of substantial leverage, and adopting performance-based fees, which increase with fund gains but do not necessarily decrease with losses. Thus the funds have operated with little transparency (even to their investors) and without board oversight.

By the 1990s, deregulation of banking and financial services led to the dramatic growth of PE and other private investment pools. In the 1970s, Congress passed laws allowing pension funds and insurance companies to invest in stock and high risk bonds for the first time (Employment Retirement Income Security Acts (ERISA), 1974 and 1978). In the 1980s, it allowed savings and loan banks to invest in risky commercial activities, including bonds rated as 'high risk' ('junk bonds'), and hence more likely to default. The Reagan administration further relaxed enforcement of antitrust and securities laws, and corporate raiders grew more powerful after the Supreme Court struck down state anti-takeover laws in 1982 (Jarrell 1983). In turn, the emergence of large pools of liquid capital for junk bonds facilitated leveraged buy-outs (LBOs), in which investors bought companies with a small down payment and borrowed the rest by using the assets of the acquired company as collateral. This high leverage model, which often led to financial distress or bankruptcy, became a central building block of the PE model of the 1990s.

Banking deregulation continued with the 1999 Gramm–Leach–Bliley Act, which repealed the Glass–Steagal Act of 1933 and allowed, for the first time since 1929, the consolidation of commercial banks, investment banks, securities firms, and insurance companies. Then in 2004, the SEC allowed investment banks to hold less capital in reserve, thereby facilitating greater use of leverage in trading activities (Lowenstein 2004). Lax regulation also aided the development of new financial instruments—commercial mortgage-backed securities (used to securitize debt which PE funds lever on the firms they acquire) as well as collateralized debt obligations, credit default swaps, and other derivatives. Congress explicitly excluded these financial instruments from regulation under the 2000 Commodity Futures Modernization Act. Taken together, these legal changes dramatically increased the pools of capital available for investment in PE and HFs and speculation, a practice which the 2011 Dodd–Frank Wall Street Reform and Consumer Protection Act is intended to curb.

Private equity and HFs also take advantage of US tax laws. By using high leverage in buying companies, for example, the interest on debt may be subtracted from taxable income, whereas retained earnings or dividends are taxable as profit. The profits from their portfolio investments are defined as 'carried interest', and this is treated as capital gains and taxed at a 15 per cent rate, rather than the top rate of 35 per cent for corporate or individual taxes (Fleischer 2008; Marples 2008; GAO 2008a: 72). In addition, most PE and HFs avoid other taxes by registering offshore (Jickling and Marples 2007: 6).

The Dodd–Frank act now requires PE and HFs with more than $150 million in assets to register with the SEC and report basic organizational and operational information, such as size, types of services, clients, employees, and potential conflicts of interest (PriceWaterhouseCoopers 2011). Legislative attempts to tax carried interest as ordinary income had failed as of the end of 2011 (Rubin et al. 2011). These minimal requirements stand in contrast to the European Union's (EU) Alternative Investment Funds Managers Directive. The latter instructs member states to adopt much more extensive reporting requirements as well as substantive rules to limit the use of leverage and implement risk management systems (European Parliament and Council 2011).

United States regulations governing SWFs are also limited in scope and have largely encouraged SWF investment in the USA. SWFs are completely exempt from taxation (Article 892 of the US Internal Revenue Code), giving them a major advantage over other private investors. When the China Investment Corporation (CIC) invested in Morgan Stanley in response to the financial crisis, for example, it avoided the 30 per cent withholding tax which other foreign investors must pay unless they are covered by a special treaty (Fleischer 2009). The US government has focused more on SWFs as a threat to national security, leading Congress to pass the Exon–Florio Amendment to the Defense Production Act of 1950. These established the Committee on Foreign Investment in the US (CFIUS), which reviews foreign acquisitions and may stop private sector transactions (Crocker 2008), such as the 2006 attempt by state-owned Dubai Ports World to acquire six major US ports (AP News 2006).

Labour Market Regulation

The USA is also well-known for its weak labour market protection compared to its European counterparts. US employment law is based on the 'employment-at-will' doctrine, which means that employers may hire or fire employees at will—although firms do worry about individual lawsuits and the reputational effects of relying on layoffs to adjust workforce levels. At the collective level, US labour laws have established a decentralized industrial relations system in which employees may gain union representation only by winning a majority of votes in elections at the workplace or firm level. This system works to limit union power by requiring high levels of union resources, both for administering existing contracts and organizing new members. While industrial unions were successful in the post-Second World War period in organizing a large percentage of workers in manufacturing and negotiating 'pattern' contracts, which applied across firms, those patterns have largely broken down as union power has eroded and union density has fallen—now to only 7 per cent of the private sector workforce—a bit less than the estimated workforce now employed by companies owned by PE.

Two aspects of the US labour institutional environment are particularly relevant to the role of new financial intermediaries. First, unlike their European counterparts, US workers and unions have no information or consultation rights so they typically do not have advance notice, and cannot influence, the change of ownership of a corporation. Second, the US pension system is a decentralized employer-based system, though some unions control members' pension funds under the provisions of the Taft Hartley Law. Public employers also have pension funds covering the majority of public sector employees. Unions and public sector officials have a fiduciary responsibility to ensure that these multi-billion dollar funds have adequate returns, and many have invested in PE and HFs in an attempt to achieve high returns. Pension funds invest an average of 8.8 per cent of their portfolios in PE, while public pension funds invest 6.8 per cent in HFs (Ederet et al. 2011)

This system has created dilemmas for US unions. While they invest in PE to gain high returns for retired members, they also encounter PE investors who take over unionized firms and may find themselves fighting these new owners over downsizing or derogation of contract rules. The result is that the US labour movement as a whole has not developed a unified position or public approach to new financial intermediaries.

Growth and Business Models of Funds

This weak regulatory environment governing capital and labour markets has created a space for new financial intermediaries to operate with few constraints. In the following sections, we examine the LBO model of PE, which has the most direct effect on management and employment relations, before turning to HFs and SWFs.

Private Equity

Private equity firms draw on the legacy of the LBO model of the 1980s, exemplified by Kohlberg, Kravis, and Roberts' (KKR) purchase of the Houdaille Corporation in 1979 and RJR Nabisco for $31.1 billion a decade later (Anders 2002; Baker and Smith 1998). Their actions were justified by ideas developed in 'agency theory' by finance economists to explain how firms can best maximize shareholder value (Jensen and Meckling 1976). According to agency theory, the 'managerial' model of the firm is deficient because shareholder ownership is too dispersed to effectively control managerial decisions. Professional managers (the agents) are free to pursue their own agendas rather than maximizing value for shareholders (the principals). Traditionally, it is argued, managers used their power to control labour and extract value through the production process. They used some of the company's retained earnings to induce diverse stakeholders to contribute to enterprise productivity and to finance investments in new technologies, worker skills, or labour peace and cooperation (Chandler 1990; Lazonick 1992). However, financial economists argue that in the short-term, managers did not maximize value for the company's current shareholders.

By contrast, LBOs and corporate takeovers in theory solve the principal–agent problem by concentrating ownership in a few hands so that shareholders have greater influence over managerial decisions. In addition, loading acquired companies with debt makes it necessary for managers to focus on cost-cutting and short-term profits to meet debt repayments and maximize returns to shareholders. For a time, this model collapsed in the scandals of the 1980s, with the indictment of leading figures such as Michael Milken (Akerlof et al. 1993) and the publication of scathing critiques such as *Barbarians at the Gates*. Investors became wary of these deals and the junk bond market collapsed.

Size, Scale, and Scope of Private Equity in the USA

By the late 1990s, however, a second wave of LBOs emerged among investors with large pools of private capital. PE firms raised capital through funds in which investors (the so-called limited partners) commit a certain amount of money and pay management fees to the PE firm (the general partner). The limited partners provide most of the capital while the general partner manages the fund and makes all of the decisions. Limited partners include primarily pension funds (or 'workers' capital), as well as insurance companies, endowments, and wealthy individuals.

Increasing access to pension funds enabled PE firms to expand the scale and scope of their operations and to become global in their investment activities in the 2000s. Data from PE data provider Pitchbook show that between 2003 and 2007, the number of annual PE transactions increased by 375 per cent (from 665 to 2,490 deals), while the value increased by nine fold ($66 billion to $607 billion). Deal activity fell dramatically during the financial crisis, but by 2010 the value of deals approached its 2005 level (Figure 2.1). These data are broadly consistent with estimates using Capital IQ data, reported

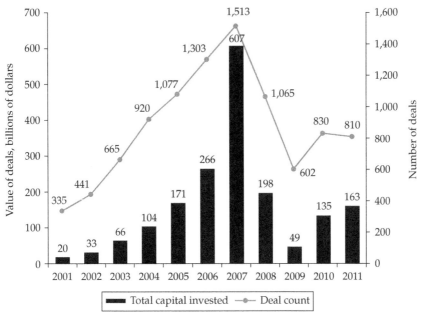

Figure 2.1 *Number and value of annual private equity deals in the USA*
Source: Pitchbook (2011).

by Strömberg (2008) and Kaplan and Strömberg (2009: Figure 2 and Table 1)

The types of PE transactions also changed in the 2000s. In the 1980s, LBOs focused primarily on large public firms in mature industries such as manufacturing and retail. By the 2000s, buy-out activity spread to a wide range of industries, including information technology, healthcare, financial services, utilities, infrastructure, business to business, and other business to consumer activities. Similarly, in the 1980s, LBOs of publicly-traded firms taken private represented almost half of the value of all transactions, but this fell to about one-third in the 2000s. By contrast, secondary transactions—in which one PE fund sells a privately-held company to another PE fund—rose from 2 per cent of transaction value in the 1980s to one-third in the 2000s (Kaplan and Strömberg 2009: Table 1).

Impact on Firms, Employment, and 'Workers' Capital'
The most comprehensive analysis of the employment and productivity effects of PE in the USA draws on industry data on PE transactions (Capital IQ) and the US Census Bureau's Longitudinal Business

Database, which covers the entire non-farm private sector (Davis et al. 2008; Davis et al. 2009; Davis et al. 2011). In the 2011 paper on PE and employment, the data consist of 3,200 PE-owned firms (with 150,000 establishments), acquired in PE transactions from 1980 to 2006. The research examined employment at PE-acquired establishments for five years before and after the PE transaction and compared these with control establishments, which were comparable in age, size, and multi-establishment status.

The findings are instructive. In PE-acquired establishments, gross job destruction was substantially greater than in the control establishments. The average cumulative five-year employment difference was 6.4 per cent in favour of the controls, with half of this due to the greater pace of closings of PE establishments. The authors found modest declines in employment in PE establishments relative to controls in manufacturing, but employment fell by nearly 12 per cent in PE-owned retail establishments relative to controls. Two years post-buy-out, these negative employment effects persisted at the firm level—with PE-owned firms showing 3.62 per cent lower employment—despite the fact that PE created somewhat more jobs than the controls at greenfield sites.

With respect to productivity in manufacturing, Davis et al. (2009) found confirmation of the agency theory view that PE ownership improves performance. Labour productivity was higher in target firms than in controls. Notably, almost three-quarters (72 per cent) of this differential was due to productivity improvements in the continuing establishments of these firms, including downsizing or closing of less productive establishments and the reallocation of activity to more productive establishments. In addition, target firms were much more likely to close establishments with lower productivity than were the controls. Unfortunately, it is not possible with these data to distinguish between productivity increases due to investments in employee skills, technology, and work organization and those due to work intensification.

For the limited partners—which are overwhelmingly the pension funds of union and public sector workers—the higher than average returns proclaimed by PE have been seriously challenged by recent evidence. A *New York Times* analysis found that pension funds with a third to over half of their money in alternative investments (PE, HFs, and real estate funds) had returns that were more than one percentage point lower than those funds that avoided these risky investments—and they paid almost four times more in management fees (Creswell

2012). Scholarly evidence also raises serious questions. An econometric study by Kaplan and Schoar (2005) of PE funds between 1980 and 2001 that had reached the end of their life found that PE returns averaged 93–97 per cent of the S&P 500. Median returns were 80 per cent of the S&P 500. Using the same data, Phalippou and Gottschalg (2009) reached similar findings but identified several features of the data, including self-selection bias, that upwardly bias the results. More importantly, the standard industry practice of measuring results using the internal rate of return (IRR) has been seriously questioned because calculations make the questionable assumption that cash proceeds from the sale of an operating company can be reinvested at the same IRR over the entire life of the PE fund. Using a modified IRR, Phalippou and Gottschalg (2007) estimated returns for the top 25 per cent of PE firms that were about half of those reported using the IRR. Moreover, the limited partners 'accept extreme illiquidity and leverage (debt) risk relative to the S&P' (Higson 2010: 7) (for fuller discussion see Appelbaum and Batt 2012: 24–7). In sum, the stated benefits of PE investments for workers' capital and the retirement income of middle-class Americans are highly suspect.

Management and Employment Relations
The labour relations strategies of PE firms take advantage of the weak US labour laws and labour movement, which provide few constraints on managerial prerogative; but PE firms do not uniformly seek to eliminate or marginalize unions. Their attitudes vary from hostile to pragmatic to indifferent. As long as unions do not get in the way of making anticipated returns, PE firms can live with them; if not, they fight them. Where labour cost savings are not a major source of higher returns—as in the $40 billion buy-out of Texas Utility Corporation (TXU)—then union contracts are not a major obstacle. But in old-line manufacturing plants or distressed industries such as steel, layoffs and deep concessions in work rules, healthcare, and pensions have been common. Overall, however, our case evidence shows that whether or not PE is hostile or willing to negotiate, it has gained the lions' share of wealth from buy-outs while workers hold on to diminished jobs with lost income and welfare security.

The steel industry, for example, is considered a positive case of PE investment because, without it, most believe the industry would have collapsed. Between 1998 and 2003, in the context of the Asian crisis, cheap steel imports, and global over-capacity, forty-five US steel companies declared bankruptcy, shut down eighteen mills, and laid-off

55,000 steelworkers. Over 210,000 retirees and their dependants lost their retiree healthcare benefits (USWA 2004). In 2001, investment banker Wilbur Ross approached the steelworkers to make a deal, and with their backing, created ISG as a parent company to buy the major steel companies out of bankruptcy at bargain prices (LTV, US Steel, Bethlehem, Georgetown, and Weirton). The bankruptcy proceedings allowed the pension plans covering over 250,000 employees, with $10 billion in underfunded benefits, to be terminated and turned over to the US Government's Insurance program, the Pension Benefit Guarantee Corporation.

The Steelworkers Union welcomed Ross because he was willing to save the mills and, unlike the legacy companies tainted with years of union hatred, he was straightforward and pragmatic. Negotiations were purely about money. The union accepted layoffs of 20 per cent in exchange for management layoffs of 40 per cent. Ross accepted the union's plan for reorganizing the plants, which streamlined job grades and led to large productivity gains. The contract maintained full-time work hours, overtime pay, and seniority provisions; set lower base wages plus an incentive bonus plan and profit-sharing; provided less comprehensive healthcare than previously; and retained important non-monetary clauses such as the maintenance of standard contract protections, a neutrality clause, and limits on pay for top managers. The union gained an expanded role in implementing the work redesign and running the plants, an extensive training programme, health and safety committees, a 'layoff minimization plan', and a union nominee to the ISG Board of Directors. Active union members were folded into the Steelworkers Pension Trust, a less generous multi-employer defined benefit pension plan than the one they had previously (USWA 2002).

Hardest hit were laid-off workers over fifty-five, who received $50,000 severance pay, and retirees whose health insurance was covered by a new trust with contributions contingent on corporate profitability. In 2005, Ross sold all of the plants to Mittal Steel for $4.5 billion, making an estimated fourteen times his investment in less than three years (Gross 2005). The mills continue to operate competitively, with collective bargaining negotiations occurring in 2012. While the deal between Ross and the Steelworkers Union saved the industry, the bittersweet pill is that Ross's profits almost exactly equal the losses sustained in the pension and health care programmes for retirees.

In a more hostile union case, the anti-union company Olmet Aluminum, backed by PE firm Matlin Patterson, filed for bankruptcy and gained a court order to void a steelworker union contract; but union militancy led to a nineteen-month massive corporate campaign against the company and PE firm, which ended with a satisfactory contract covering 1,500 workers (Business Wire 2005; Business Wire 2006).

These distressed buy-outs are a tiny fraction of PE activity. In other cases, PE has acquired healthy companies, and while they have negotiated decent union contracts, they have left the companies with huge debt loads that undermine the sustainability of the enterprises. For example, in 2007 a PE consortium of KKR, the Texas Pacific Group, and the PE arm of Goldman Sachs acquired the Texas utility company TXU (now Energy Future Holdings) in the largest PE buy-out in history—worth $48 billion. They negotiated with the union (the International Brotherhood of Electrical Workers), and the contract ensured union recognition and no job losses for three years (Beeferman 2009; Kosman 2009: 10–11). But their economic model failed, and by early 2012, the company continued to owe some $20 billion of the $40 billion in debt from the original buy-out; and credit default swap traders were betting that the company would default in the next three years (Anderson and Creswell 2010; Childs and Johnsson 2012).

In another high profile case in 2006, a consortium of investors (Bain Capital Partners, KKR, LLC, Merrill Lynch Global PE, Citigroup Inc., Bank of America Corporation, and HCA Chief Executive Officer (CEO) Dr Thomas F. Frist) acquired Hospital Corporation of America (HCA), the largest for-profit healthcare organization in the USA, providing approximately 4–5 per cent of all hospital services nationwide and employing 190,000 people. The PE owners negotiated in good faith with its unions (the Service Employees International Union and the National Nurses Union) and even signed neutrality agreements allowing the unions to organize new members in typically non-union southern states. But as in the Texas utility case, the real money is not in the union contracts. PE owners have already extracted their initial investment though financial engineering while leaving the hospital chain with a huge debt overhang. The PE owners initially invested $4.5 billion in the $21 billion deal. In 2010, they repaid themselves $4.25 billion in dividends by issuing junk bonds and loading the company with additional debt. Then in March, 2011, they issued a successful initial public offering (IPO) worth $3.8 billion IPO. While the owners more than recouped their initial investment, HCA is now saddled with $26 billion in debt—$12 billion more than the company's assets (Kosman 2011; Reuters 2011; Terry 2011). More importantly, HCA is currently under investigation for Medicare fraud—billing for unnecessary and costly interventional cardiology procedures that raise profits and can endanger patient healthcare. Prior to PE ownership, HCA had settled the largest Medicare fraud case in history ($1.7 billion) with the Justice Department in 2000. The current investigation raises serious questions about the failure of HCA under PE ownership to reign in these kinds of practices (Abelson and Creswell 2012).

In other cases, hostile PE owners have marginalized unions or fought union strikes and closed plants. In a Teamsters Union case, for example, PE firms KKR and CD&R purchased US FoodService from Dutch supermarket chain Royal Ahold in 2007. Management—union relations were cooperative under Ahold, but the new owners refused to consider the union's offer to work together on productivity improvements. Instead, they pursued a campaign of cost-cutting and work intensification; started shifting work to non-union worksites; and launched an anti-union campaign against one organizing drive that led to over 200 violations of the National Labor Relations Act.

In another case, the PE firm Brynwood Partners bought Stella D'Oro Biscuit Company, a historic Italian-style bakery located in the Bronx, in 2006. It immediately demanded cuts in wages and benefits from the plant's 130 members of the Bakery, Confectionary, Tobacco Workers, and Grain Millers Union. After failed negotiations, the workers struck for eleven months, and won the strike in 2009 when the National Labor Relations Board ruled that the firm must reinstate workers with two months back pay. But the PE firm sold the company to Lance, Inc., a North Carolina employer with an anti-union reputation, who moved the plant to Ohio with no offer of jobs to the former workers.

In sum, the available case record shows that whether PE firms negotiate or not with unions, the outcomes are similar, with the earnings of PE owners coming at the expense of workers rather than an increase in efficiency.

Private Equity, the Economic Crisis, and Financial Distress
Private equity investments were very much affected by the financial crisis and the economic recession, which in turn had negative effects for the limited partners and led to a series of bankruptcies in portfolio companies. Practitioner accounts, corroborated by the available empirical evidence, suggest that PE is highly cyclical (Kaplan and

Strömberg 2009: 137–43). The number of deals fell by more than half between the second quarter of 2007 and the second quarter of 2009 (from 737 to 302), while deal volume declined from a high of $168 billion in the fourth quarter of 2007 to a low of $7.5 billion in the second quarter of 2009. The number and volume of deals both recovered somewhat after the trough, and the value of deals in 2011 was close to its 2005 levels (Figure 2.1) (Pitchbook 2011).

The recession made it difficult to find opportunities for investment, and PE funds continued to have large amounts of 'dry powder'—funds committed by limited partners that must be invested or returned along with the relevant management fees. Estimates of dry powder as of November 2011 ranged from $376 billion (Preqin 2011: 5) to $436 billion (Pitchbook 2011: 1). PE funds have also had difficulty exiting from their mature portfolio firms (Ernst and Young 2011). Pitchbook estimated that 4,300 portfolio firms owned by PE in 2011 can be characterized as 'mature portfolio investments'. Related to this, PE funds have increased their use of secondary buy-outs (sales to other PE firms) (Preqin 2011: 3), in part to solve this problem. The PE firm which sells the portfolio company is able to exit and pay distributions to limited partners, while the PE firm which buys the company can use up some of its dry powder. One of the largest of these deals was the 2010 LBO of MultiPlan Inc., a healthcare business which creates medical networks for major healthcare insurers. The company was acquired by PE firms BC Partners and Silver Lake Partners from Carlyle Group and Welsh, Carson, Anderson, & Stowe in a transaction which valued the company at $3.1 billion (Lattman 2010).

Secondary buy-outs are problematic for the limited partners who often partner with more than one PE firm and may find themselves on both sides of the secondary buy-out, to their disadvantage. Returns to the limited partners in most PE funds proved disappointing in 2008, 2009, and 2010, which has made raising new funds challenging. The number of funds that closed and the amount of total capital raised declined throughout 2011. Despite this tough fundraising environment, over 300 PE funds were seeking commitments in 2011, the same as in the peak year of 2007.

More important for managers and employees is the pattern of distress and bankruptcies experienced by PE-owned companies. Even before the recession, bankruptcy rates of LBOs were higher than those of comparable publicly-traded firms, according to the most exhaustive study of this issue (Strömberg 2008). Strömberg found that PE firms acquired in LBOs between 1970 and 2007 had an average net debt to enterprise value of 67 per cent and an average net debt to EBITDA (earnings before interest, taxes, depreciation, and amortization) of 5.4, compared to 14 per cent and 1.1 for comparable publicly-traded firms. For the LBOs that occurred between 1970 and 2002, the rate of bankruptcy or reorganization was twice as high as it was for publicly-traded companies.

Strömberg's analysis does not cover the period of the financial crisis and its aftermath. Since then, many companies acquired by PE have been forced to seek bankruptcy protection—including Simmons, Reader's Digest, Harry and David's, and Fortunoffs Jewelry. Several restaurant chains owned by PE firm Sun Capital—Friendly's ice cream, SSI Group (Grandy's and Souper Salad restaurants), and Real Mex (El Torito Restaurant and Chevys Fresh Mex)—all entered bankruptcy in late 2011. Other major retail chains were unable to emerge from bankruptcy and were liquidated (Linens 'n Things and Mervyns). Indeed, the largest US bankruptcy of 2011 was NewPage Corporation, owned by PE firm Cerberus Capital Management (Hals et al. 2011).

The risks of financial distress associated with high levels of leverage are well-known. They include the costs of reorganization, legal and trustee fees, the loss of business, and higher future borrowing costs (Platt 2009: 13). Yet, PE firms tend to ignore these costs because they are largely protected from the effects of isolated instances of financial distress or bankruptcy among operating companies in the fund's portfolio. The legal structure governing PE funds limits these partners' losses to the equity invested in the distressed portfolio company. If a portfolio company defaults on its loans, the PE owners lose only the equity that was initially used to buy that company.

While the US PE industry had not fully recovered from the recession by the end of 2011, it pointed to several positive signs of improved performance, including an increase in billion dollar LBO deals. Through November 2011, US PE firms closed thirty-three deals over $1 billion (Pitchbook 2011). PE firms also had successfully re-financed much of the huge volume of bonds scheduled to mature in coming years. While helpful, these 'amend and extend' agreements (sometimes referred to as 'amend and pretend') have allowed some shaky companies to escape bankruptcy or restructuring, at least temporarily, but may have required them to cut employment and reduce prices and may have left them too weak to undertake new investments or projects (Hals et al. 2011).

Hedge Funds

The value of assets held by the HF industry worldwide grew massively in the last two decades—from $20 billion in 1995 to $1.92 trillion in 2007. While the financial and economic crisis led to a fall in value to $1.33 trillion by the first quarter of 2009, HFs rebounded by 2010; total assets under management in 2012 were estimated at $1.76 trillion (BarclayHedge 2012). While the industry is known for mega-funds which wield enormous power in financial markets, it is striking that the structure of the industry is relatively un-concentrated, with 25 per cent of the assets held by nineteen firms in a population of 5,000 (Fruhan 2010: 3–4).

The Rise of US Hedge Funds and their Business Models

The classic model of a HF, as developed in the USA by Alfred Winslow Jones in 1949, included three characteristics: 'hedging' market investments by holding both long and short positions, using leverage (debt) to improve returns, and paying managers based on incentives tied to performance (Temple 2001: 46). Over the last twenty years, however, HFs have taken on very different forms, using dozens of portfolio strategies and asset classes. The potential for large performance-based pay for managers has favoured the adoption of high risk and high leverage models of investment (Temple 2001: 46–7); and many HFs today take either short or long positions in any type of security or market and use leverage and performance-based pay for managers. In addition, they are typically domiciled in an offshore tax haven, have a limited number of wealthy investors, and operate in relative secrecy.

For the purposes of this study, most HFs are unlikely to have a direct effect on corporate governance or employment relations. A useful typology of funds, developed by Goldman Sachs in a 1998 guide, identified four types of funds: (a) equity funds—following the Winslow Jones model; (b) arbitrage funds, which exploit inefficiency in financial markets; (c) directional funds, which operate in a wide variety of markets, such as global macro markets; and (d) event-driven funds, which target extreme corporate events, such as mergers or bankruptcies (Temple 2001: 51). Event-driven funds also include 'activist funds', which seek to influence corporate board decisions when they believe that a firm is under-valued (Coggan 2011: 31). These funds make up a relatively small portion of the HF industry, but are the most likely to influence management decision-making because they make their returns by closing the gap between a company's stock that is under-valued and what it would be worth if the company changed its strategy, which may also involve changing its corporate governance (Fruhan 2010: 15).

Implications for Firms and Workers

Recent research on HF shareholder activists suggests that they seek to influence the governance or operations of a target firm via one of two approaches: indirectly by helping to bring about the takeover of a target firm, or directly by insisting on changes in governance or operational policies in the existing firm. Schor and Greenwood (2009), for example, analysed the demands of large shareholders of public corporations as indicated in their filings of Schedule 13D with the SEC for the period 1993–2006.[1] Schor and Greenwood found that HF activism using 13D filings was four times the level of non-HF investors, and it increased dramatically from the late 1990s onwards. The SEC filings contained nine categories of planned initiatives, which focused on capital structures, governance issues, business strategies, sales of assets, influence over merger and acquisition activity, and proxy contests (Schor and Greenwood 2009: 8).

Compared to non-HF activists, HF activists were more likely to seek ownership changes as a means of securing higher than average returns (Schor and Greenwood 2009). Activists increased the likelihood of a takeover by 11 per cent; and the firms they took over earned 26 per cent higher monthly returns compared to their counterparts that were not acquired. In sum, HFs were more likely to become activists in order to secure the takeover of a target firm and aimed to achieve their abnormal returns in this way. This approach changes the operating conditions of the target firm by inserting a new owner with a new set of governance practices and employment policies; or if ownership remains unchanged, the threat of takeover may induce changes in operating or employment policies. Another study, using the same SEC Schedule 13D data for the period 2003–05, examined changes in corporate governance and operations demanded by HFs. The authors identified a similar list of initiatives which HFs sought to implement, and 60 per cent of the 151 initiatives by HF activists were successful in achieving changes (Klein and Zur 2006).

Recent examples of successful HF activism include the industrial company Ameron International Corporation and the Barington Capital Group. James Mitarotonda, head of Barington, had attempted to get Ameron to make several strategic and operational changes, including focusing on its core business, cutting expenses and executive compensation, and buying back its own stock. When Ameron was slow to respond, Barrington ran a year-long proxy contest which resulted in his election to Ameron's Board of Directors (Barr 2011). In another case, activist HF Elliott Management, which acquired a 5 per cent ownership stake in Iron Mountain, attacked the company for its expansion strategies, which were losing money. Elliott Management demanded four new directors on Iron Mountain's board and insisted that the company maximize shareholder value by focusing on its mature real estate business and becoming an operator of a real estate investment trust (REIT), which would lower costs and US tax obligations (Mellor 2011). Iron Mountain subsequently agreed to give Elliott one board seat, commit $2.2 billion to share repurchases and dividends, explore becoming a REIT, and sell the company's digital archiving business (de la Merced 2011).

Hedge funds may also affect the governance and operations of companies by investing in distressed debt—firms that are close to, or already in, bankruptcy. HFs may provide loans to companies in trouble on the assumption that they will get the company at a bargain from investors who panic and want to sell cheaply. These HFs typically have specialized knowledge in bankruptcy laws and the ability to negotiate with other classes of creditors, which allows them to position themselves with equity rights in the restructured company. HFs that purchase distressed debt play a mixed role in these companies—allowing them to return to operation and save jobs while making large profits by preying on the most disadvantaged or powerless economic actors.

Hedge Funds since the Advent of the Financial and Economic Crisis
Since the financial crisis, investor satisfaction with returns has been low and reached its lowest levels in 2012 (Preqin 2012). HF investment in distressed debt has yielded the highest returns compared to other strategies—with average overall returns of 3.9 per cent in 2011 (Or and Barr 2011). In this way, HFs may fill a void in the supply of capital where traditional sources such as commercial banks are unwilling to take risks. Small and mid-sized companies, unable to compete in bond markets for credit, have turned to HFs to borrow billions for needs ranging from on-going operations to new strategies and innovations. While filling a needed role in the post-crisis period, HFs charge high interest rates—of 12.5 per cent or more. Moreover, they are known for their short time horizons, raising questions about

whether they will quickly foreclose on loans which fall in arrears—a strategy referred to as 'loan to own' (Ahmed 2011).

An important example of a distressed investment is Yellow Roadway Worldwide, one of the key remaining companies in the long-haul trucking industry. The case is illustrative of the role of PE and HF investment in avoiding bankruptcy and the difficult situation that the Teamsters Union faced in negotiating agreements to keep the company alive over five years. Ironically, the company faced bankruptcy to begin with because its owner copied the high leverage strategies of PE firms before the financial crisis to buy two other companies; and then the recession hit. The company's share price fell from $60 to $0.37.

The Teamsters Union represented 25,000 of the company's workforce in 2011, down from 45,000 in 2008. The union saved the company by agreeing to three rounds of contract concessions. In 2009, the union took a 10 per cent wage cut and suspension of cost-of-living increases in exchange for an option of a 15 per cent stake in the company. The resulting savings of $250 million annually were not enough to convince the company's lenders (a group of traditional institutions led by J.P. Morgan Stanley) to refinance. The union then agreed to the suspension of pension payments for eighteen months and an extra 5 per cent wage cut, which saved Yellow Roadway an estimated $50 million a month through 2010. These concessions were contingent upon the company gaining a better deal with its banks and a conversion of a $450 million bond debt to equity (interview with Teamsters' Strategic Research & Campaigns Department).

Hedge funds entered the picture in early 2010 when they purchased the company's distressed debt and demanded a third concession package if the company was to undergo a comprehensive restructuring which included a resolution of the union pension liability issue, a new injection of capital, and a debt reduction. Because the union could not obtain the identity of any of the investors it had little leverage in negotiating, and it was only through third party actors that a negotiated agreement was finally reached.

After a third union concession was accepted by Yellow Roadway Board in September, 2010, the company finally turned a corner. In exchange for the concessions, the union insisted on a new management team and board of directors, which the HF investors supported. Subsequently, the union played a key role in the recruitment, interviewing, and hiring of a new CEO; and it chose two members of the nine-person board of directors. By 2011, the company was out of immediate danger of collapse and able to focus on operations. The union was cautiously optimistic about the future. This represents another example of a bittersweet experience of unions and alternative investors—while PE and HF funds saved the company, workers ended up with substantial losses in wages and pensions.

Sovereign Wealth Funds

Sovereign wealth funds are viewed as passive, long-term, stable investors; and since the 2007 recession many US firms—especially distressed ones—have sought out SWF funds (McCormick 2008; Rose 2008). SWFs have appeared to save several large troubled American banks, including Citigroup, Merrill Lynch, and Morgan Stanley, which received more than $32 billion in investment from SWFs from China, Korea, Singapore, and United Arab Emirates (Langford et al. 2009). In 2011, the US government and AIG were allegedly seeking SWFs to take over a large portion of the US Treasury's 92 per cent stake in AIG (Guerrera and Braithwaite 2011); and SWFs from Kuwait and Singapore expressed interest in the deal (Kansas 2011).

The size of the SWF global market rose sharply before the financial crisis in 2007, and then fell precipitously in 2008–09 (TheCityUK 2011). Assets under management (AUM) of all SWFs increased by 11 per cent in 2010 to a record $4.2 trillion, with an additional $6.8 trillion held in other sovereign investment vehicles, such as pension reserve funds and development funds. While the number of transactions increased by 50 per cent from 2010, the average value of transactions decreased by 23 per cent, which suggests that SWFs are now making more, but smaller, deals. Investments in the USA are largely concentrated in financial institutions (81 per cent) and real estate companies and properties (10 per cent) (Monitor Group 2011; Bortolotti et al. 2009). Overall, however, the data available on the size and investments of SWFs are very limited and uneven (GAO 2008b).

Estimates of the size and influence of SWFs expand greatly when these estimates include government-sponsored corporations or entities. For instance, the government of the United Arab Emirates manages the Abu Dhabi Investment Authority (ADIA) as a sovereign saving fund. ADIA holds minority stakes in Citigroup Inc. (4.9 per cent), Apollo Management (9 per cent), and Hyatt Hotels Corporation (10.9 per cent). Similarly, Istithmar World, the PE arm of Dubai World, controls a 100 per cent stake in Barneys New York, a 100 per cent stake in Loehmann's, a 10 per cent stake in Perella Weinberg Partners (a financial services boutique), and a 33.3 per cent stake in Education Media and Publishing Group International (Butt et al. 2007).

Evolving Nature of Sovereign Wealth Fund Strategies and Post-Crisis Activity

Similar to other types of funds, SWFs engage in diverse investment strategies and tactics.[2] Kunzel et al. (2011) identify three types of SWFs with distinct objectives and investment horizons: savings (designed for long-term objectives), stabilization (to insulate the national budget), and pension reserve funds (for unspecified pension liabilities). Dyck and Morse (2011) distinguished two objectives of SWF investment: financial portfolio versus domestic developmental agendas, with the latter particularly important for Middle Eastern and Asian SWFs. Political objectives and cultural differences also influence SWF investment behaviour (Johan et al. 2011).

In recent years, SWFs have shifted from low-risk to higher-risk/ higher-return strategies (Weiss 2008). In addition, dissatisfied with fund performance during the financial crisis, they have begun to take more direct and proactive roles as investors. The investments of Qatar Investment Authority, for example, earned it a seat on the board of Veolia Environment and director-level representation at Harrods in the UK (Monitor Group 2011: 23). SWFs have also expanded their involvement in PE firms, from investors in funds to minority owners in the firms themselves. The ADIA bought a 9 per cent stake in Apollo Management and a 7.5 per cent stake in the Carlyle Group. The Kuwait Investment Authority and the Government of Singapore Investment Corporation have gained a 5 per cent stake in the Texas Pacific Group (Zuckerman 2011); and China Development Bank was seeking a minority stake in the same PE fund (Sender 2011).

Sovereign wealth funds also invest in private companies through innovative arrangements such as Exchange Traded Funds. BlackRock is the largest money manager in the world, with $3.35 trillion in AUM. As of 2011, BlackRock owned 5 per cent or more of over 42 per cent of all traded companies. Also, it is the largest shareholder of one in five US corporations, including AT&T, Chevron, ExxonMobil, GE, IBM, and JP Morgan Chase (Davis 2012). Several SWFs hold a significant minority stake in BlackRock, including CIC, Kuwait Investment Authority, the Government Pension Fund of Norway, and the Singapore Government Investment Corporation and Temasek (Martin 2010; Sender 2010).

While SWFs appear to be expanding their influence over their investment targets in the USA, they are constrained by the Exon–Florio Amendments and CFIUS described earlier (Rose 2008). To shun political attention, SWFs have avoided acquiring more than 10 per cent of a company or have willingly forgone voting rights as the CIC did when it bought shares of the Blackstone Group (de Swann 2010). A recent Government Accountability Office report (2009) concluded that, although there are no laws that specifically target SWFs, certain sectors are tightly regulated and monitored for foreign ownership—banking, communications, transportation, natural resources and energy, agriculture, and defence. Nonetheless, SWFs have invested in sensitive industries via their investments in PE. One example is the investment of the Mubadala Development Company (Abu Dhabi) in the Carlyle Group, which has extensive holdings in defence-related firms and firms with government contracts. In 2007, Carlyle sold a 7.5 per cent stake in its general partnership to Mubadala, and in 2010 Mubadala made an additional $500 million investment. Around the time of Mubadala's initial investment, the Carlyle Group bought Kinder Morgan (one of the largest pipeline transportation and energy storage companies in North America), ARINC (a leading provider of communications and integration systems to government agencies and transportation networks), and Allison Transmission (provider of all vehicle suppliers to the Pentagon). None of these transactions had been reviewed under CFIUS, suggesting the inadequacy of US laws to regulate SWF activity (SEIU 2008).

The China Investment Corporation (CIC)

The CIC provides a case in point of increased SWF activity in the US economy and, in particular, investment in PE and HF intermediaries. With a total of $374.3 billion AUM, CIC is one of the most active and powerful SWFs worldwide. Around 21 per cent of its portfolio was invested in alternative funds in 2010 and, of that, 42 per cent was invested in North America (CIC 2010). CIC's investment in US PE and HFs includes $3 billion in Blackstone Group with non-voting rights in 2007 and $5 billion in Morgan Stanley in the same year (Singh 2008). In early 2008, CIC contributed $3.2 billion to a $4 billion PE fund with JC Flowers & Co. primarily focused on the US financial sector.

CIC investment in PE and HFs has accelerated in the post-crisis period, including a $1 billion investment in Oaktree Capital Management LP, which was one of the firms involved in the Public–Private Investment Partnership—the government programme designed to rid banks of toxic assets (Strasburg and Carew 2009). This investment aims at distressed debt and other fixed-income assets. With this investment and an additional $2 billion in funding, CIC is expected to increase its HF portfolio (Strasburg and Carew 2009). In addition to alternative investments, CIC is investing directly, although as a minority shareholder, in corporate shares. In February, 2011, CIC filed its full list of investments in publicly-traded US stocks with the SEC for the first time.[3] According to the filing, CIC owns $9.6 billion worth of shares in a variety of companies ranging from Bank of America and Citigroup to Apple, Coca-Cola, and Johnson & Johnson.

Although CIC seems to be interested in non-voting stakes or straightforward investment opportunities, how much influence it may have on the investment strategies or investment targets is an open question due to the complexity of deal structures and limited data disclosure. CIC uses its PE firms to act on its behalf as when it used Blackstone to buy Morgan Stanley's troubled property loan portfolio in Japan in 2011 (Sender and Anderlini 2011). PE firms, such as JC Flowers & Co. and Oaktree Capital Management LP, have no obligation or motivation to reveal their investment targets. Hence, as Jeffrey Garten, Yale professor and former Commerce Department official, said, 'It's going to be harder to trace, and harder to decide whether the (SWFs') investments are worth worrying about' (Rugaber 2008).

Impact on Firms and Workers
At a global level, a few studies have investigated the impact of SWFs on firm performance, as measured by the effect on the target firm's share price. The general conclusion is that the involvement of SWFs had a positive influence on the target firm's performance over a short-term horizon, but a negative, or neutral at best, effect on longer-term share price performance (Goncalves and Fernandes 2011; Bortolotti et al. 2009). None of these studies provide breakdowns by country.

We were unable to identify studies of the impact of SWFs on labour and employment relations. However, two studies of global SWFs examined governance changes at target firms and came to two different, almost opposite, conclusions. Kotter and Lel (2008) found that the target firm's governance, including CEO turnover, do not change significantly in the three-year period following a SWF investment, thus concluding that SWFs are passive investors. By contrast, Dewenter et al. (2009) found that target firms experience one or more events indicative of SWFs monitoring or influence. They concluded that SWFs are often active investors monitoring firm management, influencing firm decisions, engaging in network transactions, and influencing government decisions related to the target firm.

Conclusions

In this chapter, we examined the features of the US regulatory framework which have shaped the behaviour of financial intermediaries. PE, HFs, and SWFs have been exempt from registration and reporting requirements, have not been required—as banks are—to hold reserves, and have faced no limits on their use of leverage. US financial market regulations have allowed these intermediaries to operate with virtually no public oversight or transparency to investors. Deregulation of financial services from the 1970s onwards made possible the growth of large pools of private capital. The preferential tax treatment of debt relative to equity and of carried interest further encouraged the expansion of PE, HFs, and SWFs. While the Dodd–Frank financial reforms of 2010 instituted registration and reporting requirements for PE and HFs (but not SWFs), the law did not change the tax code or limit business practices such as the use of high leverage on which the industry has relied. The lax financial regulatory environment is coupled with a weak union movement and labour laws that provide few mechanisms for labour to challenge or negotiate over new forms of management introduced by PE and activist HFs.

These intermediaries have had differential effects on the management and employment practices of the firms in which they have invested. SWFs generally have had long time horizons, have taken a passive approach to investment, and have stayed out of the limelight to avoid political attention. By contrast, HFs have had a much shorter time horizon, typically turning over investments in eighteen months or less. Most HFs do not appear to have a direct effect on the internal operations of their target firms, with the exception of activist HFs, which have grown in the 2000s but still represent a small share of all HF investments. PE is still not able to take over the largest US firms—a Microsoft or Johnson & Johnson, for example—but HFs can take positions in such companies that enable them to exert influence on business strategy. Activist HFs have primarily affected the corporate governance structures and strategic direction of the companies they target; and they significantly increase the probability that those companies will be taken over by another corporation, yielding substantially higher returns for HF investors. These takeovers clearly lead to changes in management strategies and operations, but exactly how these changes affect employment levels and labour conditions in unknown. Notably, where unions exist, HF investors undermine existing norms of collective bargaining because they hold considerable power but their identities are not revealed to the union.

Compared to HFs and SWFs, PE intermediaries clearly have the most direct impact on management decision-making, operations, and employment relations in portfolio firms. They restructure the operations of acquired companies without oversight from outside investors, regulators, or the public. While much of PE activity continues to focus on financial engineering, some PE managers have used consultants with specific industry expertise who are then deployed to work in portfolio companies in those industries. More importantly, as HFs and SWFs are increasingly incorporated into large multi-purpose asset management firms, often headed by PE firms, the funds available for activist intervention in portfolio firms has increased.

The outcomes for managers and employees in PE-owned portfolio companies are highly diverse and depend on a range of contingent factors, including industry conditions, the size and strategy of the PE firm, the assets of the portfolio company itself, the direction of the stock market, and general economic conditions that influence interest rates at which funds for LBOs can be borrowed and the market success of portfolio firms. At one extreme, a handful of PE firms specialize in turning around companies and have a reasonable record of negotiating with unions. The more powerful players in the industry have undertaken large LBOs, which have saddled healthy companies with high levels of debt and have resulted in bankruptcies, and losses to creditors, suppliers, and workers. Still pending are a series of LBOs from the 2005–07 period, which have huge debt loads, much of which PE has been able to refinance. But slow economic growth persists, and the future of investments made at the height of the real estate boom is uncertain. Some analysts anticipate high rates of financial distress and bankruptcy for portfolio companies although the effects on the large PE firms are likely to be muted. The most reliable econometric analyses show net employment losses are much higher in PE-owned establishments and firms compared to similar enterprises not owned by PE, and they are concentrated in services, finance, insurance, and real estate. Related research shows that higher productivity found in PE-owned firms is due primarily to the closing of less productive units and reallocation of workers to more productive sites. It is unclear whether productivity improvements are achieved via investments in skills and technology or the compliance of employees, afraid for their jobs, with work intensification. The evidence on PE's track record with unions is mixed, with some negotiating with them and others marginalizing them. In both cases, however, workers have usually lost wages and health and pension benefits, while PE owners have gained via financial engineering and the use of leverage that often threaten the overall viability of an enterprise.

One of the key lessons from the US experience is that the regulatory environment does not constrain the kind of financial engineering and risky behaviour of PE firms which results in bankruptcy or the extraction of high levels of value even as the organization struggles to exist. Indeed, PE owners may resort to dividend recapitalizations, in which more debt is piled onto the portfolio company in order to pay the PE owners a large dividend and help them recoup their original investment, despite the increased risk of distress for the firm. Not only do such actions undermine the argument that PE returns are due to improvements in firm performance, but in several instances PE firms have been accused by creditors of 'bleeding-out' the company and causing it to become insolvent. Among others, Sun Capital faces such an accusation in relation to the bankruptcy of the Mervyn's department store chain, and Apax Partners and TPG Capital face a similar complaint in the case of TIM Hellas (Appelbaum et al. 2013; Primack 2011).

The evidence we have reviewed suggests that several regulatory changes are needed to curb the destructive outcomes associated with some types of financial intermediary activity. Beyond the recently-enacted reporting requirements, two substantive reforms are particularly warranted: one, elimination of preferential tax treatment for debt relative to equity which would reduce the incentives for excessive use of leverage and, two, treatment of the carried interest earned by principals in some financial intermediaries as ordinary income for taxation liabilities.

In the cases we reviewed, the excessive use of debt is a primary cause of PE's short-term focus on cost-cutting and work intensification, and in some cases of financial distress and even bankruptcy. The threat of bankruptcy did not appear particularly worrisome in the bubble economy of the 2000s, when credit was readily available, stock prices were generally rising, and the higher risks faced by highly leveraged firms were more than offset by the very high payoffs from successful portfolio companies. In the period since the advent of the financial and economic crisis—and the instability and uncertainty of markets in at least the intermediate term—analysts expect many firms, highly leveraged in the pre-crisis years, to face distress, restructuring of their debts, and bankruptcy when that is not possible.

One approach to reducing the excessive use of debt is to reduce the preferential treatment which debt receives in the US tax code. Another solution, adopted by the EU in its reforms for NIFs, is to limit the amount of leverage which can be used, although there is on-going discussion over what that limit will be. Proposed legislation to limit the preferential tax treatment given to financial intermediaries has repeatedly failed to pass one or both houses of Congress. The Obama administration's proposal would redefine the carried interest that PE and HF managers receive as ordinary income subject to higher tax rates. While this is unlikely to modify the risky behaviour adopted by financial intermediaries, it would begin to redress the serious problem of inequality in compensation between the highly-paid executives employed by financial intermediaries and ordinary Americans. These tax proposals are modest reforms in the context of an economy in which median family income has been stagnant since 1995 while financial sector incomes have massively increased.

NOTES

1. Investors who buy 5 per cent of the shares of a corporation are required to file this report and typically become activist shareholders soon thereafter.
2. For detailed asset allocations of each SWF, see Monitor Group's SWF database <http://www.monitor.com/tabid/202/L/en-US/Default.aspx>, which covers investment activities of 33 SWFs from 1981 to the present.
3. A full list of CIC investment is available at <http://www.sec.gov/Archives/edgar/data/1468702/000095012310009135/c95690e13fvhr.txt>).

BIBLIOGRAPHY

Abelson, R. and Creswell, J. (2012). 'Hospital chain inquiry cited unnecessary cardiac work', *New York Times*, 6 August, accessed 26 September 2013, <http://

www.nytimes.com/2012/08/07/business/hospital-chain-internal-reports-found-dubious-cardiac-work.html?pagewanted=1&wpisrc=nl wonk&_r=2>.

Ahmed, A. (2011). 'Bank said no? Hedge funds fill a void in lending', *New York Times*, 8 June, accessed 26 September 2013, <http://dealbook.nytimes.com/2011/06/08/bank-said-no-hedge-funds-fill-a-void-in-lending/>.

Akerlof, G., Romer, P., Hall, R., and Mankiw, N. (1993). 'Looting: The economic underworld of bankruptcy for profit', *Brookings Papers on Economic Activity*, 2: 1–73.

Anders, G. (2002). *Merchants of Debt: KKR and the Mortgaging of American Business*. Washington: Beard Books.

Anderson, J. and Creswell, J. (2010). 'For buyout kingpins, the TXU utility deal gets tricky', *Wall Street Journal*, 28 February.

AP News (2006). 'House panel votes to block ports deal', *FOX News*, 9 March, accessed 26 September 2013, <http://www.foxnews.com/story/0,2933,187147,00.html>.

Appelbaum, E., and Batt, R. (2012). 'A Primer on Private Equity in the United States: Development and Impact on Firms, Workers and Employment Relations', Washington: Center for Economic and Policy Research, <http://www.cepr.net/documents/publications/private-equity-2012-02.pdf>.

Appelbaum, E., Batt, R., and Clark I. (2013). 'Implications of financial capitalism for employment relations research: evidence from breach of trust and implicit contracts in private equity buyouts', *British Journal of Industrial Relations*, 51 (3): 498–518.

Baker, G. and Smith, G. (1998). *The New Financial Capitalists: Kohlberg Kravis Roberts and the Creation of Corporate Value*. New York: Cambridge University Press.

BarclayHedge. (2012). 'Hedge Fund Industry: Assets Under Management', accessed 26 September 2013, <http://www.barclayhedge.com/research/indices/ghs/mum/HF_Money_Under_Management.html>

Barr, A. (2011). 'Activist hedge fund wins Ameron board seat', *Market Watch*, 30 March, accessed 26 September 2013, <http://www.marketwatch.com/story/activist-hedge-fund-wins-ameron-board-seat-2011-03-30>.

Beeferman, L. (2009). 'Private equity and American labor: Multiple, pragmatic responses mirroring labor's strengths and weaknesses', *Journal of Industrial Relations*, 51 (4): 517–27.

Bortolotti, B., Fotak, V., Megginson, W., and Miracky W. (2009). 'Sovereign Wealth Fund Investment Patterns and Performance', Working Paper, Noman: University of Oklahoma.

Burrough, B. and Helyar, J. (1990) *Barbarians at the Gate: The Fall of RJR Nabisco*. New York: Harper & Row.

Business Wire (2005). 'News from USW: Steelworkers embark on week-long New York protest tour: Union spotlights unfair treatment by

Ormet, MatlinPatterson', 11 July, accessed 26 September 2013, <http://www.businesswire.com/news/home/20050711005586/en/News-USW-Steelworkers-Embark-Weeklong-York-Protest>.

Business Wire (2006). 'News from USW: USW reaches tentative contract agreements with Ormet for Ohio and Louisiana facilities', 30 June, accessed 26 September 2013, <http://www.businesswire.com/news/home/20060630005455/en/News-USW-USW-Reaches-Tentative-Contract-Agreements>.

Butt, S., Shivdasani, A., Stendevad, C., and Wyman, A. (2007). 'Sovereign wealth funds: A growing global force in corporate finance', *Journal of Applied Corporate Finance*, 19 (1): 73–83.

Chandler, A. (1990). *Scale and Scope: The Dynamics of Industrial Capitalism*. Cambridge: Harvard University Press.

Childs, M. and Johnsson, J. (2012). 'KKR's TXU buyout facing 91% odds of default: Corporate finance', *Bloomberg Business Week*, 19 January, accessed 26 September 2013, <http://www.bloomberg.com/news/2012-01-19/kkr-s-txu-buyout-facing-91-odds-of-default-corporate-finance.html>.

CIC (2010). *Annual Report*. Beijing: China Investment Corporation (CIC).

Coggan, P. (2011). *Hedge Funds, What They Are, What They Do, Their Risks, Their Advantages*. Hoboken: Wiley and Sons.

Creswell, J. (2012). 'Pensions find riskier funds fail to pay off', *New York Times*, 1 April.

Crocker, T. (2008). 'What banks need to know about the coming debate over CFIUS, foreign direct investment, and sovereign wealth funds', *The Banking Law Journal*, May: 457–67.

Davis, G. (2012). 'Finance capitalism 2.0: How BlackRock became the new JP Morgan', in: LERA. *64th Labor and Employment Relations Association Annual Meeting*. 7 January, Chicago.

Davis, G., Haltiwanger, J., Jarmin, R., Lerner, J., and Miranda, J. (2008). 'Private equity and employment', in: Gurung, A. and J. Lerner (eds.). *Globalization of Alternative Investments*. 1, The Global Economic Impact of PE 2008, New York: World Economic Forum, 43-64.

Davis, G., Haltiwanger, J., Jarmin, R., Lerner, J., and Miranda, J. (2009). 'Private equity: Jobs and productivity', in: A. Gurung and J. Lerner (eds), *Globalization of Alternative Investments*. Working Papers, 2, The Global Economic Impact of PE 2009, New York: World Economic Forum, 27–43.

Davis, G., Haltiwanger, J., Jarmin, R., Lerner, J., and Miranda, J. (2011). 'Private Equity and Employment', NBER Working Paper, 17399, Cambridge: National Bureau of Economic Research, accessed 26 September 2013, <http://www.nber.org/papers/w17399>.

de la Merced, M. (2011). 'Iron mountain reaches truce with Elliott', *New York Times*, 'DealBook', 19 April, accessed 26 September 2013, <http://dealbook.nytimes.com/2011/04/19/iron-mountain-reaches-truce-with-elliott/>.

de Swann, J (2010). 'China goes to Wall Street: Beijing's evolving U.S. investment strategy', *Foreign Affairs*, 29 April, accessed 26 September 2013, <http://www.foreignaffairs.com/articles/66398/jc-de-swaan/china-goes-to-wall-street>.

Dewenter, K., Han, X., and Malatesta, P. (2009). 'Firm value and sovereign wealth fund investments', *Journal of Financial Economics*, 98 (2): 256–78.

Dyck, A. and Morse, A. (2011). 'Sovereign Wealth Fund Portfolios', Chicago Booth Research Paper, 11–15 / MFI Working Paper, 2011-003 / Rotman School of Management Working Paper, 1792850, 1 February.

Eder, S., Zuckerman, G., and Corkery, M. (2011). 'Pensions leap back to hedge funds', *Wall Street Journal*, 27 May, accessed 26 September 2013, <http://online.wsj.com/article/SB10001424052702303654804576347762838825864.html>.

Ernst and Young (2011). *Return to Warmer Waters: How do private equity investors create value?* Study of 2010 North American Exits, Ernst and Young, accessed 26 September 2013, <http://www.hvca.hu/wp-content/uploads/2011/12/Return-to-Warmer-Waters.pdf>.

European Parliament and Council (2011). 'Directive 2011/61/EU on Alternative Investment Fund Managers and amending Directives 2003/41/EC and 2009/65/EC', 8 June, accessed 26 September 2013, <http://europa.eu/legislation_summaries/internal_market/single_market_services/financial_services_transactions_in_securities/mi0083_en.htm>.

Goncalves, N. and Fernandes, G. (20119). 'Sovereign Wealth Funds: Investment Choices and Implications around the World', Working Paper, Lausanne: IMD International, accessed 26 September 2013, <http://papers.ssrn.com/sol3/papers.cfm?abstract_id=1341692>.

Fleischer, V. (2008). 'Two and twenty: Taxing partnership profits in PE funds', *New York University Law Review*, 83: 1–58.

Fleischer, V. (2009). 'A theory of taxing sovereign wealth', *New York University Law Review*, 84: 440–513.

Fruhan, W. (2010). 'The Hedge Fund Industry', Background Note 208-126, April, Cambridge, MA: Harvard Business School.

GAO (2008a). *Recent Growth in Leveraged Buyouts Exposed Risks That Warrant Continued Attention.* Report 08-885, Washington, DC: Government Accountability Office (GAO).

GAO (2008b). *Sovereign Wealth Funds: Publicly Available Data on Sizes and Investments for Some Funds Are Limited.* Report 08-946, Washington, DC: Government Accountability Office (GAO).

GAO (2009) *Sovereign Wealth Funds: Laws Limiting Foreign Investments Affect Certain US Assets and Agencies have Various Enforcement Processes.* Report 09-608, Washington, DC: Government Accountability Office (GAO).

Goldberg, L., Pozen, R., and Hammerle, M. (2010). 'Note: Disclosure, Regulation, and Taxation of Hedge Funds versus Mutual Funds in the U.S.', 28 August, Cambridge, MA: Harvard Business School.

Gross, D. (2005). 'The bottom-feeder king: Never mind hedge funds. Wilbur Ross gets rich the unfashionable way: In steel plants, textile mills, and other stuff nobody wants', *New York Magazine*, 'Money & the Mind', 21 May, accessed 26 September 2013, <http://nymag.com/nymetro/news/bizfinance/columns/moneyandmind/10279/>.

Guerrera, F. and Braithwaite, T. (2011). 'US woos sovereign funds in AIG sale', *Financial Times*, 13 February, accessed 26 September 2013, <http://www.ft.com/intl/cms/s/0/890244ac-3792-11e0-b91a-00144feabdc0.html#axzz2g3srRXYH>.

Hals, T., Zeidler, S., and Humer, C. (2011). 'Insight: New bankruptcy ripples may emerge', *Reuters*, 11 October, accessed 26 September 2013, <http://www.reuters.com/article/2011/10/11/us-bankruptcy-idUSTRE7995RH20111011>.

Higson, C. (2010). 'Does PE Outperform or Underperform? The PE Performance Puzzle', London: Coller Institute of Private Equity, London Business School.

Jarrell, G. (1983). 'State anti-takeover laws and the efficient allocation of corporate control: An economic analysis of Edgar v. Mite Corp', *Supreme Court Economic Review*, 2: 111–29.

Jensen, M. and Meckling, W. (1976). 'The theory of the firm: Managerial behaviour, agency costs and ownership structure', *Journal of Financial Economics*, 3 (4): 305–60.

Jickling, M. and Marples, D. (2007). *Taxation of Hedge Fund and PE Managers*. Report Code RS22689, 5 July, Washington, DC: Congressional Research Service.

Johan, S., Knill, A., and Mauck, N. (2011). 'Determinants of sovereign wealth fund investment in PE', in: AEA, *AEA Annual Conference 2012*. Chicago.

Kansas, D. (2011). 'AIG share sale: Kuwait, Singapore funds express interest', *Wall Street Journal*, 18 May, accessed 26 September 2013, <http://blogs.wsj.com/marketbeat/2011/05/18/aig-share-sale-kuwait-singapore-funds-express-interest/>.

Kaplan, S. and Schoar, A. (2005). 'Private equity performance: Returns, persistence, and capital flows', *Journal of Finance*, 60 (4): 1791–823.

Kaplan, S. and Strömberg, P. (2009). 'Leveraged buyouts and PE', *Journal of Economic Perspectives*, 23 (1): 121–46.

Klein, A. and Zur, E. (2006). 'Entrepreneurial Shareholder Activism: Hedge Funds and Other Private Investors', NYU Law and Economics Research Paper, 06-41, October.

Kosman, J. (2009). *The Buyout of America: How PE Will Cause the Next Great Credit Crisis*. New York: Penguin Group.

Kosman, J. (2011). 'Bain's huge HCA IPO gain', *New York Post*, 11 March, accessed 26 September 2013, <http://www.nypost.com/p/news/business/bain_huge_hca_ipo_gain_QQsVgFa3EOtBy4GohMc5dI>.

Kotter, J. and Lel, U. (2008). 'Friends or Foes? The Stock Price Impact of Sovereign Wealth Fund Investments and the Price of Keeping Secrets', Working Paper, Washington, DC: Federal Reserve Board.

Kunzel, P., Lu, Y., Petrova, I., and Pihlman, J. (2011) 'Investment Objectives of Sovereign Wealth Funds—a shifting paradigm', Working Paper, Washington: International Monetary Fund.

Langford, G., Garcia, D., and Lerman, A. (2009). 'Sovereign Wealth Funds: Real Estate Partners in Growth?', New York: Deloitte Touche Tohmatsu, accessed 26 September 2013, <http://www.deloitte.com/assets/Dcom-UnitedStates/Local%20Assets/Documents/us_re_sovereignrealestatepartners_040809.pdf>.

Lattman, P. (2010). 'Buyout-shop swap multiplan in $3.1 Billion LBO', *Wall Street Journal*, 'Deals & Deal Makers', 9 July, accessed 26 September 2013, <http://online.wsj.com/article/SB1000142405274870360900457535539278755872.html#>.

Lazonick, W. (1992). 'Controlling the market for corporate control: The historical significance of managerial capitalism', *Industrial and Corproate Change*, 1 (3): 445–88.

Lowenstein, R. (2004). *Origins of the Crash: The Great Bubble and its Undoing*. London: Penguin.

McCormick, D. (2008). 'Under secretary for international affairs David H. McCormick testimony before the joint economic committee', 13 February, US Treasury Department Office of Public Affairs.

Marples, D. (2008). *Taxation of PE and Hedge Fund Partnerships: Characterization of Carried Interest*. Report RS22717, 8 July, Washington,DC: Congressional Research Service.

Martin, M. (2010). *China's Sovereign Wealth Fund: Developments and Policy Implications*. Report R41441, 23 September, Washington: Congressional Research Service, accessed 26 September 2013, <http://www.fas.org/sgp/crs/row/R41441.pdf>.

Mellor, C. (2011). 'Iron mountain hit by hedge fund attack', *The Register*, 11 March, accessed 26 September 2013, <http://www.theregister.co.uk/2011/03/11/iron_mountain_attacked_by_hedge_fund/>.

Monitor Group (2011). *Braving the New World: Sovereign Wealth Fund Investment in the Uncertain Times of 2010*, SWF Report,.

Or, A. and Barr, A. (2011). 'Hedge-fund assets reclaim pre-crisis level: Aim higher', *Wall Street Journal*, 10 March, accessed 26 September 2013, <http://online.wsj.com/article/SB1000142405274870413220457619039244633456.html>.

Phalippou, L. and Gottschalg, O. (2009). 'Performance of private equity funds', *Review of Financial Studies*, 22 (4): 1747–76.

Pitchbook (2011). *The Private Equity Breakdown 4Q2011*. Report, Seattle: Pitchbook.

Platt, H. (2009). 'The PE myth', *Journal of Business Valuation and Economic Loss Analysis*, 4: 1–17.

Preqin (2011). 'PE spotlight', Newsletter, November, 7(11).

Preqin(2012). 'Hedge fund spotlight', Newsletter, August, 4(8).

PriceWaterhouseCoopers (2011). 'A Closer Look: The Dodd–Frank Wall Street Reform and Consumer Protection Act', August, PriceWaterhouseCoopers.

Primack, D. (2011). 'Killing the 500-shareholder rule', *Fortune*, 'Term Sheet'. 8 December, accessed 26 September 2013, <http://finance.fortune.cnn.com/2011/11/08/ending-the-500-shareholder-rule/>.

Reuters (2011). 'Popular IPO values HCA at $30–$31 a share', *Reuters*, 9 March, accessed 26 September 2013, <http://archive.chicagobreaking-business.com/2011/03/popular-ipo-values-hca-at-30-31-a-share.html>.

Rose, P. (2008). 'Sovereign wealth funds: Active or passive investors?', *Yale Law Journal*, 118, Pocket Part 104, accessed 26 September 2013, <http://yalelawjournal.org/the-yale-law-journal-pocket-part/scholar-ship/sovereign-wealth-funds:-active-or-passive-investors?/>.

Rubin, R., Sloan, S., and Talev, M. (2011). 'Obama proposes tax on bonds: Carried interest for wealthy', *Bloomberg Business Week*, 13 September, accessed 26 September 2013, <http://www.businessweek.com/news/2011-09-13/obama-proposes-tax-on-bonds-carried-interest-for-wealthy.html>.

Rugaber, C. (2008). 'Funds transparency woes could worsen', *AP Business*, 3 March, accessed 26 September 2013, <http://www.boston.com/news/education/higher/articles/2008/03/03/funds_transparency_woes_could_worsen/?page=2>.

Schor, M. and Greenwood, R. (2009). 'Investor Activism and Takeovers', Working Paper Series, Cambridge, MA: Harvard Business School, accessed 26 September 2013, <http://ssrn.com/abstract=1003792>.

SEIU (2008). 'Sovereign Wealth Funds and PE: Increased Access, Decreased Transparency', April, Washington: Service Employees International Union (SEIU).

Sender, H. (2010). 'BlackRock stakes for Slim and Norges Bank', *Financial Times*, 21 November, accessed 26 September 2013, <http://www.ft.com/intl/cms/s/0/64e5e48a-f58d-11df-99d6-00144feab49a.html#axzz1jxinGCR4>.

Sender, H. (2011). 'CDB seeks to join TPG stake purchase', *Financial Times*, 22 May, accessed 26 September 2013, <http://www.ft.com/intl/cms/s/0/8e4d7f2a-849b-11e0-afcb-00144feabdc0.html#axzz1f2ObvWGX?.

Sender, H. and Anderlini, J. (2011). 'CIC set for up to $200bn in fresh funds', *Financial Times*, 25 April, accessed 26 September 2013, <http://www.ft.com/intl/cms/s/0/51d8e878-6f2d-11e0-952c-00144feabdc0.html>.

Singh, K. (2008). 'Sovereign wealth funds: Some frequently asked questions', *Corner House Briefing*, 38, Dorsett: The Corner House, accessed 26 September 2013, <http://www.thecornerhouse.org.uk/resource/sovereign-wealth-funds>.

Strasburg, J. and Carew, R. (2009). 'Oaktree to receive $1 Billion from CIC', *Wall Street Journal*, 28 September, accessed 26 September 2013,

<http://compliancesearch.com/wallstreetjobreport/current-affairs/oaktree-to-receive-1-billion-from-cic/>.

Strömberg, P. (2008). 'The new demography of PE', in: A. Gurung A. and J. Lerner (eds), 'Globalization of Alternative Investments', Working Papers, 1, *The Global Economic Impact of PE Report 2008*. New York: World Economic Forum, 3–26.

Temple, P. (2001). *Hedge Funds: The Courtesans of Capitalism*. Chichester: Wiley and Sons.

Terry, K. (2011). 'Big IPO for HCA hospital chain, but buyers' remorse remains a distinct possibility', *Money Watch*, 14 March, accessed 26 September 2013, <http://www.cbsnews.com/8301-505123_162-43842687/big-ipo-for-hca-hospital-chain-but-buyers-remorse-remains-a-distinct-possibility/?tag=bnetdomain>.

TheCityUK (2011). *Financial Market Series: Sovereign Wealth Fund*, accessed 26 September 2013, <http://www.thecityuk.com/assets/Uploads/Sovereign-Wealth-Funds-2011.pdf>.

USWA (2002). 'Summary: Proposed agreement between International Steel Group, Inc., and the United Steelworkers of America', December, United Steelworkers of America (USWA).

USWA (2004). 'Steel industry restructuring: Steel crisis, bankruptcies, pension plan terminations, and consolidation', in: IG Metall, USWA—IG Metall seminar. 11—15 October, Sprockhovel: United Steelworkers of America (USWA).

Weiss, M. (2008). *Sovereign Wealth Funds: Background and Policy Issues for Congress*. CRS Report for Congress RL34336, 03 September, Washington, DC: Congressional Research Service.

Zuckerman, G. (2011). 'Kuwait and Singapore acquire slice of TPG', *Wall Street Journal*, 2 April, accessed 26 September 2013, <http://online.wsj.com/article/SB10001424052748703806304576236424131916608.html>.

3

Financialization, New Investment Funds, and Weakened Labour: The Case of the UK

ANDREW PENDLETON AND
HOWARD GOSPEL

Introduction

The activities of new investment funds (NIFs) are more extensive in the UK than any other European country and in most respects come second only to the USA. The UK is notable for being the home for a large number of private equity (PE) and hedge fund (HF) managers, and is also an important regional centre for the management of sovereign wealth funds (SWFs) based elsewhere. Investments by these funds in portfolio companies operating in the UK are also the largest in Europe.

Private equity, and to a somewhat lesser extent HFs, has been controversial in the UK. There was a heated public debate in the mid-2000s on the impact of PE and the extent to which it secured returns at the expense of employees and taxpayers. With the onset of the financial crisis from 2007 onwards, the level of activity and the salience of these funds declined somewhat, but company failures attributed to the PE business model meant that PE continued to be controversial. Financial instability has also raised concerns about HFs. The takeover of Cadbury in 2010, in which activist and event-driven HFs played a part, re-awakened political debates about ownership, takeovers, and the distribution of returns from corporate activity. SWFs have attracted much less public interest, but this may change as the scale and focus of their activities in the UK continues to develop. SWFs now own the flagship London department store Harrods and have significant ownership stakes in other well-known British companies and institutions such as the supermarket chain J.Sainsbury and Heathrow Airport.

The UK has been seen as an especially favourable locale for NIF activity because of the nature of its regulatory and taxation regimes. The broader business and financial context in the UK has also provided a favourable environment for NIF activities to develop. We provide an outline of this context, prior to considering key features of the regulatory and fiscal regimes. We then proceed to outline the main dimensions of activity of PE, HFs, and SWFs respectively. The possible impact of NIF activity on work, employment, and labour relations are then considered. The bulk of the evidence relates to PE, in part because it is easier to trace the direct role of PE than the other investment funds and in part because academic research has concentrated on PE. The chapter then considers the impact of the financial crisis, and illuminates this with some short case studies. These show that PE in particular does not inevitably have adverse effects on labour but elements of the business model render PE-backed firms vulnerable during adverse economic circumstances.

The UK Context

In the UK, PE, HFs, and SWFs have come to prominence in the last fifteen years, though they are by no means new. The UK is second only to the USA in terms of the size of funds managed from the country, though not all monies invested in these funds are generated in the UK, and the funds themselves are typically registered offshore. The UK is also the second largest site of NIF portfolio investments, including SWF investments.

There are several important contextual features which help to explain why the UK is such an important centre for raising and investing capital by NIFs. The UK has been an important global centre for 'finance capitalism' for many years, exemplified by the prominent and longstanding role of the City of London in global asset management (Kay 2012). A variety of features underpin this position, including a well-developed network of financial support services and intermediaries along with a stable and 'business friendly' regulatory environment. Since 'Big Bang' in the mid-1980s, when barriers to entry to the City were substantially removed, London has become more open to overseas financial intermediaries and similar actors (Augar 2001).

A broader context is the national 'business system'. The UK, along with the USA, has been characterized as a liberal market economy

(LME), notable for a reliance on markets to coordinate economic activity rather than relational or regulatory means (Hall and Soskice 2001). In this respect, the UK differs from most of the other countries in this book, some of which (especially Germany and Japan) have been said to take the form of coordinated market economies (CMEs). A key aspect of the emphasis on markets in the UK has been a concern amongst a broad coalition of financial services firms, supported until recently by all political parties, to maintain low, and even to reduce, regulatory barriers to business operations. The over-riding philosophy has been that market discipline functions as an effective alternative to formal regulation (Fioretos 2010). As a result, a distinguishing characteristic of the UK is the near absence of regulatory obstacles to foreign takeovers of UK companies. There are also few restrictions on the movement of capital in and out of the country. Employment protection is also viewed as being relatively weak (Venn 2009), with limited regulation facilitating the restructuring activities of NIFs. At the same time, business law and regulation is viewed as stable and transparent, with the rights and obligations of investors clearly established (Kay 2012).

Well-developed equity markets in the UK, in the form of high liquidity, transparency, and minority investor protection, have offered opportunities for NIFs to acquire ownership stakes in listed companies. In some cases PE has taken listed firms private, as in the case of Boots the Chemist and Four Seasons Health Care, which will be discussed below. Activist HFs and SWFs have been able to acquire often sizeable stakes in companies listed on the London stock market, such as National Express and Sainsburys. In addition, liquid equity markets have facilitated exits for NIFs via share sales (in the case of HFs) and flotations (for PE), and have provided *ex ante* encouragement for NIF acquisitions. Groh et al. (2012) argue that investor protection, corporate governance arrangements, and the size and liquidity of equity markets have been the key differences between the UK and other European countries, and help to explain why the UK has persistently been near the top of their Private Equity Attractiveness Index.

Although well-developed equity markets have facilitated NIF activity, paradoxically a recent contraction in the main equity markets has provided opportunities for some NIFs such as PE. The number of companies listed on the London Stock Exchange has reduced substantially from nearly 1,700 UK listed companies in 2000 to around 1,000 in 2012. The recent Kay Report on Short-Termism has suggested a number of reasons for this, including the costs of listing, the more favourable tax treatment of debt (against equity), regulatory changes for insurance and pension funds reducing the amount invested in equities, the cost of equity capital (due to the high cost of financial intermediation), the cost burden of extensive information disclosure, and the growth of an ethos emphasizing transitory ownership and trading arising in part from the development of diversified financial corporations based on the US model (Kay 2012: 24–7). As a result, private, rather than public, ownership has become more attractive, and this has provided fertile territory for the operation of PE fund managers.

These developments are reflected by major changes in the ownership of those companies that remain listed. Whereas in 1990 ownership of the listed sector was dominated by domestic insurance and pension funds and by individual shareholders, by 2010 these accounted for just 25 per cent of the market value of UK quoted shares (Central Statistical Office 2012). Ownership by pension funds, in particular, has shrunk from over 30 per cent to just 5 per cent. In part, this reflects a change in investment strategies of pension funds away from equities to other asset classes such as PE and HFs. In part, it reflects the growth of outsourcing of pension fund management, the emergence of 'other financial institutions' such as HFs, and of increased investment from outside the UK by investors such as overseas PE funds, HFs, and SWFs (Kay 2012). The Norwegian SWF, for instance, is now one of the biggest holders of UK company shares. In fact, the largest ownership group recorded in official statistics is now 'rest of the world': this includes overseas NIFs and holdings by asset managers whose head office is based outside the UK but who manage assets from UK offices. The US firm BlackRock is currently the largest asset manager in the UK market (Kay 2012: 31).

These changes in the nature of corporate ownership in the UK have profound implications for corporate governance. The now traditional picture of passive institutional shareholders is giving way to a more complex picture of activist and interventionist as well as quiescent governance. Some of these investors have relatively long-term time horizons and are primarily concerned with enhancing the value of portfolio firms; others are more short-termist and focus on changing the distribution of corporate returns. These changes in ownership and governance have a variety of knock-on effects on the management of employment and labour.

New Investment Funds in Practice

Private Equity

Although venture and development capital funds are by no means new, PE buy-outs took off in the UK in the 1980s. Prior to 1981, the Companies Act prohibited the use of assets of target firms as security against leverage incurred by acquisitors; repeal of this aspect of company legislation facilitated the development of buy-out funds and activity (Gilligan and Wright 2010). Activity grew substantially, and the UK became the second largest centre for PE activity from the mid-1980s onwards. There have been a number of peaks of activity: the late 1980s, the late 1990s, and the mid-2000s prior to the beginning of the credit crunch in summer 2007. The value of PE buy-outs rose steadily during the period, with particularly marked growth in the mid-2000s. The number of very large PE buy-outs rose in the 2000s (e.g. Boots and EMI), but these are still relatively few in number and have decreased since the onset of the economic crisis.

The UK has the next largest PE sector after the USA, and five of the largest PE houses by capital raised are based in the UK (Apax Partners, Permira, Pantheon, 3i, and Charterhouse). Over the ten years to 2010, these PE firms raised £349 billion pounds. There are currently 403 PE firms based in the UK, of which just under half specialize in buy-outs (EVCA 2012). The buy-out houses had £217 billion of funds under investment in 2011. Overall, the total investment of all PE funds (including venture capital (VC) but not including external debt) in 2011 accounted for 0.59 per cent of gross domestic product (GDP) (EVCA 2012).

PE buy-outs as a proportion of all merger and acquisition (M&A) deals in the UK has risen steadily, reaching a peak of around 60 per cent in 2007 (CMBOR 2008). The scale of PE deals also rose during the 2000s culminating in the acquisition of a Financial Times Stock Exchange (FTSE) 100 company (Boots) by the US fund KKR in 2007. At this time, around 1,300 UK businesses received PE funding each year. The British Private Equity & Venture Capital Association (BVCA) has estimated that PE funding accounts for the employment of around 3 million people in the UK or approximately 20 per cent of private sector employees (BVCA 2011). Since 2007, the number of buy-outs mounted by UK PE houses has declined from 383 to 233 companies, and the number of mega-buy-outs (over £300 million) has fallen from 21 to 10 (with just four in 2009) (EVCA 2012).

Most investments by value by UK PE houses are in buy-outs (81 per cent in 2011) rather than in new ventures (4 per cent) or in investments for growth (9 per cent).[1] About half of new investments by value by UK funds were invested in UK firms, with most of the rest going elsewhere in Europe. Communications, computer and consumer electronics, consumer goods and retail, and care and financial services have been the main sectors of investment by value in 2011. Overall, over 60 per cent of the largest PE-backed firms are in consumer services (BVCA 2012).

Following extensive public and political criticism of PE funds in 2007, a set of voluntary guidelines was accepted by the PE industry in the form of the so-called Walker Code.[2] These guidelines require that a portfolio company should publish its annual report and accounts on its website within six months of the end of the fiscal year, including information on the identity of the PE owners and managers, and provide an annual business and financial review similar to those provided by listed companies. PE houses should also publish information on their structure, investment approach, and UK investee companies, along with summary information on the investor base. In addition, information should be regularly provided to the trade association, the BVCA, which should monitor the operation of the guidelines. As for labour, the guidelines recommended that a PE firm should ensure timely and effective communication with employees especially at times of 'strategic change', either directly or through its portfolio company. Although these requirements are not legally binding, the Guidelines Monitoring Group reported in 2009 that all thirty-two PE firms covered were fully compliant.[3]

Hedge Funds

The UK has the largest concentration of HF managers outside the USA, with around 20 per cent of global HF assets managed by London-based fund managers (TheCityUK 2012b). Approximately 80 per cent of European HF investments are managed from London. At the end of 2008, there were just over 800 HFs operating out of London with around $300 billion of assets under management (AUM). Five of the largest HFs by assets are UK-based: Brevan Howard Asset Management, Man Investments, Barclays Global Investors, Bluebay Asset Management, and Bluecrest Capital Management. About 40,000 people are directly employed in the HF industry in the UK.

However, the funds themselves are typically registered offshore for tax treatment.

Most HFs operate directional strategies and are now important actors in UK equity markets. They currently account for 37 per cent of average daily trading on the UK market, followed by other high frequency traders (28 per cent) (Kay 2012: 38). Around 10 per cent of HFs operate 'event-driven' strategies, attempting to take advantage of 'special situations', such as M&As or divestitures. Around 15 per cent operate a mixture of investment approaches. Only a small proportion are activist funds, with the main activist HF managers based in the UK including The Children's Investment Fund (TCI) and Audley.

Activist and event-driven HFs grew in importance in the management and governance of UK companies in the mid-2000s (Becht et al. 2010). A prime example is the intervention of US HFs in the UK confectioner Cadbury; this encouraged significant changes of strategy by the company and led ultimately to its takeover by US food company Kraft in 2010. The first encounter was with US activist HF, Trian Fund Management, run by Nelson Peltz. The fund built up ownership of around 3 per cent in Cadbury Schweppes in 2007 and started to lobby for improvements in performance and changes in company strategy and structure. In particular, Trian pressurized Cadbury to demerge its largely North American beverage division. This campaign was supported by a number of other activist HFs and the Qatari SWF. At the time of Peltz' intervention, Cadbury embarked on a programme to raise profit margins by reducing the workforce by 7,500 employees and by closing 15 per cent of its factories. In October 2007, the company announced that its plant in Keynsham, near Bristol, would be closed with the loss of 500 jobs and production transferred to Poland. It was also announced that 200 jobs would go from the Bourneville plant in Birmingham. Various parts of the business in North America and Europe were sold off. Finally, Peltz and others successfully pressurized Cadbury to appoint new senior managers and board members whom they thought would be sympathetic to their views of the future of the company.

Cadbury's reduced size made it vulnerable to a hostile takeover, which came in the form of bid from US food multinational Kraft in 2009. At this point, HFs started to buy Cadbury shares in anticipation that the price would rise and that Kraft would be successful in its bid. Holdings by HFs and short-term traders rose to over 30 per cent by early 2010. The sale of their shares to Kraft then expedited the takeover. Initially Kraft said that it would keep the Keysham plant open but, within a month of the finalization of the deal, it announced that the factory would indeed be closed. The UK Business Minister subsequently referred to a 'lack of straight dealing' by Kraft.

A classic case of activism occurring in late 2012 was the break-up of industrial materials company Cookson into two separate companies, one focusing on performance materials (Alent PLC) and the other on ceramics (Vesuvius PLC). Alent is viewed as a high-growth business, whereas Vesuvius is seen as a more mature, stable business. The break-up was instigated by the Swedish activist fund Cevian which had built up a 20 per cent stake in Cookson from autumn 2011 and had secured a non-executive director on the company's board at the Annual General Meeting (AGM) in May 2012. It argued that breaking-up the conglomerate would enhance shareholder value. At the AGM nearly a third of investors had voted against the remuneration report after questions had been raised by Cevian and other activist investors about the size of share awards to the Chief Executive Officer and finance director.

UK-based activist HFs have often conducted their activism in countries other than the UK. Thus TCI played a leading role in the break-up and sale of ABN Amro (see Chapter 6 on the Netherlands) to Royal Bank of Scotland (RBS). Although TCI appeared to withdraw from activism during 2009–10, it has recently resumed activist acquisitions in Australia, India, and Japan, seeking to acquire stock which it perceives to be discounted because of poor corporate governance. In addition, activist HFs have been involved, along with major institutional investors, in the so-called 'shareholder spring' in the UK during 2012, whereby investors challenged executive pay deals in a substantial number of companies.

Sovereign Wealth Funds

The UK does not operate a SWF—unlike Norway and more recently France. However, it is an important centre for SWF operations, with most major funds operating a London office. London's important role emanates from its well-developed asset management and support service base, the openness of the UK to SWF activity, and the important international role of English commercial law (TheCityUK 2012a). The UK is also an important target of SWFs, accounting for 49 per cent of such funds invested in Europe over the period 1995–2009. For its part, the UK government has actively welcomed SWF investment and management activity in the UK. It is also the case that the absence of a 'public interest' criteria in UK takeover regulation facilitates SWF investments in the UK.

SWFs are not a homogenous entity, and distinctions may be drawn between those which acquire their funds from commodities, such as oil, and those whose assets are transferred in from states' foreign exchange reserves, budget surpluses, or privatization receipts (TheCityUK 2012a). Within the group of commodity-based SWFs, there is variation in the balance of objectives, between stabilization of national income and long-term wealth creation. Commodity-based SWFs using funds for wealth creation typically have a long-term approach to investment decisions, as they do not have to meet the liabilities faced by other major institutional investment funds such as pension funds and insurance companies (Preqin 2012). Equity investments are especially important, with around 40 per cent of total SWF investments in this asset class (Walker 2011). The long-term focus of SWF investment decisions provides some synergy with PE, and investments in the latter have been increasing. For instance, Apax Partners' Europe VIII fund has attracted nearly 25 per cent of its fundraising to date from China Investment Corporation (CIC), the Australia Future Fund, and the Government of Singapore Investment Corporation (Preqin 2012). An increasing number of SWFs have also been investing in HFs.

Most SWFs hold relatively small stakes in UK companies (between 1 and 3 per cent), but there are examples of larger stakes and these have given rise to media anxiety about the takeover of national assets by overseas funds. For example, in 2012, the Qatar Investment Authority (QIA) had a 25 per cent stake in the supermarket company J. Sainsbury, and there has been persistent speculation that this SWF will mount a formal takeover bid. QIA also held a 20 per cent stake in the London Stock Exchange and a 7 per cent stake in Barclays Bank. The Singaporean SWF, Temasek, holds an 18.8 per cent in Standard Chartered, a UK banking and finance group. SWFs are also starting to acquire significant interests in British land and property because property tends to generate predictable cash flows which are uncorrelated with equity movements. For instance, the Norwegian SWF has recently acquired a 50 per cent stake in the Meadowhall shopping complex in Sheffield and acquired 25 per cent ownership of London's Regent Street in 2010. The Abu Dhabi fund has recently acquired a 15 per cent stake in Gatwick Airport and (along with CIC) a significant share in the parent company of Thames Water.

The Regulatory Environment

The regulatory environment in the UK has had a substantial impact on the extent of activity by NIFs, in terms of number of funds, capital raised, and the volume of investment in portfolio companies. 'Light touch' regulation and taxation of funds and their investors have encouraged the development of funds, whilst limited 'hard law' regulation of takeovers has facilitated investments in UK portfolio companies. The latter has also been assisted by weaker labour regulation than is common in much of Europe. This section reviews salient features of the regulatory regime.

Regulation of Funds and Portfolio Companies

Investment Funds

Until recently there was no specific regulation of PE and HFs, but such funds were subject to general aspects of company, securities, and competition law. NIFs have fewer obligations to disclose information on their activities than other types of funds. In essence, they are treated as collections of private investors, and, as they do not usually seek retail market monies, for the most part they are not covered by regulations governing the sale of investment products. The fund managers of HFs operating in the UK have been required to register with the Financial Services Authority (FSA) and to be approved as 'fit and proper' to conduct investment business, but the funds themselves are not usually registered in the UK. Since the Walker Review of Private Equity there has been a degree of voluntary disclosure by PE funds (Walker 2007).

From 2013 the implementation of the European Union (EU) Alternative Investment Fund Managers' Directive changes the regulatory environment. HFs will be overseen by the newly-established Financial Conduct Authority, one of the successors to the FSA. Fund managers above a certain size (€100 million AUM for leveraged funds, €500 million for unleveraged funds) will require authorization by the financial regulator. Authorization will be based on disclosure of information about the fund manager, including the size and leverage of the funds under its control. Fund managers are required to disclose ownership of portfolio companies above various thresholds as well as the nature and source of leverage. They will be prohibited from taking dividends from portfolio companies where this puts the capital adequacy of portfolio companies at risk. This particular element of the Directive is directed against 'asset stripping'.

A large number of SWFs manage significant segments of their investments from London. As SWFs do not raise funds in the UK, they are not covered by the regulatory framework governing other NIFs. In response to criticisms that they put non-commercial aims, such as achieving political influence, ahead of investment returns, SWFs have adopted self-regulation in the form of the so-called Santiago Principles. These principles distinguish between the strategic interests of the sovereign state and the commercial, asset management objectives of the SWF (Walker 2011). The extent to which they influence behaviour in the UK is unknown.

Tax Law

The UK has scored consistently highly in the European Private Equity and Venture Capital Association (EVCA) benchmarking survey of national tax and legal environments for PE. Key features are tax transparency of limited partnership fund structures for domestic and non-domestic investors, with no tax liable on the fund itself. In practice, management fees and carried interest are not usually liable for value added tax. The EVCA Survey identified various fiscal incentives for R&D expenditure in investee firms, but also notes that corporation, capital gains tax (CGT), and income tax rates are somewhat above the European average (EVCA 2008).

The tax treatment of PE has received considerable attention in the UK. It was a major issue in a parliamentary investigation in 2007 (Treasury Select Committee 2007). Two issues have attracted particular interest. One is the taxation of the returns to general partners of PE funds; the other is the corporation tax treatment of debt within investee companies.

First, because general partners invest in the fund (typically 1–3 per cent of the fund's value), their return (carried interest) is viewed as a capital gain on a business asset. This has been controversial because payments might alternatively be viewed as a return for services and hence might be subject to income tax. Until 2008, the CGT treatment was very generous, with the tax liability tapering to 10 per cent after two years, as compared with the marginal income tax rate for higher rate taxpayers of 40 per cent. Following public outcry, the government abolished business assets taper relief in 2008 and replaced it with a flat CGT rate of 18 per cent (now 28 per cent for higher income taxpayers). However, this is still substantially lower than the highest marginal rate of income tax. In addition, the capacity to offset potential capital gains with business expenditure means that general partners usually pay little CGT.

The second area of controversy here is that interest payments on debt used by PE funds to acquire companies can be set against corporation tax paid by the investee company, given that the debt is typically loaded onto the balance sheet of the acquired companies. It has been suggested that this practice may have an adverse effect on UK tax revenues, with firms owned by PE houses paying low levels of corporation tax.

However, there are some perceived limitations of UK tax law from a PE perspective. One is that the most recent all-employee share ownership plan—the Share Incentive Plan—cannot attract tax benefits for employees when the employing company is under the control of another (i.e. PE fund). EVCA has also drawn attention to the limited concessions for executive incentive schemes, whereby schemes are either unavailable for PE-backed firms, too small in terms of rewards, or are unapproved for tax purposes (meaning that tax charges are liable on the exercise of options rather than the sale of the underlying shares) (EVCA 2008).

Takeovers

As far as mergers and takeovers of listed companies are concerned, there are significant elements of self-regulation via the City Takeover Panel. This has traditionally applied relatively permissive rules. In recent years, however, takeover regulation has become more legally-based, in part responding to EU directives. But the UK is still a relatively open country for M&As, including hostile takeover bids.

In the UK, there is no generalized 'public interest' criteria to be considered when M&As are mounted, and government can only intervene in exceptional circumstances (e.g. where national security or where press plurality is threatened). Instead, the Office of Fair Trading can refer cases to the Competition Commission when there is likely to be a 'substantial lessening of competition'. Previously, ministers could refer cases on grounds of promoting 'the balanced distribution of industry and employment'. From 1990 until 2002, the government noted that it would pay particularly close attention to 'the degree of state control of the acquiring company'. Dubai Port World's 2006 takeover of P&O might have fallen foul of this provision if it had still been in force.

The UK government recently conducted a consultation on corporate governance with an important focus on takeovers. The context to this was the takeover of UK companies by overseas companies and the role of HFs in provoking or facilitating changes of ownership which are often widely seen as detrimental to UK employees and communities. The case of Cadbury's acquisition by Kraft in 2010 was an important backdrop. The main union confederation, the Trades Union Congress (TUC), called for the creation of an independent M&A commission and for the introduction of an economic test for whether M&As should be allowed to proceed. This economic test would take into account whether the takeover would be beneficial for the target company and also in the interests of employees, local communities, and the wider economy. As a result of this consultation, the government announced a further review into short-termism. This led to the publication of the Kay Review, referred to earlier, in 2012 (Kay 2012). At the time of writing, the policy response by government has yet to be announced.

However, in autumn 2011, the Takeover Panel made a number of amendments to the Takeover Code to transpose the European Takeover Directive into domestic practice. These were mainly concerned with ensuring greater transparency, but a potentially important new requirement gives employee representatives (or all employees where there are no representatives) in target companies the right to incorporate their view in the formal response to the acquiring company. This is not likely to affect many PE transactions, because the Takeover Code applies to listed companies, whereas PE is often involved in buy-outs of unlisted firms. However, public-to-private transactions will be affected by this new requirement. It remains to be seen in what ways they are affected.

Labour Regulation

Discussions of business regimes highlight the importance of institutional complementarities (Hall and Soskice 2001; Milgrom and Roberts 1995). In the UK, an emphasis on markets as the primary means of coordinating economic activity extends to labour law and employment protection. Although the weakness of employment rights can be overstated, it is nevertheless the case that barriers to restructuring imposed by labour law tend to be weaker than in many other European countries. It is possible that the relative ease of restructuring makes the UK an attractive site for PE and activist HF activity. Furthermore, it may influence the type of activity, with NIFs more willing to embark upon transactions which require restructuring than in countries with stronger employment protection.

Employment Protection

Based on the Organization for Economic Cooperation and Development (OECD) employment protection index, the UK has the lowest level of employment protection in Europe, and is higher only than the USA and Canada within the OECD (Venn 2009). On transfer of undertakings, it is important to note that PE takeovers, as share transactions, are not viewed as a change of control which triggers employee rights to information and employment protection under the EU Directive on Safeguarding Employee Rights in the Event of Transfer of Undertakings (transposed into UK law as the Transfer of Undertaking Protection of Employment Regulations or TUPE).[4] When shares are sold and the ownership of the company transfers to new owners, this is deemed to have no impact on the contractual relationship between the company and employees being sold: the legal relationship remains unchanged and is identical before and after a sale. If a purchaser subsequently wishes to change any employment conditions, they can do so in exactly the same way as if no sale had occurred.

Worker Voice and Representation

UK employees have rights to information and consultation in various situations, the most relevant here being collective redundancies and M&As. This is not through any specially created legal channel, such as a works council, though these may be established under UK law derived from the EU Information and Consultation Directive. It should be noted that these have not been much used. As stated above, from 2011, a potentially important new requirement in the Takeover Code gives employee representatives (or all employees where there are no representatives) in target companies the right to incorporate their view in the formal response to the acquiring company.

Trade unions also have certain rights to information and consultation in collective bargaining situations. However, the law here is weak and not much used. In the private sector, union membership has fallen to below 20 per cent, the areas covered by collective bargaining have become limited. Bargaining seldom takes place at company level where it most matters for corporate governance (Workplace Employment Relations Survey 2013). It is perhaps significant that in the UK unions have had to resort to public relations campaigns, as seen in the case of the acquisition of the Automobile Association (AA). British unions have therefore not been as successful in organizing networks of union representatives as is the case with German works councils. Nor do there seem to be cases where unions have developed relationships with specific PE firms and helped establish 'beauty contests' between competing PE houses to see which one offers the best deal for employees at the target firm, as has occurred in some cases in the USA (Beeferman 2009).

Impacts on Labour and Employment

The debate on the effects of PE and HFs in the UK has been highly polarized. By contrast, there has been very little debate over the role of SWFs. On the one hand, parts of the financial and academic community argue that the UK benefits from intervention by these funds because they can assist restructuring of under-performing companies. The PE trade association, the BVCA, argues that long-term employment has grown under PE acquisitions and in the majority of cases industrial relations are conducted amicably with employees. On the other hand, trade unions and others have criticized PE and HFs on the grounds that they maximize returns to their funds at the expense of employees and other stakeholders. The TUC and large member unions, such as UNITE and GMB, have been highly critical of PE in particular, and have mounted a number of political campaigns to change regulatory policy (Clark 2009).

The fundamental argument made against PE in particular is that high returns to investors, coupled with high management fees charged by general partners, require significant shifts of value from other stakeholders such as employees and taxpayers (Watt 2008). On top of this, the substantial role of leverage in the PE model of acquisition restricts the amount of 'free cash flow' available for other stakeholders and forces managers to seek efficiencies in running investee companies. As we will see in case studies later in this chapter, in some sectors debt pressures are intensified by the practice of 'sale and leaseback' of properties, with the capital windfalls from selling property often claimed by fund managers as a special dividend, thereby taking capital out of the investee company. The case against PE, then, is that the financing model places pressures on employment and wages. Furthermore, it has been argued that it is a risky business model which places employment at risk in economic downturns and when credit becomes more expensive. Lack of transparency means that value transfers from labour and other stakeholders may well not be evident until after they have taken place. The argument against activist HFs is similar in that they are said to aim to put pressure on firms to increase returns to shareholders by direct resource transfers (share buy-backs, special dividends, etc.) and by restructuring (which may involve divestments and redundancies).

Against these claims, it is argued that well-publicized cases of employment loss after NIF interventions tend to be isolated cases where the 'fundamentals' of the companies concerned are already uncertain. Besides this, the claims in favour of PE are twofold. The first is that the duration of PE investments, linked to the lifetime of the PE fund, tends to be several years. As a result, managers in investee companies have the time to implement strategies, which lay the basis for long-term job creation. This is contrasted with the pressures arising from share price movements and quarterly reporting for publicly-listed companies, which force managers into short-term responses (Kay 2012). It also contrasts with the shorter-term perspective of activist HFs. The second is that PE-backed companies acquire better and more incentivized managers, placed there by the fund managers, who implement better quality business strategies and practices. Thus, PE-backed companies are likely to be more successful, thereby encouraging long-term employment growth. It is also argued that better management will use higher quality human resource practices, which will improve the working conditions of employees (BVCA 2012).

Despite the importance of NIFs in the UK, there have been only a limited number of academic studies of their impact. Part of the problem has been that information and data have not been readily forthcoming from the firms themselves. However, as will be listed below, there have been a number of studies of the effects of PE ownership of portfolio companies. Unfortunately, there is very little research to date into the labour effects of HFs and SWFs.

The Evidence Base—Case Study and Econometric Studies

In the past few years, there have been several case studies of PE and HF involvement in UK companies (Clark 2009; Wilke et al. 2009; Gospel et al. 2010). The PE case studies include a wide variance in employment and industrial relations outcomes. In many cases, PE

firms and the new management they install have continued prevailing approaches to work and employment. In other cases, an
adversarial situation has arisen and trade unions complain that they
have not been informed about the acquisition and about subsequent
restructuring plans which have led to a deterioration in terms and
conditions.

One of the best-known cases is that of the AA, which was acquired
by CVC Capital Partners in 2004. Shortly after acquisition, the company derecognized the GMB union, made a significant number of
redundancies, and substantially changed working patterns. However,
how far these developments can be blamed on PE is open to debate,
since it is difficult to judge what the counterfactual situation would
have been. Following the initial restructuring, the company recorded
an increase in employment.[5]

Anecdotal information on HF interventions suggests that there is
rarely direct contact between worker representatives and HFs and
that the activist plans of HFs do not intervene as deeply into employment conditions and industrial relations. However, the Cadbury case
shows how labour and employment may be affected by HF activism.
In that case, these interventions were associated with changes of strategy and divestments by the company, and these in turn had adverse
effects on employment. The subsequent sale of the company to Kraft
may have resulted from the initial HF interventions and was certainly
affected by HF interventions during the actual takeover process.
Nevertheless, it is difficult to isolate the effects on employment and
jobs in that company because the linkages are indirect.

We know of one case study of the impact of SWF activity on labour
in the UK (Wilke et al. 2009). This concerns Dubai Ports World's
takeover of P&O in 2006. This attracted some attention in the UK
and considerably more in the USA because of fears that major ports
would fall under foreign control. In the immediate aftermath of the
takeover, there was some reduction in ferry operations, some changes
in pension arrangements, and a seemingly greater desire on the part
of management to deal with a works council rather than the trade
unions. However, some of the changes may have occurred anyway
and unions continued to be recognized.

There are several quantitative studies of PE portfolio firms in the
UK, mainly conducted under the aegis of the Centre for Management
Buy-out Research at Nottingham University[6] (see Wright et al. 2009;
Gilligan and Wright 2010, and Bacon et al. 2013 for overviews). For
the most part they use material collected from the PE sector as well

as portfolio companies' annual published accounts and cover the several waves of PE-backed buy-outs since the early 1980s. The evidence is mixed with some studies showing employment reductions and others indicating little change. The studies also suggest that the nature of buy-outs affects what happens subsequently.

Amess et al. (2008) compare the employment effects of leveraged buy-outs (LBOs) and traditional acquisitions against a large control group. They find a 4.5 per cent fall in employment in the immediate aftermath of LBO transactions, but insignificant effects in the longer run. By contrast, traditional acquisitions significantly reduce employment compared with the control group for up to three years post-transaction. They break down the LBO group into those backed and those not backed by PE. The PE-backed group have no significant employment changes relative to the control group, but the non-PE-backed group show significant falls. Cressy et al. (2007) compare forty-eight UK PE-backed buy-outs with a matched sample of eighty-four companies over a five-year period and find that employment falls in the PE sample over four years. However, they find that job cuts are associated with higher operating profits, which in turn contribute to job creation. Amess and Wright (2007) compare the employment effects of management buy-outs (MBOs) and management buy-ins (MBIs) (PE is more usually associated with the latter) and find that MBIs have a small negative impact on employment whereas MBOs have a positive effect. They find that wage growth is slower in both MBOs and MBIs than in comparable firms.

Goergen et al. (2011) argue that previous studies do not clearly distinguish private equity mounted buy-outs from those mounted by either internal or external managers with VC or PE fund support. They suggest that PE buy-outs ('institutional buy-outs') are likely to have more adverse effects on employment than MBOs and MBIs because they typically replace the incumbent management and are thus more likely to break implicit contracts with employees. They also make greater use of leverage, which can restrict the proportion of returns that are available for labour. The authors find that institutional buy-outs have lower turnover and profit per employee pre-buy-out than a sample of matched firms but this difference becomes insignificant after the buy-out. At the same time, employment growth becomes significantly lower than the matched firms after the buy-out, though there is no significant change in profitability. Meuleman et al. (2009) show that UK buy-outs backed by more experienced PE firms and buy-outs of divisions have higher growth in employment than other types of PE-backed buy-out, while Weir et al. (2008) show that public-to-private buy-outs tend to experience employment declines.

A survey of buy-outs and buy-ins in the UK and the Netherlands finds that employee involvement, job flexibility, and training all increase after the buy-out (Bacon et al. 2008). However, it has been shown that PE-backed buy-outs are less likely to use high commitment work practices than buy-outs which are not backed by PE. Amess et al. (2007) find that employees in buy-out firms have more discretion over their work practices than comparable workers at non-buy-out firms.

There are fewer studies focusing on the impact of NIF on industrial relations. The evidence to date indicates little impact overall on the incidence of collective labour institutions but that, equally, these institutions have little impact on buy-outs and restructuring. One study suggests finds that 5 per cent of buy-outs remove union recognition at the buy-out, but the level of union recognition subsequently increases back to pre-buy-out levels (Bacon et al. 2004). A survey of buy-out firms with more than fifty employees in 2008 found that the incidence of any form of consultation committee increased from 42 to 59 per cent in LMEs (the LME sample being mainly UK firms) (Bacon et al. 2010). The incidence of joint consultative committees, works councils at establishment level, and a European works council was unchanged. Consultation during the buy-out itself, however, was minimal: in 59 per cent of cases employee representatives were not informed about the buy-out and in only 4 per cent of cases were they consulted. The authors argue that, whilst there does not appear to be a need to provide specific protection for information and consultation after buy-outs, there could be a case for a requirement for greater information disclosure to, and joint consultation with, employee representatives during the buy-out itself (Bacon et al. 2010: 22).

It is difficult to summarize the evidence-based papers, especially given different data sources and methodologies. Nevertheless, we would conclude as follows. The evidence we have on HFs and SWFs is very limited and it is difficult to draw definitive conclusions. However, case study material suggests that they can have significant indirect effects. As for PE, it is clear that at the time of acquisition, PE houses do not consult with employees, but also that after acquisition for the most part they do not change industrial relations arrangements. There is some evidence that acquisition by PE does initially have a negative effect on employment. However, there is some evidence that in the longer term they may have a more positive effect on employment.

The Financial and Economic Crisis since 2007

The number of PE deals in the UK fell significantly with the beginning of the credit crisis in 2007, though there has been some recovery since 2010. The value of buy-outs fell dramatically, from £68 billion in 2007 to £6.3 billion in 2009 (CMBOR 2010). In 2009, there were only nineteen buy-outs valued between £50 and £500 million. Public-to-private buy-outs fell to fifteen, whilst secondary buy-outs fell to twenty-seven. The use of funds by PE houses shifted somewhat. from mounting buy-outs to providing capital for growth and mezzanine funding: 62 per cent of funding allocations went to buy-outs in 2011 compared with 93 per cent in 2008; 20 per cent was used for growth capital and nearly 13 per cent for mezzanine funding in 2011 compared with 3 per cent and zero respectively in 2008 (EVCA 2012).

The value of funds raised by PE houses fell from $46 billion to £5.6 billion in 2009. It subsequently increased to £9 billion in 2010 and £16 billion in 2011 but is still a long way below 2007 and 2008 levels (EVCA 2012). A major shift in investors has taken place with the role of SWFs in PE increasing from 4.5 per cent of capital raised in 2008 to just under 16 per cent in 2011. At the same time allocations from pension funds reduced from over 36 per cent to just over 23 per cent (EVCA 2012).

The expectation is that PE-backed companies would be highly vulnerable to the recession from 2007 because of their high levels of leverage. Yet, there is evidence to the contrary. Wilson et al. (2012) find that PE buy-outs experienced higher growth, productivity, profitability, and improved working capital management, relative to comparable private and public firms during the recession. They attribute this in part to PE firms taking timely action to assist their investee companies. According to this study, there appears to be little difference between PE-backed firms and matched private companies in the annual change in employment from 2007 to 2009.

A smaller-scale study of larger PE-backed companies by the BVCA (2012) finds that overall employment grew during 2010 by 1.2 per cent compared with a decline of 0.2 per cent in FTSE All Share companies. 'Organic' employment (i.e. excluding the effects of acquisitions and divestments) grew by 0.2 per cent compared with a decline of −1.3 per cent in the economy as a whole. They also exhibited an improvement in their debt to EBITDA (earnings before interest, tax, depreciation, and amortization) ratio since acquisition (from 7.9 to 7.0) (BVCA 2012).

A major area of difficulty for PE funds since 2007–08 has been exit. The opportunities for a successful initial public offering (IPOs) have been considerably reduced, despite the growth in asset values during 2009, and several major IPOs were postponed in 2010. The value of IPOs dropped in 2009 to less than £0.5 billion, and further still in 2010, though with recovery to around £2 billion in 2011 (Kay 2012: 23). Similarly, the opportunities for selling firms to other PE houses have also been reduced, although the first quarter of 2010 saw an increase in secondary buy-outs (CMBOR 2010). Faced with these difficulties, and with a decline in returns, some PE firms have faced pressures from investors for withdrawal of their funds. However, as the market recovered in 2010, these pressures subsided. Also, the unattractiveness of the IPO route for exiting businesses provides an opportunity for PE to acquire businesses through trade sales.

Overall, the credit crisis has posed considerable challenges for the PE business model. Reliant on high levels of leverage in most cases, restrictions on the supply of credit have inhibited refinancing deals leading to costly increases in debt. In turn, this has added to the difficulties in exiting investments. On the other hand, the crisis has created new opportunities for PE funds focusing on turnaround situations.

Evidence on the response of activist HFs to the financial crisis is harder to come by. US data suggest that HFs significantly reduced their equity holdings during the crisis, especially in volatile and liquid stock (Itzhak et al. 2012). However, there is no comparable information for the sub-group of HFs with activist strategies in the UK. Anecdotal evidence suggests that UK activist HFs became more quiescent: the main UK activist fund TCI retreated from activism during 2007–09. More recently, activist funds have become more active again, though so far no cases have hit the headlines in the same way as Cadbury. The crisis created opportunities for some HFs, such as those specializing in purchasing distressed debt. However, the recent decline in the number of M&As has limited the potential for those HFs focusing on special events.

Similarly, SWFs were reluctant to invest in UK companies during the recession and retreated from others, as seen above. The case of the Dubai funds has also raised another spectre viz. that some SWFs may have overreached themselves in terms of involvement and acquisition and this may have future restructuring implications. However, substantial SWF investments have continued in financial services, in retail, and in infrastructure.

The challenges faced by NIFs in the economic and financial crisis can be illustrated by some well-known cases in the UK drawn from the retail and social care sectors. Before the global financial and economic crisis, the retail sector was attractive to PE for several reasons—rising consumer demand, an absence of foreign competition, and significant property assets. Social care was attractive for similar reasons—apparently assured income streams and in some cases substantial real estate portfolios.

In retail, the case of Focus exemplifies the pressures arising from the recession, and the potential impacts on labour. The company was established in the 1980s, as a privately-owned, do-it-yourself home improvement chain. In 1998, Duke Street Capital made a £68 million investment in the company which was used, along with borrowings, to buy two competitors, Wickes and General Mills. In 2002, Duke sold a stake to Apax Partners for £340 million, and Apax was said to have made a further £120 million investment in the business. On the basis of this, Focus grew to be the second largest home improvement chain in the UK, with around 430 stores and 4,000 employees. However, in 2005, the recently acquired Wickes, which was the most profitable part of the business, was sold on to another competitor. Through this and other sales and dividends, the two PE firms were reported to have taken £1 billion out of the business by the mid-2000s.

However, by this time, Focus was beginning to suffer. Its key problems were debt servicing, rents on those stores which had been sold and leased back, and the sale of the most profitable part of the company. In early 2007, another PE house, Cerberus Capital, bought Focus in a £225 million deal, which involved it acquiring the debt at a considerable discount and buying the equity for a nominal sum. Cerberus was said to have injected an undisclosed amount of new capital into the company. However, by this time, with the onset of recession and a downturn in the home improvement market, pressure on the company had grown. In an attempt to recoup its mounting losses, Cerberus began to sell stores, closed others, and made staff redundant. This was to no avail, and, in early 2011, Cerberus put Focus into bankruptcy. Subsequently, the administrator sold 55 stores, employing 900 staff, to competitors and closed 125 stores, purportedly employing around 2,000 staff. Two other aspects of PE ownership are notable from a labour perspective. First, in an unusual move, in 2008, the UK regulator, the Pension Protection Fund, ordered Duke Capital to make a retrospective payment of £8 million into the company pension scheme. The case was that the sale of Wickes and the resultant dividend had benefited the PE owner, but had significantly weakened the employee pension scheme which had been shifted onto the weaker remaining part of the company. Second, in 2012, an employment tribunal found that the company had failed to consult with employees and their union at the time of redundancy and 2,000 staff were awarded compensation payments as a result.[7]

Turning to social care, the case of Southern Cross Care Homes illustrates the kind of problems which the PE model can experience when economic conditions become unfavourable. Southern Cross was founded in 1996 and at its peak in the late 2000s was the UK's biggest care operator, with 31,000 residents and 40,000 staff. Before its collapse in 2011, it went through a number of owners. In 2002, the then top management, backed by West Private Equity, acquired the company in an £80 million MBO. Subsequently, in 2004, a secondary buy-out of the business by the management and Blackstone Capital followed at a price of £162 million. Blackstone later acquired Nursing Home Properties (NHP) for £564 million and the Ashbourne Group of care homes for £85 million. This in turn led to a competition enquiry by the UK Office of Fair Trading which cleared the acquisitions.[8]

As is common in PE-acquired businesses with substantial property assets, the care homes themselves were sold (to NHP, by now part-owned by Qatar SWF QIA). In turn, NHP sold off around half the homes to other landlords. These sales generated a substantial return for Southern Cross, but meant that a sizeable proportion of future income from patients' fees had to be devoted to property rents. Meanwhile, these rental contracts stipulated annual increases which, in the view of the trade union GMB (which represented about a quarter of Southern Cross's employees), were in excess of market norms.[9] At the same time, with the pressure on public finances arising in the recession, local authority funding was being capped. In addition, occupancy rates in Southern Cross homes were falling. This was in part attributed to poor standards of accommodation (and low assessments in inspections by the regulator, the Care Quality Commission) stemming from low investment by Southern Cross and NHP. In the meantime, Blackstone had exited, having floated the company at the end of 2007.

Southern Cross responded to this squeeze by seeking to renegotiate rents, but was largely unsuccessful. The developing situation received considerable adverse press publicity and was widely seen as a case of asset stripping and of the vulnerability of the 'sale and lease-back' model. Ever-mounting difficulties in 2011 led to the collapse of the company and the transfer of its care home operations to other care operators (some of which, as will be seen below, were also owned or about to be acquired by PE). In the run-up to the collapse, homes were closed, wage cuts threatened, and around 3,000 staff made redundant.

Equally, NIFs equity can provide injections of capital which can rescue failing businesses. Four Seasons Health Care is a good case in point. Until the late 1990s, Four Seasons was a small Scottish operator of care homes. In the early 2000s, it grew rapidly, largely by acquisitions, and in 2007 it was acquired by the Qatar SWF for £1.4 billion, with advice from a HF, Three Delta. The Qatar fund itself put up only £50 million and the rest was funded by debt, a significant proportion of which came from RBS (which was massively extending investment activities at the time). In this context, Four Seasons further expanded, acquiring more homes and running up more debt. However, it received a number of unfavourable inspection reports[10] and the Qatar fund, fearing bad publicity and having fallen out with Three Delta, began to lose faith in its investment. At this point, a number of HFs, specializing in distressed debt, began to short the company and buy debt at a discounted rate. In late 2009, RBS (now largely owned by the UK government) was pressured to intervene and took a 40 per cent stake in the company's debt, with the UK taxpayer taking a big write-off of the debt which had been run up under Qatari ownership. This enabled the company to continue to operate and indeed to take over some of the homes previously run by Southern Cross.

In effect, a 'white knight' investor was required and this emerged in summer 2012 in the somewhat unlikely person of Guy Hands, whose Terra Firma PE fund had recently suffered a debacle with the acquisition of the EMI music group. At the time, Terra Firma was said to need to use up unspent money and was looking to switch from glamorous 'growth' acquisitions to buying 'distressed' companies which nevertheless offered relatively safe prospects. Terra Firma paid £825 million, supported by Goldman Sachs and Barclays.

Now the UK's largest care operator, Four Seasons seems to offer securer care for its 20,000 residents and 30,000 staff. The company has also moved into higher dependency care, which is a growth part of the sector and offers higher profits. It has also announced that it will seek a 50 per cent balance between owned and rented properties, so as not to be over-exposed to rental costs. In labour terms, Four Seasons has never recognized trade unions, unlike many larger employers in the sector, and this policy continues. The unions concede that jobs are now more secure, but that wages in the company are increasingly polarized between top management and employees.[11]

Conclusions are difficult to draw from a small number of cases. Nevertheless, we suggest the following. First, it is clear that PE, HFs, and SWFs have become increasingly interlinked, with SWFs investing in PE and with HFs looking to take advantage of events which involve PE. Second, in recession, falling demand, high levels of debt, and the 'sale and leaseback' model can constitute a real threat to the existence of fund-backed companies. Third, acquisition and involvement by NIFs, especially where high levels of debt and property sales are utilized in the business model, can clearly have negative effects on employment and terms and conditions. However, the intervention by PE and SWFs can also support growth and help save distressed companies.

Conclusions

The UK represents a case in which a broad variety of employment outcomes have resulted from PE, HFs, and (to a lesser extent) SWF investment. These have been moderated by both the strategies of the funds and the regulatory context in which they operate. The UK has represented an important area of activity for PE investors, as shown by the large number of funds and the extent of their activity. This is to be explained by several factors: the openness of the City of London and its connections with New York; the demand for PE due to corporate restructuring and opportunities for activist HFs; a friendly legal and tax framework; and the relative weakness of industrial relations-type constraints. SWFs have also found the UK fertile ground because of the more general openness of the British economy.

In terms of labour outcomes, it would seem that fund involvement does not mean either an automatic 'win–win' situation for both sides nor an inevitable 'zero-sum' situation where workers are negatively affected. Rather, outcomes appear to be dependent on factors such as the type of fund and its strategy, its willingness to work with employees, and the possibility of adverse public scrutiny and criticism. Overall, PE has had more effect than HFs, except in certain key situations HFs can have a significant effect on the fate of a company and have major employment implications. SWFs have had the least effect.

As for PE, it is clear that at the time of acquisition, PE houses do not usually consult with employees, but also that after acquisition they do not usually change industrial relations arrangements. There is good evidence that the acquisition of a company by PE does initially have a negative effect on employment; this undoubtedly creates disturbance for the employees concerned; however, there is some evidence that in the longer term they may have a positive effect on employment. It is uncertain whether they have an effect on wages, benefits, and other aspects of working lives.

NOTES

1. In 2011 UK PE funds invested in 233 buy-outs and 377 new ventures (EVCA 2012).
2. These apply to both PE funds and their portfolio companies, where the latter were acquired in a public-to-private transaction exceeding £300 million and more than 50 per cent of revenues are generated in the UK and there are more than 1,000 full-time employees or in a secondary transaction in excess of £500 million and 50 per cent of revenues come from the UK and where there are more than 1,000 employees.
3. <walker-gmg.co.uk>
4. 2001/23/EC. This replaces Directives 77/187/EC (the Acquired Rights Directive) and 98/50/C.
5. See I. Clark (2009), 'Private Equity and Union "Recognition" at the AA', mimeo University of Birmingham, provides the story from the GMB perspective. We would like to thank Ian Clark for discussions about this case, and also Mike Wright, University of Nottingham for the provision of other information and also for discussions. See also Work Foundation (2007), *Inside the Dark Box: Shedding Light on Private Equity*, Work Foundation. London.
6. This centre is now based at Imperial College, London.
7. See the following: the Insolvency Service, Annual Report and Accounts 2011—2012, London, Stationery Office, p. 22 and <http://www.pen-sionprotectionfund.org.uk/transferredschemes/pages/alltransferred-schemes.aspx>.
8. For various government reports, see,<http://www.oft.gov.uk/OFTwork/mergers/decisions/2005/blackstone.; http://www.dh.gov.uk/health/2012/12/provider-failures/>; <http://www.cqc.org.uk/media/cqc-warns-southern-cross-healthcare-it-failing-protect-safety-and-welfare-people>.
9. GMB Union (2011).

10. See various Care Quality Commission reports for 2008 and 2009.
11. For an earlier statement of the company's opposition to trade unions see Central Arbitration Committee, Case Number TURI/487/2006 Community v Four Seasons Health Care; *The Guardian* 11 December 2012. <http://www.gmb.org.uk/gmb_campaigns/gmb_campaigns/southern_cross.aspx>.

BIBLIOGRAPHY

Amess, K. and Wright, M. (2007). 'The wage and employment effects of leveraged buy-outs in the U.K.', *International Journal of Economics and Business*, 14 (2): 179–95.

Amess, K., Brown, S., and Thompson, S. (2007). 'Management buy-outs, supervision and employee discretion', *Scottish Journal of Political Economy*, 54 (4): 447–74.

Amess, K., Girma, S. and Wright, M. (2008). 'What are the Wage and Employment Consequences of Leveraged Buy-Outs, Private Equity and Acquisitions in the UK?', CMBOR Occasional Paper, London: Centre for Management Buy-Out Research.

Augar, P. (2001). *The Death of Gentlemanly Capitalism*. London: Penguin.

Bacon, N., Wright, M., and Demina, N. (2004). 'Management buy-outs and human resource management', *British Journal of Industrial Relations*, 42(2): 325–347.

Bacon, N., Wright, M., Demina, N., Bruining, H., and Boselie, P. (2008). 'HRM, buyouts and private equity in the UK and the Netherlands', *Human Relations*, 61 (10): 1399–433.

Bacon, N., Wright, M., Scholes, L., and Meuleman, M. (2010). 'Assessing the impact of private equity on industrial relations in Europe', *Human Relations*, 63 (9): 1343–70.

Bacon, N., Wright, M., Ball, R., and Meuleman, M. (2013). 'Private equity, HRM, and employment', *Academy of Management Perspectives*, 27 (1); 7–21.

Becht, M., Franks, J., and Grant, J. (2010). 'Hedge Fund Activism in Europe', ECGI Working Paper Series in Finance, 283/2010, May, <http://papers.ssrn.com/sol3/papers.cfm?abstract_id=1616340>.

Beeferman, L. (2009). 'Private equity and American labor: Pragmatic responses mirroring labour's strengths and weaknesses', *Journal of Industrial Relations*, 51: 543–56.

BVCA (2011). *BVCA Private Equity and Venture Capital Report on Investment Activity 2011*. London: British Venture Capital Association (BVCA).

BVCA (2012). *BVCA Annual Report on the Performance of Portfolio Companies IV*. London: British Venture Capital Association (BVCA).

Central Statistical Office (2012). 'Ownership of UK Quoted Shares', London: Central Statistical Office.

Clark, I. (2009). 'Private equity in the UK: Job regulation and trade unions', *Journal of Industrial Relations*, 51: 489–500.

CMBOR (2008). 'The Impact of Private Equity-backed Buy-outs on Employee Relations', Nottingham: CMBOR.

CMBOR (2010). *European Management Buy-Out Review*. Nottingham: CMBOR.

Cressy, R., Munari, F., and Malipiero, A. (2007). 'Creative Destruction: Evidence that Buy-Outs Cut Jobs to Raise Returns', University of Birmingham Working Paper, Birmingham: University of Birmingham.

Djankov, S., La Porta, R., Lopez-de-Silanes, F., and Schleifer, A. (2008). 'The law and economics of self-dealing', *Journal of Financial Economics*, 88 (3): 430–65.

Dore, R. (2008). 'Financialization of the global economy', *Industrial and Corporate Change*, 17: 1097–112.

EVCA (2008). *Benchmarking European Tax and Legal Environments*. Brussels: European Venture Capital Association (EVCA).

EVCA (2012). *Pan-European Private Equity Performance Benchmarking Study*. Brussels: European Venture Capital Association (EVCA).

Fioretos, O. (2010). 'Capitalist diversity and the international regulation of hedge funds', *Review of International Political Economy*, 17: 696–723.

Gilligan, J. and Wright, M. (2010). *Private Equity Demystified: An Explanatory Guide*. London: ICAEW.

GMB Union (2011). *The Cross we have to Bear, the Greedy, and the Gullible*. Wimbledon: GMB Union.

Goergen, M., O'Sullivan, N., and Wood, G. (2011). 'Private Equity Takeovers and Employment in the UK: Some Empirical Evidence', ECGI Finance Working Paper, 310, August.

Gospel, H., Haves. J., Pendleton, A., Vitols, S., and Wilke, P. (2010). *The Impact of Investment Funds on Restructuring Practices and Employment Levels*. Luxembourg: Publications Office of the European Union.

Groh, A., Liechtenstein, H., and Lieser, K. (2012). *The Global Venture Capital and Private Equity Country Attractiveness Index: 2012 Annual*. Navarra: IESE Business School.

Hall, P. and Soskice, D. (2001). *Varieties of Capitalism: The Institutional Foundations of Comparative Advantage*. Oxford: Oxford University Press.

Itzhak, B., Franzoni, F., and Moussawi, R. (2012). 'Hedge fund stock trading in the financial crisis of 2007–2009', *Review of Financial Studies*, 25 (1): 1–54.

Kay, J. (2012). *The Kay Review of UK Equity Markets and Long-Term Decision Making*. London: Department of Business, Innovation, and Skills (BIS).

La Porta, R., Lopez-de-Silanes, F., Shleifer, A., and Vishny, R. (1998). 'Law and finance', *Journal of Political Economy*, 106: 1113–55.

Lazonick, W. and O'Sullivan, M. (2000). 'Maximising shareholder value: A new ideology for corporate governance', *Economy and Society*, 29(1): 13–35.

Meuleman, A., Amess, K., Wright, M., and Scholes, L. (2009). 'Agency, strategic entrepreneurship, and the performance of private-equity-backed buy-outs', *Entrepreneurship Theory and Practice*, 33: 213–39.

Milgrom, P. and Roberts, J. (1995). 'Complementarities and fit: Strategy, structure, and organisational change in manufacturing', *Journal of Accounting and Economics*, 19: 179–208.

Preqin (2012). *The 2012 Preqin Sovereign Wealth Fund Review*. London: Preqin.

TheCityUK (2012a). *Sovereign Wealth Funds*. London: TheCityUK.

TheCityUK (2012b). *Hedge Funds*. London: TheCityUK.

Treasury Select Committee (2007). *Private Equity*. Tenth Report of Session 2006–07, Vol. 1, Report together with formal minutes, HC567-1, London: Treasury Select Committee, House of Commons.

Venn, D. (2009). 'Legislation, Collective Bargaining and Enforcement: Updating the OECD Employment Protection Indicators', OECD Social, Employment and Migration Working Paper, 89, Paris: OECD, <http://www.oecd.org/els/workingpapers>.

Walker, D. (2007). *Guidelines for Disclosure and Transparency in Private Equity*. London: BVCA.

Walker, D. (2011). 'The agency challenge and stewardship opportunity', Speech to the International Forum of Sovereign Wealth Funds, May, Beijing.

Watt, A. (2008). 'The impact of private equity on European companies and workers: Key issues and a review of the evidence', *Industrial Relations Journal*, 39 (6): 548–68.

Weir, C., Jones, P., and Wright, M. (2008). 'Public to Private Transactions, Private Equity and Performance in the UK: An Empirical Analysis of the Impact of Going Private', Working Paper, Robert Gordon University and University of Nottingham.

Wilke, P., Vitols, S., Haves, J., Gospel, H., and Voss, E. (2009). *The Impacts of Private Equity Investors, Hedge Funds and Sovereign Wealth Funds on Industrial Restructuring in Europe as Illustrated by Case Studies*. Report to European Commission: Employment, Social Affairs and Equal Opportunities.

Wilson, N., Wright, M., Siegel, D., and Scholes, L. (2012). 'Private equity portfolio company performance during the global recession', *Journal of Corporate Finance*, 18: 193–205.

Work Foundation (2007). *Inside the Dark Box: Shedding Light on Private Equity*, London: Work Foundation.

Workplace Employment Relations Survey (2013). '2011 WERS First Findings', London: Department for Buiness, Innovation, and Skills.

Wright, M., Gilligan, J., and Amess, K. (2009). 'The economic impact of private equity: What we know and what we would like to know', *Venture Capital: An International Journal of Entrepreneurial Finance*, 11 (1): 1–21.

4

Ambivalent Finance and Protected Labour: Alternative Investments and Labour Management in Australia

MARK WESTCOTT AND
JOHN MURRAY

Introduction

New investment funds (NIF) have become increasingly visible in Australia over the last decade. Their development is a reflection of Australia's well-developed sophisticated and open financial system which accommodates investment in alternative financial products. However, the market for corporate control in Australia has been less active than in other countries with relatively liberal financial markets, thereby providing fewer opportunities for NIF acquisitions (Dignam 2005; Dignam and Galanis 2004). This situation invites two broad questions around the operation of NIFs in Australia. One, to what extent did these funds increase in size and significance over the course of the 2000s and how far did their activities focus on Australian assets, including Australian corporates? Two, how far have the prevailing financial and labour market regulatory regimes influenced the investment strategies of these funds? In this chapter we present broad conclusions about the implications for labour and industrial relations of the growth in alternative investment in Australia, and consider the impact of the financial and economic crisis of the late 2000s.

This chapter identifies three broad trends in the Australian financial sector with the apparent potential to significantly affect labour management within companies operating in Australia. First, over the last two decades there has been significant growth in funds under management in Australia. Much of this growth has been generated domestically due to the rise of superannuation funds. Second, the Australian financial sector has increased in size and importance since the 1980s. The liberalization of Australia's financial market allowed foreign banks and funds to penetrate the Australian market. Australia has consequently become a base for institutions which invest in both Australian and international assets. Third, Australia is a destination for investment from international sources. Thus, Australia's stable and sophisticated financial markets have attracted investment from global funds seeking to diversify their investment base.

The chapter argues that, notwithstanding these significant changes in the Australian financial landscape, the pressures on labour management in Australian companies stemming from alternative investments have been relatively diffuse. This is a consequence of the moderating role of both corporate and labour market regulation and the relative size and concentration of the Australian corporate sector. The inability of new owners to make significant reductions in labour costs and the capacity of incumbent directors to defend against hostile takeovers limits the potential to make acquisitions aimed at extensive restructuring. Concentration in the Australian listed sector also limits mergers and acquisitions (M&A) activity. In the 2000s, the top ten companies listed on the Australian Securities Exchange (ASX) accounted for between 39 and 49 per cent of total market capitalization (World Federation of Exchanges 1997–2010).

The chapter identifies the institutional environment for alternative investments in Australia, with particular focus on the relevant financial and labour market regulation. This is followed by sections on private equity (PE), hedge funds (HFs), and the Australian sovereign wealth fund (SWF), the 'Future Fund' (FF). The impact of these funds on labour management is considered in a section which presents cases and examples in order to draw out the significance of the regulatory regime in Australia. Particular consideration is given to the period since the financial crisis, beginning in 2007–08. The final section presents concluding remarks.

Contexts

The last twenty-five years has been a period of change in both financial and labour market regulation in Australia. In conjunction with these regulatory changes, Australia's financial sector has grown and altered in significant ways as a result of both domestic and international investment flows. The sector continues to be dominated by a small number of Australian-owned banks despite the presence of well-developed non-bank financial institutions. Despite being a medium-sized player in international markets, lacking the mass of markets elsewhere in the world, the Australian financial sector possesses depth, sophistication, and liquidity (Parliament of Australia 2001a: 17).

Australian financial markets are significantly interconnected with capital markets in the USA, Europe, and Asia. According to data from the World Investment Report, in the years 2001–09 there was on average AU$26 billion in foreign investment entering Australia each year, with substantial variations from year to year. This accounted for just over 2 per cent of global foreign direct investment flows (Sanyal 2011). The Australian corporate sector displays a high rate of foreign investment and ownership. A breakdown of ownership across the listed sector shows that approximately 42 per cent of listed Australian companies are owned by foreign institutions, with this foreign investment most likely to be in non-financial corporates (ASX 2010; Black and Kirkwood 2010).

In September 2011 the assets held by banks, registered financial corporations, and insurance and superannuation funds were valued by the Reserve Bank of Australia at AU$4.26 trillion (RBA 2011). The listed sector, financial and non-financial, was valued at approximately AU$1.5 trillion dollars in 2009 (ASX 2010: 10). While the financial sector is dominated by four Australian-owned banks, these banks source much of their finance from international wholesale funding markets (Brown and Davis 2010; IMF 2006). Non-bank financial institutions or non-authorized deposit-taking institutions (non-ADIs) such as merchant banks, insurers, and finance companies are well developed in Australia. Corporate financing is sophisticated as a consequence of the strength of the financial services sector. Australia is the second largest issuer of asset-backed securities and has the world's fourth largest funds management sector (Brown and Davis 2010).

Financial Market Regulation

The regulation of financial markets and products in Australia has been designed to encourage the deepening of the market while maintaining protection for investors. These two aims have not always been complimentary, yet there remains no fund-specific or financial-product specific regulation in Australia. Over the last fifteen years there have been a number of parliamentary reviews into various parts of the financial sector, reflecting both systemic and ad hoc concerns by government. As well as responding to specific corporate financial failures, during the later 1990s and 2000s governments have displayed an interest in establishing Australia as a centre for global finance.

Regulatory protections in the Australian financial system have been significantly altered since the 1980s in order to encourage freer flows of financial capital into and around the Australian economy. The most substantial changes in the regulation of the Australian financial sector occurred in the late 1990s following the Wallis Committee report in 1997. The committee's report recommended the adoption of a 'twin peaks' regulatory framework with separate regulatory institutions suggested for prudential regulation of financial institutions and the conduct of business regulation and supervision. The result was the creation of the Australian Securities and Investments Commission (ASIC) in 2001 to oversee conduct of business and market supervision, along with the Australian Prudential Regulation Authority in 1998 to ensure the prudential requirements of authorized deposit-taking institutions (ADIs). The Reserve Bank of Australia (RBA) lost the prudential oversight of banks but remained central to ensuring systemic stability (Davis 2011; Llewellyn 2006). All three groups are represented on the Council of Financial Regulators which provides a forum for cooperation and collaboration between these different regulators.

There were also changes to the regulation of business conduct in the 1990s. These were a consequence of the Corporate Law Economic Reform Program (CLERP) which commenced in 1997. The outcomes of this process have had important impacts on financial services regulation. The CLERP reforms resulted in the Financial Services Reform Act in 2001. One of the primary consequences of this legislation was the introduction of a single licensing regime for financial market participants whether offering financial products or services (Council of Financial Regulators 2011: 6). Those participants who are wholesale intermediaries (that is those not dealing with retail clients) are required to hold a license, but the legislation makes an explicit attempt to avoid unduly burdening these participants with respect to their dealings with wholesale clients.

PE and HFs operating in Australia are required to have an Australian Financial Services Licence (AFSL) issued by the ASIC. Whilst there is only one category of licence, each individual licence can have different conditions attached to it depending on the product, the services offered, and whether market participants service retail clients (Commonwealth of Australia 2009; McNally et al. 2004). As most HFs do not offer direct access to retail customers, they usually have fewer specific requirements attached to their AFSL as their investors are considered to be 'better placed to monitor and manage their investments without government regulation' (McNally et al. 2004: 59).

In addition to the broad regulatory infrastructure of the Australian financial sector, there have been some government initiatives aimed specifically at the investment funds sector. In 1998 the Managed Investments Act was introduced to increase investor protection in managed investment schemes by allowing for a single entity to be responsible for both the management of the investment and the trustee functions of the fund (hitherto carried out separately) (Parliament of Australia 2002a: 5). Other legislative changes reflect an agenda to encourage foreign investors and financial institutions to see Australia as a potential base for activities (Commonwealth of Australia 2009). For instance, two amendments were made to taxation laws in the 2000s to encourage investment in Australia from abroad (Parliament of Australia 2002b).[1] The timing of both these amendments coincided with the significant growth of both PE and HFs in Australia.

The question of whether the government should develop specific regulation for alternative investments arose in two separate parliamentary enquiries in the 2000s. In examining the role of HFs following the Asian financial crisis in the late 1990s, the RBA noted that whilst the activities of these funds could possibly impact on financial stability, 'we are probably inclined to think it would be too difficult to regulate them and that you can probably achieve most of what you want by relying on disclosure rather than regulation.' (Parliament of Australia 2001b: 88). Similarly, when considering the impact of PE on the Australian economy, both the RBA and ASIC believed the regulatory framework was robust enough to adequately safeguard both investors and the economy (Commonwealth of Australia 2009). The regulators have adopted the view that, as long as investors have adequate information about the nature of the investment strategies and the business plans of their investment fund (which are ensured through proper disclosure), there is no need for fund-specific regulation.

Some commentators have expressed a view that single licensing is not effective in minimizing systemic risk, especially that arising from HF activity. Bianchi and Drew argue that, 'while an AFSL licence-holder must report their minimum solvency requirements to

ASIC, the effectiveness of this disclosure to regulators is cumbersome compared with the speed of catastrophic financial events' (Bianchi and Drew 2010: 11). Whilst individual funds and financial market participants may comply with their licensing requirement, this does not ensure that the totality of their activities does not create a systemic risk, particularly if there is some mimicking of risky investment strategies across the sector.

Labour Market Regulation

Concurrent with liberalization in financial markets has been a deregulation in Australia's labour markets. This has seen the retreat of the state from some areas of industrial relations and its incursion into others with the abolition of compulsory arbitration and the development of statutory individual contracting. The broad effect of these changes has been to significantly remove the capacity for multi-employer bargaining and to reduce the capacity of trade unions to induce collective bargaining when employers are resistant (Cooper and Ellem 2009). This changing regulatory framework allowed owners and managers to re-engineer their work arrangements and reduced union capacity to resist these initiatives.

The replacement of the Workplace Relations Act (1996) with the passage of the Fair Work Act in 2009 (FWA) slowed this trend. The FWA establishes a regulatory framework more conducive to collective bargaining, including provisions for good faith bargaining, and, while it does not explicitly contain a mechanism for union recognition, the Act provides trade unions with some scope to pursue workplace orders (which amount to a legal determination) from the federal tribunal. The FWA also allows the federal tribunal, Fair Work Australia, to make determinations on working conditions for low pay workers (Cooper and Ellem 2009). This legislation re-regulates some areas of industrial relations (providing greater scope for unions to bargain with employers) and in doing so narrows the capacity for unilateral changes to employment conditions in workplaces where unions are present. In this sense the legislation could be viewed as a constraint on business owners and operators who are aiming to extract value by reducing the costs of labour.

Perhaps more important, in the market for corporate control are the legal obligations to maintain employment conditions for workers, including accrued leave and redundancy pay, during transfers of control. Industrial law seeks to ensure that transfer of business cannot be used as a mechanism for subverting employment conditions, and in this respect the FWA contrasts significantly with the Work Reform Act (WRA). Industrial law in Australia had historically supported a stance that employers could not renege upon their employment obligations by transferring ownership. Transmission of business provisions introduced in the WRA generally provided more flexibility for purchasers of businesses to change existing employment conditions (Hardy 2007). However, the FWA contains a tightening of the transfer of business provisions. Generally, when a transfer of business occurs (where there is a consistency across operations and assets of old and new owners), employment instruments which cover the workforce remain in place under the new ownership regime.[2] Moreover, any new employee engaged by the new owners must be employed under the same conditions as existing employees until a new enterprise agreement is created and employee consent is required for early termination of an agreement. Judicial tests have been developed over the last decade to ascertain when a transferred business ceases to be the successor of the previous owners and ultimately the issue of whether new owners are covered by transfer of business arrangements would be determined through the courts.

Regardless of the terms under which an employee is engaged, all employers are obliged to pay contributions towards their employee's superannuation.[3] Currently employers must contribute a proportion of an employee's ordinary earnings every quarter to a superannuation fund or retirement savings account that complies with the relevant superannuation legislation. Consequently, within this regulatory framework, there is relatively little capacity for a new business owner, investment fund or otherwise, of an Australian business to dramatically reduce their labour costs while maintaining their existing workforce. The only real avenue for substantial reductions in labour costs would come through reducing employee numbers. However, if new owners undertook this course of action, they would be bound to comply with redundancy provisions in the FWA and the relevant industrial instrument if they are deemed to have a strong enough connection to the previous employer.

Around the same time as the federal government amended tax legislation to attract foreign investment funds, there was some loosening in industrial law which enabled new business owners to restructure working arrangements to reduce costs. In combination with the relatively low costs of credit, deregulation provided an opening for activist investors to enter the Australian market. Regulation was amended to encourage investment funds, and, at the same time, traditional protections of employment conditions were loosened. This window of opportunity was very short, with the introduction of the FWA limiting the capacity to wind back employment conditions. As is shown shortly, there is little evidence that this favourable climate for activist investors resulted in any significant attempts by funds in Australia to extract returns by diluting employment costs.

New Investment Funds

A significant development in the Australian funds sector in the last twenty years has been the steady growth of investment funds created to cater for the retirement incomes of Australian workers, referred to as superannuation funds. The growth of these funds has created a steady supply of financial capital to be deployed in various investment vehicles.

The impetus for the growth of these funds was the introduction of compulsory employer superannuation contributions in 1992.[4] This legislation built upon and extended initiatives by the then federal Labor government and the trade union movement as part of the award system in 1987. Australian employers are required to contribute the equivalent of 9 per cent of their employee's salary as a superannuation contribution. As a consequence there has been a massive increase in the funds management industry in Australia. In 1993 the volume of assets in managed funds totalled AU$263, 974 million, of which around 84 per cent was in pension funds. In 2011 the amount in managed funds was AU$1,886,134 million, with superannuation funds holding 70 per cent of unconsolidated assets in managed funds (ABS 2011). The growth in the managed funds industry is illustrated in Figure 4.1.

The growing stock of funds available for investment, combined with the relatively small scale of the Australian corporate sector, has resulted in superannuation fund managers turning to alternative investments such as PE and HFs as part of the diversification of their investment portfolios. Large superannuation funds invest in PE (with an average commitment level of 6 per cent of assets in 2008), and in HFs, (with average allocation of 2.5 per cent in 2008) (Evans 2008, 2010). While the larger superannuation funds commit only a small proportion of their funds to PE and HFs, this still represents a substantial amount. The largest single sources of funds, at 60 per cent

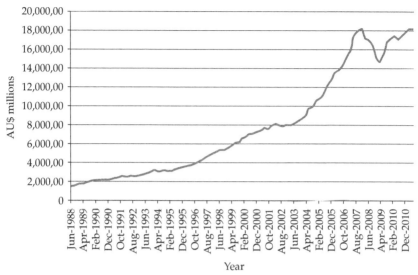

Figure 4.1 *Managed funds industry, Australia, 1988–2011*
Source: ABS (2012a).

of total draw-downs, for venture capital (VC) and later stage PE were domestic superannuation funds (ABS 2012a: 6).

In addition to the growth in domestic funds under management, the flows of foreign investment into Australia have increased over the last decade. Foreign investment in Australia doubled over the course of the 2000s growing from AU$856,704 million in 2001 to AU$2,030,032 million in 2011. While direct investment accounted for between 23 and 26 per cent of the overall total for the decade, portfolio investment grew from around 54 per cent to just under 60 per cent of foreign investment, with a drop in 2008 (ABS 2012b). The growth in funds available for investment from both within and outside Australia has created opportunities for alternative investment vehicles to emerge. While these investment activities still remain relatively limited in extent, they have certainly grown in size and prominence particularly over the 2000s.

There is a great deal of inter-connection between PE and HFs in Australia. PE managers and HFs have formed consortia to buy distressed debt. According to the RBA, around 70 per cent of global investors in loans used by PE to fund buy-outs are HFs (RBA 2007). The Australian FF is also an important institution in the alternative investment landscape. This fund, which has AU$74 billion in assets, has 16 per cent of its assets (some AU$11 billion) allocated to alternative fund managers (ATC 2011: 11). The remainder of this section considers PE, then HFs, and SWFs in turn.

Private Equity

Private equity and VC continue to be relatively small players in the Australian financial sector. An analysis of Australian VC investment in the late 1990s shows a slow but steady growth in investment between 1996 and 2001 (Bivell 2003). However, the early 2000s saw a substantial increase in PE funds raised as well as funds committed for investment as shown in Table 4.1.

Figure 4.2 is based on a different data set, collected by the Australian Bureau of Statistics (ABS), which also illustrates the significant growth in both commitments to, and draw-downs of, PE funds in years up to 2007–08. However, it shows a larger amount of funds raised than the Australian Private Equity and Venture Capital Association (AVCAL) data.

The growth in funds generated and invested during the 2000s represented a significant expansion in this asset class. The AVCAL data show that the amount invested by PE in 2008 was more than double the amount invested in 2001. Nonetheless, this level of investment remains small in the context of the Australian corporate sector as a whole.[5]

The nature of PE investment practices in Australia also changed over the 2000s. As shown in Table 4.1, the proportion of funds invested in later stage or mature business grew relative to funds invested in start-up businesses. The average size of PE transactions also increased. Between 1999 and 2004, the average PE transaction was AU$42 million; in 2006 this had increased to AU$917 million (RBA 2007: 60).[6]

The number of companies acquired and the value of acquisitions is shown in Table 4.2. These data suggests that while buy-outs by PE were small in number, the value of these transactions was greater than other avenues of business acquisition. They nonetheless remain small in comparison to equity raisings. While the total new investment in companies by PE in 2008 and 2009 was just over AU$1 billion, in 2009 AU$106 billion of equity was raised through public markets in Australia (ASX 2010: 7).

PE involvement in M&As during the last decade has remained low in terms of both the number and the value of M&As as a proportion

Table 4.1 *Private equity Australia: investments by fiscal year, 2001–2012*

	2001	2002	2003	2004	2005	2006	2007	2008	2009	2010	2011	2012
Venture capital (AU$ million)	396.51	144.07	220.62	119.69	65.68	110.76	150.57	210.21	209.95	186.92	126.45	121.58
Private equity (AU$ million)	1219.61	1224.9	828.85	807.43	1384.32	3297.61	6357.26	4179.25	2268.69	1629.74	3711.12	2800.78
Total (AU$ million)	1616.12	1368.97	1049.47	927.12	1450.00	3408.37	6507.83	4389.46	2478.64	1816.66	3837.57	2922.36

Source: AVCAL (2010a), AVCAL (2012).

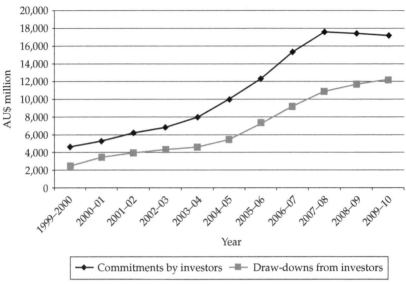

Figure 4.2 *Venture capital and later stage private equity funds, 1999–2010*
Source: ABS (2012b).

of overall activity in Australia. According to AVCAL, the number of
PE deals as a proportion of all M&As declined from 5 per cent in 2006
and 2007 to 2 per cent in 2009 and 2010. The deal value of PE M&A
activity, which can be volatile due to the presence of large individual
transactions, remains below the 13 per cent peak of 2007 (AVCAL
2010b: 4).

The impact of the global financial crisis on PE in Australia can be
seen in the difficulty PE funds have experienced in exiting from their
investments. This is illustrated in Table 4.3. Notably, since 2006–07
value secured by trade sales has been greater than value generated
though initial public offerings (IPOs). According to the ABS, there
were no exits via IPOs in 2008–09, and in that financial year the PE
industry reported write-offs of around AU$250 million.

In sum, PE investment in Australia grew from a relatively low base
during the 2000s and has been impacted by the global financial crisis.
Even at its peak in 2006 and 2007, PE represented only a small proportion of corporate funding. Despite the relatively small amount of
activity in PE, it is the changing nature of the activity that has raised
questions about the impact of the PE business model on employees in
acquired firms. These effects are set out later in the chapter.

Table 4.2 *New investment in investee companies*

	2004–2005		2005–2006		2006–2007		2007–2008		2008–2009		2009–2010		2010–2011	
	No. of companies	Value (AU$ million)	No. of companies	Value	No. of companies	Value	No. of companies	Value	No. of companies	Value	No. of companies	Value	No. of companies	Value
Pre-seed & seed	41	19	51	31	40	26	42	31	22	19	—	—	—	—
Start-up and early	55	137	43	77	37	58	50	169	36	90	20	39	11	14
Expansion	45	257	118	681	107	536	135	1137	49	537	38	334	39	504
Turnaround	6	78	10	205	5	—	15	225	11	199	8	70	2	51
Late	5	45	—	—	—	—	—	—	—	—	—	—	—	—
LBO/ MBO/MBI	24	303	37	481	52	1075	39	661	14	158	14	348	9	211
Total	176	839	259	1475	241	2359	281	2223	132	1003	96	800	90	791

Note: Value always given in million Australian dollar (AU$)
Source: ABS (2012a).

Table 4.3 *Investment by venture capital and later stages private equity investment vehicles in investee companies (in AU$ million)*

	1999–2000	2000–01	2001–02	2002–03	2003–04	2004–05	2005–06	2006–07	2007–08	2008–09	2009–10	2010–11
Investments at beginning of year	1,998	2,480	2,729	3,194	3,338	3,092	3,532	4,665	6,939	8,315	7,903	8,912
New vehicles and projects	684	685	586	472	465	839	1,475	2,359	2,223	1,003	799	791
Follow-on investments	165	202	314	194	162	183	307	446	547	675	444	286
Unrealized gains in investee companies	245	-84	73	29	50	254	453	557	-438	-1,068	495	226
Trade sales	137	87	135	69	241	291	334	392	476	618	450	1409
Initial public offers	353	171	120	76	428	246	345	360	411	0	155	—
Buy-backs		21	10	67	60	35	36	53	12	64	81	—
Write-offs	45	72	71	123	50	49	22	40	50	249	40	39
Left the industry	77	203	172	216	144	215	366	243	6	91	5	48
Investments at end of year	2,480	2,729	3,194	3,338	3,092	3,532	4,665	6,939	8,315	7,903	8,912	8694
Difference between amount invested at beginning and end of year	482	249	465	144	-246	440	1,133	2,274	1,376	-412	1009	-218

Source: ABS (2012a).

Hedge Funds

As noted by the Organization for Economic Cooperation and Development (2007: 19), there is a particular fuzziness around the HF label. HFs are generally referred to as 'managed funds that use a wider range of financial instruments and investment strategies than traditional managed funds, including the use of short-selling and derivatives to create leverage, with the aim of generating positive returns regardless of overall market performance' (McNally et al. 2004: 57). HFs traders and managers make use of a wide range of investment strategies with the broad aim of ensuring returns during both expansions and contractions in the share market (AIMA and ASSIRT 2002). In Australia, there has been a growth in institutions employing these investment strategies and calling themselves HFs.

There is a distinction between the operation of HFs that are based in Australia and the interests of HFs in the Australian corporate sector. The Australian Trade Commission reported that the amount of funds under management in HFs in Australia increased markedly (from a very low base) during the 2000s from AU$2 billion of assets under management in 2000 to AU$70.3 billion in 2007 (ATC 2008: 3). The value of assets under management fell in 2008, but recovered slightly in 2009 and 2010 (ATC 2011: 5).

It has been estimated that in June 2012 there was AU$42.8 billion of assets managed by the HF sector in Australia. This represented 3.6 per cent of Australia's investment management industry (Triple A Partners/Basis Point Consulting 2012). Whilst still a comparatively small segment, as some commentators have noted, HFs can become market leaders as they can adopt a substantial position on a particular investment strategy due to their use of leverage, which may then be mimicked by other market participants (Rankin 1999). The effect of HFs is, however, difficult to decipher as much of the activity in the Australian industry is in 'fund of funds' HFs.

It is also important to recognize that HF assets are not necessarily generated within Australia. Indeed the development of a HF industry in Australia is not synonymous with an increasing interest by HFs in Australian equities or financial products. Since 2001, the Australian federal government has actively sought to establish Australia as a global financial centre. Australia is the second largest centre for HF management in Asia (behind Hong Kong) with around eighty-five investment managers (ATC 2011). As with PE, Australia is a relatively attractive base for HFs operations due to its well-established financial market infrastructure and its proximity to emerging and developed markets in Asia. Conversely, the comparatively small size and concentrated nature of the Australian listed sector provides limited opportunities for investment in Australian assets.

The vast majority of Australian-based HFs invest outside Australia. Around 85 per cent of the funds managed by HFs are allocated to global markets with the rest allocated to Australian markets (ATC 2011). The investment strategies most likely to be associated with activist HFs, namely event-driven approaches and distressed debt strategies, are not extensively used among Australian HFs. Around 2.5 per cent of HF assets invested in the Australian market are classified as corresponding to event driven and an insignificant number (less than 1 per cent) associated with distressed debt strategies (ATC 2011: 4).

Although institutional investors such as superannuation funds invest in HFs, the largest category of investors in HFs in Australia is high net worth individuals and retail investors (ATC 2011). Retail investors can access HF products usually through master trusts or wrap platforms, and the accessibility of HFs to retail investors has increased in recent years. This has attracted greater regulatory scrutiny since the financial crisis (ASIC 2010). As discussed earlier, the client base that HFs target has repercussions for their licensing requirements.

The Australian government has come under some pressure to examine the regulation of both HFs and their investment activities in the light of fund and corporate failures in the last five years. Following the collapse of the Basis Yield Alpha fund in August 2007, questions were raised about the access of retail investors to HF products. A danger highlighted by this collapse was that some retail investors who had invested in different investment platforms did not know that they were investing in a HF (Washington 2008). The collapse of this fund spurred ASIC to develop new disclosure obligations for HFs (particularly those with retail clients). In February 2011 ASIC released a consultation paper proposing that HFs provide greater information in their product disclosure statement about key features and risks (ASIC 2011). This intervention was not an attempt to limit the client base of HFs but to generate more information about products so that customers could assess risk appropriately.

The practice of short-selling by HFs, and its potential impact on companies, gained some attention following the failure of an

Australian listed childcare company ABC Learning in 2008. This company suffered a sharp decrease in share value in February 2008 that was attributed by the Chief Executive Officer (CEO) to the short-selling of company equities by HFs (Bartholomeusz 2008; Poisel and Terrett 2009). While this contention was arguably spurious, it created some discussion about market manipulation by HFs (Bartholomeusz 2008; Schwab 2008).[7] Short-selling of equities, not just by HFs, was seen as contributing to the effects of the global financial crisis in Australia, most notably the rapid decline in stock prices on the ASX in the later part of 2008. The federal government introduced a ban on short-selling of stock in September 2008. This ban was relaxed in November of the same year, but the short-selling of financial stocks remained in place until May 2009 (Brown and Davis 2010).

There is little evidence of HF activism in Australia so far but there has recently been some speculation that distressed debt investing may become more prominent. The potential impact on labour of distressed debt investment is considered later in the chapter.

Sovereign Wealth Funds

As with HFs, the activities of SWFs in Australia are difficult to track. Variance in the reporting standards that different governments impose on their own SWFs, coupled with the tendency of SWFs to invest in other managed funds, can obscure the investment activity of particular SWFs. In practical terms, this means that we know relatively little about the holdings of foreign SWFs within Australia. As a result, this section focuses on the closest equivalent of an Australian SWF, the 'FF'. In particular it considers the development and operation of this fund and its impact on the Australian corporate sector.

The FF was created by the passage of the *Future Fund Act 2006.* This Act sets out the powers and responsibilities of the FF Board of Guardians, who are empowered to make decisions on how to invest the FF (Commonwealth of Australia 2006: Part 4, Section 35). The Act establishes the board as a body corporate to provide a separate legal identity from the government with a statutory responsibility for managing investments, enabling the Board to hold investments in its own name and on behalf of the Commonwealth (Parliament of Australia 2005: 3).

The FF can be viewed as a quasi-SWF. Unlike the large SWFs established in other commodity rich countries, it was not established using windfall gains made by changes in commodity prices, and nor is it designed to smooth the effect on the domestic economy of decreases in commodity prices. Instead, the FF was established to 'make provision for unfunded superannuation liabilities that will become payable during the period when an ageing population is likely to place significant pressure on the Australian government's finances' (Future Fund 2006: 3). All earnings from the FF are thus reinvested.

Government interference in the investment strategies of the FF is limited by the Act, but the minister responsible can set out expectations for returns, the tolerance of risk, and broad guidelines on the allocation of financial assets (Commonwealth of Australia 2006: Part 3, Section 18:4). The investment mandate for the FF from the government remains unchanged since its inception and includes a requirement that the Board 'act in a way that minimizes the potential to effect any abnormal change in the volatility or efficient operation of Australian financial markets; and is unlikely to cause any diminution of the Australian government's reputation in Australian and international financial markets' (Future Fund 2010a: 114).[8]

The financing of the FF has created particular corporate governance issues notably regarding the influence of the fund over specific Australian corporations. Seed capital of AU$18.0 billion for the FF was provided out of accumulated budget surpluses (Parliament of Australia 2005: 5). Following the initial seed capital, the federal government transferred capital of AU$51.3 billion to the FF from budget surpluses in 2005–06 and 2006–07 and some of the proceeds from the sale of Telstra (the formerly state-owned telecommunications company). The government's remaining 2.1 billion shares in Telstra, valued at AU$8.9 billion, were transferred to the FF in February 2007 (Future Fund 2007: 8). The transfer of ownership gave the FF a 16.8 per cent share in Telstra and made it the largest shareholder in the company, but with a specified escrow period during which the FF was prevented from selling their stake in the company (Future Fund 2007: 79). The relationship between the FF and Telstra is discussed in greater detail below.

The establishment of the FF presented some initial challenges, both political and financial. Questions have been raised in the Australian Senate about the strategies of the fund and its investment mandate. Specific issues have included whether FF investment is 'responsible' (as the FF legislation prohibits investment in companies performing any activity deemed illegal in Australia), and the potential implications of various government policy proposals on the assets held in the FF. For example, will changes to competition policy for the telecommunications industry reduce the value of the FF holding? Other issues raised have been whether the fund should engage in short-selling practices, and whether investments should be managed in a manner beneficial to participants in the Australian financial market more generally.

In its early years there has been tension between the transfer of a narrow range of assets into the fund and the need to pursue diversification of investments so as to reduce risk and fulfil the investment mandate. In light of the challenges in investment markets as a result of the financial crisis so soon after its establishment, the FF was fortunate to be 'cash-heavy' in its formative stages. This provided protection against the erosion of wealth as equities markets fell, as well as allowing for the necessary liquidity to make acquisitions as opportunities became available.

The FF took an activist approach to its relationship with Telstra, attracting a lot of media interest in the process. In 2007 the FF joined a protest vote against the remuneration report at the company's Annual General Meeting (AGM) against a lack of transparency with regard to executive incentives. This resulted in an Australian record 66.2 per cent vote against the remuneration report (Future Fund 2007; Korporeal and Sainsbury 2007; Telstra 2007). The previous year Telstra had faced a similar protest vote, when a majority of non-government shares voted against the remuneration report for similar reasons, (Sainsbury 2006). The motion on the remuneration report in 2007 was deemed non-binding and Telstra adopted the report despite the outcome of the vote, with the Chairman singling out the FF for criticism.

A series of events spanning late 2008 and early 2009 escalated hostilities between the FF and Telstra.[9] Reports appearing in the *Australian Financial Review* in April 2009 suggested that the FF, having sustained an estimated AU$2 billion loss in the first months since its Telstra holding came out of escrow, was engaged in coordinating a campaign by institutional shareholders to put pressure on Telstra board members and oust its Chairman (Williams 2009b, 2009c). The latter subsequently resigned at the following board meeting, with the CEO bringing forward his departure date at the same meeting (Williams 2009a). However, the new Telstra Chair and CEO also found themselves in conflict with the FF. At the Telstra AGM in 2010, the FF voted against all three motions put to shareholders (Future Fund 2010c). These motions related to the remuneration report, changes to the company's constitution, and the appointment of a director.[10]

Sovereign wealth funds are generally held to be benign owners due to the long-term nature of their investment. The activism of the FF in its relationship with Telstra appears to be considerably different, with the FF determined to defend the value of its shares. FF representatives argued repeatedly in Senate Estimates, and in their own publications, that their relationship with Telstra was not exceptional, that their behaviour was in line with their investment mandate, and that they were defending and enhancing value.

Implications for Firms and Workers

There are few studies that investigate the impact of different alternative investment classes on labour in Australia. This is largely due to the relatively small market for corporate control and the strength of protection offered to labour under Australian industrial law. Nevertheless, a higher incidence of buy-out activity in the lead-up to the financial crisis served as evidence that NIFs were becoming more active in the market for corporate control. The relatively small and concentrated nature of the Australian listed sector creates a situation where a small number of transactions can have a substantial impact on a large section of the labour force.

Burgeoning public awareness and political debate around the impact of PE as an investment class developed in 2006 following the attempt by a consortium of Australian and international funds to buy out the Australian listed company Qantas Airways (which had been government owned until 1992).[11] In response, the Australian Federal Parliament established a committee of inquiry to assess the impact of PE on the Australian economy (Commonwealth of Australia, 2007). Although most submissions to the inquiry focused on whether the use of debt in PE deals heightened the risk of financial instability, a small number of trade unions (mostly with members working for Qantas) made submissions focusing on operational changes that might result from PE ownership. For example a submission by the Australian Manufacturing Workers Union stated that it was, 'concerned that the very high rates of return required to finance PE debt-driven buy-outs can threaten target companies' long-term interests and provision of decent employment conditions and security to employees' (AMWU 2007: 3). The bid was ultimately unsuccessful, although the Qantas board have subsequently pursued a number of the strategies outlined in the takeover proposal.

A successful PE bid for a large and mature Australian company, Myer, was made in March 2006. Then part of the Coles-Myer group, Myer Pty Ltd, was purchased for AU$1.4 billion by a PE consortium led by Texas Pacific Group's Asia-based fund. The collective agreements covering employees in Myer's distribution centres and retail stores were due to expire soon after PE took control of the company. The new owners could have made use of 'WorkChoices' legislation, which allowed employers to effectively de-recognize unions and install a bare minimum set of employment conditions for their workforce, in an attempt to reduce unit labour costs across the company (Westcott 2009). However, the operating partners and senior executives in the company chose instead to enter into a new agreement with the unions representing these workers. The labour management strategy pursued by the owners was to encourage and reward performance whilst simultaneously seeking greater flexibility in staff utilization (Westcott and Pendleton 2013). Myer's owners seemed to embrace the 'classic' PE disciplines—greater accountability, defined and measureable performance indicators, regular reporting, and well-defined financial targets (Jones 2008)—rather than attempt to leverage existing employment conditions as a source of value. The value gains made by the management team mainly came from reducing costs and increasing efficiencies in other areas of the business such as supply chain, warehousing and distribution, and business information systems (Westcott and Pendleton 2013).

Myer was returned to the public market through an IPO in November 2009. The company was re-listed with an initial value of AU$2.4 billion, although the share price dropped immediately following its float. The timing of the float into a market where asset prices were falling and the share market overall was losing value following the financial crisis no doubt effected the Myer share price. In contrast during the 'bull market' conditions prior to the crisis PE arguably did not need to pursue vigorous turnaround strategies based on reducing costs (labour included) as value could be realized through other means (Folkman et al. 2009).

The impact of the financial crisis on asset values and profitability may be driving PE investors to rely more heavily on 'leveraging' labour in order to generate value gains (Folkman et al. 2009). Some of the current difficulties in extracting value are illustrated by the particular problems faced by some PE funds in Australia. In 2011 two well-known retail companies owned by PE funds passed into administration largely due to their inability to service debt requirements.

The first, REDgroup Retail Pty Ltd (which included Australian book retailers Borders and Angus & Robertson, as well as New Zealand book retailer Whitcoulls), owned by Private Equity Partners, was put into voluntary administration in February 2011. At the time, REDgroup operated 116 stores and employed 2,327 employees (Ferrier Hodgson 2011a).[12] The administrators negotiated the sale of two REDgroup stores as well as the online business. However, between February and July the administrator closed 140 stores and 2,064 employees were made redundant (Ferrier Hodgson 2011b). The possibility that this company would face trading difficulties was foreshadowed several months earlier. In July 2010 REDgroup announced that it would likely be in breach of two of its debt covenants, reporting debt liabilities of AU$131 million (Speedy 2010). The company reported a AU$43 million loss for 2009–10 with earnings of AU$27million (Greenblat 2010). Despite press coverage blaming REDgroup's high debt for its demise, the company defended the PE ownership model. It argued that its business failure was due to competition from online booksellers exempt from the Australian goods and services tax (REDgroup Retail 2011: 19).

A second PE-owned retail company purchased in the pre-crisis boom, the Colorado group, passed into voluntary administration in March 2011. This company had been acquired in a hostile takeover by a Hong Kong-based PE fund, Affinity Equity, in November 2006 for a reported AU$430 million (Ahmed 2011; Ferrier Hodgson 2011c). When placed into voluntary administration, Colorado's debt amounted to around AU$400 million with Affinity having an exposure of AU$135 million. At that time the company controlled five different clothing and footwear brands and operated 434 stores across Australia with a total workforce of 3,800 (Ferrier Hodgson 2011c). Unlike REDgroup, the Colorado group was reorganized under administration and re-launched as Fusion Retail Brands. In all 139 stores were shut and 1,042 staff made redundant as part of this 'workout' process (Ferrier Hodgson 2011d, 2011e).

In both these cases, few operational changes had been undertaken by PE owners. The decline in consumer spending in Australia in 2010 and 2011, the high levels of debt servicing required, the inability to mark-up asset valuations in a weak market, and the corresponding lack of interest in trade sales combined to push these companies into insolvency.

Falling revenues and asset valuations, coupled with high debt servicing, contributed to the near collapse of another high profile pre-crisis PE buy-out in Australia, that of the Nine Entertainment Company. The media company was sold to CVC Asia Pacific in three separate transactions between 2006 and 2007 for an estimated AU$5.6 billion (Ahmed and Shoebridge 2011). Mediocre financial results in this venture resulted in CVC being forced by its creditors, including HFs holding around 40 per cent of the senior debt, to re-capitalize. This resulted in a debt for equity swap, with HFs Apollo Global and Oaktree Capital taking a 95 per cent equity stake in the company. The recapitalization meant CVC Asia Pacific lost its entire investment of AU$1.9 billion (Hume 2012).

Some commentators have suggested that a new market for distressed debt or non-performing loans may open another avenue for NIFs (Blake Dawson and Pricewaterhouse Coopers 2009). Currently, however, non-performing loans remain concentrated among the major Australian banks. It has been estimated that these carry around AU$11 billion in defaulted loans (Perkis 2010: 204). In the past, banks have not sold these loans, but changes to capital requirements as a consequence of the Basel II framework could have profound impacts on distressed debt sales (Perkis 2010). The purchase of non-performing loans may have the effect of creating symmetry in the risk–return profile of managers and creditors, especially in cases where debt is exchanged for equity. In such cases new owners effectively have an incentive to return the business to viability, as they will only realize a return on their equity when the resuscitated business is sold. However, there remains a possibility that buyers of distressed debt seek to sell-on this debt (at a premium) rather than taking on an activist role to restructure the acquired company (Perkis 2010).

The positions taken by HFs and PE can be complementary or conflicting in the context of debt sales, refinancing, and work-outs. For example, a hedge fund may purchase corporate debt at a low face value with the aim of making a gain as a creditor though a favourable scheme of arrangement if the company moves into bankruptcy. In this case the investor has no real interest in reviving the company. PE funds may see the purchase of debt as a pathway to taking equity in a failing company, which can then be restructured with the aim of a future sale when the company has been turned around. However, in the case of Nine Network Pty Ltd, it was HFs which swapped debt for equity at the expense of the PE fund which had bought the company. The market for debt of distressed companies has become more visible in the post-financial crisis environment as a number of companies purchased with relatively cheap debt in the late 2000s attempt to refinance.

Isolated cases, like Alinta Energy, highlight that HFs and PE funds may adopt short-term positions (seeking a premium on cheap debt from new owners) or longer-term positions (swapping debt for equity and assuming ownership) in the same deal (Lee 2011; Range 2011).

Could distressed debt investing be to the detriment of workers in the companies whose debt is sold? Corporate law dealing with insolvency and bankruptcy combine with employment protection during business transfers to make it difficult to restructure companies via changes in employment whilst in administration. However, there is scope for investors who buy companies in voluntary administration to avoid full liability for the leave and severance entitlements of existing employees. Existing contracts and collective agreements for employees cannot be changed, or terminated, during this process, unlike Chapter 11 bankruptcy in the USA (Petit 2008). However, the administrator may recommend a scheme of arrangement for the continued operation of the company that affects how and when outstanding employee entitlements are paid. In cases where an arrangement alters the legislated priority of payment of employee entitlements, changes are allowable if approved by a majority of employees affected (Commonwealth of Australia 2010). Consequently cases may arise where accumulated entitlements of employees are forgone in order to keep distressed businesses operating.

The recent difficulty exhibited by PE funds in the Australian corporate environment suggests two important conclusions. First, the absence of any reported systematic initiatives to restructure the labour force or alter employment conditions in companies bought out by PE funds suggests that this is not an avenue that these funds can or wish to pursue. There is limited capacity for new business owners to change current employment conditions. When businesses fail employees are second only to secured creditors, and their accrued entitlements are protected to some extent whilst in voluntary administration. If labour has captured value in the company (through staffing levels, work rules, or payment levels), it is difficult for owners and management (funded by alternative investments or otherwise) to appropriate this value by changing ownership. Second, the regulatory framework places restrictions on the capacity of consortia to buy distressed debt and then remove employee entitlements as a liability on the balance sheet or implement turnaround strategies based on squeezing labour costs. These regulatory arrangements, along with Australian banks' historical reluctance to sell non-performing loans, may explain the lack of 'activism' among investors in debt markets to date (Duran 2011). It seems that generating value from distressed debt may be more likely to come from financial engineering (by securing a large discount on the face value of debt) than from squeezing the labour force.

Conclusions

The past decade has seen a significant growth in alternative investments in Australia, albeit from a comparatively small base. PE and HFs have grown as a consequence of domestic factors, especially the growth of superannuation funds, and international factors such as increases in foreign portfolio investment. These funds attracted media and public attention, especially prior to the global financial crisis, but have thus far attracted little academic study of their potential impact on companies and their labour management. The evidence presented in this chapter represents a first attempt to bring together data from different sources and begin to build a picture of the Australian situation. As such we can make no definitive statements regarding impact but can set out some tentative results.

It appears that in Australia the direct impact of NIFs on labour management leads to little change in prevailing patterns of labour management in the industries in which they operate. This may be due in part to the nature of investment and the investment cycle but more important is the Australian regulatory environment. Investment in Australia from foreign sources doubled between 2001 and 2008. The greatest proportion of this investment, and an increasing proportion prior to the financial crisis, is portfolio investment. Foreign investment in Australia has come about as a result of large funds and financial institutions diversifying their investments globally. Australia has a well regulated and stable financial market, and governments in the 2000s have sought to make Australia a global centre for financial services. Prior to the financial crisis in 2008 Australia, like much of the developed world, experienced steady increases in asset prices (both corporate and property). During most of the 2000s, investment returns were strong in a relatively low-risk financial setting. Alternative investments, through financial engineering and good market analysis, could provide returns with little need for activism or, in the case of PE, significant labour force reorganization.

There are some indications that releasing value in the post-crisis period may require more dramatic corporate restructuring and this could lead to more sustained attempts to leverage value from labour. A number of PE funds have liquidated or written down assets, raising questions over the capacity of PE funds to earn above market returns. However, the capacity to leverage labour is currently constrained in Australia. The web of regulation in both labour and corporate law currently allows few opportunities for the costs of labour to be reduced in the short term after a change in ownership. This inevitably restricts the choices for investment funds looking for corporations to 'turn around' in order to create value. In companies which employ workers covered by collective agreements, a change in ownership does not provide an opportunity to alter the formal employment contract. Transfer of Business provisions in labour law stipulate that employment instruments remain in place until their termination or expiry. Under the FWA, once an agreement has expired employers must engage in genuine bargaining with an employee representative if their employees request another agreement. Companies are also obliged to pay a superannuation contribution for their employees. These contributions are paid into a superannuation fund and as such are not held as assets of the firm. Employers are obliged to pay redundancy pay for permanent employees in larger organizations, meaning that labour shedding can have a potential up-front cost. This labour regulation regime restricts the options that are open to NIFs which acquire corporate assets. Indeed, the few examples of PE buy-outs of Australian companies suggest that there have been few changes in the management of waged workforces.

In the wake of the financial crisis, the Australian economy has remained relatively robust with both economic growth and employment levels remaining comparatively healthy. However, if demand for Australian commodities falls and economic conditions deteriorate, there may well be a reconsideration of the regulatory framework around the investment activities of alternative funds and whether the existing nexus of labour and corporate regulation should be relaxed in order to allow 'renewal' of business operations.

NOTES

1. See Taxation Laws Amendment (Venture Capital) Act 2002 and Tax Laws Amendment (2006 Measures No. 4) Act 2006. The 2002 amendment set out that the 'carried interest' of VC general partners would be treated

as capital gains and not income. As noted by the Senate when the 2006 amendments were introduced, 'under the proposed changes foreign investments in sectors that are traditionally not land-rich (such as retail, financial services, or information technology sectors) will avoid capital gains tax' (The Senate 2006: 5).

2. These can be found in Part 2 Section 8 of the FWA.
3. Employers are legally obliged to pay superannuation contributions for employees, regardless of whether they are full-time, part-time, or casual, if they are paid AU$450 or more in a month. (See Guide to superannuation for employers at <http://www.ato.gov.au/content/00249857.htm>).
4. As required by the Superannuation Guarantee Charge Act, 1992 and the Superannuation Guarantee (Administration) Act, 1992.
5. The Senate enquiry into PE reported that in the financial year 2006/2007 PE funds were equivalent to around 10 per cent of new equity raised.
6. One or two large transactions can have a disproportionally large effect on the average transaction size due to the relatively small size of the Australian corporate sector.
7. ABC Learning was placed in receivership in November 2008. It was reported that ABC had 16,500 employees when it went into receivership and that around 700 employees were made redundant or resigned in the three months following (O'Sullivan and Carson 2009).
8. Since the establishment of the FF, further nation-building Funds have been established, the Building Australia Fund, the Education Investment Fund (reorganization), and the Health and Hospitals Fund (Nation-building Funds Act 2008). These Funds are governed by the FF Board, with different investment mandates that specify lower benchmark returns and negligible risk.
9. In late 2008, Telstra submitted a non-compliant bid document in response to a call for tenders by the federal government to construct a National Broadband Network (NBN) in Australia. The non-compliant bid document led to the exclusion of Telstra from the tender process and was associated with a fall of more than AU$6 billion in market value in a single day as analysts predicted that the government would be compelled to separate Telstra in order to build the NBN without their participation (O'Sullivan 2009).
10. The Corporations Act was amended in 2011 introducing a 'Two Strikes' test whereby if a company's remuneration report attracts a negative vote of 25 per cent or more at two successive AGMs, a motion to determine whether the directors need to stand for re-election will be put to the meeting (Corporations Amendment (Improving Accountability on Director and Executive Remuneration) Bill 2011).
11. Ironically the bid by a PE consortium (which included Australian investors such as Macquarie Bank as well as international funds including Texas Pacific Group) for Qantas in 2006/2007 was unsuccessful

in part due to a US hedge fund not accepting the takeover offer in time as they anticipated that the bidders would increase the price of their offer.

12. There were another fifty-two Angus and Robertson stores operated as franchises.

BIBLIOGRAPHY

ABS (2011). 'Managed Funds Australia', cat. no. 5655.0, Time Series Spreadsheets, Canberra ACT: Australian Bureau of Statistics (ABS).

ABS (2012a) 'Venture Capital and Later Stage Private Equity, Australia 2010–2011', cat. no. 5678.0, Canberra ACT: Australian Bureau of Statistics (ABS).

ABS (2012b) 'International Investment Position', Australia: Supplementary Statistics, Calendar Year 2011, cat no. 5352.0. Canberra ACT: Australian Bureau of Statistics (ABS).

Ahmed, N. (2011). 'Colorado Group teeters as lenders ponder debt extension', *The Australian*, 23 March, <http://www.theaustralian.com.au/business/opinion/colorado-group-teeters-as-lenders-ponder-debt-extension/story-e6frg9if-1226026349226>.

Ahmed, N. and Shoebridge, N. (2011). 'Hedge funds launch assault on Nine's owner', *Australian Financial Review*, 16 December, 37.

AIMA and ASSIRT (2002). *Hedge Fund Booklet*, <http://www.asx.com.au/documents/products/Assirt_Hedge_Fund_Booklet.pdf>.

AMWU (2007). *Submission to Inquiry into Private Equity Investment and its Effects on Capital Markets and the Australian Economy*. May. Granville NSW: Australian Manufacturing Workers Union (AMWU).

ASIC (2010). '10-12AD Margin lending licensing commences', Media Release, 1 February, <http://www.asic.gov.au/asic/asic.nsf/byheadline/10-12AD+Margin+lending+licensing+commences?openDocument. Canberra ACT: Australian Securities and Investments Commission (ASIC)>.

ASIC (2011). 'Hedge Funds: Improving Disclosure for Retail Investors', Consultation Paper 147, Canberra ACT: Australian Securities and Investments Commission (ASIC).

ASX (2010). 'Capital Raising in Australia: Experiences and Lessons from the Global Financial Crisis', ASX Information Paper, 29 January, Sydney, NSW: Australian Securities Exchange (ASX).

ATC (2008). *The Hedge Fund Industry in Australia*. Sydney, NSW: Australian Trade Commission (ATC).

ATC (2011). *Australian Hedge Funds*. Sydney, NSW: Australian Trade Commission (ATC). <http://www.austrade.gov.au/ArticleDocuments/2792/Australian-Hedge-Funds-2011.pdf.aspx>. Australian Trade Commission (ATC).

AVCAL (2010a). *Market Observations: Australia and New Zealand.* Sydney, NSW: The Australian Private Equity and Venture Capital Association Limited (AVCAL).

AVCAL (2010b). *2010 Yearbook. Australian Private Equity and Venture Capital Activity Report—October 2010.* Sydney, NSW: The Australian Private Equity and Venture Capital Association Limited (AVCAL).

AVCAL (2012). *2012 Yearbook. Australian Private Equity and Venture Capital Activity Report—November 2012.* Sydney, NSW: The Australian Private Equity and Venture Capital Association Limited (AVCAL).

Bartholomeusz, S. (2008). 'When hedge funds attack', *Business Spectator*, 26 February, <http://www.businessspectator.com.au/bs.nsf/Article/When-hedge-funds-attack-C79U3?OpenDocument&src=srch>.

Bianchi, R. and Drew, M. (2010). 'Hedge fund regulation and systemic risk', *Griffith Law Review*, 19 (1): 6–29.

Bivell, V. (2003). *Australian Venture Capital Investment 1996–97 to 2001–02.* Sydney, NSW: Private Equity Media.

Black, S. and Kirkwood, J. (2010). 'Ownership of Australian equities and corporate bonds', *Reserve Bank of Australia Bulletin*, September Quarter 2010: 25–33.

Blake Dawson and Pricewaterhouse Coopers (2009). 'Distressed Investing in Australia: A Guide for Buyers and Sellers' Sydney, NSW and Melbourne VIC: Blake Dawson and Pricewaterhouse Coopers, <http://www.pwc.com.au/deals/assets/Distressed-Investing-Apr10.pdf>.

Brown, C. and Davis, K. (2010). 'Australia's experience in the global financial crisis', in: R. Kolb (ed.), *Lessons from the Financial Crisis: Insights and Analysis from Today's Leading Minds.* New York: John Wiley & Sons, 357–44.

Commonwealth of Australia (2006). *Future Fund Act 2006.*

Commonwealth of Australia (2007). *Private Equity Investment in Australia.* The Senate Standing Committee on Economics.

Commonwealth of Australia (2009). *Inquiry into Financial Products and Services in Australia.* Parliamentary Joint Committee on Corporations and Financial products and Services in Australia, November.

Commonwealth of Australia (2010). *The Regulation, Registration and Remuneration of Insolvency Practitioners in Australia: The Case for a New Framework*, The Senate Economics References Committee, September.

Cooper, R. and Ellem, B. (2009). 'Fair work and the re-regulation of collective bargaining', *Australian Journal of Labour Law*, 22 (3): 284–305.

Council of Financial Regulators (2011). 'Review of Financial Market Infrastructure Regulation', Consultation Paper, October.

Davis, K. (2011). 'The Australian financial system in the 2000s: Dodging the bullet', in: H. Gerard and J. Kearns (eds), *The Australian Economy in the 2000s.* Conference 15–16 August, Sydney: Reserve Bank of Australia, 301–54, <http://www.rba.gov.au/publications/confs/2011/index.html>.

Dignam, A. (2005). 'The takeovers panel, the market efficiency principle and the market for corporate control—an empirical study', *Company and Securities Law Journal*, 23 (1): 58–64.

Dignam, A. and Galanis, M. (2004). 'Australia inside-out: The corporate governance system of the Australian listed market', *Melbourne University Law Review*, 28 (3): 623–53.

Duran, P. (2011). 'Distressed debt traders are gentlemen: report', *Australian Financial Review*, 8 March.

Evans, J. (2008). 'Study of Australian Superannuation Fund Attitudes to Private Equity Investing', Australian School of Business Research Paper, 2008ACTL02.

Evans, J. (2010). 'Hedge Fund Survey of Australian Superfunds', AIMA and UNSW, <http://www.aima-australia.org/forms/AIMAAUST2010SuperannuationHedgeFundSurvey.pdf>.

Ferrier Hodgson (2011a). 'REDgroup Redundancies Fact Sheet 30-5-11', <http://www.ferrierhodgson.com/en/Media/Ferrier%20Hodgson%20Press%20Release%20-%20REDgroup%20Fact%20Sheet%2030-5-11.aspx>.

Ferrier Hodgson (2011b). 'Final Angus & Robertson bookstore closures 5-7-11', Press Release, http://www.ferrierhodgson.com/en/Media/Ferrier%20Hodgson%20Press%20Release%20Fact%20Sheet%205-7-11.aspx.

Ferrier Hodgson (2011c). 'Fact Sheet: Colorado Group', Press Release, 30 March, http://www.ferrierhodgson.com/en/Media/Fact%20Sheet%20-%20Colorado%20Group%20-%20March%202011.aspx.

Ferrier Hodgson (2011d). 'Colorado Group Restructure—14-6-11', <http://www.ferrierhodgson.com/en/Media/Press%20release%20Colorado%20Group%20-%2014-6-11.aspx>.

Ferrier Hodgson (2011e). 'Fusion Retail Brands Limited', Press Release, 20 September, <http://www.ferrierhodgson.com/en/Media/FH%20Press%20Release%20-%20Fusion%20Fact%20Sheet%2021911.aspx>.

Folkman, P., Froud, J., Johal, S., and Williams, K. (2009). 'Private equity: levered on capital or labour', *Journal of Industrial Relations*, 51 (4): 517–28.

Future Fund (2006). *Annual Report 2005–06*. Melbourne VIC: Future Fund Board of Guardians.

Future Fund (2007). *Annual Report 2006–07*. Melbourne VIC: Future Fund Board of Guardians.

Future Fund (2010a). *Annual Report 2009–10*. Melbourne VIC: Future Fund Board of Guardians.

Future Fund (2010b). *Statement of Investment Policies*. Melbourne VIC: Future Fund Board of Guardians. Melbourne VIC: Future Fund Board of Guardians.

Future Fund (2010c). 'Future Fund votes against resolutions at Telstra AGM', Media Release, 19 November. Melbourne VIC: Future Fund Board of Guardians.

Greenblat, E. (2010). 'Bookstore chain looks for condensed version', *The Sydney Morning Herald*, 18 November: 6.

Hardy, T. (2007). 'Protection of Employees in a Transmission of Business: What is Left in the Wake of WorkChoices and Subsequent Statutory Amendments', Working Paper, 42, Centre for Employment and Labour Law, Melbourne: The University of Melbourne.

Hume, M. (2012). ''Lenders' deal averts Nine bankruptcy', *Financial Times*, 17 October, <http://www.ft.com/cms/s/0/be032610-183e-11e2-8 0af-00144feabdc0.html#axzz2A70Emh7X>.

IMF (2006). *Australia: Financial System Stability Assessment.* IMF Country Report No. 06/372, Monetary and Capital Markets and Asia and Pacific Departments, 8 September, Washington, DC: International Monetary Fund (IMF).

Jones, D. (2008). 'Issues in MBOs: a case study', Private Equity and Venture Capital Workshop, 26 February 2000, Centre for Continuing Legal Education: University of New South Wales.

Korporeal, G. and Sainsbury, M. (2007). 'McGauchie defies Murray on Sol', *The Australian*, 8 November, <http://www.smh.com.au/business/ mcgauchie-follows-sol-out-20090508-ax5t.html>.

Lee, T. (2011). 'Recharged Alinta energy in the hunt for customers', *The Australian*, 1 April, <http://www.theaustralian.com.au/archive/ business-old/recharged-alinta-energy-in-hunt-for-customers/ story-e6frg97o-1226031618881>.

Llewellyn, D. (2006). 'Institutional Structure of Financial Regulation and Supervision: The Basic Issues', World Bank Seminar: Aligning Supervisory Structures with Country Needs, Washington, DC, 6–7 June.

McNally, Chambers S., and Thompson, C. (2004). 'The hedge fund industry in Australia', *Reserve Bank of Australia (RBA) Financial Stability Review*, September: 57–65.

OECD (2007). *The Implications of Alternative Investment Vehicles for Corporate Governance: a Synthesis of Research about Private Equity Firms and Activist Hedge Funds.* Paris: OECD (Steering Group on Corporate Governance).

O'Sullivan, M. (2009). 'It takes two to tango', *Sydney Morning Herald*, 9 January, <http://www.smh.com.au/business/it-takes-two-to-tango-20090109- 7dok.html>.

O'Sullivan, M. and Carson, V. (2009). 'ABC collapse cost 700 their job', *Sydney Morning Herald*, 24 March, <http://www.smh.com.au/business/ abc-collapse-costs-700-their-jobs-20090323-97iu.html>.

Parliament of Australia (2001a). *The Opportunities and Constraints for Australia to Become a Centre for the Provision of Global Financial Services.* Report of the Senate Select Committee on Superannuation and Financial Services, Canberra, ACT: Parliament of the Commonwealth of Australia

Parliament of Australia (2001b). *International Financial Markets: Friends or Foes.* House of Representatives Standing Committee on Economics,

Finance and Public Administration, March, Canberra, ACT: Parliament of the Commonwealth of Australia

Parliament of Australia (2002a). *Report of the Review of the Managed Investments Act 1998*. Parliamentary Joint Committee on Corporations and Financial Services, December, Canberra, ACT: Parliament of the Commonwealth of Australia

Parliament of Australia (2002b). 'Taxation Laws Amendment (Venture Capital) Bill 2002', Bills Digest No. 78 2002-03, <http://www.aph.gov.au/binaries/library/pubs/bd/2002-03/03bd078.pdf>.

Parliament of Australia (2005). 'Future Fund Bill', Explanatory Memorandum, House of Representatives, December, Canberra, ACT: Parliament of the Commonwealth of Australia.

Perkis, D. (2010). 'Corporate restructuring: The impact of credit derivatives and distressed debt investing', *Journal of Banking and Finance Law and Practice*, 21: 185–213.

Petit, C. (2008). 'Rejection of Collective Bargaining Agreements in Chapter 11 Bankruptcies: Legal Analysis of Changes to 11 U.S.C. Section 1113 Proposed in H.R. 3652. The Protecting Employees and Retirees in Business Bankruptcies Act of 2007', *Congressional Research Service Report for Congress*, Washington, DC.

Poisel, T. and Terret, A. (2009). 'Transparency and disclosure: Implications of the bear raid on ABC Learning Centres', *Company and Securities Law Journal*, 27 (3): 139–65.

Range, J. (2011). 'Alinta's debt for equity swap deal set to go', *Australian Financial Review*, 15 March: 16.

Rankin, B. (1999). 'The impact of hedge funds on financial markets: Lessons from the experience of Australia', in: Reserve Bank of Australia (ed.), *Capital Flows and International Financial System*, Reserve Bank of Australia Conference, 9–10 August: 151–63, <http://www.rba.gov.au/publications/confs/1999/rankin.pdf>.

REDgroup Retail (2011). 'Submission to the Productivity Commission Inquiry into the Economic Structure and Performance of the Australian Retail Industry', May, <http://www.pc.gov.au/__data/assets/pdf_file/0007/109771/sub089.pdf>.

RBA (2007). 'Private equity in Australia', *Financial Stability Review*, March: 59–73, Reserve Bank of Australia (RBA).

RBA (2011). 'Assets of financial institutions: Statistical tables', Sydney: Reserve Bank of Australia (RBA), <http://www.rba.gov.au/statistics/tables/index.html#assets_liabilities>.

Sainsbury, M. (2006). 'Telstra won't say how high hurdles are', *The Australian*, 15 November, <http://www.theaustralian.com.au/business/telstra-wont-say-how-high-hurdles-are/story-e6frg8zx-1111112522744>.

Sanyal, K. (2011). 'Foreign Investment in Australia: Recent Developments', Background Paper, Australian Parliamentary Library, 1 April, <http://

www.aph.gov.au/About_Parliament/Parliamentary_Departments/ Parliamentary_Library/pubs/BN/1011/ForeignInvestmentAust>.

Schwab, A. (2008). 'Facts fail to bear out Groves' hedge fund claim', *Crikey*, 29 August, <http://www.crikey.com.au/2008/04/29/facts-fail-to-bear-ou t-groves-hedge-fund-claims/?wpmp_switcher=mobile>.

The Senate (2006). 'Tax Laws Amendment (2006 Measures No. 4) Bill 2006 [Provisions]', Standing Committee on Economics, October.

Speedy, B. (2010). 'Booksellers covenant warning', *The Australian*, 30 July 2010: 23.

Telstra (2007). 'Results of general meeting', *ASX Report*, 7 November.

Triple A Partners/Basis Point Consulting (2012). *Australian Hedge and Boutique Fund Directory 2012*. Sydney: Basis Point Consulting.

Washington, S. (2008). 'Basis Capital fund collapse provides insight into investor risks', *The Age*, 8 January, <http://www.theage.com.au/ business/basis-capital-fund-collapse-provides-insight-into-investor-risks-20080108-1kv1.html#ixzz1ezscZGmQ>.

Westcott, M. (2009). 'Private equity in Australia', *Journal of Industrial Relations*, 51 (4): 529–42.

Westcott, M. and Pendleton, A. (2013). 'Private equity and labour management: The case of Myer', *Journal of Industrial Relations*, 55 (5): 723–42.

Williams, P. (2009a). 'Who killed McGauchie?', *Australian Financial Review*, 9 May: 27.

Williams, P. (2009b). 'Future Fund raises heat on Telstra chair', *Australian Financial Review*, 17 April: 48.

Williams, P. (2009c). 'Murray calls time on Telstra chairman', *Australian Financial Review*, 16 April: 1.

World Federation of Exchanges (1997–2010). 'Statistics 1997–2010', <http:// www.world-exchanges.org/statistics/annual>.

5

Financialization and Ownership Change: Challenges for the German Model of Labour Relations

JAKOB HAVES,
SIGURT VITOLS, AND
PETER WILKE

Introduction

Germany has long been seen in comparative political economy as a country with a distinctive institutional structure and path of industrial development relative to liberal market economies (LMEs) like the UK and US (Vitols 2001).[1] Already, at the beginning of the twentieth century, the term 'organized capitalism' was used to describe the close interlinks between a small number of large banks and industrial companies which were organized as cartels with the support of the German state (Höpner 2005). Since the 'take off' period of industrialization, financial markets have been less developed than in other countries, in part because of numerous financial crises, in part due to the critical attitude of the state towards the stock market (e.g. during the National Socialist period). Correspondingly, banks have played a particularly important role in the financing and corporate governance of companies. The number of listed domestic companies has remained modest, with almost all SMEs and many large-sized firms deciding to remain private.

After the Second World War this coordination on the capital side was matched by coordination on the labour side (Thelen 1991). In the 1950s and again in the 1970s, legislation was passed granting workers comparatively strong co-determination rights, both on the shop floor through works councils and on supervisory boards of large companies through employee representatives. A strong system of coordinated collective bargaining based mainly on industry-level agreements developed in the 1950s and 1960s.

Not surprisingly, in the varieties of capitalism literature, Germany is therefore seen as an archetypical case of a coordinated market economy (CME) (Hall and Soskice 2001). This type of institutional structure is seen as particularly supportive of high-quality manufacturing production in so-called 'medium-tech' industries, such as automobiles, machinery production, and chemicals. This type of production is said in turn to rely on 'patient' capital, that is financing with a long time horizon and modest expectations for profitability, as well as on skilled production workers, in the context of implicit contracts with management investing heavily in firm-specific skills.

Starting in the mid-1990s, however, changes in some of these institutions precipitated a debate in comparative political economy regarding the extent to which the German model has been transformed. These positions vary quite widely: on the one extreme, some commentators see a strong tendency to convergence on the Anglo-American LME model, while the other extreme sees only marginal changes in the post-war German model (Beyer 2003; Höpner and Streeck 2003; Thelen 1999). A key part of this debate is the role of financialization in forcing changes in the German model through a number of channels. First, large German banks are seen as losing interest in the traditional 'Hausbank' model of relational finance in long-term relationships, moving instead to the market-oriented model used by US investment banks. Second, a change in the structure of shareholdings, namely a decrease in the number of large shareholdings and an increase in the significance of foreign institutional investors, is seen as exerting pressure on German companies to focus more on (short-term) financial returns and less on long-term industrial goals.[2] Third, private equity (PE) and hedge funds (HFs), which were almost unknown to the public in Germany before the late 1990s, are seen as intensifying this pressure on companies for financial performance (Fichtner 2009; Huffschmid et al. 2007). Further, these aspects of financialization are seen as exerting pressure on the coordinated system of collective bargaining and on the 'implicit contracts' that exist between management and labour in many German companies (Bahnmüller et al. 2011; Jackson 2005).

This chapter addresses this debate by focusing on the role of the three types of new investment funds (NIFs)—private equity (PE), hedge funds (HFs), and sovereign wealth funds (SWFs)—on the German economic model and system of labour relations. Here we take the position that the German economy has in some respects moved closer to the LME model, in particular a weakening of the Hausbank model and corresponding increase in the role of institutional investors, which has strengthened the orientation of large listed German companies towards 'shareholder value'. PE and HFs have also played a role in this transformation through pressure on listed companies for higher profitability. This financial pressure has been one factor contributing to the erosion of the coordinated system of collective bargaining and the shrinking of the so-called core labour force, which enjoys long-term employment security and good working conditions.

At the same time, the extent of change should not be exaggerated. The number of German companies listed on the stock exchange, where pressures for financialization are largest, has remained modest in comparison with the LMEs. Very few small and medium-sized enterprises (SMEs) are listed and many leading large companies (e.g. Bosch and Bertelsmann) have explicitly chosen to remain private. Many banks—especially the group of municipal savings banks and cooperative banks—remain committed to the Hausbank principle and continue providing relational finance to SMEs. Furthermore, although union density and the degree of collective bargaining coordination has eroded somewhat, the legal framework for co-determination has not been weakened and worker representatives remain quite strong in most large and many medium-sized companies. Whereas the NIFs have played a certain role in creating this pressure, nevertheless Germany has proved to be only partially hospitable to these actors. Levels of PE activity are below the European average; HF activity has severely receded since the financial crisis and the overall evidence is that activist HFs have not been particularly successful in Germany. After an initial period of controversy, PE investors have likely become more cautious and have at least partly adapted to local practices such as consulting labour. In all, the NIFs can be seen as one among a number of factors contributing to incremental change in the German CME.

The Institutional Context of the German Model

In this section, the German system of corporate finance is outlined and the role of what has traditionally been called 'patient' capital is discussed. Similarly, the German system of employment protection and industrial relations is outlined. The strong pressures on these are considered.

The Financial System and Patient Capital—a Changing Environment

As mentioned above, banks played a particularly important role in the financing and corporate governance of industrial companies in the twentieth century. This has occurred partially as a result of 'accident'—particularly through a series of financial crises which hindered the development of financial markets—and partially through design (Höpner and Krempel 2004). Despite these crises, there was a fairly stable institutional structure in the large firm sector, where a small number of large banks not only provided loans to companies, but also had significant shareholdings in these companies and appointed key members of their supervisory boards. In the first half of the twentieth century, this structure in conjunction with state-supported cartels was characterized as 'organized capitalism'. Although product markets were to some extent liberalized in the 'social market economy' established after the Second World War, weakening the power of the cartels, nevertheless the key role of banks in corporate governance remained and the label 'Deutschland AG' (Germany Inc.) was used by many to characterize the system. The two bank sectors which mainly lent to smaller companies—the municipal savings banks and cooperative banks—generally did not own shares nor have representatives on the boards of these smaller companies. Nevertheless both large companies and SMEs were seen to have access to sufficient capital in Germany due to these institutions.

Starting sometime in the 1990s, however, a series of developments triggered a discussion on the extent to which this system was being threatened. As discussed in the introduction, these factors included a change in the orientation of large banks, a change in the shareholder structure towards foreign and dispersed ownership, and increasing activity by NIFs in Germany. Network analyses of bank–company interlinkage show a significant decrease in the density of cross shareholdings since the mid-1990s. Most of the increase in share ownership was accounted for by so-called institutional investors, such as pension funds and mutual funds, which prioritize shorter-term financial goals (above all increases in share price), thus contrasting with the longer-term perspectives with a mixture of financial and industrial goals which were said to characterize 'patient' German investors. These new investors were seen to place demands on German companies to pay more attention to increasing share price, for example by returning cash to shareholders (rather than hoarding it for hard times), improving financial transparency, managing profitability expectations through investor relations departments, and prioritizing quarterly earnings. A further development was that more and more companies had an investor base made up mainly of financial investors with small shareholdings. As a result these companies were exposed for the first time to the threat of hostile takeovers by outside investors willing to pay a premium for shares (Höpner and Jackson 2006).

These changes were in part introduced by design through a series of legislative reforms designed to make the German stock market operate more like stock markets in the USA and the UK. Starting in 1990, the German legislator passed four different Financial Market Promotion Laws (*Finanzmarktförderungsgesetze*) designed to bring the country's financial system more in line with the LME model. Each of these laws has included a package of measures to reform securities, banking, and company law. Important measures included the following: the creation of a regulatory agency specifically dedicated to securities market regulation (on the model of the US Securities and Exchange Commission); the definition of insider trading rules and penalties; the authorization of derivatives, share buy-backs, and the use of stock options for executive remuneration; and corporate governance measures designed to strengthen the rights of minority shareholders, for example the principle of 'one share one vote' and limits on the influence of banks.

These legislative measures were also in part designed to encourage the development of PE and, to a lesser extent, HFs. The attitude of legislators towards SWFs has however been more restrictive. The changes affecting each type of fund are discussed in turn.

Regulation of Private Equity
German legislation has had as one of its explicit aims the creation of a more 'friendly' environment for financing industry, including PE. In particular the second and third Financial Market Promotion Laws (passed in 1994 and 1998 respectively) improved the legal structures and operating conditions for PE considerably.

However, although the European Private Equity and Venture Capital Association (EVCA) 2008 benchmarking report gives Germany high marks in some areas (specifically in the freedom of insurance companies to invest in PE and in the availability of a 'PE-friendly' fund structure—the GmbH & Co KG), in other respects EVCA sees Germany as being significantly below the European average. High levels of taxation are a key factor in this respect. The EVCA bench-marking report is rather critical of Germany on the grounds that various provisions of German tax law are significantly less favour-able to investors than in most other European countries. The corpo-rate tax rate, top personal tax rate, and taxation of stock options are all above the European average. There are less pure fiscal Research & Development (R&D) incentives for companies and net interest payments on debt are only partially deductible. The tax rate for car-ried interest is roughly in line with the European average. Only the taxation of performance-based incentives is more favourable than the European average. According to EVCA, this means that Germany is somewhat less attractive than most European countries as a location for PE investment.

The onset of the economic and financial crisis saw a partial political *volte-face* and re-regulation of financial markets. Of major importance in this respect are the attempts to regulate investment funds on a European level, as seen in the Alternative Investment Fund Managers Directive, which was adopted by the European Parliament and the Council in November 2010. The Directive came into force in July 2011 and the Member States had until July 2013 to transpose the directive into national law. This directive led to substantial new regulatory obligations for PE investments. PE funds now need a licence from the German Federal Financial Supervisory Authority (BaFin). To gain this, they need to prove that portfolio and risk management are handled separately. Moreover, all PE firms now need a depository, the primary function of which is to separate asset safe-keeping and management functions. The intention of this is to avoid conflicts of interest and better to protect investors. In concrete terms, this means that the depository controls the valuation of PE funds' assets. In addition, PE firms are subject to minimum capital requirements, and fund manager performance-related payments are to be made in the form of shares/units in the fund which they are obliged to retain for a certain period. Last, but not least, the Alternative Investment Fund Managers Directive introduced new transparency requirements for PE, such as the need to inform investors and supervisory authorities about fund transactions. When the value of a transaction exceeds a certain threshold, the target company's directors and works council must be informed of the buy-in.

When PE acquires more than 50 per cent of the voting rights of a non-listed company they now have to comply with wide-ranging information and consultation obligations towards the company, its shareholders, and the regulatory authorities. Among others this includes the presentation of a particular strategy for preventing conflicts of interest, the impact on the future business of the non-listed company and the likely repurcussions on employment, including any material change in the conditions of employment. Furthermore, the Directive includes specific provisions prohibiting asset stripping in order to protect the capital of a non-listed company.

Regulation of Hedge Funds

Another measure designed to support the financial industry in Germany was the authorization of the establishment of HFs in 2004. However, the regulations covering HFs remained strict in comparison with other countries. For example, in the interests of protecting smaller investors, only funds-of-funds (which in theory have diversified risk more than single HFs) can be publicly marketed. Directors of HFs also have to register with the regulatory authority and prove that they have a certain level of experience. As a result, relatively few HFs have been established in Germany. Thus, when we analyse the activities of HFs we are essentially looking at investments of foreign funds in German companies.

Changes favourable for activist HF activity in Germany have also been limited. Germany is now a leading exemplar of the 'one share one vote' principle, due to the elimination of multiple voting rights, voting caps, and other measures which privileged inside investors. On shareholder rights indexes overall, however, Germany only receives moderate marks (Siems 2008), meaning that it is somewhat of an average case regarding the ease with which activist investment funds can pressure company management to make changes.

Constraints on Sovereign Wealth Fund Investment

The legislation most directly relevant for SWF activity in Germany is the foreign trade law (*Aussenwirtschaftsgesetz*), which was recently modified. As of 2009, the Economics Ministry has the right to vet foreign investors, such as SWFs, which seek to acquire more than 25 per cent of the equity of a German company. The Ministry has the right to veto these investments in limited circumstances, for example in arms production. To date, the practical relevance of the law has been limited. There have been several long-term investments by Middle

Eastern SWFs in large German companies (e.g. Thyssen Krupp AG, Daimler AG, Volkswagen AG, and others) since the 1970s.

Labour Regulation

In the German system of labour relations, strong legal rights for workers and their representatives to employment protection, information, consultation, and co-determination, as well as an extensive system of vocational training, underpin an implicit contract between management and workers. Long-term job security is exchanged for workers' willingness to invest in firm-specific skills. On the one hand, management and owners are expected to have a long-term orientation whereby they will accept temporary financial losses in order to maintain employment. On the other hand, trade unions are expected to make compromises in times of crisis and not to exercise their full bargaining power during upturns.

However, in recent decades, this implicit contract has come under pressure. There has been a substantial rise in precarious employment, and thus the percentage of workforce ('core' workforce) covered by this contract, which is particularly strong in large manufacturing firms, has shrunk substantially. The proportion of workers in so-called 'normal' employment (full-time, tenured work) decreased from 74 per cent in 1990 to 66 per cent in 2011.[3] Furthermore, even within this core, this implicit contract has been modified somewhat as 'shareholder value' notions have influenced management behaviour. PE and HFs have played a role in bringing pressure for shareholder value to Germany. Nevertheless, the nature of labour regulation and the strong position of works councils and trade unions in these 'core' companies impose constraints on the strategies which NIFs can implement.

Employment Protection

According to data compiled by the Organization for Economic Co-operation and Development (OECD), Germany scores above the OECD average with regard to overall employment protection (2.6 versus 2.2 on a scale of zero to six).[4] In the case of collective dismissals, Germany has among the strongest levels of protection within the OECD (3.8 versus an average of 2.6), for example through the length of the procedure involved. As a result, collective dismissals are typically costly. However, employment protection for temporary workers is considerably weaker and individual dismissal protection is in line with the European average.

Information, Consultation, and Co-determination Rights

Workers in Germany enjoy extensive information, consultation, and co-determination rights, conditional on the size and legal form of the firm. The main channel of information for most workers is through the works council. In principle, a works council can be elected in any establishment with five or more regular workers, as defined by the Works Constitution Act. In most companies in the core industrial sectors with more than 100 employees there will be a works council. However, due to a relatively low rate of organization in smaller plants, about 44 per cent of West German and 36 per cent of East German private sector workers were represented by a works council (Ellguth and Kohaut 2012). Works councils enjoy extensive rights to information on economic issues and consultation and co-determination rights on many employment-related matters.

A second channel for worker rights is representation on supervisory boards. In companies with more than 500 employees, one-third of supervisory board members are employee representatives; in companies with more than 2,000 domestic employees, half of the supervisory board members are employee representatives. However certain types of company (e.g. media) are exempted from this requirement. Roughly one-quarter of workers in Germany are employed at companies with board level employee representation (BLER).

In cases of NIF activities, BLER is an important source of information for worker representatives. Also important for restructuring is the requirement in German law that existing agreements between management and works councils continue to apply even when a plant has been sold. In larger companies works councils are often involved in the process of selling a plant or division. For instance, they may seek to identify potential purchasers who are acceptable to the works council.

Trade Unions and Collective Bargaining

Germany has a strongly unified labour movement with over four-fifths of union members belonging to one of the affiliates of the German Trade Union Confederation, the Deutscher Gewerkschaftsbund. Although some employers have company collective bargaining agreements with a union (e.g. Volkswagen), multi-employer bargaining is the norm in Germany. Union density has decreased over the past few decades to less than one-quarter. However, in the industrial core, trade union membership still is comparatively high (above 60 per cent), and since collective agreements apply to companies with a low union membership rate, a significantly higher percentage of the workforce is covered by binding agreements. This percentage has decreased in what was the former West Germany from 70 to 54 per cent and in the former East Germany area from 56 to 37 per cent between 1996 and 2011 (IAB 2012: 1).

Trade unions negotiate over a wide variety of wage and working condition. According to labour law, there is a strict division of labour between issues negotiated with works councils (at plant or company level) and with trade unions. However, trade unions have managed to attain a strong degree of influence within companies by running slates of candidates for works council elections. Trade unions also are involved in the process of electing board-level candidates for company boards.

Summing up

Due to comparatively strict labour regulation, Germany is considered as a relatively difficult market for NIFs, since restructuring measures and possible collective redundancies are more difficult to push through than in countries with less co-determination and protection for workers. However, in practice, this assessment is not always true. Indeed, as we will see, there are some examples where PE investors see German co-determination structures as a positive asset and a chance to come to a cooperative agreement with employee representatives which can help implement restructuring measures.

New Investment Funds in Germany

There are significant differences in the economic importance, organizational structure, and visibility between the three types of NIFs in Germany. PE is most significant, as in addition to investment by foreign PE funds there is a domestic PE community which has grown significantly in the past two decades. German HFs are almost non-existent, and, although foreign activist HFs moved into Germany in the early 2000s, this activity has receded drastically since the financial crisis. Finally, according to the definition used in this study, Germany does not have a SWF of its own, but foreign SWFs have increased their investments in Germany in the past decade.[5]

Private Equity in Germany

The PE community in Germany, represented by the German Private Equity and Venture Capital Association (Bundesverband Deutscher

Kapitalbeteiligungsgesellschaften, BVK), is diverse, composed of three distinct types of investment funds with different interests and traditions. Historically, the first type of funds which appeared were SME funds (in part state-owned), which invest patient capital in traditional SMEs, followed by VC funds (mainly for start-ups) and finally by buy-out funds. At the end of 2012, 187 funds were members of the BVK, and it is estimated that another 30 funds are active in Germany but not members of the BVK. Most of the larger members are subsidiaries of US- or UK-based PE funds such as Carlyle and Permira.

The number of portfolio companies of PE funds in Germany has only slightly increased since 2001. In 2012 PE funds held investments in 6,622 companies, compared to 5,758 investments in 2001 (see Table 5.1). However, this statistic masks a significant increase in the average PE deal size up until the financial crisis; so-called 'mega buy-outs' (i.e. buy-outs with equity investments of over €300 million) were almost unknown in Germany up until the 2000s, but became increasingly frequent up until 2008. As a result, the total sales of PE portfolio companies in Germany tripled between 2001 to 2010, while the number of employees working in these quadrupled. In all, approximately 3 per cent of the German workforce is employed at PE portfolio companies; in comparision, in the UK, PE portfolio companies employ around 20 per cent of the private sector workforce (see Chapter 3 on the UK for details).

During most of the 1990s, PE investment volumes in Germany remained fairly constant at the relatively low level of about €500 million a year (see Figure 5.1). In the wake of the global dot.com boom starting in the late 1990s, PE investment quadrupled between 1997 and the 2000/2001 dot.com peak. The bursting of the dot.com bubble saw the PE branch experiencing its first major crisis, with investment

Table 5.1 *Number of companies, sales, and employment at private equity funded companies in Germany, 2001 and 2010*

	2001	2010
Companies	5,758	6,622
Total sales (€ billion)	67.5	202.4
Employees	345,600	1,189,700

Note: Figures do not necessary include all PE funds that are members of the BVK. Thus these figures can only give an estimation of PE investments in German companies.
Source: Bundesverband Deutscher. Kapitalbeteiligungsgesellschaften (BVK) statistics.

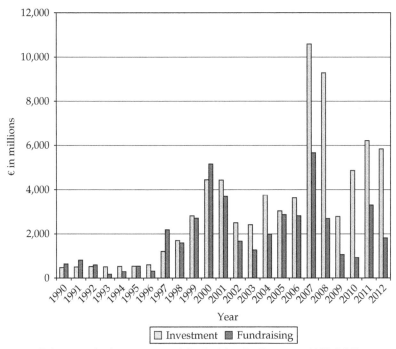

Figure 5.1 *Private equity investment and fundraising in Germany, 1990–2012*
Source: BVK data, <www.bvkap.de>.

volumes declining significantly in 2002 and 2003. The market recovered somewhat between 2004 and 2006, though investment volumes remained far below those of 2000/2001. The situation changed however in 2007 and 2008, with the German PE market experiencing an unprecedented boom and the money invested by PE firms in German companies rose to over €10 billion in 2007. Even though slightly receding in 2008 on account of the first effects of the crisis, some €9 billion still went into new investments.[6] Subsequently, however, 2009 saw the PE market collapsing, hit hard by the effects of the economic and financial crisis. In Germany, investment volumes dropped to their lowest level for ten years. Though the market recovered somewhat in 2010 and 2011, investment levels still remained well under those of the immediate pre-crisis years. Investment declined again in 2012 and, according to industry sources, the outlook for 2013 and beyond is characterized by uncertainty (BVK 2013).

In the past decade the dominant proportion of investments made by PE firms in Germany was in the field of buy-outs, representing 87 per cent of the total value of PE deals in the 2007 boom. By contrast, venture capital and other investment forms only accounted for a very small share of total investment volumes.[7] The effects of the economic and financial crisis greatly impacted the buy-out segment, leading to its collapse in 2009, particularly in large deals (€150–300 million) and mega-deals (>€300 million).

Hedge Funds

The founding of HFs in Germany was first allowed with the introduction of the so-called 'Investment-Modernisierungsgesetz' (Investment Modernization Law) in 2004. Since then HFs have been established in Germany as 'Sondervermögen mit zusätzlichen Risiken' (special assets with additional risks) under specific legal restrictions. These funds are allowed to use leverage and short-selling strategies but the general public is not allowed to invest in them. Shares of these funds can only be acquired in the form of a private placement, for instance by institutional investors. However, funds-of-funds which are registered with the German financial regulatory authority BaFin can be offered to private investors.

Almost a decade after the passage of the law, there are very few HFs which are headquartered in Germany. As of February 2013, there were only thirteeen single HFs and four funds-of-funds registered with the regulatory authority (BaFin). The German Investment Fund Association, which uses a definition of a HF which also includes German subsidiaries in Luxembourg, lists twenty-two HFs open to the public at the end of 2012, with total assets under management of €650 million. None of the German HFs can be characterized as having an activist approach.

There are relatively few statistical studies of HF activity in German companies. However, these suggest that activist HF involvement has been modest in comparison with other countries, particularly the LMEs, and was highly concentrated in the mid-2000s. Achleitner et al. (2010) have analysed ninety-six cases of HF investments in listed German companies between 1998 and 2007; in total 90 per cent of the identified investments took place in the last three years of this period (2005–2007). Using a different data source and methodology, Becht et al. (2010) identify forty-three instances of HF activism in Germany between 2000 and 2008; their data, which cover fifteen European countries, suggest that Germany is somewhere in the middle in terms of active HF involvement. Extending the analysis to 2010, Drerup

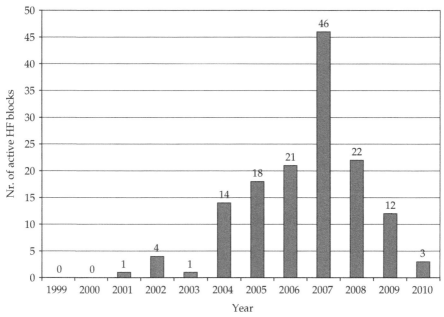

Figure 5.2 *Active hedge fund blocks in top 100 German listed companies, 1999–2010*
Source: Drerup (2012: Table 2.

(2012) finds 142 'active' HF blocks amongst the top 100 German listed firms, with the first block identified in 2001, rising to a peak of forty-six blocks in 2007, and falling to just three blocks in 2010 (see Figure 5.2). Goyer (2011) finds that HF activity in Germany is significantly lower than in France in the 2000s.

Sovereign Wealth Funds

Evidence regarding the extent of SWF activities in Germany is limited. A report by the Deutsche Bank identified a total of €5.1 billion SWF investments in German companies between 1995 and mid-2008; by way of comparison the figure for SWF investments in UK companies in the same time period was €26 billion. An analysis of SWF investments in listed companies identified 149 investments in 833 listed companies (i.e. 18 per cent of the listed companies examined) at the end of 2007. Of these, seventeen were large investments (i.e. ownership stakes of at least 1 per cent of total shares in the company) (Fernandes 2011). Examples of long-term investments of SWFs as minority shareholders are the investments of Kuwait and Abu Dhabi in Daimler (7 per cent and 9 per cent of shares respectively), Dubai VAE with 2.2 per cent of Deutsche Bank's stock, and the recent investment of Qatar in Volkswagen AG (25 per cent).

Relative Importance of New Investment Funds

Private equity has been growing in importance in Germany over the past few decades, particularly in mid-sized companies (*Mittelstand*) in traditional sectors, but it remains below the European average relative to GDP and well below its peak activity before the crisis. Given that about 3 per cent of the German workforce is employed in PE portfolio companies, the impact of PE on the employment system overall can be seen as modest. Up until the crisis, activist HFs played a role in several cases in influencing the corporate governance and strategy of listed German companies. However, activist HF activity has receded significantly since 2007–08. SWF investment in Germany has been modest to date, although it may increase substantially in the future.

Outcomes and Effects of New Investment Funds on Companies

As in many other European countries, the debate on the effects of PE and HFs in Germany has been highly polarized. Some voices in the financial and academic communities have long argued that Germany has a need for more activity from these types of funds. In addition to the lack of risk capital for start-ups, it is argued that buy-out capital is necessary to help deal with the succession problem for SMEs. Furthermore, it has been argued that PE is needed to help Germany in the transition to a more shareholder value-oriented capitalism. For example, it can help conglomerates to spin-off non-core businesses and assist banks in exiting from large shareholdings in industrial companies. These observers have also argued that PE and activist HFs can help change corporate governance in a more shareholder-value friendly direction. In contrast, trade union and other observers have greatly criticized PE and HFs. The Social Democratic politician Münterfering received considerable publicity, within and outside Germany, when he characterized these types of funds as 'locusts' in 2005 (Bockenheimer 2010; Lutz and Achleitner 2009; Schlesier et al. 2012).

These differing positions have been reflected in different research findings on the employment and industrial relations effects of these funds. On the one hand, on its website the BVK lists a number of case studies where PE investments have led to positive results, including employment growth. On the other hand, the trade union-related Hans Böckler Foundation has published case studies of PE and HF investments which document disrespect for rights of information, consultation, and co-determination along with negative effects on employment and working conditions. However, as with all case study-based information, a key question concerns the representativeness of the cases. Econometric studies on a larger number of PE deals and HF interventions could in principle address this problem of representativeness, but to date there have been very few of these studies (BVK 2006; Kamp 2007; Lutz and Achleitner 2009).

Econometric Studies

With regard to the effects of PE on employment, Lutz and Achleitner (2009) report that there are no German studies using archival data comparing PE-backed and matched companies. Studies based on archival data are said to be less subject to bias than survey-based data. There are two survey-based studies in Germany on this topic. The first study, which was done by the Deutsche Beteiligungs AG in cooperation with the *Finance* magazine (2004), compared the growth and employment levels of portfolio companies with companies not funded by PE. Forty-five buy-outs which had taken place between 1997 and 1999 were matched with similar companies. According to the study, the portfolio companies studied developed nearly twice as fast as the other companies over the same period. While the turnover of the portfolio companies increased on average by 7.4 per cent a year, it only rose by 3.9 per cent in the other companies. As regards employment, headcount in the portfolio companies grew on average by 4.5 per cent a year, while the comparable figure for the other companies was just 2.2 per cent (Deutsche Beteiligungs AG/FINANCE 2004).

The second study looking at the consequences of PE investments on companies and their employees in Germany was conducted by the BVK in conjunction with PwC (PWC/BVK 2005). The study, which was based on a survey of 198 PE firms and 128 companies financed by them, showed that median employment growth in portfolio companies excluding turnaround situations was 4.4 per cent. Although turnaround investments resulted in a median employment decrease of 28.6 per cent, the study underlines the fact that, particularly for companies in financial difficulties, the growth in business after a PE investor had come on board was above average, with such companies showing average earnings before income and tax growth of 56.7 per cent between 2000 and 2004. On this basis, the study concludes that it is better to 'sacrifice' a certain proportion of headcount during restructuring rather than to risk insolvency and the subsequent loss of all jobs. Notwithstanding the methodological limitations of surveys based on self-reporting, we should take note that both studies were conducted by the PE sector itself.

Regarding HFs, there are a number of studies regarding impact on share price and operating performance, but none on employment outcomes. A study by Bessler et al. (2008) identified 324 events involving announcements of HF block holdings between 2000 and mid-2007. This study identified significant short-term positive abnormal returns in share price; for example, for the period 80 days before and 80 days after the announcement, cumulative abnormal returns were 10.4 per cent. However, returns were much higher for smaller illiquid stocks than for companies with a larger, more dispersed shareholder base. Furthermore, estimates of whether or not there are significant long-term effects depend on the model specification.

A second study already mentioned above looks at activist HFs in a number of European countries (Becht et al. 2010). This study finds that there are positive stock price returns to investor activism in Germany of 3.8 per cent or 6.1 per cent after the announcement of an activist HF block holding (10 days before to 10 days after the announcement or 20 days before to 20 days after the announcement, respectively); the difference in short-term returns between Germany and Europe as a whole are not statistically significant. Long-term returns are not examined in the study.

A third study comparing share price developments in sixty-seven HF and 159 PE targets in Germany between 1993 and 2007 found a significant average short-term increase in share price of 4.5 per cent (Mietzner and Schweizer 2011). However, after a 250 day holding period, the abnormal return was –2.5 per cent for PE targets and –21.5 per cent for HF targets. The authors speculate that the difference is due to the inability of activist HFs to implement significant changes to corporate governance in the German legal environment.

A further study on HF activity (Drerup 2012) examined 278 HF shareholdings between 1999 and 2010. The study finds short-term positive abnormal returns in share price following announcement of a HF block holding. However, abnormal returns in the following year are negative, leading to a net zero result in share price over the long run. Furthermore, the study finds no significant changes in operating performance, leverage, or cash holdings, suggesting that the success of activist HFs which have been observed for the USA are 'not easily transferrable to the German capital market' (Drerup 2012: 1). A doctoral dissertation looking at 133 German HF events between January 2008 and April 2010 came to essentially the same conclusion (Stadler 2010). All in all, these studies suggest that, although activist HFs have a short-term impact on share price, the long-term impact on 'real' performance may be negligible.

There are no econometric studies on the impact of SWF investments on German companies.

Case Studies

In the past few years a considerable number of case studies of PE and HF involvement in German companies have been published. These cases identify both positive and negative effects on companies and their employees, making it difficult to draw generalizable conclusions. Where they are present, works councils are typically involved in negotiating restructuring in both positive and negative situations.

Most PE case studies report that business development in portfolio companies has been positive in the medium term, whereby positive business development is not always synonymous with employment growth. One example of this is the case of Grohe, a manufacturer of bathroom fittings. The company was acquired in 1999 by BC Partners, only to be sold five years later in the context of a 'secondary buy-out' to a consortium led by the Texas Pacific Group. While in the hands of the PE funds, Grohe was subject to comprehensive restructuring, resulting in large redundancies and plant closures in 2005. Nevertheless the company recovered in the wake of the restructuring, showing a major improvement in profitability. This development was accompanied by continuing redundancies. Though employment levels have picked up again since 2010, they are still well below the level at the time of the buy-out in 2005.

There are also examples of where a buy-out has led to both growth in sales and profits but also in employment. A recent example for PE investment in Germany is the case of the KION Group, a forklift producer with more than 20,000 employees worldwide. The case is interesting because it illustrates the active involvement of employee representatives in the buy-out process as well as in management decisions during the crisis.

In 2006 KION was spun off from Linde AG and sold to a consortium of KKR and Goldman Sachs for a price of about €4 billion. The decision in favour of the private investor was supported in principle by KION's employee representatives. In the subsequent bidding process, in which several international PE firms put in offers to acquire KION, the employee representatives were continually informed by Linde's management. Each bidder consortium had to answer questions posed by the works council, which was able to draw up a list of its preferences and to exclude certain candidates. Moreover, the works council was also able to require that the future purchaser should finance at least 20 per cent of the purchase price with its own equity.

Under the new management, corporate strategy became focused on the initial public offering (IPO) planned for the medium-term, resulting in restructuring measures designed to increase market share through acquisitions, holdings, and joint ventures. Following the buy-out by KKR and Goldman Sachs, KION was at first able to grow, leading to the creation of some 1,000 new jobs. However, the crisis hit KION hard and the company had to cope with a 55 per cent drop in turnover which resulted in the partial closure of a German plant and the complete closure of a UK plant in 2009.

In reaction to this situation KION management, the investor and the works council all agreed on a recapitalization, including new funds provided by KKR and Goldman Sachs and the issuing of a bond enabling the refinancing of loans totalling more than €1 billion, as well as opening up new lines of credit amounting to more than €110 million. Due to these cooperative negotiations between management, investors, and employee representatives, KION was able to get through these difficult economic times. In August 2012 the state-run Chinese company Weichai Power took a major stake in KION (the biggest Chinese investment in Germany to date), which solved the most urgent financial problems and—according to the works council—laid the foundations for a future IPO.

Detailed cases of activist HF investment are scarce in comparison to PE cases. Case studies of HF interventions show that there is rarely direct contact between HFs and worker representatives and that the restructuring plans of HFs do not explicitly focus on changes to employment conditions and work organization (Wilke et al. 2009). However, the German industrial relations system can moderate the impact of activist HFs on companies, as illustrated by the case of an investment by a HF consortium in the photofinishing company Cewe Color, where the works council and trade union worked together to ward off an activist HF.

Cewe Color is active in the processing of digital and analogue photos, but also related products such as photo calendars, books, and gift articles. The company has thirteen locations in twenty-four European countries and has around 3,100 employees. In 2005, the company came into the sights of institutional investors including several HFs. For these investors, the company was an interesting target because it had high liquidity, very low debt, and seemed to be under-valued. Under the lead of the US investor Guy Wyser-Pratt three HFs purchased a stake of just under 20 per cent in Cewe Color.

In the following year, the management and investors worked together reasonably amicably. However, in the autumn of 2006, the HF managers lost patience with the company's management. They blamed the management (in particular the Chief Executive Officer) for mismanaging the company and ignoring the interests of shareholders. In their eyes, the transition from analogue to digital photography was for the most part completed and thus the company should liquidate its equity reserves and pay out a special dividend to shareholders. The HFs demanded a dividend of €5 per share, whereas management offered a dividend of €1.20 per share. These disagreements marked the beginning of a fierce conflict between Cewe Color management and the activist HFs. This conflict was mainly argued out in public, which was quite new for Germany. Additionally, both sides made extensive use of the media, which was a familiar tactic for activist HFs but again not a common strategy for the company management. The climax of this conflict was reached in early 2007 when the HFs sued the management and the Chairman of the supervisory board for collusive behaviour to influence the share price with the aim of forcing out the HFs.

To resist the plan of the HFs to pay out a special dividend to the investors and to vote some board members out of office and replace them with others supportive of the HF strategy, Cewe Color's management acted in concert with its workforce, the works councils, and the unions. With the backing of the employees, the management was able to take the high ground in the media and public opinion. Prior to the critical shareholders meeting, the unions and works councils called on the employees to demonstrate against the HFs in support of management. More than 1,700 workers answered the call. In the media the conflict was characterized as 'Oldenburg vs. New York'.

This positive publicity for management was an important factor in winning over the remaining shareholders and restraining the plans of the HFs.

Detailed case studies on the impact of SWF investments on German companies and employment relations are scarce. Gospel et al. (2011) looked at three cases of SWF investments in Germany: Ferrostahl, an engineering company based in Essen, in which a 70 per cent stake was purchased by Abu Dhabi's IPIC from MAN in 2009; Mauser AG, one of the world's leading packaging companies, which was purchased by Dubai's DIC in 2007; and Almatis, a producer of specialized aluminium oxide, which was also purchased by Dubai's DIC in the same year. In the first two cases, employment increased after SWF investment. In the case of Almatis, however, turnover dropped by 80 per cent and major restructuring ensued.

After the Financial Crisis: The End of Financialization in Germany?

Since the onset of the financial crisis new PE investment and, in particular, activist HF activity has decreased considerably in Germany. Is this an indication that the process of financialization has been reversed? The following analysis suggests that in some ways the process may have been halted. However, financialization is a multifaceted process, and in other ways has continued. Furthermore, it is not a linear process, thus some tendencies may be stunted for an extended period of time due to the financial and economic crisis.

In the case of PE, the unfavourable macroeconomic situation experienced over the last few years has contributed to a drastic slowdown in fundraising, investment, and divestment activity. Private and institutional investors exercise greater caution in the selection of their investments, and the readiness of banks to provide loans for very large and highly leveraged company takeovers has decreased. Furthermore, the IPO route, which is generally considered to be the most lucrative exit channel, has become more difficult and the number of IPOs has been drastically reduced. Nevertheless, it would be wrong to speak of the end of PE in Germany, but rather of a refocusing of activity in smaller and medium-sized buy-outs, with less leverage and at lower purchase prices. Surveys indicate that many institutional investors would like to increase their allocation to PE in the medium-term, as PE is seen as an investment class which can offer higher returns than public equity (i.e. the stock market) and risk diversification. PE has already shown a phoenix-like ability to recover after the dot.com crisis to rise to new highs and has also recovered to a certain extent since the 2008/09 financial crisis.

Furthermore, the financial crisis appears to have intensified the pressure on PE to achieve financial returns in the companies in which it is already invested. Here the debt incurred during most buy-out deals play a key role. The interest payments which have to be met regularly considerably narrow the financial resources available to companies during the downturn. A particularly extreme case is the automobile supplier industry. PE had invested heavily in a number of 'Tier 1' suppliers in Germany (i.e. suppliers with direct relations with the car manufacturers). Due to the tendency of manufacturers to outsource production and R&D, these Tier 1 suppliers presented a 'growth story' which interested PE firms. The availability of low-interest loans often led PE firms to acquire automotive supplier companies without adequately taking the risks involved into account. A series of company owners took advantage of the boom years to sell their companies to PE investors at high prices. The loans taken out by the investors to finance these acquisitions were for the most part then transferred to the companies. In combination with decreased demand, these high levels of debt were behind an above-average rate of insolvencies in the German automotive sector during the crisis (Scheuplein 2012).

For several German companies owned by PE investors, the debt situation remains a threat. Companies acquired by PE investors before the onset of the crisis, in the context of a leveraged buy-out, will be increasingly feeling the effects of this debt burden over the next few years. Even now there are the first signs of companies rescheduling their debt, with payment periods being extended. The more a company is burdened by debt, the more probable it is that measures will be taken in the future to cut costs, including via employment reductions and restructuring measures.

Additionally, PE firms are beginning to re-appraise and change their business models due to the crisis effects. One trend is towards a greater focus on existing portfolio companies. According to a survey of 170 PE investors active in Germany, 90 per cent of participants stated that the greatest change in their business models over the coming years would be a stronger focus on a more active portfolio management (PwC 2012). This strategy aimed at 'streamlining' and

'nursing' the existing portfolio is logical in times when new investments and exits involve difficulties and when the financial situation
of a number of portfolio companies makes it necessary to become
more actively involved. More active portfolio management means
that several funds have had to find new ways of restructuring and
increasing the value of their portfolio companies during the crisis.

Similarly, SWF investments have been seen as fairly benign in terms
of pressure on employment and working conditions, since SWFs generally acquire controlling interests in companies for strategic rather
than financial reasons. However, with a deterioration in company
performance during the crisis, it appears that SWFs are reappraising
this strategy and increasing pressure on their portfolio companies for
financial performance, including reducing employment and labour
costs (Wilke et al. 2009).

Less certain is the long-term future of activist HFs in Germany. In
the Anglo-Saxon countries, there has been something of a revival of
their activity in the past year. However, this has not been the case in
Germany. The studies cited above suggest that, overall, German institutional arrangements do not provide fruitful ground, as short-term
increases in share prices are not followed up by long-term improvements in operative performance and shareholder value. If this
perception is shared by the HF community, we may see a further refocusing of activist HFs on countries with more hospitable institutional
environments such as the UK and the USA.

Aside from NIFs, other indicators suggest that at least some aspects
of the process of financialization have continued in Germany. As mentioned above, large domestic shareholdings continue to decrease in
significance, as new records have been set for the percentage of shares
held by foreign institutional investors. The largest thirty listed companies are now majority-owned by foreign investors. Furthermore, the
financing patterns of non-financial companies have continued to shift
during the crisis away from bank financing towards market-based
finance, such as bonds and short-term commercial paper raised by
their own financial companies (Deutsche Bundesbank 2012).

In the employment area, the tendency towards increasing use of
precarious labour has once again resumed after a dip during the
height of the crisis. In 2008/09 some forms of precarious employment decreased as fixed-term contracts were not renewed and the use
of temporary agency workers reduced. With subsequent economic
recovery, however, companies have increased their use of these forms
of labour in an effort to retain flexibility and reduce labour costs.

While large manufacturing firms retain their core workforce of highly skilled long-term workers, this core continues to shrink at many firms. Although the relationship between financialization and these labour market developments is complex, certainly the pressure for greater financial returns on companies plays a role in these developments.

Conclusions

The role of NIFs in Germany has been very controversial regarding their economic and employment effects. In the words of the German academics Lutz and Achleitner (2009), NIFs have been seen by many as either 'angels' or 'demons'. Particularly before the financial crisis, NIFs were seen by many as the spearhead of financialization in Germany and the transition to a LME, including related Anglo-Saxon style employment relations (Fichtner 2009; Huffschmid et al. 2007). Since the crisis, however, this view has receded as the banks have taken centre stage. The opposing view saw NIFs as a key force which could improve the supply of risk capital and help modernize an economy based on traditional manufacturing. Both sides found plenty of ammunition to support their arguments in the form of case studies, which showed outcomes anywhere from massive employment growth to plant closures and bankruptcy. The lack of serious econometric studies on the matter does not help clear up this controversy.

This chapter has intended to take a more balanced view that NIFs have been one—but only one—aspect of the process of financialization in Germany. Although the NIFs rose to significance and caught the public attention in the past decade and a half, at the same time there have been a number of parallel changes, including a change in the strategies and behaviour of large banks and the rise of political currents favouring public policies which encourage neo-liberalism. Furthermore, especially in comparison with the LMEs, Germany represents a mixed case, presenting both opportunities and challenges for PE, HF, and SWF investors. On the one hand, there is a demand for PE (not least due to ownership succession in private companies and an increasing concentration on core competencies in large firms) and opportunities for activist HFs in a financial system which has traditionally not been strongly oriented towards shareholder value. On the other hand, the legal and tax framework is less friendly than in other countries. Employees also have comparatively strong information and decision-making rights, particularly in larger companies.

The German case shows that PE, HF, and SWF involvement does not necessarily lead to either a 'win–win' situation for both sides or to situations where workers are negatively affected. Rather, the outcomes appear to depend upon the economic and financial context, the willingness of investors to take into account the interests of employees, and the ability of trade unions and worker representatives to assert their rights. The case studies examined above show how German institutions for representing worker interests can have a moderating effect on the impact of NIFs.

The labour market data on Germany would appear to support this view. The trend towards precarious employment relations has been a slow and long-term development which has continued through the financial crisis, despite a decrease in PE and HF activity in Germany. More and more companies are using temporary agency workers and fixed contracts. Nevertheless, one should not exaggerate the extent of these changes. The 'normal' employment relationship, of full-time and tenured work, is still the predominant form of employment in Germany, and OECD statistics show that job tenure has been remarkably stable over the past decade and is among the highest among the OECD countries. Together with the stability and use of the institutions of vocational training, this suggests that the implicit contract between management and labour, even if it has been eroded, has not disappeared. At any rate, the strength of the German economy throughout the Eurozone crisis and the performance of the export economy, suggest that the German model of high-quality, medium-technology manufacturing has survived the various financial and institutional changes that have taken place in the past decade and a half.

NOTES

1. In this chapter, between 1949 and 1990, 'Germany' is used to refer to the Federal Republic of Germany.
2. The German business newspaper *Handelsblatt* reported that average foreign ownership of the DAX 30 (largest listed) German companies increased to 55.8 per cent in 2010 (Sommer 2011).
3. Own calculation based on data from the IAB (<www.iab.de>).
4. The latest data on the Employment Protection indicator is from 2008 (available at <http://www.oecd.org/employment/emp/oecdindica-torsofemploymentprotection.htm>). Since then, employment dismissal legislation has not been substantially revised.

5. There is some state ownership of companies, but this tends to operate through state-owned (e.g. Kreditanstalt für Wiederaufbau) or regional banks (Landesbanken).
6. One needs to bear in mind that the investment amounts listed only represent the capital actually owned by the PE firms. The actual amounts of funds used in buy-outs are usually two or three times higher, as buy-outs are generally 50–70 per cent financed via bank loans in order to achieve the desired 'leverage'.
7. This includes seed capital and rescue capital, but also minority holdings by a PE investor.

BIBLIOGRAPHY

Achleitner, A-K., Betzer, A., and Gider, J. (2010). 'Do corporate governance motives drive hedge fund and private equity fund activities?', *European Financial Management*, November, 16 (5): 805–28.

Bahnmüller, R., Faust, M., and Fisecker, C. (2011). *Das kapitalmarktorientierte Unternehmen: Externe Erwartungen, Unternehmenspolitik, Personalwesen und Mitbestimmung*. Forschung aus der Hans-Böckler-Stiftung, Band 135, Berlin: edition sigma.

Becht, M., Franks, J., and Grant, J. (2010). 'Hedge Fund Activism in Europe', ECGI Working Paper Series in Finance, 283, May, <http://papers.ssrn.com/sol3/papers.cfm?abstract_id=1616340>.

Bessler, W., Drobetz, W., and Holler, J. (2008). 'Capital Markets and Corporate Control: Empirical Evidence from Hedge Fund Activism in Germany', Discussion Paper, Giessen: University of Giessen.

Beyer, J. (2003). *Vom Zukunfts- zum Auslaufmodell? Die deutsche Wirtschaftsordnung im Wandel*. Wiesbaden: Westdeutscher Verlag.

Bockenheimer, J. (2010). 'Entdeckung der Sanftheit', *Süddeutsche Zeitung*, 'Finanzinvestoren', 31 March, <http://www.sueddeutsche.de/geld/finanzinvestoren-entdeckung-der-sanftheit-1.10501>.

BVK (2006). *Zukunft sichern durch Buy-out*. Berlin: Bundesverband Deutscher Kapitalbeteiligungsgesellschaften (BVK).

BVK (2013). 'Private Equity-Prognose 2013: Erwartungen der deutschen Beteiligungsgesellschaften zur Marktentwicklung', February, Berlin: Bundesverband Deutscher Kapitalbeteiligungsgesellschaften (BVK).

Deutsche Beteiligungs AG and FINANCE (2004). 'Economic Impact of Private Equity in Germany', *Finanz Studien*, Reihe im F.A.Z.-Institut, Frankfurt.

Deutsche Bundesbank (2012). 'Long-term Developments in Corporate Financing in Germany: Evidence Based on the Financial Accounts', Monatsberichte, January: 13–27.

Drerup, T. (2012). 'Much Ado About Nothing: The Effects of Hedge Fund Activism in Germany', 9 December, <http://ssrn.com/abstract=1718365>.

Ellguth, P. and Kohaut, S. (2012). 'Aktuelle Ergebnisse aus dem IAB-Betriebspanel 2011', *WSI-Mitteilungen*, 4.

EVCA (2008). *Benchmarking European Tax and Legal Environments*. Brussels: European Private Equity and Venture Capital Association (EVCA), <http://www.evca.eu/uploadedFiles/Executive_Summary_Benchmark_2008.pdf>.

Fernandes, N. (2011). 'Sovereign Wealth Funds: Investment Choices and Implications around the World', IMD International, <http://ssrn.com/abstract=1341692>.

Fichtner, J. (2009). 'Activist Hedge Funds and the Erosion of Rhenish Capitalism: The Impact of Impatient Capital', Working Paper, 17, CCGES CCEAE: York University / Université de Montréal.

Gospel, H., Haves, J., Pendleton, A., Vitols, S., Wilke, P., Catero, B., Duman, A., Dunin-Wasowicz, S., Engelen, E., Korpi, T., and Pradelle, P. (2011). *The Impact of Investment Funds on Restructuring Practices and Employment Levels: Company Case Studies*. 18 January, Dublin: Eurofund.

Goyer, M. (2011). *Contingent Capital: Short-term Investors and the Evolution of Corporate Governance in France and Germany*. Oxford: Oxford University Press.

Hall, P. and Soskice, D. (2001). *Varieties of Capitalism: The Institutional Foundations of Comparative Advantage*. Oxford: Oxford University Press.

Höpner, M. (2005). 'Sozialdemokratie, Gewerkschaften und organisierter Kapitalismus in Deutschland: 1880-2002', in: *Kölner Zeitschrift für Soziologie und Sozialpsychologie*, Sonderheft, 45: 196–221.

Höpner, M. and Jackson, G. (2006). 'Revisiting the Mannesmann takeover: How markets for corporate control emerge', *European Management Review*, 3: 142–55.

Höpner, M. and Krempel, L. (2004). 'The politics of the German company network', *Competition and Change*, 8 (4): 339–56.

Höpner, M. and Streeck, W. (2003). *Alle Macht dem Markt?* Fallstudien zur Abwicklung der Deutschland AG, Frankfurt/New York: Campus.

Huffschmid, J., Köppen, M., and Rhode, W. (2007). *Finanzinvestoren: Retter oder Raubritter?: Neue Herausforderungen durch die internationalen Kapitalmärkte*. Hamburg: VSA.

IAB (2012). 'IAB-Aktuell', 01 June, Institut für Arbeitsmarkt- und Berufsforschung (IAB), Nürnberg.

Jackson, G. (2005). 'Stakeholders under pressure: Corporate governance reform and labour management in Germany and Japan', *Corporate Governance: An International Review*, 13 (3): 419–28.

Kamp, L. (2007). 'Zum Einfluss von Private Equity- und Hedge-Fonds auf die Wirtschaft', *WSI Mitteilungen*, 11: 596–603.

Lutz, E. and Achleitner, A.-K. (2009). 'Angels or demons? Evidence on the impact of private equity firms on employment', *Zeitschrift für Betriebswirtschaft (ZfB)*, Special Issue Entrepreneurial Finance, 5: 53–81.

Mietzner, M. and Schweizer, D. (2011). 'Hedge funds versus private equity funds as shareholder activists in Germany: Differences in value creation', *Journal of Economics and Finance*, 37 (1): 1–28.

PwC (2012). *Private Equity Trend Report 2012. Learning to Live with the new Reality*. PricewaterhouseCoopers International Limited (PwC).

PwC and BVK (2005). *Deutsche Unternehmen Profitieren Maßgeblich von Private Equity*. Berlin: Pricewaterhouse Cooper (PWC) and Bundesverband deutscher Kapitalbeteiligungsgesellschaften (BVK), <http://www.bvk-ev.de/media/file/54.equity_portfolio.pdf>.

Scheuplein, C. (2012). 'An die Wertschöpfungskette gelegt: Die finanzgetriebene Restrukturierung in der deutschen Automobilzulieferindustrie und ihr Scheitern', *PROKLA*, 42 (1): 49–64.

Schlesier, M., van Doorn, T., Achmedowa, K., and Häßelbart, M. (2012). *Die größten Finanzinvestoren und deren Geschäfte: Heuschrecken oder harte Sanierer*. Hamburg: Books on Demand.

Siems, M. (2008). 'Shareholder protection around the world ('Leximetric II')', *Delaware Journal of Corporate Law*, 33: 111–47.

Sommer, U. (2011). 'Rekordwert: Ausländische Investoren greifen nach DAX-Konzernen', *Handelsblatt*, 'Finanzinvestoren', 19 January, <http://www.handelsblatt.com/finanzen/boerse-maerkte/boerse-inside/rekordwert-auslaendische-investoren-greifen-nach-dax-konzernen/3767590.html>.

Stadler, M. (2010). 'Shareholder-Aktivismus durch Hedge Fonds: Empirische Untersuchung für Deutschland', Doctoral thesis, 19 March, Department of Economics, Berlin: Technische Universität Berlin.

Thelen, K. (1991). *Union of Parts: Labor Politics in Postwar Germany*. Ithaca, NY: Cornell University Press.

Thelen, K. (1999). 'Why German employers cannot bring themselves to dismantle the German model', in T. Iversen, J. Pontusson, and D. Soskice (eds), *Unions, Employers, and Central Banks: Wage Bargaining and Macro-Economic Regimes in an Integrating Europe*. New York: Cambridge University Press.

Vitols, S. (2001). 'The origins of bank-based and market-based financial systems: Germany, Japan, and the United States', in W. Streeck, and K. Yamamura (eds), *The Origins of Nonliberal Capitalism: Germany and Japan*. Ithaca: Cornell University Press, 171–99.

Wilke, P., Vitols, S., Haves, J., Gospel, H., and Voss, E. (2009). *The Impacts of Private Equity Investors, Hedge Funds and Sovereign Wealth Funds on Industrial Restructuring in Europe as Illustrated by Case Studies*. Report to European Commission: Employment, Social Affairs and Equal Opportunities.

6

Contested Financialization? New Investment Funds in the Netherlands

EWALD ENGELEN

Introduction

The Netherlands has been harder hit by the global financial and economic crisis than many might have thought. During the first, financial phase of the crisis, the Dutch government was forced to inject capital into its banking system to the tune of well over 25 per cent of its gross domestic product (GDP), making it one of the biggest European victims of the bankruptcy of Lehman Brothers in September 2008. Initially, the Dutch economy, unlike the Dutch treasury, appeared to have remained largely unscathed from the fall out of the financial meltdown. This was very much in line with popular and academic literatures, which see the Netherlands as the proverbial seventeenth state of the German Federal Republic. However, since the outbreak of the second, political phase of the crisis in October 2009 when the Greek Prime Minister Papandreou announced that the Greek budget deficit was three times as large as expected, Germany and the Netherlands have moved in opposite directions. While Germany has been able to maintain momentum, resulting in continuous, albeit low, economic growth and declining unemployment, the Dutch economy has drifted into recession territory, resulting in rising unemployment, rising state indebtedness, growing budget deficits, and an accumulation of austerity measures adding up to €52 billion (or well over 15 per cent of the state budget) over four years.

This chapter is not about providing an explanation for the diverging fates of Germany and the Netherlands during the crisis, but uses these observations to qualify the tendency to lump these political economies together as embodiments of what Hall and Soskice have called 'coordinated market economies' (CMEs), which are then contrasted with the USA and the UK as typical examples of 'liberal market economies' (LMEs) (Hall and Soskice 2001).

This chapter presents the Netherlands as a hybrid political economy, standing in-between the CME and LME models. It combines, in an idiosyncratic and path-dependent manner, properties of both systems. The chapter explains how and why this hybrid political economy has impacted upon the rise and fall of Anglo-American new investment funds (NIFs) in the Netherlands. The claim made here is that Anglo-American NIFs have barely affected Dutch labour markets, despite their sizeable penetration of the Dutch economy and a noisy public debate over their activities and impact. High accessibility through open capital markets has not translated into an erosion of employment, industrial relations institutions, and working conditions because these are legally determined at the sectoral or national level.

The structure of the chapter is as follows. The next section outlines the hybrid character of the Dutch political economy, embedding this discussion in the financialization literature. The following section presents the regulatory framework which governs the scope of activities of Anglo-American NIFs in the Netherlands and discusses the extent and nature of changes in this in response to the crisis. The subsequent section provides a profile of the type of NIFs active in the Netherlands and the nature of their activities. Then, the social consequences of NIF activities are discussed, drawing attention to two case studies to explore employment effects. The final section concludes with a discussion of the implications for theory.

A Hybrid System

The Netherlands is known for combining an export-oriented economy with a well-developed welfare state with corporatist characteristics (Katzenstein 1985, 2003; Visser and Hemerijck 1997). In terms of product and labour market regulation, the Netherlands is often seen as similar to Germany, whilst its welfare state is often viewed as comparable to those found in the Scandinavian countries (Esping-Andersen 1990). As such, it features prominently as an example of a CME in Hall and Soskice's *Varieties of Capitalism* (Hall and Soskice 2001).

However, over the last two decades, this characterization has become increasingly questionable. First, since the late 1990s, a number of deregulatory measures have been pursued in an explicit attempt to mimic the so-called 'Danish model', making it easier for employers to hire and fire workers while enhancing the potential for temporary workers to gain full social rights. This is reflected in the Netherlands' standing in the Organization for Economic Cooperation and Development (OECD) Employment Protection Index where, with a score of 2.23, it is grouped together with countries like Brazil, the Czech Republic, and Ireland. This is well above the score of typical LMEs such as the UK (1.09) and the USA (0.85), but far below those of typical CMEs like Germany (3.8), Belgium (2.61), and France (3.0) (OECD 2008).

Second, the CME characterization ill fits some other notable properties of the Dutch political economy, such as its openness to international capital flows (Amable 2003). Inward- and outward-bound foreign direct investment is around 75 per cent and 100 per cent of GDP respectively. Moreover, most of these are portfolio investments, reflecting the high degree (around 80 per cent) to which Dutch shares and (sovereign) bonds are foreign-owned (FESE 2008).

This is reflected in the prevalence of Anglo-American NIFs in the Netherlands. In fact, the Netherlands was one of the first continental European targets of private equity (PE) funds and activist hedge funds (HFs) (Engelen et al. 2008). Moreover, their activities have remained at a relatively high level since their first involvement in the Netherlands from the mid-1980s onwards (PE) and early 2000s (HFs) (Bruining et al. 2005). In a recent comparative study by EVCA, the Netherlands scores just below the UK and Sweden as the third most attractive location for PE and venture capitalists in Europe (EVCA 2011).

A further indicator of financial openness is the importance of the Dutch trust industry for facilitating tax management by multinational corporations and, as of late, regulatory arbitrage by large US- and UK-based banks (Risseeuw and Dosker 2011). According to the Financial Stability Board (FSB), the Dutch share in the $60 trillion 'shadow banking system' rose from 6 to 8 per cent between 2005 and 2010, making it the third largest venue for fiscal and regulatory arbitrage worldwide (FSB 2011).

A third attribute that makes the Dutch political economy stand out from its CME neighbours is the size of its banking sector. Before the 2008 crisis, total Dutch banking assets reached five times GDP, although after the crisis they have shrunk to four times. This is comparable to Switzerland, the UK, and Ireland—world champions in terms of excessively large banking sectors (Engelen et al. 2010; DNB 2012). Although Dutch banks suffered severely during the crisis—two banks were nationalized and several others received substantial capital support from the state—Dutch institutional investors, especially pension funds, are still formidable financial players. These funds are unique in corporatist Europe in the sense that they are mandatory pre-funded old age insurance funds that have assets under management of €830 billion, well over 120 per cent of Dutch GDP (Ebbinghaus 2011). The largest have invested substantial sums—around 10 per cent of assets under management—in NIFs (mostly HFs, Funds-of-Funds, and PE funds).

A final indicator of financialization and hybridization is the size of the Dutch structured finance market (the root cause of the crisis in the USA in the form of repackaged (sub-prime) mortgages). The combination of high mortgage debts (125 per cent of GDP), low non-mandatory private savings, and high loan-to-value ratios has resulted in a so-called 'funding gap' of nearly €500 billion. This has made Dutch banks heavily reliant on short-term inter-bank funding through the asset-backed commercial paper-market and led to the development from the late 1990s of a securitization market that has become the world's fourth largest in absolute terms. In relative terms it is comparable to that in the UK (Aalbers et al. 2011). This is increasingly recognized by international organizations like the OECD, the International Monetary Fund, and the European Commission, as a source of instability in the Dutch economy.

Hall and Soskice's LME–CME distinction may be used to predict two distinct modes of financialization, defined by the level of openness of these institutional configurations to the forces of financialized capital. In the case of LMEs, *consensual financialization* would be expected because the underlying logics and coalitions—high factor mobility, short-term profit maximization, dependence on financial metrics—are largely in alignment with the goals, interests, and techniques of financial elites. In the case of CMEs, one would expect instead a mode of *contested financialization*, as the very same goals, interests, and techniques of financialization clash head-on with the logics of loyalty, voice, and reciprocal commitments that are the hallmark of CMEs. This results in a more limited penetration of financialization and more public controversy about its effects (Hall and Soskice 2001; Streeck 1992, 2009).

Based on the foregoing, the Netherlands is best understood as a case of *compartmentalized financialization*, which has the following attributes: (i) high openness to Anglo-American investors and capital flows; (ii) easy acceptance of financial metrics, conventions, and objectives at the ownership level; and (iii) limited effects on corporate governance, social welfare, and employment rights as a result of strong labour market regulation and a well-developed welfare state. The expectation derived from this is that the Netherlands should have an intermediate level of penetration (between LMEs and CMEs) by NIFs, should have experienced a lower impact in terms of negative labour outcomes than in LMEs, and should have witnessed a lower level of public controversy over those outcomes than in CMEs (Engelen et al. 2010; Engelen and Konings 2010).

The Regulatory Context

In this section there is a short description of the regulatory context that shapes the activities of NIFs in the Netherlands. We provide an outline of Dutch capital market regulation, taxation, and labour market regulation. We also refer to economic citizenship rights in the Netherlands more broadly and describe how the legislator has responded to political calls for more financial market regulation.

Capital Market Regulation

Foreign investment funds aiming to invest in firms established under Dutch law face no discriminatory regulation vis-à-vis domestic firms. They possess the same legal rights to purchase equity in unlisted firms as other investors. Purchasing shares in listed firms is only subject to notification requirements once the ownership share reaches certain thresholds. In addition, these requirements do not discriminate between types of investors (HFs, PE, SWFs (sovereign wealth funds), institutional investors, or retail investors) or their nationality. Buyers of publicly-traded equities have to inform the Financial Markets Authority of the size of their stake once it crosses a threshold of 3 per cent of outstanding shares. This threshold was recently lowered from a level of 5 per cent in response to high profile cases of HF activism. The 5 per cent threshold was seen to allow HFs to build up ownership positions undetected. There is as yet no related obligation to divulge 'intent' in the Netherlands.

A further piece of securities market regulation relevant for investors is the requirement to make a public bid for a listed firm once a stake has reached a 30 per cent threshold. The reasoning is that the purchase of such a large stake suggests takeover intent, which is relevant information for other shareholders and hence has to be divulged to ensure an orderly bidding process. Moreover, under new legislation the board is granted a much longer response time (up to six months).

Dutch corporate governance used to be known for its limited minority shareholder protection (La Porta et al. 1998). Since the early 2000s, shareholders have gradually gained more rights, in line with international trends (Gourevitch and Shinn 2005). Control rights over the board of directors used to be shared between an independent board of supervisors and the works council, with the latter mainly composed of union members. Since the early 2000s, the legislator has shifted the balance of power squarely from the supervisors to share-holders. Shareholders gained the right to put unsolicited items on the agenda of the General Shareholder Meeting (GSM) if they possessed more than 1 per cent of outstanding shares. The two-tier board model is no longer mandatory for large limited liability corporations, whilst the right to appoint members of the supervisory board has been allocated to the GSM, albeit with a binding right of suggestion for the works council (though rarely used in practice).

Of course, NIFs do not function only as investors but also as suppliers of asset management services. In that guise NIFs have to obtain a license from the Dutch financial markets regulator and from that point are listed on a public register. Until recently, Dutch capital market regulation distinguished between retail clients and wholesale clients but made no distinction between domestic or foreign funds. If a fund had less than 100 participants and if the size of the participations did not exceed €50,000, NIFs were not required to obtain a licence. Nor did they have to register in any other way. In response to the European Alternative Investment Fund Managers Directive of 2011, this has changed recently. According to a new Act in force from July 2013, all NIFs active in the Netherlands will fall under the supervisory jurisdictions of the financial markets regulator and the Dutch Central Bank, no matter the size of their investments, the status of their clients, or their nationality. Moreover, and this goes beyond European Union (EU) regulation, the Dutch government had the legal right to cap performance fees if it felt incentives had resulted in excessively risky behaviour by fund managers (Ministerie van Financiën 2012).

Licences are granted if funds can demonstrate expertise, provide transparency, produce a professional prospectus to potential customers, and practise regular reporting. Following the EU NIF Directive, EU-based NIFs that pass these requirements elsewhere gain a 'passport' to operate in the Netherlands and other European jurisdictions. Non-EU-based NIF's will, from July 2013 onward, have to apply for a licence from the Dutch financial markets regulator and will have to fulfil all legal requirements, irrespective of whether they are supervised in their country of origin. The Netherlands has no specific legal restrictions on the ability of NIFs to go short (except under exceptional circumstances), invest with borrowed capital (leverage), or buy derivatives (AFM 2005).

Despite some public debate in 2008 on the need to establish an equivalent of the US Committee of Foreign Investment in the United States (CFIUS), there is as yet no regulation in the Netherlands that explicitly targets SWFs. Since SWF activity in the Netherlands is restricted to mainly small portfolio stakes in Dutch publicly-listed firms, there has—as of yet—been no pressing political reason to regulate SWF activity in any way. This could change if Asian SWFs invest in the Netherlands on a larger scale.

Taxation

Taxation arrangements impact upon the activities of NIFs in the Netherlands in three main ways. One, in order to enhance the attractiveness of the Netherlands as the location for foreign investment funds, in 2008 the Ministry of Finance introduced a special legal entity, a so-called Exempted Investment Fund. Under this facility, funds that operate in the Netherlands are exempted from corporate taxation if the fund serves as a collective investment vehicle and has an open-ended nature. This exemption is granted on a case-by-case basis by the Dutch revenue service. There has been some lack of clarity whether NIFs are eligible since many involve investments by partners and can hence be seen as serving tax management purposes. The revenue service is currently in the process of defining threshold indicators to determine whether a fund is eligible for exemption.

Two, the Netherlands has introduced new legislation for the taxation of so-called carried interest, that is, the pre-determined share of the return on investment of a fund that is allocated to the general partners of the fund (typically 20 per cent). In mid-2008, the Ministry of Finance presented plans to tax the 'carry' of PE and HF partners as income instead of wealth. This explicitly addressed wider societal concerns over the mild fiscal treatment of foreign PE funds operating in the Netherlands. The proposal would have resulted in an increase in effective taxation from a 1.2 per cent wealth tax to a 52 per cent income tax. Of course it could only apply to domestic PE funds and would not affect foreign NIFs. Despite heavy lobbying by the Dutch branch organization, the plan became law in January 2009, though in a milder form. Under specified conditions, the 'carry' can be booked as corporate gains and is taxed at 25 per cent. This is a substantial increase on the previous taxation arrangements though much lower than the 52 per cent income tax initially envisaged.

The third relevant element of taxation concerns the fiscal treatment of debt. In many jurisdictions, interest can be deducted from the profits liable for corporate gains taxation. The Netherlands is no different. According to some news reports, Anglo-American PE funds in particular were abusing the lenient fiscal treatment of debt by burdening portfolio firms with excessive debt. In August 2008, a Dutch daily newspaper reported that Anglo-American PE funds had received €400 million from the Dutch revenue service as fiscal compensation for losses booked in 2007 by portfolio firms (*De Volkskrant* 2008). Several attempts to balance the fiscal treatment of equity capital versus debt capital have since been launched, but have stumbled over international tax treaties as well as fears about unwanted side effects (Vleggeert 2009). A high profile state committee in early 2010 made a set of recommendations for a more equal treatment of debt and equity capital to diminish the attractiveness of highly leveraged buy-outs. But nothing has since been heard of these proposals. It is unclear to what extent the proposals will gain political traction in the near future. Although left-wing Dutch parties advocated similar measures in their election manifestos, the recently established 'blue—red' coalition of conservatives and social democrats failed to include them in their coalition agreement.

Labour Regulation

The Netherlands has been trying to adopt the Danish model of 'flexicurity' in an attempt to break down the barrier between 'insiders' and 'outsiders' (SER 2010; Wilthagen and Tros 2005). Of the Dutch labour force of seven million, around one million are self-employed and around one million have 'non-standard' contracts (part-time work, temporary work (Souren 2008)). However, the latter have the same set of social rights and protection as full-time workers, including pension savings, sickness pay, access to training, and disability insurance. It is the category of the self-employed that is increasingly seen as eroding the integrity of Dutch social protection, giving employers a means of avoiding strict and costly social security arrangements. Although several plans have been presented to close this 'gap', the consensus on how to do so is not yet forthcoming since there is stalemate between labour unions and employer organizations, each of whom claim to represent the interests of the self-employed.

Despite a low level of unionization (21 per cent), the Netherlands is known for collective wage agreements, negotiated by peak-level labour unions and employer organizations, that are extended across their sectors by legal extensions. This results in a coverage ratio of 79 per cent, just below Sweden (90 per cent) but well above Germany (61 per cent) and much higher than the other cases discussed in this volume. As a result, employers and labour unions have been able, through peak negotiations at the Foundation of Labour and the Socio-Economic Council, to rise above partisan interests and agree on wage rises well below annual changes in average profitability. This used to result in low unemployment figures (until 2012, when unemployment rapidly increased from 6 per cent to 7.5 per cent in mid-2013 as a result of misguided austerity policies) and a competitive export sector (Visser and Hemerijck 1997).

The Netherlands is also known for its well-developed set of citizenship at work rights: these are largely on a par with German co-determination laws (Engelen 2000, 2004; Rogers and Streeck 1995). Under the Dutch Works Council Act, workers possess strong information and co-determination rights. Firms with more than fifty employees have to facilitate the establishment of a works council if the workforce expresses an interest in having one. In practice, this means that less than half of all firms with more than fifty and less than 100 workers have a council. This share rapidly increases above the 100-worker threshold. While most works councillors are union members, works councils are legally required to represent the full workforce, irrespective of union membership, in regular meetings with management. Works council rights are strongest in the domains of human resource management (HRM) and employment relations. Their rights are advisory on issues relating to business strategy, substantial investments and divestments, and the future of the firm. As was noted above, under new corporate governance legislation, works councils have recently gained the right to suggest candidates for half the seats on the supervisory board. However, it is the GSM that has the final say (Engelen 2004).

Unique to the Netherlands is the legal right of shareholder representatives and labour unions to demand a legal inquest by the

Corporate Chamber of the Amsterdam Court in cases where there is an irreconcilable conflict between management and other 'stakeholders' over strategic decisions that have substantial effects on the continuity of the firm (Van der Sangen 2003a, 2003b). Recently two cases involving foreign NIFs have been brought before the Corporate Chamber. One involved the British PE fund Apax and the Dutch publishing house PCM, and the other involved the Dutch company Stork and two American activist HFs, Centaurus and Paulson. Although the NIFs concerned were largely exonerated of the claims made by disgruntled unions and shareholders, these cases clearly damaged the public standing of NIFs. Moreover, a number of instances of shareholder activism concerned attempts by shareholders to initiate just such an enquiry into mismanagement against the wishes of the incumbent management (see the subsection 'Hedge Funds' below).

Profile of New Investment Funds

In this section, we present a brief overview of the size and nature of the activities undertaken in the Netherlands by NIFs, distinguishing between Dutch and foreign NIFs. I first discuss PE funds, then (activist) HFs, and finally SWFs.

Private Equity Funds

In line with its high degree of financialization, the Netherlands has a sizeable domestic PE industry. Dutch PE funds participate in more than 1,300 firms worldwide, 1,050 of which are located in the Netherlands. More than 70 per cent of all managed capital is invested in the Netherlands. Dutch portfolio firms managed by domestic PE funds employ 350,000 workers and generate a total turnover of €82 billion. The overall size of the Dutch PE market in 2010 in terms of invested capital was €2.0 billion, compared to €11 million in 1985. Almost half of this, €0.9 billion, can be traced to foreign PE funds. Since the mid-1990s the Netherlands has become an increasingly attractive arena of operation for foreign PE investment, especially from the USA and the UK. However, the amount of invested foreign capital has shrunk since the crisis to €0.5 billion (NVP 2011).

Table 6.1 provides an overview of the overall size of the PE industry in the Netherlands. Since there are some year-to-year inconsistencies in the reporting by the Dutch industry organization, these figures

Table 6.1 *Private equity funds in the Netherlands: domestic and foreign, 2003–2011*

	2003	2004	2005	2006	2007	2008	2009	2010	2011
Assets under Management (€ euro)	7.8	8.4	13.5	20.4	22.5	23.3	23.3	24.3	25.0
Number of firms	1200	1200	1200	1300	1350	1300	1330	1360	1407
Employment (thousand)	400	400	400	420	354	351	350	400	350
Total turnover (€ euro)	66.5	66.5	66.5	67.5	75.0	112.5	108.0	109.0	83.0

Source: Based on NVP annual reports 2003–11.

should be treated with some caution. Nevertheless the trend they illustrate is obvious: growing assets under management, a growing number of investee firms, and—up until 2008—a growing share of employment and turnover. Since 2008, employment and turnover of investee firms have declined, in line with the overall performance of the Dutch economy.

Initially PE investments mostly concerned seed and expansion capital and had domestic origins. However, from the mid-1990s onward, the amount of capital targeted at larger buy-outs started to surpass seed and expansion capital. Buy-outs really took off from 2001 onwards. This was mainly due to a small number of very large buy-outs conducted by foreign PE funds. Most buy-outs in the Netherlands are private-to-private and involve mid-sized firms, generally in close cooperation with incumbent management. Large public-to-private buy-outs conducted by foreign PE funds have been relatively rare in the Netherlands. From 1985 until the outbreak of the crisis in 2008, only thirteen of these buy-outs took place. This type of transaction is almost exclusively conducted by large Anglo-American PE funds such as Apax, Centaurus, and Kohlberg, Kravis, and Roberts (KKR), sometimes in collaboration with Dutch PE funds such as Amsterdam-based Alpinvest.[1]

Table 6.2 gives an overview of the amount of capital deployed by foreign PE funds in the Netherlands along with some indicators illustrating their importance for the Dutch economy. Due to data constraints only the most recent years are given. In 2010, foreign PE funds invested in 40 Dutch firms, with 50,000 employees and some €27 billion in turnover (equivalent to 4.6 per cent of GDP) (NVP 2011). These figures encompass participation in every financing phase, from

New Investment Funds in the Netherlands   187

Table 6.2 *Foreign private equity funds in the Netherlands, 2007–2011*

	2007	2008	2009	2010
Total investment (€ euro)	2.3	1.4	0.1	0.9
Number of firms	20	25	30	40
Employment	29,000	31,000	30,000	50,000
Total turnover (€ euro)	—	28.5	27.0	27.0

Source: Based on NVP annual reports 2007–10.

seed capital to public-to-private buy-outs. However, between 50 to 70 per cent of overall annual investment goes to buy-outs. PE funds are most active in producer services, consumer goods and services, and retail. Well over 60 per cent of annual investment goes to these sectors. In terms of numbers of firms the distribution is more even (EVCA 2011; NVP 2011). The figures illustrate that deep-pocketed foreign PE funds have dominated the market for large buy-outs, leaving domestic PE funds the much smaller markets for seed capital and other earlier financing phases. These funds have scaled back their activities since the start of the crisis.

Hedge Funds

The domestic HF industry in the Netherlands is negligible, consisting of little more than thirty funds with approximately €1.5 billion assets under management. Most of these funds pursue long/short equity strategies, while some do automated trading and other quantitative strategies. The same is true for the global population of HFs, where long/short strategies also predominate (IFSL 2011). Given the large share of foreign ownership of Dutch shares and bonds (over 80 per cent), we assume that part of that ownership derives from foreign HFs pursuing portfolio investments. These investments, though, do not substantially differ in size, scope, and intent from regular portfolio investments made by institutional investors (pension funds, insurers), investment funds, and other professional asset managers.

More relevant for our purposes are the activities of foreign 'event-driven' or activist HFs. These are HFs which attempt to use the voice rights of shares to initiate material changes in managerial strategy or corporate governance, either through closed consultations, public actions, or by igniting a shareholder revolt during a GSM. The first signs of HF activism in the Netherlands were in 2004. In that

Table 6.3 *Hedge fund activism in the Netherlands, 2004–2011*

Year	Number of Hedge funds	Firm	Aim	Successful or not
2004	5	Shell	Remuneration	Yes
		CSM	Voting rights	Yes
		Unilever	—	—
		Laurus	—	—
		PinkRocade	—	—
2005	2	Versatel	—	—
		ASMI	—	—
2006	4	Stork	Divestment	—
		ArcelorMittal	Divestment	No
		Ahold	—	—
		Euronext	—	—
2007	5	Akzo Nobel	—	—
		Nutreco	—	—
		ABN Amro	Mismanagement	Yes
		Dico	—	—
		Philips	Retained earnings	—
2008	4	Atos	Divestment	—
		Alanheri	—	—
		Exendis	—	—
		ASMI	Mismanagement	Yes
2009	0	—	—	—
2010	3	Endemol	Strategy	Yes
		Oce	Merger	—
		Draka	Takeover	—
2011	4	ASMI	Mismanagement	No
		Batenburg	—	—
		Beheer	Control	No
		Holland Colours	Divestment	Yes
		TNT		

Source: De Jong, A. et al. (2007); Author's research based on digital archive <www.fd.nl>.

year, five publicly-quoted firms were targeted by activist investors, followed by two in 2005, four in 2006, and three in 2007. The crisis of 2008 put a temporary halt to their activities. From 2010 onwards there are new signs of HF activism (see Table 6.3).

Activism is driven by the availability of investor capital, by excess capital in corporate targets, and facilitated by corporate governance regimes with strong minority owner protection. Although there were no instances of shareholder activism in the Netherlands in 2009 due to the crisis, event-driven HFs returned in 2010. However, whereas the majority of activist HFs before the crisis came from the USA and the UK, since then they have increasingly been replaced by domestic activists. Before the crisis the HFs concerned were accused of acting in concert, although attempts to prove this have failed. The owner-ship stake from which they launched their activism ranged from less than 1 per cent to more than 10 per cent but most had around 5 per cent. In many instances, the activists focused on issues arising from managerial strategy, such as mergers, divestments, or control issues. The crisis does not seem to have changed that. In contrast to recent instances of shareholder activism in the UK (Barclays) and the USA (Citigroup) over pay packages, there has as of yet been no activism in the Netherlands over executive remuneration in the financial sector.

Sovereign Wealth Funds

Although there have been heated public debates in the Netherlands about the need to set up a CFIUS-like agency or a special code of con-duct for SWFs to regulate substantial stockholdings, no such initia-tives have yet occurred. Most SWF investments in the Netherlands are small (less than 1 per cent) and are not aimed at control. There were seventy-four known investments in Dutch publicly-quoted firms during 2002–07 by the twenty largest SWFs, of which twelve exceed the 1 per cent threshold (Fernandes 2011). Much more substantial are direct investments by Asian firms, such as the holding in ECT, the largest container terminal operator in Rotterdam, by Hutchinson Port Holdings of China. However, firm-to-firm investments are in general viewed as forms of state capitalism and are taken to fall outside the scope of this chapter.

Given their small size and conventional nature, these investments have largely remained below the political radar. The high tide of political contestation over the rise of SWFs in the Netherlands on the back of the crisis seems to have passed, although in the euro-crisis Asian SWFs have increasingly been approached by peripheral gov-ernments as potential buyers of state assets in an attempt to alleviate debt burdens. Instead, the increasing number of Dutch envoys to places like Hong Kong, Taiwan, and Mainland China suggest a will-ingness to open the country for Chinese investments. It remains to be seen whether this depoliticized stance towards SWFs will survive a politically salient future takeover, such as the one that is curently being undertaken by the Mexican telecoms giant Américo Móvil of former state firm KPN.

Social Consequences

In this section, I discuss the labour outcomes of the activities of foreign NIFs. I first discuss the impact of PE funds before focusing on activist HFs. Given the conventional portfolio stakes of SWFs, this section will not provide a separate discussion of their impact.

Private Equity Funds

Since there are no standardized longitudinal data available on the labour outcomes of PE buy-outs in the Netherlands, it is not easy to assess their effects. Most relevant in this context is work done by the Rotterdam-based team of Hans Bruining and the UK-based team of Mike Wright. In a 2005 paper, they used the Centre for Management Buy-out Research database, which traces buy-outs since the late 1970s and now contains records of well over 16,000 buy-outs in the UK and Europe, to investigate the performance of forty-five Dutch buy-outs of more than €7.5 million. Their conclusions were threefold. There was (i) no erosion of so-called high commitment HR policies; (ii) no decrease in job protection, work conditions, employment rights, or employment levels; (iii) no noticeable effect on voice rights, level of unionization, or the effectiveness of the works council (Bruining et al. 2005).

According to these authors, the potentially detrimental effects of buy-outs were largely absorbed by features of the Dutch industrial relations system determined at the sector and national level. Given the high degree of labour protection in the Netherlands, Dutch firms are 'institutionally protected', limiting the scope of manoeuvring for capital providers (Bruining et al. 2005). Over and above that, Bruining and colleagues report increases in the quality of HRM policies after the buy-out which cannot be explained by Dutch employment and industrial relations arrangements (Bruining et al. 2005). This suggests a 'ratcheting-up' effect of buy-outs on HRM policies. However, this dataset includes both PE and non-PE buy-outs and hence the conclusion that PE buy-outs are responsible for this ratcheting-up effect is on shaky foundations.

More recent research has shown that PE buy-outs in the Netherlands have beneficial effects on the quality of entrepreneurial and administrative management of the firm in question (Bruining et al. 2011). However, a comparison of the effects on HRM practices of PE and non-PE buy-outs in the UK and the Netherlands has demonstrated that PE buy-outs in the Netherlands lead to a weakening of HRM practices, suggesting that the positive effects observed in the 2005 study were due to non-PE buy-outs. This research contrasts with that in the UK. Hence Bacon et al. conclude that their findings offer support for concern about 'the adverse implications of PE and buy-outs for the European social model given the spread of Anglo-American practices into mainland Europe' (Bacon et al. 2008: 1427). Their tentative explanation is that in the Netherlands PE funds focus primarily on buying out distressed firms, resulting in trade unions and works councils being willing to collaborate in cost-cutting exercises in order to save jobs, whereas in the UK PE funds tend to select under-invested firms to enhance value, resulting in the opposite effect, that is, improved HRM practices (Bacon et al. 2008: 1427).

An interesting case of PE activity in the Netherlands concerns the department store chain Hema. Declining profitability of its parent group Vendex KBB from the early 2000s onwards led to a public-to-private buy-out by a coalition of Dutch PE firm Alpinvest and US PE firm KKR. The PE owners awarded themselves a special dividend, financed by loans, and sold some real estate. In early 2007 it was decided to sell the Hema part of the business, resulting in its acquisition by a group of funds led by UK-based PE firm Lion Capital. High levels of debt incurred to finance the acquisition meant that Hema made losses in 2007 and 2008. Lion attempted to sell Hema in 2009 but it proved impossible for PE funds to raise the funding required. The sale was cancelled and Lion increased its equity stake. Since 2007 there have been several trade union campaigns about deteriorating employment conditions at Hema. In 2009 the FNV Bondgenoten union organized a successful one-day strike to increase wages at a central distribution depot and took legal action against the company. Since then industrial relations have become more peaceful. The growth strategy adopted by the company has paid off with new store openings and some increase in employment.

Despite some traces of deteriorating employment and industrial relations, there has been hardly any overt opposition by trade unions to PE activities. Some local Dutch labour unions did rally around specific ownership events involving PE funds. They claimed that public-to-private buy-outs burdened firms with debt, resulting in declining investments, higher throughput, and declining employment conditions. However, no concerted attempt has been made by peak-level unions systematically to counter the claims made by PE lobby organizations about the beneficial effects of PE fund buy-outs. Nor have they tried to leverage their position in the influential

Socio-Economic Council to initiate more restrictive legislation for foreign PE funds.

Union acquiescence could be due to a lack of resources, a lack of interest, or a lack of clear-cut proof of detrimental effects on working conditions and employment. Moreover, since the crisis, Anglo-American PE funds, which used to dominate the market for large buy-outs, have radically diminished their Dutch presence, thereby lessening the need for Dutch labour unions to rally around 'victims' of foreign PE buy-outs. It is much easier to mobilize around foreign buy-outs than it is to mobilize against domestic PE funds.

The latest development in PE activities in the Netherlands is their increasing presence in (newly) privatized domains of the Dutch welfare state. As a consequence of attempts to enhance female labour market participation many European governments have established policies for providing childcare facilities. While the Netherlands was a latecomer in this area (Esping-Andersen 1999), and is still known for its high share of female part-time workers (Visser 1999), since 2005 fiscal subsidies have given a large boost to the number of children in pre-school and after-school childcare. This has turned childcare into a growth industry, which, because of its steady income stream, has proved to be attractive to Anglo-American PE funds. The most notable case is that of Providence Equity Partners, owner of the Estro Group, the biggest childcare provider in the Netherlands with over 600 facilities. While childcare is offered by private companies, it is strongly reliant on state subsidies. Recent cutbacks in these subsidies have therefore had significant consequences for the business model of large childcare providers, forcing Estro for instance to renegotiate the covenants on its bank loans.

Recently PE funds have also moved into Dutch healthcare. On the back of a partial privatization of Dutch healthcare in 2005, PE funds are actively participating in the wave of consolidation this has set in motion. Most of these PE funds are of domestic origin. When current restrictions on for-profit business models are lifted, as is currently being debated in the Dutch Parliament, foreign PE funds and care and cure providers can be expected to enter the Dutch market in larger numbers.

Hedge Funds

Identifying the effects of HF activism is even harder than for PE funds. Given the limited number of cases and their one-off nature, it is not easy to link instances of activism to long-term consequences for industrial relations, HRM practices, and employment numbers. This is due to multi-causality and uncertain causal linkages. HFs reach their stated objectives in only half of the cases they become involved in. Moreover, most of these cases deal with corporate governance issues followed closely by strategic issues like mergers or divestments. Although critical for the long-term future of corporations, they are several times removed from the determination of employment conditions. The general target of activist HFs is improving 'capital efficiency' rather than transforming employment policies. Even when activist HFs succeed in parachuting friendly managers onto the board of directors, it is mostly for limited duration, that is until the mission is accomplished. So, even more than is the case with PE buy-outs, employment conditions in firms subject to HF activism tend to be determined almost completely by the general institutional environment or by exogenous variables only tangentially related to the motives of the HF in question. This too is because of the nature of the intervention. Once the 'event' has been triggered and the anticipated wealth effects have been realized, activist HFs generally leave the scene and are hence no longer directly responsible for what happens next (Brav et al. 2008; Clifford 2008; Klein and Zur 2006, 2009). In addition, labour effects are constrained by Dutch employment and industrial relations institutions.

This is clearly demonstrated by the extreme case of the involvement of activist HF The Children's Investment Fund (TCI) in ABN Amro. The initial target was a large and ambitious, but under-performing bank that was pressed by its activist suitor to replace its management or embark on a merger to enhance its capital efficiency. This resulted in a series of moves by the incumbent management which ultimately led to the largest cross-border bank takeover ever, finalized before the deepening of the financial crisis in September 2008. The subsequent nationalization of the Dutch remainder of ABN Amro and Fortis, combined with a sharp drop in financial activities after the crisis and the crisis response of enhanced regulation, resulted in tens of thousands of job losses. In the UK, the Royal Bank of Scotland, which had acquired the wholesale arm of ABN Amro, also encountered severe economic difficulties and had to be nationalized. However, it is stretching causality to ascribe these losses directly to TCI, even though its actions triggered the subsequent series of events.

Conclusions

I began this chapter with the expectation that the hybrid nature of the Dutch political economy would result in a compartmentalized mode of financialization. This would be shown by (i) an intermediate level of NIF penetration; (ii) a low level of NIF impact in terms of labour outcomes; and (iii) a low level of public contestation over their activities.

The first of these expectations is clearly borne out. The Netherlands is indeed hospitable to foreign NIFs and has hence become one of the larger European markets for Anglo-American PE funds and event-driven HFs. However, the crisis of 2008 seems to have changed all that. Foreign PE funds appear to have sold most of their stakes, while HF activism seems to have shifted to domestic raiders. This is not due to legal and regulatory changes, but to the re-nationalization of capital as a result of the on-going euro-crisis. Nevertheless, there are also signs of Dutch 'gold-plating' of EU directives so as to control Anglo-American NIFs more effectively. Moreover there still is the possibility that continuing political discussions about the causes of the crisis will ultimately result in stricter fiscal treatment of debt financing and the 'carry' of HF and PE partners. Whether this indicates a shift to a more contested mode of financialization, as befits a CME, remains to be seen.

While the crisis has affected the deployment of Anglo-American NIFs in the Netherlands, they have not disappeared from the scene. After dropping off in 2009, the following two years saw activism at almost pre-crisis levels, due to the huge cash reserves of many publicly-quoted firms. Nevertheless, a larger share of that activism is by other investors than HFs and is now initiated to a larger extent by domestic funds. The same is true for foreign PE funds. They too have become regular players in the Dutch market for corporate control, even though they have scaled back their investments—from €2.3 billion in 2007 to €0.9 billion in 2010. This is largely due to a noticeable decline in public-to-private buy-outs. Despite this, Anglo-American PE funds have simultaneously moved into newly privatized sectors like childcare and, to a more limited extent, healthcare. What remains uncertain is the post-crisis fate of Dutch firms that were subjected to highly leveraged buy-outs. Many of these firms were taken over with borrowed capital in the form of secured five-year loans which will have to be rolled over from 2013 onwards. While debts of up to 90 per cent of total assets were normal before the crisis, PE funds may find it difficult to renew those loans against similar conditions, given the de-leveraging of banks, the re-nationalization of capital, and the flight to safety of investors.

In terms of labour outcomes, too, my expectations have largely been corroborated up to this date. Despite data problems, the conclusion that buy-outs have not had a significant negative effect on industrial relations and work relations in most cases. This is due to the fact that labour market regulation and economic citizenship rights are determined at the national and sector level and are hence non-negotiable at the firm level. This diminishes the freedom of action of owners as well as managers. This is corroborated by the case of a retail firm (Hema) subject to serial buy-outs. However, on the basis of econometric analysis, Bacon et al. (2008) found traces of eroding HRM practices in Dutch firms subject to PE buy-outs. This could be attributed to the fact that in the Netherlands, foreign PE funds are mainly targeting distressed firms and, in these cases, labour unions may be more willing to accept harsher working conditions in exchange for securing employment. HF activism proved to be too fleeting to attribute particular labour outcomes to it with confidence, as was suggested in the extreme case of ABN Amro and TCI. Moreover, strong employment losses in this case were at least partially attributable to exogenous variables such as the declines in bank profitability and the size and amounts of financial transactions in the wake of the crisis.

Finally, in terms of public controversy a more mixed picture emerges. Before the crisis there was a striking mis-match between the lack of robust empirical evidence for negative labour impacts of Anglo-American NIFs and the strong negative tone of public discussions about them. An earlier analysis of newspaper reporting and public statements of Dutch politicians between 2000 and 2007 suggested a powerful coalition of liberal commentators, politicians, and labour union officials, backed by a network of 'old boys' and their interlocking directorates, that tried to whip up public sentiment against these newcomers (Engelen et al. 2008). Moreover, this stood in stark contrast to policy initiatives to market the Netherlands internationally as a safe haven for investors, as a result of strong lobbying from financial interests after the ABN Amro tragedy (Engelen and Glasmacher 2012).

This was partly due to contingencies. In general, the public perception of NIFs is strongly determined by high profile cases. In the Dutch setting, these were ABN Amro and TCI (for activist HFs) and the buy-out of a large publisher, home to four of the five Dutch quality newspapers, by the UK-based PE Apax in 2004. The first of these de-legitimated pro-shareholder arguments and fed a nostalgic longing for safeguards to protect Dutch companies. The latter provided a substantial segment of influential Dutch journalists with hands-on experience of the labour outcomes of PE buy-outs. But, given the lack of quantifiable detrimental employment and industrial relations effects, this clearly was 'much ado about nothing'.

The post-crisis picture is more complex. As large public to private buy-outs have disappeared (for now) things on the PE front seem quiet. The same is true for HF activism, which now either targets smaller firms or pursues defensive activist strategies such as contesting takeover bids mounted by others. Moreover, while ABN Amro continues to embarrass those politically responsible, the fallout from the crisis in the Netherlands was such that a reluctant government is increasingly being forced by Dutch voters and EU legislation to clamp down on banks, financial markets, and other financial players. Whether this will ultimately transform the Dutch case from compartmentalized into contested financialization it is too soon to tell. But it is clear that the Netherlands is retracing some of its earlier steps towards the Anglo-American model.

NOTES

1. Alpinvest was co-owned by PGGM and ABP, the two largest (public) pension funds of the Netherlands, and was subject to a management buy-out, partly financed by the US-based PE fund Carlyle Group, in early 2011. (EVCA 2011; NVP 2011).

BIBLIOGRAPHY

Aalbers, M., E. Engelen, and Glasmacher, A. (2011). ' "Cognitive Closure" in the Netherlands: Mortgage securitization in a hybrid European political economy', *Environment & Planning A*, 43 (8): 1779–95.

AFM (2005). *Hedge Funds: An Exploratory Study of Conduct Related Issues.* Amsterdam: AFM. Financial Market Authority (AFM).

Amable, B. (2003). *The Diversity of Modern Capitalism.* Oxford: Oxford University Press.

Bacon, N., Wright, M., Scholes, L., and Meuleman, M. (2008). 'The effects of private equity and buy-outs on HRM in the UK and the Netherlands', *Human Relations*, 61 (10): 1399–433.

Brav, A., Jiang, W., Partnoy, F., and Thomas, R. (2008). 'Hedge fund activism, corporate governance, and firm performance', *Journal of Finance*, 63 (4): 1729–75.

Bruining, H., Boselie, P., Wright, M., and Bacon, N. (2005). 'The impact of business ownership change on employee relations: Buy-outs in the UK and Netherlands', *International Journal of Human Resource Management*, 16: 345–65.

Bruining, H., Verwaal, E., and Wright, M. (2011). 'Private equity and entrepreneurial management in management buy-outs', *Small Business Economics*, DOI 10.1007/s11187-011-9386-8.

Clifford, C. (2008). 'Value creation or destruction? Hedge funds as shareholder activists', *Journal of Corporate Finance*, 14: 323–36.

de Jong, A., Roosenboom, P., Verbeek, M., and Verwijmeren, P. (2007). *Hedgefondsen en Private Equity in Nederland*. Rotterdam: RSM/EUR.

De Volkskrant (2008). 'Fiscus Spekt Kas van Opkoopfondsen', 21 August.

DNB (2012). *Jaarverslag 2012*. Amsterdam: De Nederlandsche Bank (DNB).

Ebbinghaus, B. (ed.) (2011). *The Varieties of Pension Governance: Pension Privatization in Europe*. Oxford: Oxford University Press.

Engelen, E. (2000). *Economisch Burgerschap in de Onderneming: Een Oefening in Concreet Utopisme*. Amsterdam: ThelaThesis.

Engelen, E. (2004). 'Problems of descriptive representation in Dutch works councils', *Political Studies*, 52 (3): 491–507.

Engelen, E. and Glasmacher, A. (2012). 'Multiple financial modernities: International financial centres, urban boosters and the internet as the site of negotiations', *Regional Studies*, DOI:10.1080/00343404.2011.624510.

Engelen, E. and Konings, M. (2010). 'Financial capitalism resurgent: Comparative institutionalism and the challenges of financialization', in G. Morgan, J. Campbell, C. Crouch, and O. Pedersen (eds), *The Oxford Handbook of Comparative Institutional Analysis*. Oxford: Oxford University Press, 601–24.

Engelen, E., Konings, M., and Fernandez, R. (2008). 'The rise of activist investors and patterns of political response: Lessons on agency', *Socio-Economic Review*, 6: 611–36.

Engelen, E., Konings, M., and Fernandez, R. (2010). 'Geographies of financialization in disarray: The Dutch case in comparative perspective', *Economic Geography*, 86 (1): 53–73.

Esping-Andersen, G. (1990). *Three Worlds of Welfare Capitalism*. Oxford: Polity Press.

Esping-Andersen, G. (1999). *Social Foundations of Postindustrial Democracies*. Oxford: Oxford University Press.

EVCA (2011). EVCA Yearbook 2011. Zaventem: EVCA.

Fernandes, N. (2011). 'Sovereign Wealth Funds: Investment Choices and Implications Around the World', 1 March, <http://papers.ssrn.com/sol3/papers.cfm?abstract_id=1341692>.

FESE (2008). 'Share Ownership Structure in Europe', December, <http://www.fese.be/_lib/files/Share_Ownership_Survey_2007_Final.pdf>, Federation of European Securities Exchanges (FESE).

FSB (2011). 'Shadow Banking: Strengthening Oversight and Regulation Recommendations of the Financial Stability Board', 27 October, <http://www.financialstabilityboard.org/publications/r_111027a.pdf>, Financial Stability Board (FSB).

Gourevitch, P. and Shinn, J. (2005). *Political Power and Corporate Control: The New Global Politics of Corporate Governance*, Princeton, NJ: Princeton University Press.

Hall, P. and Soskice, D. (2001). *Varieties of Capitalism: The Institutional Foundations of Comparative Advantage*. Oxford: Oxford University Press.

IFSL (2011). *Hedge Fund Report*. <http://www.thehedgefundjournal.com/magazine/201005/commentary/ifsl-hedge-funds-2010.php>. International Financial Services, London (IFSL).

Katzenstein, P. (1985). *Small States in World Markets: Industrial Policy in Europe*. Ithaca, NY: Cornell University Press.

Katzenstein, P. (2003). 'Small states and small states revisited', *New Political Economy*, 8: 9–30.

Klein, A. and Zur, E. (2006). 'Hedge Fund Activism', NYU Working Paper, CLB-06-017, October, <http://ssrn.com/abstract=1291605>.

Klein, A. and Zur, E. (2009). 'The Impact of Hedge Fund Activism on the Target Firm's Existing Bondholders', 21 November, <http://ssrn.com/abstract=1526527>.

La Porta, R., Lopez-de-Silanes, F., Shleifer, A., and Vishny, R. (1998). 'Law and finance', *Journal of Political Economy*, 106 (6): 1113–55.

Ministerie van Financiën (2012). *Voorstel van Wet AIFM-Richtlijn*. 19 April, <http://www.rijksoverheid.nl/ministeries/fin/documenten-en-publicaties/kamerstukken/2012/04/19/voorstel-van-wet-aifm-richtlijn.html>.

NVP (2010). 'Ondernemend Vermogen: De Nederlandse Private Equity Markt in 2009', Amsterdam: Nederlandse Vereniging van Participatiemaatschappijen (NVP).

NVP (2011). 'Ondernemend Vermogen: De Nederlandse Private Equity Markt in 2010', Amsterdam: Nederlandse Vereniging van Participatiemaatschappijen (NVP), <http://www.nvp.nl/data_files/Ondernemend%20Vermogen%202010.pdf>.

NVP (2003–2011). *Annual Reports*. Amsterdam: Nederlandse Vereniging van Participatiemaatschappijen (NVP).

OECD (2008). 'OECD Indicators of Employment Protection', Paris: OECD, <http://www.oecd.org/document/11/0,3746,en_2649_37457_42695243_1_1_1_37457,00.html>.

Risseeuw, P. and Dosker, R. (2011). *Trust Matters*. Amsterdam: SEO.

Rogers, J. and W. Streeck (1995). *Works Councils: Consultation, Representation and Cooperation in Industrial Relations.* Chicago: University of Chicago Press.

SER (2010). 'Zzp'ers in Beeld: Een Integrale Visie op Zelfstandigen Zonder Personeel', October, 4, Den Haag: SER, <http://www.ser.nl/~/media/DB_Adviezen/2010_2019/2010/b29123.ashx>.

Souren, M. (2008). 'CBS-berichten: Meer flexwerkers, maar niet op alle fronten', *Tijdschrift voor Arbeidsvraagstukken*, 24 (4): 460–4.

Streeck, W. (1992). *Social Institutions and EconomicPerformance.* London: Sage.

Streeck, W. (2009). *Re-Forming Capitalism: Institutional Change in the German Political Economy.* Oxford: Oxford University Press.

Van der Sangen, G. (2003a). 'Het enquêterecht als bron van nieuw ondernemingsrecht: Beschouwingen over de uitdijende reikwijdte van het enquêterecht I', *Tijdschrift voor Ondernemingsbestuur*, 1, <http://arno.uvt.nl/show.cgi?fid=6063>.

Van der Sangen, G. (2003b). 'Het enquêterecht als bron voor nieuw ondernemingsrecht? II', *Tijdschrift voor Ondernemingsbestuur*, 2, <http://arno.uvt.nl/show.cgi?fid=6197>.

Visser, J. (1999). *De sociologie van het halve werk.* Amsterdam: Vossiuspers AUP.

Visser, J. and Hemerijck, A. (1997). *A Dutch Miracle: Job Growth, Welfare Reform, and Corporatism in the Netherlands.* Amsterdam: Amsterdam University Press.

Vleggeert, J. (2009). *Aftrekbeperkingen van de Rente in het Internationale Belastingrecht.* Deventer: Kluwer.

Wilthagen, A. and Tros, F. (2005). 'The concept of "flexicurity": A new approach to regulating employment and labor markets', *The ICFAI Journal of Employment Law*, 3 (1), 7–24.

7

A Capital–Labour Accord on Financialization? The Growth and Impact of New Investment Funds in Sweden

TOMAS KORPI

Corporate Governance and Worker Interests

Ownership of and investments in private companies, often labelled corporate governance, is generally examined from the perspectives of owners or shareholders. While this may seem an obvious analytical starting point, it neglects the interests of workers in these issues. Corporate governance clearly affects shop floor labour relations, and may also impact on company growth, wage development, and job stability. Moreover, from the perspective of labour more generally, ownership and investment may influence business cycles, economic growth, balance of payments, and income distribution (Bergström and Södersten 1994). Investments in companies tend to be strongly pro-cyclical, and reducing this connection could smooth business cycles. Investments may of course also impact on economic growth, not only of individual companies but of the economy as a whole. Investments may also affect the balance of payments to the extent that investments are financed by foreign capital. Finally, ownership tends to be highly concentrated, and policies affecting capital formation will therefore impact on the distribution of wealth and income in society.

There are therefore several reasons why labour should have a direct interest in decisions around ownership and investment. What form such an interest may take is of course another question and a case in point is the Swedish labour movement's evolving approach to corporate governance during the post-war period. While governance issues have been high on the agenda throughout the whole period, the policies pursued have changed dramatically over time. The Social Democratic party, the political arm of the Swedish labour movement has, for instance, used public investment companies as well as tax policy to directly influence the level and direction of company investments, whilst the second arm, the trade union movement, has attempted to influence growth through the wage bargaining process. Another union initiative was the much-debated wage-earner funds, whose purpose was to strengthen employee voice within companies as well as to guarantee that company profits were reinvested. With the exception of the latter proposal, labour's policy vis-à-vis private ownership of production was often described as a compromise, as a deal struck between labour and capital to the benefit of both.

The latest phase of this evolving engagement came with the deregulation of financial markets in the late 1980s, dramatically changing Swedish corporate ownership. Among the subsequent developments is the rise of so-called new investment funds (NIFs), that is, private equity (PE), hedge funds (HFs), and sovereign wealth funds (SWFs). These funds can be seen as one dimension of the broader concept of financialization. This is the notion that the structure of contemporary market economies has shifted from long-term 'real' production towards short-term financial movements.

In the light of the vocal criticisms of NIFs heard elsewhere, the stance of Swedish labour appears strikingly different. Much of the legislation opening up Swedish markets for NIFs was in fact enacted under Social Democratic governments, and trade unions have been guardedly positive in their assessment of the funds. The purpose of this chapter is to examine the causes and consequences of these changes in Swedish corporate governance from a labour perspective. The question is posed whether the current position can be described as a new type of labour-capital accord. We do so by first reviewing the changes in the Swedish labour movement's approaches to private sector ownership and investment, paying special attention to the move towards a more market-based approach in the 1980s that triggered the growth of NIFs. Particular emphasis will be placed on the arguments of the two traditional arms of the labour movement: the Social Democratic Party and the Trade Union Confederation LO (*Landsorganisationen i Sverige*). Thereafter we consider the development of these funds, using extant data to discuss changes in investments over time as well as analyse the available evidence regarding the impact of the funds on employment, wages, and employment relations. We conclude by considering labour's current approach to corporate governance and by assessing whether this is an alternative way for organized labour to pursue its interests.

The Political Economy of Ownership and Investment

Compared to other industrialized nations, Sweden is a country with well-organized employer organizations, high union density, central-ized bargaining, strong employment protection, extensive social insurance programmes, and a long tradition of active labour market policies. While recent years have seen changes in many of these areas, Sweden in many ways is (or at least was) a typical example of what Hall and Soskice (2001) called a coordinated market economy.

The Era of Coordination

The above characterization focuses largely on the labour market and on social protection, the classic areas of bi- and tripartite bargaining. Nevertheless, during the heyday of Swedish 'coordination' this also included questions relating to ownership and investment. The inter-ests of labour generated discussions within the labour movement over issues ranging from employer prerogatives regarding the work process at the shop floor level to the legitimacy of private ownership of the means of production.

The reformist stance of Swedish labour generally led it to accept private property rights, and to strive to improve the conditions of labour within the existing system. However, this did not imply that labour relinquished all matters of ownership to business. Rather, it is frequently stated that labour's policies came to further the interest of both labour and business, in particular that of big business. Three examples may illustrate this: 'golden' shares, 'bound' shares, and 're-investment' funds. The general principle on differentiated voting rights introduced in the Swedish Companies Act (*Aktiebolagslagen*, ABL) of 1944 was that B-shares should carry the weight of one-tenth of the voting rights of A-shares. An exception was, however, made for companies that previously had introduced golden A-shares, that is shares with up to 1,000 times the votes of B-shares, and this happened to include many of the largest Swedish companies. This allowed holders of golden shares to exert voting rights disproportionate to their investment, and to retain control without a substantial capital commitment (Högfeldt 2006; Schnyder 2008).

Bound shares relates to foreign ownership of Swedish businesses, and dates back to the ABL of 1910. This stipulated that only Swedish-controlled companies could acquire real estate without obtaining government approval, and permitted companies to prove that they were not run by foreign interests through voluntary ceilings on foreign stock ownership and voting rights. While not formally prohibiting foreign ownership the law clearly discouraged it, allowing Swedish business to control companies without having to fear foreign intervention (Högfeldt 2006; Schnyder 2008).

The final example relates to government policies regarding profits and investments. The policies encompassed a multitude of instruments, one of which was re-investment funds. Throughout a large part of the post-war period, the taxation of corporate profits hovered around 50 per cent. However, firms were permitted to exempt some of their profits from tax by depositing them in an account at the Central Bank reserved for re-investment expenses. In particular among large companies, retained earnings therefore became an important source of investment financing, allowing firms to continue to expand (Bergström and Södersten 1994; Högfelt 2006; Pontusson 1992).

In addition, Swedish corporate ownership during this period was characterized by a pyramid structure, often with a bank-affiliated company at the top. Sweden could therefore be said to have had a bank-based system of business finance, in which financing was organized between companies and their house banks. Retained earnings and bank loans were the source of most corporate sector funding, with banks a particularly important source of business finance among SMEs. This system displayed clear similarities with the systems existing in many other European countries, and in particular with those of other Nordic countries (Hyytinen and Pajarinen 2001). A high degree of ownership concentration was also a characteristic of Swedish corporate ownership.

Whilst these policies furthered the interests of business, they also furthered those of labour (Högfeldt 2006; Schnyder 2008). The policies supported a core of large Swedish firms providing stable employment to increasing portions of the labour force. They also served the purpose of limiting income inequality by creating a small propertied class and discouraging the payment of dividends. Finally, the policies stimulated the creation of a fairly limited set of owners and managers, giving the labour movement a clearly identifiable partner for bargaining purposes.

The spate of legislation enacted in the period immediately after the Second World War was followed by another wave in the 1970s, and particularly important for labour's current stance vis-à-vis NIFs are two acts from the middle of the decade. The Employee Consultation and Participation in Working Life Act (*Medbestämmandelagen*, MBL) was enacted in 1975 and has since been the main piece of legislation regulating Swedish trade unions' information and consultation rights. Among the Act's provisions is a requirement that employers negotiate with unions regarding important changes to the company as well as to work and employment conditions. It also imposes an obligation on employers to inform unions regarding company developments with respect to production and economic prospects. Finally, employers are required to provide unions with opportunities to examine the accounts, budgets, and other company materials to the extent that this is necessary for unions to safeguard the interests of their members.

The Act also regulates layoff notifications in the case of shortages of work. Regulations regarding layoff and dismissal are furthermore found in the Employment Protection Act (*Lagen om anställningsskydd*, LAS) from 1974, including the requirement that there be just cause for dismissals brought about by a lack of work, and that the reasons should be related to the work of the individual employees affected. It should be noted that shortage of work not only implies a drop in sales but also changes initiated by the employer in the management of the company. Although most of the Act's provisions are mandatory, some provisions may be side-stepped through collective agreements at the sectoral and/or local level. This applies, for instance, to the order of selection for layoffs, which otherwise prioritizes seniority and age.[1]

A New Ownership Regime

This landscape began to change in the late 1970s and early 1980s. Then, in a series of steps between 1985 and 1989, Sweden deregulated the financial sector by removing or relaxing regulations on prices and interest rates, foreign ownership, and domestic and international transactions (Englund 1990). This included the elimination of bound shares as well as re-investment funds, though extremely differentiated voting rights (initially) remained.

The driving forces behind this sea-change were numerous, and are perhaps best summarized as an interaction of structural and ideological changes (Jonung 1993; Telasuo 2000). Important dimensions were the sizeable budget deficits generated by the counter-cyclical fiscal policies of a centre-right government following the oil crises in the 1970s. This was to be financed by loans, and banks were required to purchase fixed-interest government bonds. Private sector loans (to both households and business) were instead routed through alternative, unregulated, channels. The deregulatory initiatives were therefore in part motivated by a desire to simplify government debt financing and to reduce the size of the grey financial sector (Drees and Pazarbaşıoğlu 1995; Englund 1990). Technological developments, as well as increasing internationalization of Swedish companies, had furthermore made it easier for financial actors and multinationals to circumvent domestic capital regulations (Englund 1990; Wihlborg 1980). A long-term drop in investments in the manufacturing sector was also thought to be linked to the lack of credit, and it was believed that deregulation would ease this constraint as well (Bergström and Södersten 1994).

In addition, despite having remained outside of the European Community (EC) in order to be able to pursue stabilization policies focusing on full employment, access to European markets was a longstanding concern within the Social Democratic leadership (Gustavsson 1998; Magnusson 2009). Increasing integration within the EC had created a growing anxiety regarding Sweden's possibilities for trade, leading to a concern to conform to developments of EC law (Telasuo 2000). This was later coupled with a desire to be an integrated part of this evolving Europe (Carlsson 2003; Sverenius 2000). Finally, key actors within the Social Democratic government that had succeeded the centre-right coalition became convinced of the necessity of deregulation, in part due to the perceived difficulties in regulating the grey financial sector (Book 1997; Telasuo 2000). This conceptual change took place in a context in which conservative parties, parts of business, and prominent academic economists had long been pushing for deregulation (Blyth 2002; Telasuo 2000).

The series of deregulatory measures were passed against strong trade union objections (Book 1997; Telasuo 2000). While white-collar unions were less resistant, the blue-collar confederation LO was resolutely opposed to deregulation. Initially, this traditional strong Social Democratic ally argued that the development of financial markets had increased the salience of capital controls and demanded that existing regulations be retained. The LO feared that deregulation would limit the possibilities for the Swedish government to pursue stabilization policies aiming at full employment. They also worried that deregulation would increase capital outflow, which would imply decreasing domestic investment, something which in turn would result in lower employment. Nonetheless, towards the later stages of the deregulation process, the LO had grudgingly accepted most of the legislative reforms. An exception were the changes in 1989 enabling short-term capital movements, the so-called hard core, to which the LO remained critical. However, as before, these objections from the LO were disregarded by the Social Democratic Cabinet.

While these general regulatory changes set the scene for the rise of NIFs in Sweden, there was also new legislation dealing specifically with the regulation of such funds. The evolution of this legislation illustrates the importance of European developments for Swedish company law. The initial regulation of investment funds dates from the enactment of the 1974 Mutual Funds Act (*Aktiefondslagen*, AFL), coinciding with the passage of the MBL and the LAS. The AFL was based largely on guidelines developed by the EC and the Organization for Economic Cooperation and Development (OECD) in the early 1970s. In 1990 this was replaced by the Act on Collective Investment Funds (*Lagen om värdepappersfonder*, VPFL), which in part was a reaction to the EC's passage of the UCITS Directive in 1985. Although not a member of the EC at the time, Sweden nonetheless sought to adapt national legislation to that of the Community.[2] Compared to prior legislation, the most important aspect of the VPFL was that it enabled foreign-based funds to become active in Sweden. The most recent act is the 2004 Act on Investment Funds (*Lagen om investeringsfonder*, LIF), passed in response to two modifications of the original UCITS Directive in 2002 (Saalman 2005).

Hedge funds (HF) have been allowed to operate in Sweden since the enactment of the 1990 VPFL (Saalman 2005). Currently, HFs are regulated under LIF, whereby they are classified as a type of 'special' fund. There is, in other words, no separate legislation dealing exclusively with HFs, and most of the legislation applying to other funds applies to HFs as well. Obviously, laws such as the ABL, MBL, and LAS apply to the portfolio companies of HFs as well. The special fund status primarily involves investment rights and governance. The former refers to risk management, whereby special funds may deviate from the general risk requirements after obtaining permission from the Swedish Financial Supervisory Authority (SFSA). In principle, a HF may invest in any type of financial asset having obtained approval from the SFSA. The only limitations refer to equity which differs from financial instruments, for example raw materials and real estate (Saalman 2005).

Regarding governance, special funds such as HFs may, with permission from the SFSA, limit their offering to special groups of investors. These groups include, among others, professional investors, investors subscribing to a minimum specified investment, and foreign investors. Some Swedish HFs apply restrictions of this type, but others have taken the opposite tack and in effect function as mutual funds open to the general public (Saalman 2005).

The regulatory situation regarding PE is similar to that of HFs. There is no specific legislation targeted at PE firms while their portfolio companies are subject to legislation such as the MBL. However, PE funds fall outside the LIF since they are not open to the general public and do not allow the return of shares during the lifetime of the fund. They therefore do not require SFSA consent to operate. PE funds also lie outside of the VPFL, as they are considered to provide advice regarding the acquisition and management of companies rather than in relation to financial instruments. In contrast to HFs, the activities of PE funds do not require authorization nor are they the object of supervision by the SFSA (Zimdahl 2009).

By the late 1980s and early 1990s, the changes in the regulatory framework meant that significant steps had been taken away from the bank-based system of business finance. These steps set the stage for the arrival of NIFs. A final piece of the puzzle, which specifically related to PE, involved the investment strategies of the public pension funds. A new pension fund was created by government in 1996 with the specific assignment to invest exclusively in Nordic unlisted companies. In the context of a shift in governance it is notable that the fund's assets came from the dismantled wage-earner funds. In 2001 the remaining public pension funds were also allowed to make PE investments up to a maximum limit of 5 per cent of their capital. However, the pension funds may not invest directly in a company, and as a consequence the pension funds have made substantial investments in the funds of PE firms (Henrekson and Jakobsson 2008).

Yet change was not limited to the financial environment: the labour market and its organizations changed as well. This in particular applies to the trade unions and to wage bargaining. Although Swedish trade unions are still among the strongest in the world, union density has declined to around 70 per cent. There are, however, large variations according to industrial sector, occupation, and age. Density is considerably higher in manufacturing than in services, and higher in the public than in the private sector. It is also higher among white-collar than blue-collar workers and higher among older than younger workers. Consequently, while the Swedish labour force is highly unionized when taken as a whole, it is notably weaker among blue-collar service workers than elsewhere.

High union density is combined with relatively powerful organization. Swedish unions are organized according to occupation and industry rather than religious or political lines, and the vast majority of unions belong to one of three major confederations. In addition, Swedish employers also tend to be more organized than their counterparts in other countries, with many belonging to associations which, in turn, are organized into confederations. In this highly organized setting, three types of collective agreements may be distinguished: between union and employer confederations, between individual unions and employer organizations, and between local unions and individual employers. During the height of coordination, wage bargaining was carried out at the level of the confederations. Wage drift arising from local wage agreements existed, but the central agreements nevertheless set a floor.

The general trend since the early 1980s has been towards decentralization of collective bargaining. Although the confederations may still coordinate the bargaining of their member unions and local branches, individual unions now generally bargain over pay and working conditions. Employers and local unions moreover play an increasingly important role in supplementing the framework agreements signed at the higher levels through local bargaining. As will be discussed further below, these developments in terms of organization and bargaining may influence the way NIFs impact on employment, wages, and employment relations at the company level.

The Current Views of the Social Partners

The regulation of the financial sector has changed dramatically since the early 1980s. Concerning the regulation of PE, the most recent benchmarking report from the European Venture Capital Association (EVCA 2008) claimed that Sweden favours investors slightly less than the European average. Whilst Sweden was less restrictive with regard to pension funds' and insurance companies' investments in venture capital, there were also fewer tax and fiscal Research & Development

(R&D) incentives. European Private Equity and Venture Capital Association (EVCA) tersely noted that 'Sweden does not offer any tax incentives for investors, fund management companies, or funds to invest in private equity and venture capital' (EVCA 2008: 149). Further, although there were tax deductions available for key foreign personnel, there were no tax allowances for business R&D expenditure, R&D capital expenditure, or for the creation of innovative firms. Moreover, both capital gains and income taxes for individuals were higher than the European average. Sweden's position in the EVCA's ranking, and its score on the various items, has been relatively stable since the first benchmarking report in 2003.

The Swedish PE community insists that PE generates benefits for the economy in terms of growth and jobs, claiming that PE-owned companies grow faster than other companies. It also argues for various legislative changes which they believe would enhance the role of PE such as changes in taxation (NIC 2009; SVCA 2011). This contrasts somewhat with the situation for HFs where, in relation to the Alternative Investment Fund Managers Directive, business representatives argued that the Swedish special fund regulations should retain their current form (SIFA 2009).

While Swedish trade unions have expressed some concerns about the effects of PE (Berggren et al. 2003), they have nevertheless also conveyed a cautiously positive attitude to PE firms. Representatives from the LO have stated that PE may supplement ordinary ownership by introducing active owners with access to capital. The central question was not who owns the company, but how the owners acted as managers and in relation to their employees. Moreover, as the Employee Consultation Act provides Swedish unions an opportunity to be involved in restructuring processes, there is also greater legal protection than elsewhere. Finally, the social insurance system provides better protection for employees in cases of restructuring than in most other countries. Nevertheless, the LO argued that risk is unevenly distributed, with managers of PE funds less exposed to risk than employees in the portfolio companies (Independent Living Institute 2008; Thorén 2008). There have also been calls for strengthening the requirements regarding leveraging and information in line with the initial Alternative Investment Fund Managers proposal (Dagens Industri 2010).

Another issue, given the importance of first and second pillar pension funds for the PE market, concerns the development of trade union policy on pension fund investment strategy and corporate governance. The LO has formulated explicit ethical guidelines regarding their capital investments, emphasizing not only that portfolio companies should follow Swedish law (or foreign were applicable) but also that they should obey the core International Labour Organization (ILO) conventions and formulate clear policies regarding, for instance, the remuneration of senior managers (LO 2006). These ethical criteria should be applied conditional on the overarching goal of maximizing the return on pension capital while maintaining a balanced risk profile, which the LO does not see as a contradiction. This exemplifies what the LO terms a restrictive use of ownership power, as opposed to an active use involving attempts to steer companies in a particular direction. Guidelines of this kind have also been formulated by the five major public pension funds, and the LO's corporate governance policy states that similar policies should be developed by all boards on which the LO is represented (LO 2009). Hence, while the LO shies away from an active ownership role, it nevertheless attempts to use the leverage provided by pension capital to set minimum standards regarding the employment practices of portfolio companies.

New Investment Funds

Private equity, HFs, and SWFs are all active in Sweden, and their activity has been increasing since the early 1990s. PE is the most important in terms of amounts invested, although HFs had until recently attracted more publicity due to interventions in some of the largest Swedish companies. This has now changed as a number of PE funds have come under public scrutiny. In contrast, there has been very little discussion of the role played by SWFs.

Regarding the latter, the current government has expressed a generally positive attitude towards SWFs, and Invest in Sweden, a government agency promoting foreign investment in Sweden, attempts to attract investment. SWFs do not appear to be an important issue for unions, whilst the Confederation of Swedish Enterprise has been guardedly positive (Erixon 2007). Information on investments is scant and limited to media reports. These, for instance, indicate that Abu Dhabi Investment owned Swedish stock valued at SEK11 billion in 2007, including around one billion in each of Volvo, Nordea, Ericsson, H&M, and TeliaSonera. This figure amounts to less than 1 per cent of these companies' value on the stock exchange (Hässler 2007). It has also been reported that another Abu Dhabi fund, Mubadala, became a major owner of SAAB through its stake in SAAB's new owner Spyker (Kerpner 2010). The only extensive discussion of SWFs is a background report to the Swedish Globalization Council, a special commission set up by the current government (Ganslandt 2008). Although lacking information on SWF investment in Sweden, the background and final reports from the commission (Braunerhjelm et al. 2009) downplayed the importance of SWFs' investments in Sweden. In sum, despite an alarmist tone in some of the media reports, SWFs do not appear to be a major concern.

As for HFs, the number of HFs registered in Sweden has grown from just over ten in 2001 to around one hundred in 2010. Over the period 2002–07, the proportion of capital managed by HFs never-theless remained relatively stable at around 5 or 6 per cent of total assets under management (Nyberg 2006). However, few follow an activist approach, and this applies to both Swedish and international HFs. In a study of HF activism in Europe over the period 2000–08, Becht et al. (2010) identified eleven interventions by activist funds in Sweden. The funds involved were Hermes Focus Funds, Laxey Partners, Centaurus Capital, Audley Capital, Cevian Capital, and two unnamed funds. Other activist funds known to have invested in Sweden are Icahn Partners and Parvus Asset Management. All of these funds are based in either London or New York with the excep-tion of Cevian, which is based in Stockholm.

Cevian's Swedish connection was also evident in the fact that, although not ranked among the most active funds in the study, Cevian was the one with the clearest focus on Sweden. Of the total of eleven cases of Swedish activism identified, Cevian single-handedly accounted for five. The fund has been involved in a number of well-known Swedish companies, such as the car manufacturer Volvo, the telecommunications firm TeliaSonera, the retail chain Lindex, and the insurance company Skandia.

Cevian's investment strategies are exemplified by its involvement in Skandia, a company providing traditional life insurance, mutual fund savings, insurance, and banking. At the turn of the millen-nium, Skandia (founded in 1855 and the oldest company on the Swedish stock exchange) was rocked by two major crises. The first of these came in the wake of the stock market crash of 2000–02 and affected all major Swedish insurance companies providing pension insurance plans. The crash led to large losses among the companies' customers, who claimed that they had been promised large returns and had not been sufficiently informed regarding the risks involved (Swedish Financial Supervisory Authority 2004). The ambiguous regulations, inadequate information, and lack of consumer protection undermined public trust in insurance companies. The second crisis only involved Skandia, and occurred shortly afterwards in 2003 when several of Skandia's senior managers were accused of financial irregularities. The allegations attracted immense media attention, and involved large unauthorized bonuses and the provision of choice real estate at an extremely low cost (BBC 2003). On top of this came dealings in connection with Skandia's life insurance subsidiary Skandia Liv, whose profits and assets where expropriated by Skandia at the cost of Skandia Liv's share- and policy-holders (Nachemsson-Ekwall and Carlsson 2004). This led to a class action suit by the class action against Skandia Association, its 14,000 members claiming compensation for some 1.2 million life insurance customers (Kollnert and Weber 2008).

Against this background, Skandia suffered a loss of profits and drop in stock prices. By 2003, the share price had fallen to one-tenth of its 1999 value (Norén et al. 2006). Cevian believed that the share price largely reflected its poor reputation and not its potential profitability. In addition, Cevian had noted that Skandia lacked a strong owner: its ownership consisted mainly of institutional funds and no single owner held more than 5 per cent of total shares (Sunesson 2008). In a clearly event-driven move, Cevian acquired 3 per cent of Skandia's shares in December 2004. By 2005 they had increased their holdings to 3.4 per cent, and also controlled an additional 3.5 per cent of total voting rights (AFX News 2005).

A number of measures were outlined by Cevian prior to entry. Some of these (e.g. a reduction in operating costs) were initiated even before Cevian acquired a stake in Skandia, and Cevian's responsibility for them seems limited. Cevain made an impression in other ways. Most important was Cevian's active pursuit of the sale of the company. In September 2005, the South African insurance company Old Mutual announced an interest in acquiring Skandia. The bid triggered a heated public discussion about the future of Skandia and the valuation of the bid (including government intervention and legal action against Old Mutual by the Swedish Shareholders' Association) (Karlsson and Wahlström 2007; Sunesson 2008). Cevian was, however, satisfied, and pushed through the sale against the resistance of other shareholders (Sunesson 2008). In 2006, Skandia was bought by Old Mutual, an acquisition that included all of Cevian's stock.

For Cevian and its partners, the investment was clearly profitable. For Skandia's employees, the consequences of Cevian's purchase are more difficult to assess. Employment was at its lowest in 2004 after a reorganization involving layoffs in Sweden and abroad (i.e. prior to Cevian's entry) and rose thereafter. The appraisal is further complicated by realignments within the company during Cevian's period. From an employee perspective, the bottom line is probably that no aggregate employment reductions took place during Cevian's involvement.

Despite the engagement of sovereign wealth and HFs in major Swedish companies, PE funds appear to be of greater importance. PE investments in Swedish portfolio companies averaged 0.8 per cent of gross domestic product (GDP) over the period 2000–10 and, as evident from Figure 7.1, Sweden is usually placed among the top two European countries in rankings of investments relative to GDP.[3] Still, in terms of absolute size, the Swedish market is substantially smaller than the markets in France and the UK. In 2010, for instance, PE firms invested approximately €2.6 billion in Swedish portfolio companies. This made Sweden the fourth biggest market in Europe, but a far cry from the €12.7 billion invested in the UK.

The size of the Swedish PE industry is also reflected in the size of Swedish PE firms. This is illustrated in Figure 7.2, showing total investments by country of PE firm. The size of the British market is

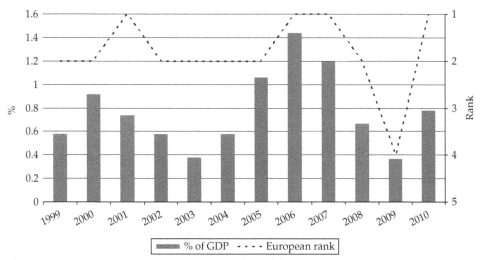

Figure 7.1 *Private equity investments in Swedish portfolio companies (% of GDP)*
Source: EVCA yearbooks.

Figure 7.2 *Investments by private equity firms from selected European countries (€ million)*

Source: EVCA yearbooks.

evident in that it requires a separate scale on the right hand side of the figure. Nonetheless, some Swedish private equity companies are large in an international context. In 2012 EQT and Nordic Capital, both with headquarters in Sweden, were ranked among the fifty largest PE firms by PEI 300.

Figure 7.2 also shows that investments by Swedish PE firms have grown dramatically, and fluctuated widely, over time. Investments remained at a relatively stable level throughout the 1990s, rising slightly towards the end of the decade. A dramatic increase occurred in 1999, and investments have trended upwards ever since. The overall upward trend does, however, include spectacular downturns in Sweden and elsewhere, as a result of the financial crises in 2000/1 and 2008/9. Swedish investment activity was roughly halved in these episodes. This cyclical pattern also applies to the combined Swedish activities of foreign and domestic equity firms, as illustrated in Figure 7.1.

The number of employees in Swedish portfolio companies has of course also varied. Throughout the period 2001–10 it fluctuated between approximately 5 and 7 per cent of the Swedish private sector workforce (Nutek 2003; SVCA 2008). The studies on which these numbers are based are not entirely comparable, so the figures should be taken only as approximations. Nonetheless, it is clear that this is a non-trivial sector of employment in Sweden.

A large part of the capital raised by Swedish PEfirms comes from abroad. Over the period 1999–2009 around 40 per cent of the equity invested in Swedish PE funds came from domestic sources, another 40 per cent came from other European countries and the remaining 20 per cent from outside the continent. These figures are roughly similar to those in other European countries, although the proportion of domestic financing was slightly lower in Sweden.

Figure 7.3 shows the average proportion of funds provided by different types of investors over the period 1999–2009. The biggest single source of equity provided to Swedish equity firms is pension funds, both foreign and domestic. Their placements account for around a quarter of the capital made available. This figure is likely to be an underestimate, since pension funds could also be involved indirectly through the second biggest source, funds-of-funds. These account for slightly more than 10 per cent, and probably include capital from pension funds. As for other sources, insurance companies and banks each provide around 10 per cent of the capital, with the remaining sources being much smaller. This distribution is again similar to the European

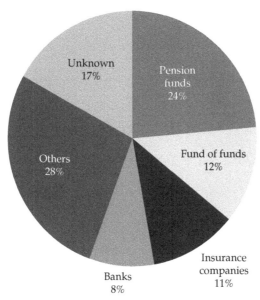

Figure 7.3 *Fundraising by Swedish private equity firms, 1999–2009*
Source: EVCA yearbooks.

average, the one major difference being that banks account for around 20 per cent of the investments in Europe.

Not only has aggregate private equity activity fluctuated over time, the character of investment has also changed. Initially, buy-outs were almost always small acquisitions, but more recently there have been more medium and large buy-outs. However, despite the rise in the average buy-out value between 1995 and 2009, small deals still make up the majority of acquisitions. In the peak year of 2007 twenty-nine of the fifty buy-outs or buy-ins had transaction values of €25 million or less.[4]

It is also interesting to note the evolving investment strategy with regards to sector. One sector that has been of great importance from the start is manufacturing. This is illustrated in Figure 7.4 showing the share of investments in manufacturing and healthcare of the total market value of buy-outs and buy-ins over the period 2000–09. Over the period as a whole, around one-third of total investments were made in the manufacturing sector. However, the manufacturing share shows a downward trend, in part because of increasing investments in healthcare. Large investments were made in the healthcare sector over the period 2004–07, during which healthcare accounted for around 40 per cent of total investments.[5] Investments in healthcare have since declined and, although not included in Figure 7.4, this coincides with an increase in investment in education. The

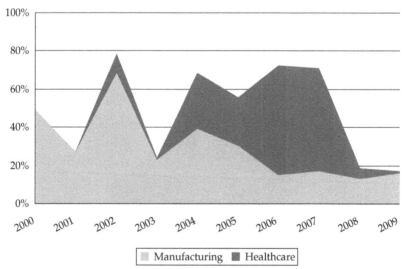

Figure 7.4 *Market value of buy-outs and buy-ins in Sweden, share of selected sectors*
Source: CMBOR.

developments in healthcare and education are both related to the part-privatization of services previously provided exclusively by the public sector.

This successive shift in investment strategy can also be illustrated through three company case studies. The first involves Callenberg, an engineering group specializing in marine electrical automation and heating, ventilation, and air conditioning (HVAC). The company, situated in Uddevalla on the Swedish west coast, was founded in 1951 and acted as a supplier to the area's shipping and shipbuilding industry during its heyday. However, competition from Asian ship-yards and reduction in oil shipments as a result of the oil crises in the 1970s led to a series of closures. Between 1975 and 1987 the number of employees in the Swedish shipbuilding industry involved in the construction of new merchant vessels went from almost 30,000 to zero (Storrie 1993). Callenberg reacted to this convulsion by broaden-ing its markets, first in the USA and then in Asia. In addition, before the crisis the company had started to specialize in system deliveries in electronics, navigation, and communication as well as services to shipping companies and shipyards abroad.

In 1999, Callenberg was acquired by Expanda as part of a bigger purchase. Expanda was a company centred on furniture and design, and its board declared Callenberg's activities extraneous to Expanda's core business and started looking for a partner (Expanda 2001). In 2001, the Swedish PE firm Segulah acquired 80 per cent of Callenberg Group, obtaining the remaining 20 per cent the following year.

According to Segulah, Callenberg lacked focus since its five dif-ferent operating entities acted largely independently (Blomberg and Oleru 2009, upon which the following account is mainly based). Segulah therefore strived to create a larger, more integrated business providing a broader set of services. The primary goal was to gain an advantage by consolidating in a fragmented industry. Callenberg lacked proprietary technology and products, so the focus needed to be on improving services. Segulah's strategy therefore involved replacing parts of the company board with executives from the field of marine engineering and with other executives with relevant indus-try expertise.

During the Segulah period, Callenberg experienced major growth. Turnover in the Callenberg Group increased by a factor of five, mostly through the acquisition of other companies. Segulah investigated alternatives with regard to acquisitions, and as a result Callenberg acquired three other companies engaged in marine engineering and HVAC operations. Profit margins also increased. Furthermore, Segulah explored financing alternatives, both with regard to issues like invoice payments as well as negotiating new bank contracts. The final change involved the introduction of incentive schemes, for example a stock options scheme offered to top management in 2003 (which reduced Segulah's ownership share to 90 per cent).

In November 2007, Segulah and all management shareholders sold their stock to the Wilhelm Wilhelmsen Group. Seen as a whole, Callenberg seems to be a success in which targeted acquisitions enabled the group as a whole to grow and consolidate. The benefits of the expansion for the parent company may, however, be limited and of a more indirect nature. Whereas employment in some of the other members of the group expanded, employment remained relatively stable at the Uddevalla subsidiary. Turnover also fluctuated, even if it grew for the group as a whole. For the Uddevalla branch, the benefits of the expansion seem to lie mainly in the fact that it is now part of a larger conglomerate.

As noted above, investments in manufacturing have been partly replaced by services of various kinds, including telecommunications. One example here is C More, the largest Pay-TV provider in Scandinavia with branches in Sweden, Norway, Denmark, and Finland. The company has its roots in one of the earliest private cable providers FilmNet which in 1997 was acquired by the French broadcasting company Canal+ (Rådet för mångfald inom massmedierna 1997). Canal+ was in turn a branch of the French Vivendi group, and the acquisition was to be the French company's Scandinavian branch. However, Vivendi accumulated substantial debt, and started looking for ways to divest (the following account is based on Schulz et al. 2008). An attempt to let Canal+ go public was unsuccessful, but in 2003 Canal+ was acquired by the two PE companies Baker Capital from the USA and Nordic Capital from Sweden, and re-named C More Entertainment. The total price of the buy-out was €70 million, with the two investors each acquiring a 50 per cent share of the company.

The primary motive for the acquisition of C More was the belief that the private TV market in Scandinavia was an area with growth potential. In addition, Sweden was about to introduce digital television, implying that households would need to sign new television contracts. A parliamentary decision had been made in 1997, and broadcasts had been initiated in 1999. A second parliamentary decision in the spring of 2003 put an end to analogue broadcasting, with regional transmitters closing down between 2005 and 2008. There was therefore an opportunity for expansion without major strategic changes, although the two investors brought in a new Chief Executive Officer, introduced new board members with industry experience, and instituted stronger financial incentives for senior management.

Within fourteen months, C More was able to expand the number of subscribers by almost 100,000 to approximately 800,000. Employment also grew, as did revenue which increased by around 15 per cent between 2002 and 2004. This led to a dramatic increase in the value of the company, and in March 2005, Kanal 5, a branch of SBS Broadcasting, acquired all shares of the C More Group for €270 million. The acquisition by Baker and Nordic took place at a very opportune moment and, since the company was fundamentally profitable, few changes were needed. The expansion in the number of subscribers and the attendant increase in company value then allowed the investors to turn a handsome profit. The takeover also appears fairly positive from an employee point of view, with overall employment increasing somewhat.

The latest change in private equity activity can be illustrated by the British private equity company 3i's 2005 acquisition of Carema, a provider of care services. Carema was originally founded in 1996 under the name of Nordvård and went through a series of mergers prior to the arrival of 3i. This process continued under the new owners, initially with the integration of the Finnish healthcare company Mehiläinen into the newly created Ambea Group. Growth continued thereafter with the acquisition of some two dozen Nordic healthcare companies. These acquisitions are also the primary explanation behind the strong growth in turnover, employment, and profits in the Swedish operation. Turnover and the number of employees doubled between 2004 and 2009, while profits (EBITA) tripled. In a secondary buy-out, 3i sold Ambea to the US-based PE company KKR and the small Swedish PE firm Triton in 2010.

Carema now supplies a wide range of care services to municipalities throughout Sweden, Finland, and Norway, mainly in the areas of elderly care, primary care, outpatient care, and occupational health services. The bulk of the group's business is in Sweden, and is an illustration of the trend towards privatization of Swedish care services. Around 20 per cent of elderly care is supplied by private providers, and the situation is similar in childcare and youth education. A large part of this is provided by PE-owned companies with Carema being one of the largest. A situation of stable or increasing demand (in the case of elderly care), in combination with an equally stable source of income from municipalities, has attracted private equity firms.

Carema's ambition has been to increase profits by increasing efficiency, and this has primarily been secured through changes to the use of staff. However, a series of recent scandals has shown that this has gone too far. The company was rocked by revelations of under-staffing, the replacement of trained personnel by untrained staff, and cases of outright maltreatment in some of its elderly care facilities (Björk 2011). Outrage was also caused by the discovery that, despite their substantial profits before interest, costly internal loans from the PE owners meant that the company paid very limited taxes (Gripenberg 2011). As a result, the Ministry of Finance has stated that they will initiate an oversight of the applicable tax rules. The issue was also debated in Parliament, with scathing critiques of the recent incidents from all sides.

Overall, these cases suggest rather mixed employment outcomes, and hint at sector differences. Yet despite the dramatic growth in the activities of NIFs in Sweden and the public interest in these issues, large-scale quantitative analyses focusing on wages, employment, and working conditions are largely lacking. The previously mentioned reports by the government agency Nutek and the industry association SVCA (Swedish Private Equity & Venture Capital Association) dealing with the PE industry are the most widely cited, and generally conclude that buy-out companies grow faster than all comparison groups. One example is the study of 117 SVCA members and other companies active in the Swedish PE market (SVCA 2008). The study examined employment changes between 2001 and 2006, and reported that median employment growth in PE portfolio companies was 10 per cent. Of the private equity companies studied, 66 per cent grew and 26 per cent shrank, and the remainder saw no change. In the comparison group of companies listed on the Stockholm Stock Exchange, the highest growth was displayed by companies on the Mid Cap list with median growth of 4 per cent. Companies on the Large Cap list showed no change, whereas those on the Small Cap list shrank by 4 per cent. PE growth was particularly strong in the venture capital segment, with seed-corn investments displaying a rise in employment of 19 per cent. Buy-out investments also grew, but here the median employment growth was 3 per cent. This was higher than in the comparison group of all active limited companies with a turnover of between SEK100 million and 10 billion.

Similar results were obtained in both earlier and subsequent studies by the SVCA. Whilst these results are suggestive, the reports point out that the reference groups are less than perfect. Buy-out and reference group companies may differ with respect to size and sector, and comparisons of PE firms with more carefully-defined control groups are necessary to achieve a more precise comparison.

An ambitious attempt at reference group construction is the study by Olsson and Tåg (2012). Using a difference-in-difference approach, they evaluated wages and employment among individuals employed in buy-out companies by comparing them with individuals in other companies that had been matched by sex, age, education, previous earnings, region, sector, firm size, and firm employment growth. The analysis covered approximately 200 private equity buy-outs between 1998 and 2004, and showed employees in buy-out companies to have a slightly lowered risk of unemployment as well as somewhat higher average wages during the four years after the buy-out. Most, but not all, of the higher earnings were related to the reduction in unemployment. At company level there was no difference in employment between the buy-out firms and their matched twins. However, employment growth was lower in those establishments that had previously been part of the buy-out company. The analysis furthermore indicated that the reduction in establishment growth was related to hiring freezes rather than layoffs.

Although the results suggest that private equity buy-outs have a positive impact on wages and employment, caution is needed when interpreting the results. An initial hiring and firing freeze may be expected in the period immediately after a takeover if workforce adjustments are suspended prior to restructuring. Such a delay to reorganization initiatives could, for instance, be the outcome of mandatory labour consultation. This interpretation is consistent with the result that unemployment risk was lowest in the first two years following the buy-out. Whilst there are no clear indications that buy-outs are detrimental to wages and employment, the fairly short follow-up period (four years) means that the long-term consequences of PE buy-outs for employees in portfolio companies remain uncertain.

A longer follow-up period was used by Bergström et al. (2007). They evaluated wages and employment in around seventy buy-out companies between 1998 and 2006 and compared them with the development in their twenty largest peers within narrowly-defined industrial sectors. As shown in Figure 7.4, manufacturing accounted for a large share of private equity investments in the late 1990s and early 2000s, and this is also the case here where around half the buy-out companies examined belonged to the manufacturing sector. A similar predominance of manufacturing companies was also reported by Olsson and Tåg (2012). Although the matching does not capture size and other differences between the PE portfolio companies and their peers (as in Olsson and Tåg 2012), it does take industry-specific developments into account. Instead, the main advantage of this study is the longer follow-up period, as it examined wages and employment over the whole holding period (i.e. pre-entry to post-exit). Despite these differences, the results reported by Bergström et al. (2007) are similar to the firm level results found by Olsson and Tåg (2012) in that there are no effects of buy-outs on either employment or wages. In stark contrast to the SVCA studies mentioned initially, the 'findings suggest that employment and wage levels in the buy-out companies have developed in line with the peer groups' (Bergström et al. 2007: 35).

There is less evidence on the impact of investment funds on working conditions and employment relations. However, a survey carried out recently among local branches of Unionen, the largest trade union in the private sector and the largest white-collar union, looked at how the PE buy-out had impacted on the companies and on employment relations (Unionen 2009). This showed that a majority of the companies had undergone changes in company management as well as cost reduction programmes. Some also had activities outsourced or sold off, although the majority had not. Instead, most had made acquisitions, and developed new markets and products. With regard to employment relations, around 80 per cent of the locals responded that opportunities for conducting union work had improved or were unchanged. However, a minority found that they had experienced a change for the worse. Most also replied that information and consultation had remained unchanged, yet there again was a large minority (30–40 per cent) who believed that access and influence had decreased.

Although these results clearly are interesting, they too would be bolstered by the use of appropriately-constructed comparison groups. As it stands, it is uncertain whether the worsening of employee relations reported by the significant minority is something specific to the buy-out companies, indicative of takeovers more generally, or part of a national trend.

A New Capital–Labour Accord?

Labour's approach to issues related to business ownership and investments has gone through a dramatic turnaround since the halcyon days of coordinated capitalism, and it could be questioned whether Sweden should still be classified as a coordinated market economy. This would in particular seem to apply to the financial sector, where regulatory changes have opened up for market-based finance and transformed Swedish ownership structures.

Deregulation (and changes in regulation in the case of the public pension funds) is also reflected in the massive increase in PE investment. This, and the rise of NIFs more generally, is one particular aspect of the broader notion of financialization. While financialization is said to encompass a wider array of financial phenomena, many of the issues linked to financialization such as debt-financed restructuring and stock option pay, also appear in connection with investment funds.

Of the NIFs examined, the activities of HFs and SWFs are difficult to evaluate due to the dearth of relevant data. More information is available regarding PE funds although there are substantial lacunae here as well.

From a legal perspective, the EVCA benchmarking index shows that Sweden could be perceived as relatively unappealing in some respects to private equity funds. Nevertheless, despite these obstacles, Sweden attracts a substantial amount of PE investment. In fact, in relation to the size of the economy, Sweden ranks about equal with the UK, widely held to be the world's second leading PE market after the USA. This suggests that either the issues mentioned by the EVCA are of lesser importance or that other factors compensate for the difficulties potentially caused by some aspects of Swedish law. In this connection it is interesting to note that the lion's share of PE investment in Sweden is made by foreign investors, that is, those that presumably would be most deterred by Swedish legislation.

Swedish trade unions have emphasized that from their point of view the crucial question is how investment funds impact on employment and other labour-related outcomes. Hard evidence is scarce, and many of the existing analyses consist of fairly simple descriptive breakdowns of trends. The positive claims made by PE interest groups have received little support, yet at the same time there does not seem to be a clear net negative impact of PE investment on employment, wages, and industrial relations. In this perspective, the guardedly positive stance among Swedish unions does not seem unreasonable.

Further caution would, however, seem advisable because the construction of the control groups and the length of the follow-up period in existing studies appear problematic. The results may moreover be sector specific. The non-effect of PE on employment and wages at the company level found by both Olsson and Tåg (2012) and Bergström et al. (2007) is interesting in the light of the sector differences identified by Davis et al. (2008) for the USA. In the latter's analysis of the employment effects of PE investment in the manufacturing sector, no differences in the evolution of employment in the buy-out and control groups were evident. This contrasted starkly with developments in other sectors (e.g. retail trade, services, and finance) where employment dropped noticeably. Reductions in employment among (mainly) non-manufacturing buy-outs were also found by Goergen et al. (2011). In the Swedish studies, manufacturing firms made up a large part of the companies examined. If the lack of a buy-out effect on employment is generic to manufacturing, it opens up the possibility of similar sector differences in Sweden as well. This is also hinted at in the case studies. No explanation is offered for the sector difference by Davis et al. (2008), yet one conjecture is that it is related to differences in production methods. Compared to manufacturing, other sectors tend to be more labour intensive, making it more likely that measures to improve profitability will come at the expense of labour.

Although there is as yet no Swedish analysis of the effects of PE buy-out by sector, it is suggestive that the reduced unemployment risk reported by Olsson and Tåg (2012) is limited to companies needing outside investment financing (see also Boucly et al. 2011 for similar results for France). If there is a reduction in unemployment due to buy-out, it would seem that such firms are more likely to be found in the manufacturing sector than elsewhere. Another indication that PE buy-outs in the other sectors may be more unfavourable for employees comes from the employment patterns in the Swedish care sector. As noted above, PE companies have recently invested heavily in this sector, and PE-owned companies supplied around two-thirds of privately-provided care in 2008 (Szebehely 2011). Although no distinction was made between PE-owned and other private care providers, the result in a recent study that staffing ratios and full-time staffing was substantially lower in private elderly care than publicly-provided care (Stolt et al. 2011) is interesting given the prevalence of PE in this sector.

If these conjectures turn out to be substantiated, this could be problematic for unions. Local co-determination, heralded by unions as a way to influence the activities of PE, is dependent on strong shop floor representation. The importance of a local union presence had been underscored by the trend towards decentralized bargaining, and it is therefore notable that unionization rates are particularly low in the private service sector. This weakness of unions would seem to limit their possibilities to avert restructuring to the detriment of labour in precisely the sector where it may be the most likely.

However, these are possibilities that need further analysis. Another problem with existing research is the exclusive focus on immediate employment outcomes of portfolio companies, disregarding the wider impact of the policy changes. Issues such as the consequences of NIFs on total investment, overall growth rates, and aggregate employment have not been examined, to say nothing of the broader societal consequences of the policy changes.

Whether this should be described as a capital–labour accord on financialization is debatable. One the one hand, many of the regulatory changes opening up in Sweden for the NIFs were made by Social Democratic Cabinets. Likewise, the blue-collar confederation LO, the largest of the Swedish trade union confederations and a longstanding ally of the Social Democrats, backed the change in the public pension funds' placement regulations allowing them to invest in stocks (a change crucial for development of the PE market). Both have also expressed a certain appreciation of PE funds and investments.

On the other hand, apart from the placement regulations, other reforms were resisted by the trade unions. Largely opposed to the regulatory changes, labour has retroactively been forced to accept them as a fait accompli and has had to adapt. In particular, the LO disagreed with the deregulation of international capital mobility that was fundamental for the ascendance of the NIFs. Furthermore, although they have voiced some appreciation for PE firms this is clearly circumscribed. The current stance of the trade unions (and maybe of the labour movement as a whole) should perhaps be summarized as making the best of a bad situation, arguing from a position of weakness rather than from one of strength. Instead of actively trying to shape the market economy to further the interests of organized labour and its members, labour is now restricted to curbing the excesses of the market. An example of this is its insistence on observance of the rather weak ILO conventions. This could of course still be labelled an accord, yet it is one radically different from the earlier compromise.

NOTES

1. In the latest version of OECD's Employment Protection Index from 2003, Sweden's overall score is similar to that of other northern European countries. Sweden's score for permanent employees is somewhat higher (i.e. more protective) and for temporary workers somewhat lower than other countries in North-Central Europe. However, with regard to collective dismissals, Sweden is among the most protective countries (OECD 2004).
2. Sweden joined the European Union, the successor of the EC, in 1996.
3. Unless otherwise stated, all estimates of the Swedish and European private equity market below draw upon the data collected by the SVCA and EVCA through their annual surveys of private equity firms. The original data are not available, limiting the analyses. It is also difficult to assess the quality of the data, yet these are the primary sources of information on the European private equity market.
4. Information kindly supplied by Mike Wright of the Centre for Management Buyout Research (CMBOR).
5. CMBOR data kindly supplied by Mike Wright.

BIBLIOGRAPHY

AFX News (2005). 'RTP Cevian fund now controls 6.9 pct of Skandia: Positive on Old Mutual bid', *Finanznachrichten*, 1 September, <http://www.finanznachrichten.de/nachrichten-2005-09/1952198-rpt-cevian-fund-now-controls-6-9-pct-of-skandia-positive-on-old-mutual-bid-020.htm>.

BBC (2003). 'Boss of scandal-hit Skandia quits', 1 December, <http://news.bbc.co.uk/2/hi/business/3252424.stm>.

Becht, M., Franks, J., and Grant, J. (2010). 'Hedge Fund Activism in Europe', Finance Working Paper, 283/2010, Brussels: European Corporate Governance Institute.

Berggren, C., Spånt, R., Mörtvik, R., and Carlsson, N. (2003). 'Fusioner och snabba klipp förödande', *Dagens Nyheter*, 12 January.

Bergström, C., Grubb, M., and Jonsson, S. (2007). 'The operating impact of buyouts in Sweden: A study of value creation', *Journal of Private Equity*, 11: 22–39.

Bergström, C. and Södersten, J. (1994). 'Kapitalbildningens politiska ekonomi', in B. Holmlund (ed.), *Arbete, löner och politik*. Stockholm: Fritzes, 241–62.

Björk, J. (2011). 'Ny kritik mot Carema', *Ttela*, 27 December, Sweden.

Blomberg, D. and Oleru, D. (2009). 'Who's in Control? A Comparative Case Study on Private Equity and Shareholder Activism', Master thesis, Stockhom: Stockholm School of Economics.

Blyth, M. (2002). *Great Transformations: Economic Ideas and Institutional Change in the Twentieth Century*. New York: Cambridge University Press.

Book, C. (1997). 'Kuppmakare och ideologiskt skifte? Om processen när socialdemokraterna avvecklade valutaregleringen', Politiska institutioner och strategiskt agerande (PISA), Working Paper, 15, Uppsala: Uppsala University.

Boucly, Q., Sraer, D., and Thesmar, D. (2011). 'Growth LBOs', *Journal of Financial Economics*, 102 (2): 432–53.

Braunerhjelm, P., von Greiff, C., and Svaleryd, H.E. (2009). *Utvecklingskraft och omställningsförmåga: En globaliserad svensk ekonomi*. Slutrapport, Globaliseringsrådet, Stockholm: Utbildningsdepartementet.

Carlsson, I. (2003). *Så tänkte jag: Politik & dramatik*. Stockholm: Hjalmarson & Högberg.

CMBOR (2010). *European Management Buy-out Review*. Nottingham: Centre for Management Buyout Research (CMBOR).

Dagens Industri (2010). 'Underkänt för svenska ordförandeskapet', 5 January.

Davis, S., Haltiwanger, J., Jarmin, R., Lerner, J., and Miranda, J. (2008). 'Private equity and employment', in J. Lerner and A. Gurung (eds), *Globalization of Alternative Investments: The Global Impact of Private Equity Report 2008*. Working Papers, 1, Cologny: World Economic Forum, 43–64.

Drees, B. and Pazarbaşıoğlu, C. (1995). 'The Nordic Banking Crises: Pitfalls in Financial Liberalization?', IMF Working Paper, 95/61, Washington, DC: International Monetary Fund.

Englund, P. (1990). 'Financial deregulation in Sweden', *European Economic Review*, 34: 385–93.

Erixon, O. (2007). 'Protektionism snubbeltråd för ekonomin', *Svenskt Näringsliv*, 7 November, Stockholm.

EVCA (2008). 'Benchmarking European Tax and Legal Environments', October, Brussels: European Venture Capital Association (EVCA).

Expanda (2001). 'Expanda renodlar: Överlåter 80 procent av aktierna i Callenberg Group', Press Release, Växjö: Expanda.

Ganslandt, M. (2008). *Internationellt statligt ägande och konkurrens*. Underlagsrapport, 17, Globaliseringsrådet, Stockholm: Utbildningsdepartementet.

Goergen, M., O'Sullivan, N., and Wood, G. (2011) 'Private equity takeovers and employment in the UK: Some empirical evidence', *Corporate Governance: An International Review*, 19 (3): 259–75.

Gripenberg, P. (2011). 'Caremas ägare tjänar halv miljard på räntorna', *Dagens Nyheter*, 14 December, <http://www.dn.se/ekonomi/caremas-ag are-tjanar-halv-miljard-pa-rantorna>.

Gustavsson, J. (1998). *The Politics of Foreign Policy Change: Explaining the Swedish Reorientation on EC Membership*. Lund: Lund University Press.

Hall, P. and Soskice, D. (2001). 'Introduction to Varieties of Capitalism', in P. Hall and D. Soskice (eds), *Varieties of Capitalism: The Institutional Foundations of Comparative Advantage*. Oxford: Oxford University Press, 1–68.

Hässler, D. (2007). 'Supershejker till Göteborg', *Realtid*, 21 December, <http://www.realtid.se/ArticlePages/200712/20/20071220200509_ Realtid358/20071220200509_Realtid358.dbp.asp>.

Henrekson, M. and Jakobsson, U. (2008). *Globaliseringen och den svenska ägarmodellen*. Underlagsrapport, 19, Globaliseringsrådet, Stockholm: Utbi ldningsdepartementet.

Högfeldt, P. (2006). 'The history and politics of corporate governance in Sweden', in R. Morck (ed.), *History of Corporate Governance around the World: Family Business Groups to Professional Managers*. Chicago: University of Chicago Press, 517–80.

Hyytinen, A. and Pajarinen, M. (2001). 'Financial Systems and Venture Capital in Nordic Countries: A Comparative Study', Working Paper, 774, Helsinki: The Research Institute of the Finnish Economy.

Independent Living Institute (2008). 'Åsa-Pia Järliden Bergström, LO-ekonomerna—LO är försiktigt positive till riskkapitalföretag', 12 April, <http://www.independentliving.org/assistanskoll/20080412-LO-f orsiktigt-positiva-till-riskkapitalforetag.html>.

Jonung, L. (1993). 'Riksbankens politik 1945–1990,' in L. Werin (ed.), *Från räntereglering till inflationsnorm: det finansiella systemet och Riksbankens politik 1945–1990*. Stockholm: SNS förlag, 287–419.

Karlsson, C. and Wahlström, J. (2007). 'Activist Fund's Impact on Blue Chip Companies in Sweden: Analysing the Implications on Capital Structure, Valuation and Credit Rating', Master thesis, Jönköping: Jönköping University.

Kerpner, J. (2010). 'Saabs nya storägare', *Aftonbladet*, 28 January, <http:// www.aftonbladet.se/nyheter/article6502320.ab>.

Kollnert, D. and Weber, E. (2008). 'Det gemensamma bästa kan inte förutsättas: En berättelse om Grupptalan mot Skandia', Bachelor thesis, Södertörns: Södertörns högskola.

LO (2006). *Responsibility and Power of Ownership*. Stockholm: Landsorganisationen i Sverige (LO).

LO (2009). 'Utveckling av LOs ägarpolicy', 05 May, Stockholm: Landsorganisationen i Sverige (LO).

Magnusson, E. (2009). 'Den egna vägen: Sverige och den europeiska integrationen 1961–1971', Doctoral thesis, Uppsala: Acta Universitatis Upsaliensis.

Nachemsson-Ekwall, S. and Carlsson, B. (2004). *Guldregn: Sagan om Skandia*. Stockholm: Bonnier.

NIC (2009). 'Obstacles to Nordic Venture Capital Funds', September, Oslo: Nordic Innovation Center (NIC).

Norén, H., Norén, U., and Wahll, H. (2006). 'Företagsanalys och shareholding: En fallstudie av Cevian Capital AB och dess förvärv', Master thesis, Göteborg: Göteborg Universitet.

Nutek (2003). 'Utvecklingen för riskkapitalbolagens portföljbolag', R 2003:11, Stockholm.

Nyberg, L. (2006). 'Är hedgfonder farliga', 24 November, Sveriges Riksbank, <http://www.riksbank.se/pagefolders/28337/061124.pdf>.

OECD (2004). *OECD Employment Outlook 2004*. Paris: OECD Publishing.

Olsson, M. and Tåg, J. (2012). 'Private Equity and Employees', IFN Working Paper, 906, Stockholm: Institutet för Näringslivsforskning.

Pontusson, J. (1992). *Limits of Social Democracy: Investment Politics in Sweden*. New York: Cornell University Press.

Rådet för mångfald inom massmedierna (1997). *Medieföretag i Sverige: Ägande och strukturförändringar i press, radio och TV*. Swedish Government Official Reports, SOU, 1997: 92, Stockholm: Fritzes.

Saalman, H. (2005). 'Hedgefonder och svensk fondlagstiftning', Bachelor thesis, Juridiska institutionen, Göteborg: Göteborgs Universitet.

Schnyder, G. (2008). 'Does Social Democracy Matter? Corporate Governance Reforms in Switzerland and Sweden (1980–2005)', Working Paper, 370, Cambridge: University of Cambridge.

Schulz, W., Kaserer, C., and Trappel, J. (2008). 'Finanzinvestoren im Medienbereich: Gutachten im Auftrag der Direktorenkonferenz der Landesmedienanstalten', Vorabfassung, Mai, Hans-Bredow-Institut für Medienforschung an der Universität Hamburg.

SIFA (2009). 'The Commission's Consultation Paper on Hedge Funds', Stockolm: Swedish Investment Fund Association (SIFA).

Stolt, R., Blomqvist, P., and Winblad, U. (2011). 'Privatization of social services: Quality differences in Swedish elderly care', *Social Science & Medicine*, 72: 560–7.

Storrie, D. (1993). 'The Anatomy of a Large Swedish Plant Closure', Doctoral thesis, Göteborg: Göteborgs Universitet.

Sunesson, D. (2008). 'Ownership Matters: A Clinical Study of Cevian Capital', Bachelor thesis, Stockholm: Stockholm School of Economics.

SVCA (2008). 'Portföljbolagsstudie 2007: Utvecklingen för riskkapitalbolagens portföljbolag 2001–2006', Stockholm: Svenska Riskkapitalföreningen (SVCA).

SVCA (2011). 'Som man sår och vattnar får man skörda', Stockholm: Svenska Riskkapitalföreningen (SVCA).

Sverenius, T. (2000). 'Vad hände med Sveriges ekonomi efter 1970?', Swedish Government Official Reports, SOU, 1999: 150, Stockholm: Fakta info.

Swedish Financial Supervisory Authority (2004). 'Livbolagskrisen', Stockholm: Finansinspektionen.

Szebehely, M. (2011). 'Insatser för äldre och funktionshindrade i privat regi', in L. Hartman (ed.), *Konkurrensens Konsekvenser: Vad Händer med Svensk Välfärd?* Stockholm: SNS, 215–57.

Telasuo, C. (2000). 'Småstater under internationalisering: Valutamarknadens avreglering i Sverige och Finland på 1980-talet. En studie i institutionell omvandling', Meddelande från Ekonomisk-historiska institutionen vid Göteborgs universitet, 78, Göteborg: Göteborgs Universitet.

Thorén, M. (2008). 'Riskkapitalister bättre än sitt rykte', Nyheter från Sveriges Radio-Ekot, *Sveriges Radio*, 28 January, <http://sverigesradio.se/cgi-bin/ekot/artikel.asp?artikel=1856855>.

Unionen (2009). *Owned by Private Equity*. Stockholm: Unionen.

Wihlborg, C. (1980). 'Exchange controls on financial capital flows in Sweden: Implications for costs to firms, effectiveness, and allocation', Swedish Government Official Reports, SOU, 1981, 52. Stockholm: Liber Förlag.

Zimdahl, C. (2009). 'AIFM-direktivet och dess effekt på private equity-branschen', Bachelor thesis, Lund: Lunds University.

8

An 'Italian Way to Private Equity'? The Rhetoric and the Reality

Introduction

Italy provides an interesting context for the operation of new investment funds (NIFs) because of its corporate ownership, corporate
governance, and industrial structure. Although Italy was not initially
attractive to private equity (PE), the strong role of internationalized
mid-sized companies and SMEs came to offer opportunities for NIFs
from the mid-2000s onwards. As a result, there was a substantial
increase in the scale of activities by PE funds in the years immediately before the onset of the financial crisis. By contrast, the activities
of other investment funds, such as hedge funds (HFs) and sovereign
wealth funds (SWFs), have been more modest, and so far these have
confined their involvement to a few large industrial and financial
groups.

There are several important features of the Italian corporate system which provide a backdrop to the operation of NIFs. Company
structure in Italian capitalism is significantly different from other
'relational systems' of ownership and governance. The number and
relative importance of large companies has declined over the last few
decades and, as elsewhere, there has been a shift from industry to
services. The backbone of Italian industry consists of a heterogene-
ous group of mid-sized companies: this group includes the so-called
pocket-sized multinationals, with at most a few thousand employees
in several countries, and other somewhat smaller companies (sometimes with only a few hundred employees) but characterized by a
strong international orientation and often listed in the 'small cap'
segment of the stock exchange. In addition, there is also a myriad of
small and medium-sized enterprises (SMEs) with commercial weaknesses in terms of research and innovation.

These various companies typically combine family ownership, production 'know-how', quality products, and under-developed managerial systems. They are therefore attractive candidates for intervention, modernization, and value creation by NIFs. Some observers have argued that PE involvement offers an opportunity to overcome the under-development of the Italian entrepreneurial structure. According to Sattin (2007), there is 'an Italian way for PE' characterized by minority shareholdings and strategies for company expansion. Pontarollo and Casè (2007), for their part, have cautiously distinguished between a 'speculative' role for PE in large-scale operations and a potentially 'virtuous' role for PE in SMEs. We discuss this distinction further in the conclusion, based on the evidence from a set of case studies.

Another distinctive feature of Italy is the structure of company ownership. In the listed sector, Italian capitalism is characterized by high ownership concentration, with most firms still mainly owned by family bloc-holders. In the group of medium-sized and smaller companies, large shareholders account for a high proportion of shares—typically between 60 and 70 per cent (Turani 2006). In large companies, corporate agreements between a narrow elite of shareholders ('patti di sindacato') allow family owners to control numerous listed and unlisted companies, often with relatively little capital. In some respects, activist HFs and SWFs may contribute to greater efficiency and transparency in the Italian system of 'closed' corporate governance (Croci 2011; Erede 2008). However, these latter investment funds have played a comparatively modest role so far, with their activities confined mainly to a few large Italian industrial and financial groups.

In this chapter, we outline the main features of the Italian context, before providing details on the growth of NIFs. Since PE is by far the most important of the three types of investment fund in Italy, the chapter focuses mainly on PE; three case studies of PE activity are considered. On the basis of the case study findings, we highlight several different forms of PE involvement in the Italian setting.

The Context

In the 1990s Italian firms started to make greater use of stock market listing due to the increased capital requirements needed to respond to global competition. As a result, the Italian system, like other bank-based systems, has been subject to the pressures of shareholder value and finance capitalism. In the 1990s, this was augmented by the structural crisis of the Italian economy, culminating in the exit of the lira from the European Monetary System and the adjustments needed to gain admission to the European Monetary Union. During this period policy-makers came to the view that the Italian economy and its companies needed to open up to markets and to modernize corporate governance and company control. What followed was a long series of legislative interventions in financial market regulation and company law, of which the most salient aspects will be discussed in what follows.

Financial Law and Institutions

Investment funds were introduced into the Italian system in 1993 (Law No. 344). The initial legislation has been significantly amended over time, considerably expanding its scope and opportunities for use. The road chosen by the legislator was that of progressive deregulation and of strengthening contractual autonomy, starting with the Consolidated Finance Act of 1998 and followed by several ministerial and legislative decrees.[1] As a consequence, the acquisition of majority shareholdings, as well as investment in quoted shares in public-to-private deals, is now permitted, and management companies can offer advisory services to target companies. Constraints on borrowing and debt of management companies, and rules regarding investment strategies of funds reserved to qualified investors, have been relaxed.[2] Also, the by-laws of investment funds which are open only to qualified investors no longer require approval by the Banca d'Italia.

What was crucial, however, was the Reform of Company Law Act of 2003, which removed all obstacles to leveraged buy-outs (LBOs). Only then did PE, which had previously played a marginal role, become significant. Furthermore, since 2010, the activities connected with holding and managing acquisitions (including those involving PE) were substantially liberalized and are no longer treated as 'reserved activities' under the control of Banca d'Italia. Subsequent company law reforms enhanced the rights and competencies of minority shareholders both regarding the nomination of members to company boards and their rights and competencies within these bodies.[3] The changes were intended to encourage direct participation by shareholders—not least by institutional investors like pension funds and HFs—and the exercise of their right to vote. However, with a few exceptions (to be discussed below), minority interests, and in particular investment funds, have so far not distinguished themselves by 'shareholder activism' in company meetings.

In contrast to the trend towards deregulation, however, legislation was adopted in 2012 to specifically regulate the activity of SWFs.[4] Similar to developments in other countries in the EU, the law grants a set of special powers to the state to protect the national interest in the defence and security sectors, as well as activities of strategic importance in the energy, transport, and communications sectors.

Turning finally to the tax regime, recent reforms have been advantageous for the funds. The corporate tax reform of 2004 rendered mergers and de-mergers tax-neutral and made the purchase of stock more favourable due to a tax exemption on profits and dividends for shareholders. The tax deduction of 84 per cent on profits was increased to 95 per cent by the Finance Act of 2008. Finally, since July 2011, the tax regime for Italian closed-end funds has shifted from taxation upon accrual to taxation at the time of realization of gains; income tax is thus levied on investors at the time when profits are realized and no longer applies to the fund itself.[5]

To summarize, the trend to decreasing regulation by the state and legislative and tax reforms, in the last ten to fifteen years, have created a conducive environment for NIFs.

Labour: Law and Institutions

In principle, Italian employees have high levels of employment protection, and this should limit the opportunities for NIFs to restructure Italian enterprises. Article 18 of the Workers' Statute of 1970 protects a worker from individual dismissal without just cause. However, the article only applies to companies with more than fifteen employees. Given the characteristics of Italian industrial structure, this means that a very large proportion of workers do not fall under its protection. In addition, there has been a recent trend to encourage more atypical work (including temporary contracts) to make the labour market more flexible.[6] These contracts lack any form of employment protection. Job insecurity is now the norm for young workers. More general, empirical research demonstrates that the Italian translation of the concept of flexicurity is 'flex-insecurity': unemployment benefits are insufficient to provide effective financial security, which means that flexibility becomes synonymous with precariousness (Berton et al. 2009).

On the other hand, the information and consultation rights of worker representatives have been strengthened through the introduction of administrative sanctions for breaches of these rights, applicable in all enterprises employing at least fifty workers.[7] However, the effectiveness of these rights continues to depend on the strength and skills of the trade unions. In addition, the Italian system of labour relations does not prescribe rights of participation in decision-making processes at the company level. The Reform of Company Law itself, despite introducing the dualistic model of board structure, explicitly rules out the possibility that employees might be part of the supervisory board. Italy thus differs from other relational-based systems of ownership and governance where worker participation in company boards has legal under-pinning.

Trade Unions and Collective Bargaining

There are twelve million trade union members in Italy—more than in any other country in the European Union. However, with half the membership made up of pensioners, overall union density among employees is 33 per cent (ICTWSS 2009). Italian unions have been weakened in recent years by a number of factors. One is the structural changes that have occurred in Italian capitalism, such as the atomization of production units. A further weakness is the persistent and growing division of the union movement. Leaving aside the explosion of autonomous unionism and the consequent fragmentation of representation in the public and tertiary sectors, the number of unions has increased: the three largest confederations (CGIL (Confererazione Generale Italiana del Lavoro), CISL (Confederazione Italiana Sindicati Lavoratori), and UIL (Unione Italiana del Lavoro)) have been joined by the UGL (Unione Generale del Lavoro), a confederation close to the right-wing parties. Also, in some larger establishments, the presence of COBAS (Confederazione dei Comitati di Base), an unaffiliated union movement, is sometimes significant. Trade union divisions have also increased in qualitative terms because over the last few years differences and competition between the three largest confederations have increased significantly.

As regards collective bargaining, it is necessary to distinguish sectoral bargaining at the national level from the company level. In the former, collective bargaining coverage is estimated to be around

80 per cent, given that it reflects the application of the *erga omnes* principle of national collective agreements. Collective bargaining at company level depends instead on the presence and force of union representation in the company. This varies considerably by sector, size, and locality. The proportion of workers covered by second-level bargaining is diminishing, with about three million in the private sector, equivalent to around 40 per cent of the total.

New Investment Funds

Until the financial crisis, the various types of investment fund in Italy had grown at different rates: HFs very slowly, SWFs initially very slowly but lately becoming more important, and PE more rapidly.

Hedge fund investment in listed Italian companies has been limited. At the beginning of the financial crisis in 2007, the value of shares possessed by HFs in listed Italian companies was estimated at €2.2 million (Mangano 2008). The value of shareholdings above the 2 per cent threshold is about half that (€1.1 million), distributed among fifty-four funds with shares in forty-one listed companies, including the Unicredit banking group, the Parmalat food company, Benetton, and Generali. In most other listed companies HF shareholdings are very small.

Until 2008 SWFs were of limited importance in Italy. Estimates at the time quantified their investments at around €1.5 billion and their presence was concentrated mainly in the luxury goods and real estate sectors (Pasca di Magliano 2009). They first became a matter of public discussion in the autumn of 2008, when the fund controlled by the Libyan Central Bank purchased 4.9 per cent of Unicredit's capital. Since then the presence of SWFs in the Italian economy has grown substantially. According to the most recent study (Alvaro and Ciccaglioni 2012), SWF hold stock in 102 listed companies in Italy, with a percentage share (35.6 per cent) much higher than that recorded by the same study for Germany (17 per cent), France (19 per cent), and the UK (25 per cent). However, the corresponding value of shareholding by the SWFs as a percentage of stock exchange capitalization, equal to 2.2 per cent, does not differ significantly from these other countries (2.0 per cent in France, 2.6 per cent in Germany, and 3.0 per cent in the UK).[8] According to data issued by the SWF Law Center (2012) the value of SWF investments in Italy is concentrated mainly in the energy (€5.2 billion), finance (€3.9 billion), and aeronautics (€2.0

billion) sectors, while the rest of their investments are distributed amongst the real estate sector (€470 million), infrastructure (€241 million), commerce (€200 million), and the car industry (€160 million).

Turning to PE, the sector has grown considerably in the past decade. According to data from the Italian Private Equity and Venture Capital Association (AIFI), the number of PE and venture capital (VC) fund managers operating in Italy increased from ninety-eight in 2002 to 188 in 2010 (of which thirteen were devoted solely to VC). In the same period, the amount of investments rose from €2.6 billion (2002) to the maximum value of €5.5 billion recorded in 2008. It then fell by more than 50 per cent in the following two years but grew again in 2011 (€3.6 billion).[9]

The rows in Table 8.1 report the total annual values of investments and show their growth until the peak of almost €5.5 million in 2008 and their collapse in the two following years, when the financial crisis reached Italy. Note, however, that the 2011 value was already close to that of 2006. Of interest for our purposes here, however, is their disaggregation. This reveals the following features in particular: the dominant role of the pan-European funds, whose resources are concentrated in a small number of large-sized investments; the weight of the funds owned by the banking sector until the financial crisis, as well as its drastic reduction in subsequent years (from 23.3 per cent in 2006 to 2.8 per cent in 2011); and a significant presence of public operators (mainly regional finance institutions) which show a striking dispersion of resources among a large number of small-sized investments.

The data in Table 8.2 and Figure 8.1 on the distribution of investments by purpose show that investments in buy-out operations have also absorbed the bulk of PE resources in Italy. In three years they accounted for two-thirds of total capital invested, reaching a peak of 78.5 per cent in 2007. The value fell to 52.6 per cent in 2008, and in this case appears to have been an anomaly connected with the exceptionally high value of turnaround investments (30 per cent) in that same year (Table 8.2 and Figure 8.1).

The next two tables illustrate the buy-out segment in more detail. Table 8.3 shows that investments in this segment were made almost entirely by independent private actors, that is, 'generalist' savings management companies (SGRs), funds other than SGRs and specifically dedicated to Italy (country funds), and the pan-European funds.

The high number of investments by these funds was due to the concentration of activity in the early, growth, and development stages.

Table 8.1 *Private equity in Italy: distribution of investments by type of operator*

	2006 Operations	2006 Investments	2007 Operations	2007 Investments	2008 Operations	2008 Investments	2009 Operations	2009 Investments	2010 Operations	2010 Investments	2011 Operations	2011 Investments
Pan-European funds	34	1,858	22	2,742	26	3,073	18	1,123	21	1,674	24	1,846
Genralist SGRs	84	736	99	749	134	1.515	90	964	116	512	129	1,169
Country funds	29	214	25	189	45	322	39	275	35	114	39	369
Italian banks	55	872	38	443	38	412	27	152	23	93	21	102
Regional/public operators	69	44	77	51	88	92	80	68	67	58	81	84
Early stage funds	21	7	41	23	44	41	29	33	30	10	32	13
TOTAL	292	3,731	302	4,197	302	5,458	283	2,615	292	2,461	326	3,583

Note: Operations refer to number of active funds. Investments are reported in million euros.
Source: Based on AIFI annual reports, 2006–11.

Table 8.2 *Private equity in Italy: distribution of investments by stage of investment*

	2006		2007		2008		2009		2010		2011	
	Opera-tions	Invest-ments	Opera-tions	Invest-ments	Opera-tions	Invest-ments	Opera-tions	Invest-ments	Opera-tions	Invest-ments	Opera-tions	Invest-ments
Early stage	62	28	88	66	88	115	79	98	106	89	106	82
Expansion/growth	105	1,094	113	786	145	837	112	371	109	583	139	674
Turnaround	25	165	14	50	26	1.636	11	416	14	51	6	7
Replacement	—	—	—	—	—	—	9	42	7	91	12	559
Buy-out	100	2,444	87	3,295	113	2,869	72	1,688	56	1,647	63	2,261
TOTAL	292	3,731	302	4,197	302	5,458	283	2,615	292	2,461	326	3,583

Note: Operations refer to number of active funds. Investments are reported in million euros.
Source: Based on AIFI annual reports, 2006–11.

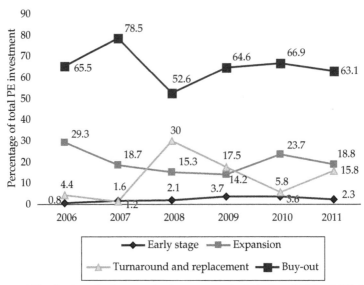

Figure 8.1 *Distribution of private equity investments in Italy from 2006 to 2011, by stage (% of total PE investment)*

Source: Based on AIFI annual reports, 2006–11.

Table 8.3 *Private equity in Italy: distribution of private equity investments by type of investment and operator[a]*

	Generalist SGRs[a]			Country funds			Pan-European funds		
	ES	E	BO	ES	E	BO	ES	E	BO
2006	3	16	55	3	12	10	13	6	20
2007	7	22	67	2	13	8	—	6	17
2008	8	34	61	7	13	14	—	1	18
2009	14	28	61	5	10	20	—	4	17
2010	33	34	62	7	14	16	—	6	20

	Early stage funds			Italian banks			Regional/public operators		
	ES	E	BO	ES	E	BO	ES	E	BO
2006	16	10	—	11	24	15	53	31	—
2007	42	4	—	7	20	8	42	35	—
2008	42	2	—	8	16	5	34	34	2
2009	29	4	—	14	13	1	38	41	1
2010	26	2	—	4	17	—	30	27	2

ES = Early stage (seed and start-up); E = Expansion (expansion and growth); BO = Buy-out
[a] SGR = Generalist savings management companies
Source: Based on AIFI annual reports, 2006–11

Table 8.4 *Private equity in Italy: distribution of the number of buy-out investments by size class*

Buy-out (only own capital)	2005	2006	2007	2008	2009	2010	2011
Small (<€15 million)	58.0	70.0	64.0	62.0	67.0	73.0	67.0
Medium (€15–150 million)	36.0	28.0	30.0	35.0	29.0	22.0	28.0
Large and Mega (>€150 & >€300 million)	6.0	2.0	6.0	3.0	4.0	5.0	5.0
Total	100.0	100.0	100.0	100.0	100.0	100.0	100.0

Source: Based on AIFI annual reports, 2006–11.

Finally, buy-outs were not just restricted to the large-sized enterprise segment or to international funds. To the contrary, Table 8.4 shows that, in all the years considered, much the largest segment consisted of smaller takeovers, in which the capital invested directly by PE funds did not exceed the threshold of €15 million. This finding highlights the largely unnoticed existence of intense buying and selling activity by small enterprises, mainly through the generalist SGRs.

Corresponding to the differential diffusion of the three types of investment funds are substantial differences in their impacts on labour and industrial relations. SWFs have had least effect and PE the most. The evidence shows that shareholdings of SWFs in individual listed Italian companies are significant, and relatively larger than in other large countries. Yet the investments are mostly recent—in part subsequent to the 2008–09 financial crisis—and they are generally not large enough to significantly alter ownership structures and/or influence ownership–management–labour relations.

Similar considerations apply to HFs. The legislative changes mentioned at the outset have substantially increased the capacity of institutional investors to exert direct influence. Nevertheless, the few empirical studies conducted on the matter show that, for the time being, the activism of institutional investors in Italy has been modest. Erede (2008) surveyed the activities of twenty-nine HFs with shareholdings above 2 per cent in around forty companies listed in 2008. He concludes that in only 25 per cent of cases is there outright activism by funds trying to get larger payouts for shareholders or changes in corporate governance (e.g. election of a fund representative to the board of directors or the board of auditors). More typical is either a passive stance or, possibly, relational strategies disguised as passive behaviour aimed at forging alliances with the management and/or the majority shareholders in order to gain exclusive advantages to the detriment of other minority shareholders. Nor does the survey by Croci and Petrella (2011), covering the period 2000–07, report empirical evidence of significant activism by HFs so that, with a few exceptions, their purchases and their 'voice' have not had a significant impact on the stock market. Overall, therefore, the HFs which have purchased shares in Italian companies have preferred to maintain a low profile, and any activism has focused on issues concerning corporate governance. There has been very little direct impact on trade union and labour relations.

Different considerations apply to the case of PE. Given the characteristics of the Italian economy, the advent of PE was a novelty, but as yet there has been very little analysis of the effects of NIFs. The evidence to date relates to financing and company performance rather than labour effects. Moreover, until the financial crisis these had been conducted solely by or in collaboration with the PE sectors' representative association, the evident purpose being to build and disseminate a positive image of the sector and its importance for the Italian economy. This was not without success: until the financial crisis, PE funds were viewed mainly in a positive light. Discordant voices were mostly confined to a few critical analyses in the academic world. The critics emphasized the speculative nature of PE within broader critiques of financial capitalism. Those in favour of PE note that it is an important backer of SMEs, and that most SMEs in Italy find it difficult to grow because of financial barriers. PE can provide SMEs with finance and management know-how. By contrast, any negative implications of PE activities often arise from larger investments where the investors mainly pursue short-term speculative goals.

However, the data set out above are not sufficient to support the claim that there is a single, distinctive 'Italian way to PE', which is oriented to SMEs with the primary objective of strengthening, modernizing, and fostering their growth. There is no doubt that a large majority of PE investments are concentrated among SMEs: according to AIFI data, in 2009 the corresponding share of investments was 75 per cent by sales (based on sales volume up to €50 million as the defining criterion) or 77 per cent by employment (based on companies with fewer than 250 employees). The data themselves are unsurprising given Italian industrial structure; on the other hand, it does not significantly differ from those for many other European countries.

Moreover, the figure also includes investments made by public funds, which probably offset the absence of private funds in the smaller size classes. Above all, the figure reported concerns the number of investments, not their amount; in Italy as in other countries buy-out investments are the dominant segment. The Italian situation is therefore just as mixed as that of other countries; this ambivalence also emerges from the three case studies outlined in the next section.

Private Equity and Labour: Three Case Studies

Due to the lack of a sufficient quantity of independent empirical research on the company-level effects of PE investments (either minority or buy-out), it is not possible to generate definitive conclusions regarding the impact of PE on employment, workers, or industrial relations. The following three case studies cannot overcome this gap on their own but they provide illuminating information on the dynamics of PE investment in the Italian institutional context and help to explain observed differences in labour and employment outcomes.

Marazzi Group

Founded in the 1930s, Marazzi is currently one of Italy's major multinational companies and the world leader in its sector (the design, manufacture, and sales of ceramic tiles with a growing presence in sanitary fixtures).[10] The Group, based in Sassuolo (Modena) in Emilia Romagna, is controlled by the third generation of the original founding Marazzi family, which holds the majority of shares in the company; it has manufacturing plants in Italy, Spain, France, Russia, and the USA, and in 2008 employed more than 6,000 staff in its plants, commercial branches, and showrooms.

Private equity investment in the company (2004) occurred on the basis of mutual interest. Filippo Marazzi saw entry by PE as the leverage that, in addition to securing the finance necessary for expansion strategies, would allow for the modernization of the management of the company and consolidation of leadership in the sector. In turn, the funds became interested in Marazzi because it was a healthy company with significant growth prospects.

In December 2004 the PE investors Permira and Private Equity Partners (Pep) bought 33 per cent of the capital of the company from the Marazzi family with the aim of going public within the next three to five years. The volume of this sale accounted for €132 million, whereas the total value of the company was estimated at €750 million. In February 2006 Marazzi went public and the funds reduced their ownership stake to 10 per cent. The two funds earned substantial profits on this sale, since Permira and Pep had bought the shares for €3.9 each and sold them for €10.25. Both investors withdrew from Marazzi in February 2007 with overall profits of €134 million over the two years. In May 2008 Marazzi was delisted in order to consolidate and expand the company. Once again Permira and Pep invested in the company (this time €250 million) and created jointly with Marazzi the new enterprise Fintiles. This company was indirectly controlled by Filippo Marazzi, with 49 per cent participation by Permira and Pep through LuxELIT.

Marazzi is a case of PE investment without debt and a minority partnership (33 per cent of shares). The decision not to use leverage was made jointly by Marazzi and the PE funds. The cash flow of Marazzi was good, but so were the prospects for growth, which required enormous financial resources. The investment goal of the PE funds was to facilitate the growth and 'globalization' of Marazzi. The absence of debt in the PE investment gave the company the flexibility to finance the strategic acquisition of Welor Kerama, the leading company in Russia, to bring already initiated strategic investments to completion (such as the doubling of factory capacity in Dallas in the United States) and to gradually modernize systems in other factories. The latter reinforced the technological leadership of Marazzi in its sector.

These developments can be traced in the company's financial data, which are available up to the first quarter of 2008. The period from 2004 to 2007 was a period of strong growth for the group. The Russian business unit achieved stellar results year after year and contributed in a significant way to the overall positive performance of the Marazzi Group: a 29.2 per cent increase in sales in 2006 (against +6.7 per cent in the group overall) and 26.1 per cent in 2007 (overall: +2.1 per cent). Earnings before interest, taxes, depreciation and amortization (EBITDA) grew by 30.7 per cent (compared to an average of 12.4) in 2006 and another 13.1 per cent in 2007 (overall: –2.9 per cent). This brought the profit margins of this business from 39.7 per cent in 2005 to 40.1 per cent in 2006 and then down to 36.0 per cent in 2007.

As already mentioned, the most evident consequence of PE investment was the reorganization of the organizational and managerial structure of the company, which was desired and supported by the entrepreneur (Peveraro 2008). The reorganization of the company was conducted along two directions: first, the 'managerialization' of the structure and, second, the adoption of principles and structures of corporate governance in view of the Marazzi stock market quotation.

Industrial relations at Marazzi have always been characterized by a cooperative style and well-developed direct relationships between unions and the family owners. From this point of view, the PE funds bring about a significant change as they are an 'invisible owner'. The shop stewards within the company, and the unions on the outside, do not have direct relationships with them, but they feel the increased PE influence, in particular in the current crisis phase. After the entry by PE no major restructuring processes took place, at least as far as the Italian plants were concerned. Factories were modernized during recent years, but this was considered part of a normal process and did not have a major impact on employment.

To conclude, the Marazzi Group is a 'virtuous case' of PE investment. The PE funds enabled the already internationally active company to continue its course of expansion and consolidation. The principal reasons for this success story are the following:

1. The family owner consciously *chose* the PE option to grow the company and become quoted, *chose* PE funds which had a clear industrial strategy, and staffed the top layer of the board with representatives of funds that had clear industrial objectives for medium- and long-term growth.
2 Marazzi retains the distinctive features of a family firm and is a technological and market leader in its sector. It was economically healthy but still had a traditional organizational structure, and showed strong potential for further growth, making it attractive for PE.
3 The absence of leverage from the PE investments. This enabled the use of cash flow to finance very large investments over a three-year period and facilitated a medium- and long-term perspective.

Seves Glassblock

Seves Glassblock is the glass brick division of the Seves Group. The latter was established in 1997 through a PE-backed management buy-out of the Florentine company Vetroarredo, whose origins date back to 1928. In 2007 the Seves Group had twenty-five factories (ten in

Europe, eight in Asia, and seven in the Americas) with a total of about 4,500 staff. Of these plants, four were part of the Glassblock Division and were located in Florence (in the region of Castello, where the head office of Seves Glassblock is based), the Czech Republic, Germany, and Brazil. At this time, Seves Glassblock produced and distributed over 36 per cent of glass bricks produced and distributed worldwide.

In April 2006 ownership of the Group was transferred to PE funds Ergon Capital Partners (Belgium), Vestar Capital Partners (Cayman Islands), and Athena PE (Italy, already a co-owner). The value of the secondary buy-out was €375 million. In 2008 the Chair and the Managing Director, who were formerly shareholders in the company with a share of 10 per cent, both suddenly left the company, which meant the loss of the management that had led the transitional and then the expansion phase. A few weeks later, at the start of November, Seves unexpectedly communicated its intention to stop the hot production stage at the Florence plant for twelve months in order to reduce the high level of stock in trade of the Seves Glassblock division. This decision was justified by the difficulties in the glass brick section following the crisis, including decreases in sales of 32.5 per cent and in the operating margin by 83 per cent over the previous two years. At the same time the company opened the procedure for an Extraordinary Wage Guarantee Fund for 87 employees at the Florence plant (those employed in the furnace area) combined with the laying-off of a further twenty workers. The announcement by Seves was in fact equivalent to the dismissal (immediate or forthcoming) of ninety-seven employees out of the total of 170 at the Florentine plant.[11]

Although these may appear modest at first glance, they were not seen that way by the parties involved for at least two reasons. The first is that they were not an isolated case but added to many other crisis situations in the Florence region The second reason is that the Seves case involved a highly specialized factory and labour force that represented 'the feather in the cap' of Florentine industry and its tradition. Since it was a request for extraordinary temporary unemployment pay, the action by Seves in November 2008 appeared to most observers as an announcement of plant closure. This explains the strong mobilization by the trade unions, which led to strikes, political mediation, and various other initiatives.

In January 2009 a first agreement was signed between Seves and the trade unions. It established the Wage Guarantee Fund for 110 employees but its status was reduced from 'extraordinary' to 'ordinary', which presupposed the re-employment of staff in the company. The closing of the plant seemed to have been averted. Seves, moreover, undertook to present a new industrial plan by 15 April 2009, based on the construction of the new blast furnace for the Florence plant. In the following months, however, the company increasingly delayed reactivation of the blast furnace and, at the same time, gradually relocated production to the Czech Republic. The Tuscany Region offered loans for the construction of the new furnace, but the company put off a decision on this. Whilst the company played for time the institutions also mobilized: the Mayor of Florence convened the City Council in front of the factory gates and went to Brussels to meet the top management of the funds that control Seves. This failed to achieve any concrete results. At the same time it emerged from the budget figures of the company that, despite being faced with an undisputed decrease in sales, the Florence plant, with revenues of €19.9 million and a gross operating margin of €2 million, was not only profitable but achieving results that were clearly better than those of the plants in the Czech Republic and Brazil, which were losing money (€12.1 million and €22.9 million, respectively, in the previous year). However, the budget included provisions for the possible closing of the Florentine site.

By the end of 2009 the affair at the Seves plant in Florence had assumed the character of a 'cat and mouse' game. On the one hand, the company negotiated and signed agreements (in June and December) on re-launching the plant. On the other hand, it continued to procrastinate over the date when production would resume. It argued that future market conditions would determine the resumption of production while simultaneously transferring abroad the dies for the manufacture of bricks. Since then the crisis has continued with the same pattern. After 20 months of 'cassa integrazione' production was started again. But only 103 workers came back, with another forty-four remaining on the books of the extraordinary wage guarantee fund. The agreement from July 2010 between Seves, trade unions, and the public institutions contained the obligation on the company to continue production for at least a further five years. But Seves shut down the melting furnace in December 2012 and once more applied for a Wage Guarantee Fund for ninety-seven of the 107 workers who had remained. As of early 2013, the PE owners have put the entire company up for sale and the fate of the plant continues to be uncertain.

To conclude, the Seves case illustrates the impotence not only of trade unions but also of local institutions. Agreements were signed but not observed by the company and there was a lack of informa-tion on the 'invisible finances' of the funds and its current financial situation. While it is not possible to prove the ultimate reasons for the investors' decision, on the basis of the economic data available, relat-ing both to the Seves Group and to the Seves Glassblock Division, the following hypothesis can be developed: beyond the difficulties gener-ated by the economic crisis, this is not so much a case of a company in crisis but of the investment in crisis. The owners faced high levels of indebtedness in its portfolio, with the Florence plant representing a means to save money and 'generate cash'.

Saeco International Group

Saeco International Group is a leading company that designs, pro-duces, and markets coffee machines for household and professional use, and automatic vending machines for hot and cold beverages and snacks. Set up in Italy in 1981 for the production of domestic espresso coffee machines, Saeco has grown successfully over the years to become a group with sixteen subsidiaries worldwide and a sales net-work in more than sixty countries.

In December 2003 the French PE fund managers Pai Partners took over ownership of the group. At that time Saeco's situation was excellent. Besides holding a market share of 30 per cent in Europe and 65 per cent in Italy, the company was distinguished by its very high profitability. At the time it had a gross operating margin equal to 20 per cent of turnover (compared with an average for the electri-cal household appliances sector of about 10–15 per cent), an EBITDA of €45 million (first half of 2003) and an overall end of year turnover of €420 million with a profit of €21 million. The acquisition took place through a LBO totalling €746 million. The equity investment amounted to €150–200 million, with the contribution of Pai Partners amounting to only €34 million. The resulting total debt on Saeco of €500–550 million was therefore higher than the entire turnover from 2003.

In March 2007 Saeco announced the closing of production at the Gaggia site of Robecco sul Naviglio (in the Milan area), which had approximately 126 employees, and its transfer to a new Romanian plant. Only the technical and commercial departments remained in Robecco, and employed just twenty-six employees. For the com-pany, production in Robecco was no longer sustainable compared to the competition, which produced at lower costs, and therefore its transfer was necessary in order to guarantee competitiveness. The trade unions insisted that in 2006 the plant in question made profits of €2 million. Therefore, they argued, the transfer of production was a response to financial rather than industrial logic, and was thus unjustified. Subsequent bargaining, nevertheless, did not lead to substantial changes in the decision. The workers were given an Extraordinary Wage Guarantee Fund and, in August 2008, the last fifty finally left the company in the form of voluntary redundancies.

In September 2008 Pai Partners was forced to re-capitalize the company with €185 million, but this did not prevent Saeco from joining countless other companies suffering from the economic crisis at the start of 2009: 740 employees (out a total of about 1,000) were granted an Ordinary Wage Guarantee Fund two days a week for three months. The trade unions managed to obtain the protection of the lowest wages, which—on the basis of the agreement that prescribes a supplement of the public wage guarantee by the company—did not fall below the threshold of €1,000 per month.

In April 2009 the crisis at Saeco was clear. It was stifled by bank debt amounting to an unsustainable €660 million, even higher than the debt generated in 2003 for the LBO. Its turnover in 2008 was over a quarter less than that of 2003 (€318 million against €420 million), and it had annual losses of over €350 million by March 2009. Its gross operating margin had dropped from €86 to €14 million and its European market share to below 30 per cent. A few months later Saeco was purchased by Philips for €170 million on the condition that €300 million of debt with the pool of creditor banks would be cancelled. The price for the rescue of Saeco was very high: a formerly healthy 'pocket-sized multinational' that exemplified the 'Made in Italy' ethos is today just a division of a Dutch multinational. Also, in the espresso coffee machines sector, which had been dominated by small and medium-sized Italian producers (Cimbali, De Longhi, Lavazza, La Pavoni), the arrival of a giant like Philips with a turnover of €27 billion and sales in sixty countries altered the equilibrium and the competition. As one commentator put it: 'if, as the competitors fear, the idea of the Dutch is to make espresso coffee machines a branch of their global business, the brand Saeco will end up, perhaps next to the Philips brand, on thousands of shelves in shops and supermarkets all over the world. A bit like what happened to San Pellegrino water which, passing to Nestlé, became the most widely sold mineral water in the world' (Scagliarini 2009). In other words, it will not only be Saeco which pays the price for its LBO.

Table 8.5 *Private equity in Italy: type and strategy of investments and industrial relations in the three case studies*

	Case 1 **Marazzi Group**	Case 2 **Seves Glassblock**	Case 3 **Saeco International Group**
Sector	Construction (ceramic tiles)	Construction (glass bricks)	Coffee machines
Type of PE-investment	Minority	Management buy-out + secondary buy-out	Buy-out
Strategy and financial crisis	Expansion Investments worldwide and in Italy	Delocalization of production abroad and closing down of the main plant in Italy Goal: access to cash	Very high indebtedness Debt restructuring (banks) Sale to foreign industrial competitor
Union / industrial relations	No influence	Collective bargaining, agreements and strikes, but powerless	Powerless

The history of this case is relatively simple. In 2003 Saeco was a healthy company, with profitability and asset values significantly higher than the average for the sector. The LBO, through which the Pai Partners Fund acquired control of the company, radically changed the very sound balance sheets and wiped out the financial health of Saeco. In the words of a financial journalist, who in October 2004 had highlighted the consequences of the operation, 'until December 2003 (Saeco) could easily be defined a happy company...was no longer so; the obvious risk of this situation is that the new management, driven by the need to generate cash in order to repay debts and interest, adopts policies that can guarantee good performance in the short term but are incapable of ensuring the competitiveness of the company in the medium–long term' (Ronchi 2004). Even before the financial collapse of 2009, the progressive loss of Saeco's market share shows what can result from PE involvement.

In the three cases summarized in Table 8.5, the trade unions and company representatives were either uninfluential in the 'virtuous' case or impotent in the others in relation to PE operations. This empirical evidence comes as no surprise in the case of Italy; indeed, it can be generalized for the country as a whole. Given the weakness of trade unions in the private sector and the limited nature of collective bargaining at company level, trade unions and their representatives have very little potential to bargain over the possible entry of funds into companies. They may be informed about the entry of PE as negotiations are underway or after the event. At best, they may be able to bargain over the restructuring which follows PE investment. However, unions generally lack the strength and expertise to do more. Moreover, company-level union representatives who can keep up with fund specialists are very much an exception, with limited time off from work and limited or non-existent support facilities.

There is a final aspect which should be emphasized. The entry of PE normally leads to a formalization of industrial relations in the company. In most cases, the well-established, although often informal, system of industrial relations typical of the small and medium-sized enterprise disappears, and thus also the power base of delegates and/or the external trade unions within the company. The owner is no longer rooted locally, but far away, and sometimes the distance makes direct contact impossible. Such a development can be seen in the case of Seves: the ownership of the company became 'invisible' and the trade unions (and other local institutions) became powerless.

The Recent Crisis and the Future of Private Equity in Italy

The figures reported previously showing the predominance of buy-out operations, suggest that the thesis of an 'Italian way to PE' should be treated with a great deal of caution. The three case studies reinforce this by showing the diversity of PE involvement in Italy. It is very likely that 'virtuous' cases like Marazzi are not isolated, but the absence of a solid body of independent research on PE prevents precise estimation of their significance and frequency for the time being. On other hand, the Seves and Saeco cases show that the speculative logic predominant until the crisis erupted certainly did not stop at Italy's borders; nor did it solely characterize the 'big deals' involving larger companies. Indeed, Seves and Saeco were two paradigmatic examples of the backbone of the 'Made in Italy' SME sector that the PE rhetoric promised to modernize and strengthen. Here the same methodological reservations apply to prevent any sort of generalization. The financial crisis and the credit crunch, however, have shown that these were no exceptions.

Table 8.6 *Private equity in the Italian press before and after the financial crisis*

Before the crisis	After the crisis
Private equity Italian-style(*Corriere Economia*, 16 January 2006)	If debts kill off Made in Italy products (*La Repubblica*, 8 February 2009)
Private equity, the benevolent barbarian(*Corriere Economia*, 30 January 2006)	Operations of recent years in Italy a boomerang (*La Repubblica*—Affari e Finanza, 9 February 2009)
Private equity, an opportunity for Italian SMEs (*Il Sole–24 Ore*, 20 March 2007)	Locust funds, now debts crush firms(*La Repubblica*—Affari e Finanza, 11 May 2009)
Private equity funds change Italian capilalism (for the better) (*La Repubblica*—Affari e Finanza, 26 March 2007)	Under the surgeon's knife of private equity. More rubble than real development (*Corriere della Sera*, 20 December 2009)
	Emilia, the repentant district. Just finance never again (*La Repubblica*—Affari e Finanza, 5 October 2009)

Note: Titles have been translated by the author from Italian to English.

The first empirical evidence in this regard is the reversal in the meaning, production, and construction of the 'PE reality' by Italian economic journalism in the space of a few months—as emerges from simple comparison of the headlines before and after the financial crisis (Table 8.6).

In turn, these and other headlines of the same tenor from 2009 onwards summarize the empirical evidence of the crisis: what hitherto had been perceived as an exception—that is, the well-known cases of acquired firms which fell into a vortex of successive sales among funds (secondary buy-outs) with a progressive increase in their indebtedness—was instead the tip of an iceberg submerged in a sea of liquidity. When that sea suddenly dried up, the iceberg of firms with financial structures damaged by LBOs by one or more PE funds emerged in its entirety.[12]

News reports on the iceberg were followed by more far-ranging analyses. Even if often partial or circumscribed, they shed more light on a reality hitherto concealed by the scant transparency of the sector, and by the difficulty, if not the impossibility, of collecting disaggregated data on unlisted companies.

A survey by the leading economic newspaper, *Il Sole–24 Ore*, examined the balance sheets of twenty-five companies subject to secondary PE transactions between 2000 and 2008. On average, a company remained in the possession of a PE fund for three or four years. At the time of secondary buy-outs by other funds, revenues had grown on average by 18 per cent, the gross operating margin by 19 per cent, and employment by 14 per cent.[13] Overall growth, however, is over-shadowed by the figure for indebtedness, which doubled between the entry and exit of the fund (+99.7 per cent). 'These debts', the authors stress, 'have not been contracted in order to invest, but in order to enable the PE funds to purchase companies. In short, they are "unproductive"—one might say "useless"—debts which tie the hands of companies when they want to invest' (Longo and Pavesi 2011). Striking in this regard is not so much the figures in themselves as the consistency with the longstanding criticism that the PE 'demon' corrodes the financial health of a company and makes it structurally fragile.

Authoritative confirmation of this is provided by a Bank of Italy study on the financial situation of the Italian companies in which PE has invested (Granturco and Miele 2011). The analysis cross-references the data collected by a questionnaire-based survey on PE funds with those issued by the Central Credit Register and the Company Accounts Data Service in 2008. Of the 263 companies on which it was possible to conduct analysis, 142 (42 per cent) were at risk; of these, forty-one were seen as 'critical' because they combined high credit risk with low profitability. It also emerges from the study that sixty companies had already decreased in value and a further seven companies were in liquidation. Overall, in every macro-sector of activity, the share of PE investee companies at risk was always higher relative to the Italian firms in the same 'risk/vulnerability' situation. One of the main reasons was high leverage (greater than 5:1) at the time of the investment.

Note that the data reported are under-estimated. The authors, in fact, emphasize that, for various reasons, the levels of indebtedness indicated by the Central Credit Register 'are certainly lower than the real ones'. But there are two further reasons. First, the survey was unable to cover all the PE fund management companies (twelve out of sixty-eight did not respond to the questionnaire) and the study does not contain information on the sectoral weight of the companies that did not return the questionnaire. Second, the data refer to 2008 and therefore reflect the repercussions of the financial crisis to only a limited extent. The authors themselves stress that, when limiting the analysis to only the companies for which the 2009 balance sheet was already available, the share of enterprises at risk rises to 46 per cent. For the aforesaid reasons, therefore, it is likely that the share of PE investee companies at risk amounts to considerably more than 50 per cent.

Overall, the consequence of the financial crisis has been the reputational collapse of PE in Italy as well as the inevitable downturn in fundraising and investment. Not surprisingly, therefore, both the association representing the sector and individual actors have sought, since the onset of the crisis, to limit the damage and to restore PE's image as rapidly as possible. The discursive strategy has been simple but nonetheless effective: the sector has indeed seen excesses, and it has sometimes lost sight of its core business under speculative pressure; yet this has been the fault not of the (good) Italian funds but of the large (bad) foreign funds, which have 'drugged' the market. This reasoning has been efficacious because it has directed attention to well-known cases such as the near bankruptcy of Ferretti; this case was characterized by the 'flight' of the Candover Fund which, rather than contributing to the company's urgent recapitalization, preferred the write-off option. It thus gave up its ownership, thereby losing the €360 million that it had invested.[14]

Even so, the entire PE sector benefited from the speculative approach which multiplied the leverage and company value. None have considered it appropriate to question the technique of the LBO, which is now acknowledged to have been used to an 'exaggerated' or even 'irresponsible' extent (Sattin 2010). Glossed over in particular is the fact that the reality of the PE sector cannot be so easily simplified, not least because 'good' (investments for expansion) and 'bad' (speculative investments) practices as a rule operate simultaneously in fund management companies.[15]

Notwithstanding the reputational crisis of PE, it would be wrong to discard it as a 'model belonging to the past'. As discussed above, the volume of investments in Italy grew again in 2011, after the halving recorded in 2009–10, almost to the level reached in 2006. From a purely financial point of view, this finding comes as no surprise: the peculiarity of PE consists, in fact, in its capacity to take advantage of phases of euphoria, exploiting liquidity and low interest rates while at the same time offering itself as an alternative source of financing in phases of crisis, in which the banks reduce resources and simultaneously tighten the criteria for access to credit. As for the speculative variant of PE, it was certainly slowed down by the crisis and the difficulties of the banking system; but high liquidity and low interest rates are only two of the three conditions that fuel it: the other one is the legal admissibility of the LBO. Not by chance, the beginning of the 'boom' of PE in Italy coincided with the deregulation of LBOs. At present, there is no indication that the legislation will be revised.

Conclusion: Four Ideal Types of Private Equity

The three types of NIFs have spread in Italy to different extents and have had differential impacts on labour and industrial relations. Currently, HFs and SWFs have limited importance, even if the latter have recorded substantial growth in recent years. As far as can be ascertained, neither of these two kinds of NIFs have had significant direct consequences on employment or industrial relations. PE, by contrast, has undergone significant development following deregulatory measures enacted around 2000. The measures taken to facilitate leveraged buy-outs (LBOs) have been especially important in this respect. The credit crunch and the financial crisis, however, have revealed the shortcomings of the predominant business model based on high levels of indebtedness of PE portfolio companies. In several cases this has resulted in the demise of the company as an independent concern. In these cases, as in the two cases examined in this study (i.e. Seves and Saeco), trade unions have proved powerless and have at best been able to secure agreements mitigating job losses.

Whilst the predominance of speculative PE is clear, it would nevertheless be an over-simplification to claim that this model applies to all cases of PE investment. However, the dearth of independent empirical research on PE makes it impossible to estimate the relative importance of 'virtuous' cases such as that of the Marazzi Group and to evaluate the statistics on smaller-scale investments and buy-outs in the SME sector.

Against this background and in light of the empirical material presented, we propose a typology consisting of four ideal types of PE as a possible basis to advance research on PE in Italy (Cattero 2012). Based on the case studies, two ideal types can be identified initially.

- The first ideal type of PE, which we call *'entrepreneurial'*, is characterized by minority shareholding and patient capital with a long-term horizon (5–10 years), which is oriented to production, maintenance of the entrepreneur's strategic leadership, and safeguarding of the company's financial health;

- The second ideal type is that of *'speculative'* PE: its typical features are control of the company via buy-out, the extensive use of leverage, a shorter time horizon (3–5 years), and the extraction of financial resources and real assets to accelerate and increase the return on capital invested.

In the first case, the company is conceived of as an economic agent which is invested in for its own development: this is the ideal type where finance is used in the service of the company, with PE providing risk capital. In the second case, the relationship is reversed, and the company serves finance: it is not solely a speculative commodity but a commodity which buys itself, with a real risk of bankruptcy through its indebtedness. In this case PE investment becomes a risk to the company.

These first two ideal types, to which the three case studies correspond, tend to coincide with the two main types of PE investment: provision of capital and expertise to support 'growth/expansion' on the one hand, and 'buy-out' investment on the other. However, the complex reality cannot be fully reduced to these two types, and not all investments in development/growth and in buy-outs fully correspond to the two types. We therefore propose a further two ideal types.

Consider first the concept of 'expansion'. The term suggests the traditional meaning of sales and employment growth, but the financialized economy—of which PE is at once a vehicle for and an expression of—has transformed values and principles and increasingly rewards the short-term view, which focuses on short-term financial growth. In these cases, PE involvement typically takes the form of a minority investment rather than a complete buy-out. This limits the capacity of PE to speculate with the assets of the company but does lead nevertheless to a greater emphasis on financial metrics and performance.

A second consideration is the large number of buy-outs in the small firm sector. In this case, it is likely that what makes the difference is the purchaser. If this is an industrial group, the buy-out may be the logical conclusion of an industrial growth strategy pursued by the company which, when a purchaser is found, disinvests and reaps the capital gain generated by the company's increased value. In these cases, PE involvement takes the form of a buy-out which aims at developing market share in the medium-run. Whilst the desired eventual outcome may be exit with healthy capital gains,

Table 8.7 *Ideal types of private equity*

SHARE OF INVESTMENT BY PRIVATE EQUITY	BUY-OUT	Industrial acquisition	Speculative
	MINORITY	Entrepreneurial	Financial expansion
		ABSENT	LOW	HIGH
			SPECULATIVE LOGIC	

shorter-term management and governance strategies are not dominated by speculative logics.

On the base of these considerations, the analysis can be refined by hypothesizing two hybrid ideal types in addition to the two initially identified (Table 8.7):

- First, an ideal type of 'financial expansion' oriented to improving the company's financial parameters. This modifies the first ideal type above in that, whilst minority investments are geared towards growth, the role of financial outcomes nevertheless becomes more important;
- Second, in the case of acquisitions we can observe a non-speculative and financially sound (i.e. low indebtedness) process of growth and expansion. Although PE takes over companies in their entirety, and a key medium-term objective is to achieve capital gains for the fund through resale, this is achieved by relying on growth in market share rather than speculative exploitation of company assets.

The typology proposed may be useful both for comparative purposes and for more systematic investigation of specific cases.

Finally, it is important to compare the logics of action and their outcomes between private funds and public agencies in the expansion segment of SMEs. Here, special attention should be paid to the Fondo Italiano di Investimento (FII), promoted since 2010 by the Ministry of Economy and Finance and subscribed to by the state-owned Cassa depositi e prestiti and the main Italian banks. With €1.2 billion raised, the FII is the largest Italian development capital fund. It is active with investments in the developmental stage of Italian SMEs which have a turnover between €10 and €100 million in order to support their growth and to consolidate and expand their market presence. After the market failure since the onset of the financial crisis, it is now the state which attempts to change the political economy with PE—the question is, will this be a more successful 'Italian way'?

NOTES

1. These include the Law Decree No. 78/2010, the Ministerial Decree No. 197/2010, and the Legislative Decree No. 141/2010.
2. The following categories are deemed to be 'qualified' investors: (i) entities and international bodies established according to international treaties implemented in Italy; (ii) institutional investors, even if not subject to tax, established in a country which allows an adequate exchange of information with Italy ('qualifying' countries included in the White List); and (iii) central banks and bodies which manage the official reserves of a country.
3. The Law for the Protection of Savings (Law No. 262/2005) and the legislative decree 27/2010, which transposed the European directive on the rights of shareholders in listed companies (Directive 2007/36/EC).
4. Law Decree No. 21, converted with amendments into Law No. 56/2012.
5. Law No. 10/2011.
6. This started with the 1997 Treu Law of the then centre-left government and was followed by the so-called Biagi Law of the second Berlusconi government (2003).
7. Legislative Decree No. 25/2007, which implements EU Directive 2002/14/EC.
8. The authors stress that these figures present lower bound estimates, in that only eleven of the sixty-four existing SWFs publish (wholly or in part) detailed information on their shareholdings in listed companies.
9. The value of PE investments based on AIFI data reported in the following sections also include the activities of foreign funds without formal bases in Italy about which it has been possible to obtain data from public sources.
10. The data for this section are drawn from Marazzi Group (2206, 2007, 2008).
11. A Wage Guarantee Fund is an intervention which for a set time covers 80 per cent of the wages of workers suspended from work due to company crises. The Ordinary Wage Guarantee Fund (*Cassa integrazione guadagni ordinaria*) is introduced in short-term situations and presupposes the return of the workers into production, whilst the Extraordinary Wage Guarantee Fund (*Cassa integrazione guadagni straordinaria*) aims at gradually getting rid of redundant staff, avoiding the traumatic social repercussions caused by collective dismissals.
12. The list of names and brands, like Saeco symbols of 'Made in Italy', would be long. Hence only the best known are cited here: IT Holding (Ferré) and Valentine in fashion and Ferretti in yacht construction.
13. However, in the absence of other information, the figure for employment does not necessarily equate with job creation.

14. Only one year previously, the Candover Fund had offloaded debts amounting to €1.2 billion onto Ferretti. The Ferretti Group, the symbol of 'Made in Italy' in the exclusive sector of luxury yacht construction, was saved by a group of banks which made it possible to restructure the debt while also acquiring ownership of the company. In January 2012 the Ferretti Group was finally sold by the banks to the Chinese Shandong Heavy Industry Group, which acquired a 75 per cent ownership share.

15. With reference only to the cases considered here, the Permira Fund can boast of its success with Marazzi. As a minority shareholder it has contributed to the latter's growth. But in the same period it also was responsible—among many other deals—for the secondary buy-out of Ferretti, from which it extracted resources to refinance the LBO, with the acumen, or perhaps simple good fortune, of reselling the majority shareholding to the Candover Fund, which purchased it with leverage of 7:1 just one year before the financial crisis erupted.

BIBLIOGRAPHY

AIFI (2006–11). 'Il Mercato Italiano del Private Equity e Venture Capital', Yearly Meetings, (AIFI) and PricewaterhouseCoopers, <www.aifi.it>.

AIFI (2011). *Yearbook 2011*. Associazione Italiana del Private Equity e Venture Capital (AIFI). Roma: Bancaria Editrice.

Alvaro, F. and Ciccaglioni, P. (2012). *'I Fondi Sovrani e la regolazione degli investimenti nei settori strategici'*, Discussion paper, 3, Roma: Consob.

Berton, F., Richiardi, M., and Sacchi S. (2009). *Flex-insecurity. Perché in Italia la flessibilità diventa precarietà*. Bologna: Il Mulino.

Cattero, B. (2012). 'Giano bifronte. L'ambivalenza asimmetrica del private equity nell'economia finanziarizzata', *Rassegna Italiana di Sociologia*, 53: 67–89.

Croci, E. (2011). *Shareholder Activism. Azionisti, investitori istituzionali e hedge fund*. Milano: Angeli.

Croci, E. and Petrella, G. (2011). 'Price Changes Around Hedge Fund Trades: Disentangling Trading and Disclosure Effects', Working Paper. Milano: Università Cattolica del Sacro Cuore.

Erede, M. (2008). 'Governing Corporations with Concentrated Ownership Structure: Can Hedge Funds Activism Play Any Role in Italy?', Annual Meeting Paper, Toronto: Canadian Law and Economics Association (CLEA).

Granturco, M. and Miele, M. (2011). 'Il private equity in Italia: una analisi sulle "imprese target"', *Questioni di Economia e Finanza*, 98, Roma: Banca d'Italia.

ICTWSS (2009). 'Database on Institutional Characteristics of Trade Unions, Wage Setting, State Intervention, and Social Pacts', Amsterdam: Amsterdam Institute for Advanced Labour Studies (AIAS).

Longo, M. and Pavesi, F. (2011). 'Borsa e fondi: più freno che sostegno', *Il Sole 24 Ore*, 12 June.

Mangano, M. (2008). 'Hedge, due miliardi su Milano', *Il Sole 24 Ore*, 2 March.

Marazzi Group (2006). *Financial Statements as of 31 December 2005*. Modena: Marazzi Group.

Marazzi Group (2007). *Annual Accounts 2006*. Modena: Marazzi Group.

Marazzi Group (2008). *Annual Accounts 2007*. Modena: Marazzi Group.

Pasca di Magliano, R. (2009). *'I Fondi di Ricchezza Sovrana: assetti, obiettivi e impieghi'*, Roma: Nuova Cultura.

Peveraro, S. (2008). *Private equity e aziende familiari. Dieci storie raccontate dai protagonisti*. Milano: Egea.

Pontarollo, E. and Casè, M. (2007). 'Il private equity e l'industria italiana', *L'industria*, 27: 679–701.

Ronchi, M. (2004). 'Troppo debito rende nervosi', *Corriere della sera*, 'Economia', 18 October.

Sattin, F. (2007). 'La via italiana al private equity', *Il Sole 24 Ore*, 6 September.

Sattin, F. (2010). 'Quale futuro per il private equity?', *Harward Business Review Italia*, 5: 67–69.

Scagliarini, R. (2009). 'La cura Philips per Saeco', *Corriere Economia*, 28 September.

SWF Law Centre (2012). *Biannual Legal Report*, 1, Spring.

Turani, G. (2006). 'Il decollo del quarto capitalismo', *La Repubblica*, 'Affari e Finanza', 1 May.

9

Private Equity and Labour in a Transition Economy: The Case of Poland

STEFAN DUNIN-WĄSOWICZ AND
PERCEVAL PRADELLE

Introduction

In 1989 Poland began a process of economic transformation with the aim of establishing a market economy. Aggressive monetary reform, privatization, and institutional reforms were undertaken to position the country for European Union (EU) membership. Due to a dynamic internal market, a qualified workforce, and favourable pricing of assets, Poland was able to attract substantial foreign direct investment (FDI), both in terms of strategic industrial acquisitions and through financial investments in the rapidly developing stock market. Following the lead of large corporations, many mid-sized companies established subsidiaries in Poland allowing them to produce for both the domestic and export markets. In addition to increasing investments from abroad, the economy was also stimulated by small local companies which quickly grew in size and market share.

Private equity (PE) firms started to play an active role in the country from the early 1990s, with financial assistance from major international financial institutions. PE investments steadily increased in the following years, spurred on by Polish accession to the EU in 2004. Numerous PE transactions in the region initially focused on acquiring assets previously owned by the state owing to the large privatization programmes in the 1990s. Although investment levels remain modest in comparison to Western Europe, Poland is now the main market for PE in Central and Eastern Europe (CEE).

The fact that the Polish government invited PE and other investment funds to participate in some privatization programmes bears witness to the rather positive image enjoyed by these funds, at least in the eyes of public officials, and of the modernizing role attributed to them. In 2011, for instance, the government invited Stephen Schwarzman, co-founder of the Blackstone Group, to visit Poland to evaluate investment prospects in the country. The involvement of PE and other funds in Polish companies has not generated much controversy. Employee organizations and Polish trade unions have not so far publicly voiced any opinion about PE and other funds, probably because of the modest involvement of these funds relative to the size of the economy. Occasional tensions between funds and employees or managers, sometimes reported in the media, have remained confined to the level of individual companies.[1] Meanwhile, hedge fund (HF) and sovereign wealth fund (SWF) activity and acquisitions in Poland have been virtually non-existent so far.

Given the lack of studies and aggregate data on the effects of PE in Poland, this chapter considers three detailed case studies of PE investment in a range of sectors: in a household appliances company, a telecoms company, and an IT company. These case studies focus on changes in employment levels, the introduction of new forms of labour organization, pay levels, the establishment of training programmes, and industrial relations. In these three companies the impact of PE on working conditions and labour has been limited. Although caution is required when generalizing from three cases, the trends and practices in the case study companies are nevertheless broadly in line with those observable among competitors and in the private sector more generally. It is concluded, therefore, that the impact of PE on labour in Poland has been neutral overall.

Institutional Contexts

Capital and labour regulation in Poland has been modelled on that in other countries, and is also shaped by the implementation of EU directives. Though they often include provisions already tried and tested in foreign jurisdictions, these regulations are not without loopholes in the Polish context.

Regulation of Capital

Regulation of Investment Funds
A domestic fund structure is provided for in Polish law in the form of Closed-End Investment Funds for non-public assets (CEIF).

This structure is relatively recent (Investment Fund Law of 27 May 2004) and is not often used in practice. Most PE funds active in Poland operate instead via Polish limited liability companies (*spółka z ograniczoną odpowiedzialnością*). In this case, a holding company based in a different European country, often the Netherlands, Luxembourg, or Cyprus, is generally the owner of the shares in the Polish company.

Although Polish insurance companies can buy shares directly in PE funds, Polish pension funds are not allowed to do so as PE is excluded from the list of authorized asset classes specified in pension legislation. However, pension funds can invest indirectly in PE if the investment vehicle is a CEIF, up to a limit of 10 per cent of the pension fund's assets (EVCA 2008; Mergermarket 2008). This restriction may to some extent limit PE activities in Poland by constraining the amount of funds available for investment.

According to Dzierżanowski et al. (2009), the recent implementation of several EU directives into Polish law resulted in easier access to capital markets for small and medium-sized companies, thereby creating more favourable conditions for the growth of PE and venture capital (VC) activities.[2]

Overall, the 2008 European Private Equity and Venture Capital Association (EVCA) benchmarking survey on legal and tax environments ranks Poland seventeenth out of twenty-seven European countries. Measuring overall PE attractiveness in twenty-five European countries, Kucharczyk (2010) awards Poland twenty-second position, while Groh et al. (2011) rank the country thirty-sixth out of a total of eighty countries on their global VC and PE country attractiveness index.

Polish law does not define HF or make any provisions regarding their activities. As a result, there are no registered HFs in Poland. Instead there are investment funds with entities applying HF strategies, such as the use of financial leverage and short-selling. These might be termed 'quasi-HFs'. The law sets investment limits for various types of financial instruments, and because the limits are less rigorous for closed-end funds, quasi-HFs operating in Poland usually take the form of closed-end investment funds. Although foreign HFs can acquire Polish financial assets without registering with the Polish financial supervisory authority, Polish institutional investors are not allowed to invest in foreign HFs. As a result, foreign HFs wishing to operate in Poland and to collect funds from investors need to register by taking the legal form of a limited liability company or of a regular investment fund (Antkiewicz 2007). In the latter case, they will adopt the CEIF form.

Shareholder Rights

International standards for the protection of shareholders' rights, such as the EU Transparency Directive, have been implemented in Polish law. However, the law suffers from ambiguities and weak enforcement, resulting in several known cases of abuses of minority sharholder rights (Dzierżanowski and Tamowicz 2002).[3] The 2005 European Bank for Reconstruction and Development (EBRD) legal indicator survey on protection of shareholders' rights awarded Poland eight points out of ten for the institutional environment, but only four out of ten for simplicity and protection of shareholders' rights. Dzierżanowski et al. (2009) note, however, that the implementation of EU directives into Polish law markedly improved the protection of minority shareholders' rights. The EBRD (2010) notes that although the situation with listed companies has improved, minority shareholders in unlisted companies may encounter difficulties enforcing disclosure of information.

Tax Law

A corporation tax rate of 19 per cent is applied to resident companies (including those with limited liability) and to permanent establishments of foreign companies. Though somewhat higher than the Central European average, this rate is nevertheless in the lower half of corporate tax rates in the European Union.[4] In addition, corporate income tax exemptions are provided to investors investing in one of the fourteen special economic zones across the country. Poland is therefore a competitive tax zone in Europe and, as observed by Klonowski (2011), across emerging markets such as Brazil, India, and China.[5]

Tax levels and cross-country variations in taxes matter since they are key criteria for PE investment decisions. Investigating the macro-determinants of PE investment in Europe, Bernoth et al. (2010) found a significant correlation for the CEE region (though not for Western European countries) between lower corporate tax rates and PE activity. Their study confirms earlier research by Groh and Liechtenstein (2009) showing the key role played by tax competition in attracting foreign investments. In fact, in its economic survey of Europe, the United Nations (2004) highlights how low corporate tax rates are used by CEE governments as a tool to attract investors.

Turning to interest payments, these can be deducted from taxes only under specific conditions. As a result, EVCA judges the legal environment for deductibility of net interest expenses as unfavourable and below the European average (EVCA 2008). This possibly limits the inflow of funds into Poland. Dividends paid by Polish companies to parent EU-based companies are exempt from tax if the parent company owns at least 10 per cent of the shares in the Polish company. Interest and royalties paid to EU-based parent companies are subject to a 5 per cent rate, but will be fully exempt from taxes after July 2013 (EVCA 2009b, 2009c).

Although tax is to be paid on a regular basis when the investment occurs via a limited liability company, domestic investors with shares in CEIFs enjoy more favourable treatment as they are exempted from paying income tax until the redemption of their shares (EVCA 2008). Furthermore, a permanent domestic establishment is required for foreign firms investing via companies, whereas this is not the case for foreign partners in CEIF PE funds (EVCA 2006, 2008). Though take-up has been low so far, it is likely that PE investments in Poland will increasingly be directed through CEIFs because of the tax advantages.

Polish law does not include any specific provision on carried interest, the tax treatment of which varies according to the situation. In cases where the fund manager is an individual, it is considered a bonus related to employment income, and is therefore subject to progressive income tax at 18 or 32 per cent. Where the fund manager is a legal person, carried interest is taxed as corporate income (19 per cent). Performance incentives for PE fund managers are compatible with Polish regulation and are commonly paid as bonuses rather than carried interest if the fund has the legal form of a CEIF and is managed by an individual (EVCA 2008, 2009b). Finally, the Polish tax system does not offer any fiscal incentives to invest in PE, HFs, or SWFs.

Constraints on Foreign Investment

According to the Economic Freedom Act of 2004, undertakings by foreign entities originating within the EU or the European Free Trade Association (EFTA) zones are regulated by the same rules as those applicable to Polish entrepreneurs. Entities from outside the EU or EFTA zones can only undertake business or acquire ownership stakes in companies having the form of a limited partnership, limited joint-stock partnership, limited liability company, or joint-stock company (in practice the large majority of firms have one of these legal forms). Government concessions are required for a limited number of sectors—defence, energy production and distribution, protection of persons and properties, radio and TV broadcasting, and air transport (Article 46).[6]

Labour Regulation

The Polish system of industrial relations is characterized by decentralization, individual employment rights, and a strong dependence on the Labour Code (Towalski 2009). In 2010, the proportion of employees in unions was 15 per cent. With the exception of the Baltic states, this is the lowest percentage in Central Europe. The fact that formerly state-owned companies all have unionized workforces is nevertheless of particular importance considering the significant participation of PE funds in privatization programmes (see the section on funds below). According to Klonowski (2011), a social package guaranteeing employment and in some cases pay increases has typically been agreed between unions and PE or other investors acquiring privatized companies.

Collective bargaining coverage in Poland is difficult to measure precisely with estimates varying between 14 and 30 per cent. Even taking the highest of these figures, Poland ranks lowest among Central European countries on this indicator (Fulton 2011). The score of 0.37 received by Poland on the European Participation Index of employees (computed by the European Trade Union Institute, where 1 is the maximum) is higher than for Romania, Bulgaria, and the Baltic states, but lower than for the Czech Republic, Slovakia, and Hungary. Overall, the country is found in the weaker participation rights group of the EU 27 (Vitols 2010).

Board representation for employees is provided for in Polish law for state-owned and partially-privatized companies, but not private companies. Works councils can be created in companies with no trade unions following the recent application of the EU Directive on information and consultation (2002/14/EC). These councils have rights to information on economic issues, but consultation rights only on employment and restructuring questions (Fulton 2011).

Overall, Polish employment protection legislation is more permissive than in most Western European countries, as measured by the Organization for Economic Cooperation and Development (OECD) index of employment protection. It is, however, slightly above the Central European and OECD averages (Venn 2009). The position of Poland on the index has remained more or less stable since the previous edition of the survey (OECD 2004), and the changes introduced subsequently (i.e. limits on the number of successive fixed-term contracts and halving of the notification periods for collective dismissals) offset each other (Venn 2009).

It has been emphasized in some earlier research, such as Shertler's (2003) work on VC investments in Western European countries, that employment protection and labour market rigidities are negatively correlated with inflows of PE investments. Whether the level of labour protection is a criterion in the investment decision of funds active in Poland remains uncertain. To date there are no studies providing in-depth investigation of the impact of employment protection legislation on PE and other investment fund activities in CEE countries. Comparing the macro-determinants of PE investment in Western Europe and in CEE, Bernoth et al. (2010) found that the most robust determinants of PE activity in both regions are financial and economic variables—namely the ratio of equity market capitalization to gross domestic product (GDP) and the ratio of commercial bank lending to GDP—but not labour variables. Trade union strength is inversely correlated with PE investments only in Western Europe but is positively related in the CEE countries. Employment protection legislation is not a robust determinant in either of the two regions.

Looking at inflows of FDI into CEE countries (which can be used as a proxy to evaluate the motivations of foreign investors), Leibrecht and Scharler (2009) find a positive correlation between FDI and the low unit labour costs characterizing CEE labour markets. However, they do not find a significant statistical relation between employment protection legislation and FDI flows. They conclude that low production costs are a key factor attracting FDI into the region, whereas the relative rigidity or flexibility of labour markets is less relevant.

To conclude, though it is frequently claimed that low levels of employment protection may assist PE and other funds investing in the country, it does not seem to be an important factor in attracting or stimulating PE activity.

Funds

While PE investment in Poland has been rising constantly until recently, to date HF and SWF acquisitions remain small and sporadic. For this reason, most of the following discussion focuses on PE.

Private Equity

Private equity in Poland has two main strands. The first is domestic and relies on capital accumulated by individuals in the early stages of privatization. These funds are frequently the investment vehicles for owner-managers of privatized companies who later partially diversified their holdings by creating PE-like organizations. The second category includes financial investors whose activities were structured as PE companies from the beginning. This category comprises four types of PE funds active in Poland:

1. funds established on the basis of initial support from international financial institutions (i.e. the European Bank for Reconstruction and Development and the International Finance Corporation) and from government agencies (e.g. the Polish–American Enterprise Fund, whose assets were managed by Enterprise Investors, one of the PE market founders in Poland);
2. funds established on the basis of an initial private capital investment in specialized funds (e.g. MCI or White Eagle Industries);
3. subsidiaries of regional funds operating across CEE (e.g. Innova Capital); or
4. so-called 'business angels' (non-institutional individual investors, grouped in the Polish Network of Business Angels) (Kornasiewicz 2004; Próchnicka-Grabias 2008).

Private equity in Poland is now well-established and most PE investors belong to the trade association (Polskie Stowarzyszenie Inwestorów Kapitałowych). Of 1,696 active PE firms with offices in Europe, twenty-five are headquartered in Poland (EVCA 2011), and about forty PE firms in total are currently investing in the country. PE activity in Poland grew steadily during the 2000s. Accounting for only 0.07 per cent of GDP in 2002, it rose to 0.22 per cent in 2007, with €1.1 billion invested in company buy-outs in that year. Total investments then decreased to €913 million in 2008 (0.17 per cent of the GDP) and to €267 million in 2009 in the aftermath of the crisis, but rebounded to €657 million in 2010 (CMBOR 2010; EVCA 2009a, 2011).

Compared with Western Europe, investment levels remain modest. In 2010 they accounted for 0.19 per cent of Polish GDP, while the European average stood at 0.32 per cent of the per country GDP (EVCA 2011). Poland is nevertheless the leading recipient of PE investment flows in CEE over the last few years, whether measured by the value of invested capital or by the number of investee companies. In

2010, it accounted for more than half of the total investments in the region with forty-four Polish companies receiving PE funding, compared to a regional average of twelve investee companies per country. The Czech Republic, Romania, and Ukraine came next in terms of amounts invested (EVCA 2011).

The leading position of the Polish market in attracting PE investments is largely attributable to the size of the country's economy. The fact that it has the biggest stock market in the region, which enlarges the scope of initial public offering (IPO) exit opportunities for potential investors, is another reason. Throughout the 1990s and 2000s, the dominant exit route nevertheless was the trade sale to a strategic investor, followed by divestment by public offering, secondary sale to another PE house, and sale to management. To date, PE funds operating in Poland have completed close to 700 exit transactions. About fifty of these took the form of IPOs, and more than 10 per cent of firms listed on the Warsaw exchange have received PE funding (Klonowski 2011).

Most PE investment in Poland is in the production and distribution of consumer goods and services (see the case of Zelmer below) and in the IT and telecommunications sector (see the cases of Sygnity and Netia, respectively). Also worth highlighting is the strong presence of PE in healthcare, which was the largest sector by value in 2009 and which underwent substantial consolidation through so-called 'buy and build' strategies. This is well illustrated by the example of the Mid Europa fund, which acquired and merged three large domestic healthcare clinic companies in 2007 (Karsai 2009).

Initially, PE acquisitions in Poland were mainly development and growth stage investments, often associated with privatization programmes after 1989.[7] However, buy-out activity rose considerably in the 2000s, becoming by far the predominant form of investment. In 2009 and 2010, buy-outs accounted respectively for 74 per cent and 79 per cent of all transactions, and mostly concerned small and mid-market investments (EVCA 2011). The average size of PE transactions has also been growing since 2000, reflecting some consolidation in the sector.

Hedge Funds and Sovereign Wealth Funds

At present, HF and SWF activity in Poland is limited and there has not been any public or political debate about their activities. There are currently a few dozen investment funds applying HF-like strategies.

This includes Polish and foreign funds operating in Poland as well as a few Polish funds operating abroad. In January 2011, the assets managed by such funds reached approximately 3.5 billion Polish zlotys, that is, 3 per cent of the total assets of 115 billion Polish zlotys managed by investment funds on the Polish capital market. This is up from 2.1 billion zlotys one year earlier (Uryniuk 2011). These funds mostly invest in shares and bonds and do some short-selling, but a number of these funds have recently started expanding their activities to cover raw materials, futures products, and currencies. At the end of 2008 the largest equity position of HFs in listed companies was only 0.4 per cent of the company's shares. HF participation in unlisted Polish companies is difficult to gauge. While data are very sparse, such participation seems to be confined to a small number of companies. Among the few known examples, it is worth mentioning Tiger Global which acquired a majority of shares in the job portal Pracuj.pl and has indirect participation in the social networking portal Nasza-klasa.pl (Grynkiewicz and Makarenko 2008).

Turning to SWF involvement in Poland, the largest of the top twenty identified equity positions in listed companies in 2008 was held by Norges Bank (the investment manager for the Norwegian Government Pension Fund), with a stake of 1.5 per cent of shares. In 2009, aborted negotiations with the Qatar Investment Authority over the purchase of the publicly-owned shipyards of Gdynia and Szczecin were widely publicized and commented on in the press. The exact reasons why the deal was not completed were not disclosed (WBJ 2009; Wiśniewski 2009). Otherwise, the Qatar Investment Authority has some involvement in the Polish real estate sector.

In 2010 talks were initiated regarding the privatization of Enea, a public energy producer and distributor. Among the potential buyers was Kulczyk Investments (the investment arm of Jan Kulczyk, a wealthy Polish business owner and entrepreneur) in partnership with the Libyan Investment Authority. The possible participation of the latter was considered problematic by the state treasury, one of a number of reasons for why no agreement was reached and the company remains in the public sector (Zasuń 2010). The Polish government itself does not own any SWF. There has been speculation that it could create a SWF in the coming years and finance it with taxed profits from the exploitation of Polish shale gas reserves.

Consequences for Labour

In view of the negligible involvement of HFs or SWFs in listed companies and given the absence of data on the few cases of participation in unlisted companies, the focus in this section is on PE investments. Whilst financial data on the volume of PE transactions in Poland is readily available, no studies have yet been carried out on the overall impact of PE activity on employment levels and working conditions. Case studies are therefore helpful to build a general picture of PE activity and its consequences for employment and restructuring practices. Three investee companies were surveyed in detail for this purpose, two of them with foreign PE funds as their main shareholder and one with a domestic PE fund as its main owner. The section below relies extensively on these three cases, although it draws on additional information and examples where appropriate.[8]

The first company, Netia, is a fixed-line phone operator that received support from the Iceland-based fund Novator Telecom (a subsidiary fund of Novator One LP) in order to secure its position in the broadband internet market and to enter the cellular market. The fund started accumulating Netia's shares in 2005 (the company was and still is listed on the Warsaw stock exchange), and acquired at the same time a 70 per cent stake in P4, a joint venture created with Netia to develop Netia's mobile network. To date P4 has been kept private. The fund exited Netia in 2009 but still owns shares in P4.

The second company, Zelmer, produces household appliances and has a share of this market in Poland of approximately 20 per cent. The Polish-American PE fund Entreprise Investors started to acquire ownership in 2005 after the company was privatized via an IPO. To date the fund is still the main investor, with close to 50 per cent of the shares.

The third company, Sygnity, exemplifies a PE-backed merger in the IT sector. The firm was created in 2007 from the merger of two organizations, Computerland and Emax. Computerland had itself been the subject of a buy-out in the 1990s, financed by the private equity fund Enterprise Investors, which resulted in a successful IPO, the growth of the company, and the broadening of the scope of its activities. Behind the merger plan was the domestic PE fund BB Investment, at that time the majority owner of Emax. Well before the financial crisis the project encountered several implementation issues in a context of declining demand for IT services. Because post-merger performance fell short of expectations, the supervisory board dismissed Sygnity's head and appointed one of the founders of the fund as the new president, who then started restructuring the company. The fund exited the company in 2010.

Employment Relations

Employment Levels

An EBRD survey conducted among a sample of PE funds investing in transition countries between 1992 and 2005 suggests that in 36 per cent of cases, PE investors resorted to operational restructuring such as changes in the strategy or organization of portfolio companies (EBRD 2006).[9] An additional 20 per cent of the transactions consisted of mergers and acquisitions, while labour restructuring entailing redundancies or retraining occurred in 14 per cent of the cases. Substantial divestments were undertaken in 9 per cent of the investments and financial restructuring (i.e. changes in the debt structure) accounted for 8 per cent. Unfortunately, the survey does not mention if these types of restructuring overlap.

Focusing on the case study companies, there are no clear trends in employment change (see Table 9.1). In two of the companies, Zelmer and Netia, headcount numbers increased during the first two to three years after the entry of the PE fund. They fell moderately at

Table 9.1 *Employment in the case study companies, 2005–2011*

		2005	2006	2007	2008	2009	2010	2011
NETIA	PE fund involvement	Entry	—	—	—	Exit	—	—
	Headcount	1,220	1,111	1,281	1,673	1,342	1,441	1,376
ZELMER	PE fund involvement	Entry	—	—	—	—	—	—
	Headcount	2,312	2,687	2,700	2,644	2,624	1,902	1,775
SYGNITY	PE fund involvement	—	Entry	—	—	—	Exit	—
	Headcount	—	3,291	3,000[a]	2,500[a]	2,600[a]	2,100[a]	1,900[a]

[a] *Note*: Authors' estimates based on information published in *Parkiet* newspaper and Sygnity Annual Reports.
Sources: Based on Annual Reports of Netia, Zelmer, and Sygnity. *Parkiet* newspaper, various issues.

Netia in the crisis years 2008 to 2010 to levels that were neverthe-less higher than those prevailing at the time of the fund entry. In Zelmer, the decrease in employment after the crisis was particularly pronounced between 2009 and 2010. This decrease is largely due to the transfer of employees to newly created companies which are financially independent and separate from Zelmer. These transfers explain approximately two-thirds of the fall in employment in the company, while the rest arose from voluntary redundancies. As for the third company, Sygnity, the workforce was reduced by approxi-mately one-quarter over a two-year period in the aftermath of the failed merger.

The case of Zelmer is particularly informative with respect to staff-ing levels and workforce composition. The company had already been restructured between 2001 and 2004 under state ownership to prepare for privatization, and substantial downsizing was not con-sidered necessary nor implemented under PE ownership. In order to cope with seasonal fluctuations, the PE fund introduced temporary workers during months of peak demand. Although the headcount of permanent workers decreased overall,[10] it was more than com-pensated for by the hiring of seasonal staff. The company therefore achieved higher employment levels and increased flexibility.

Growing use of temporary and seasonal workers, some of whom are contracted through temporary work agencies, is a general trend in the Polish economy, especially in the manufacturing sector. It is not specifically associated with PE ownership. In fact, during the last decade, Poland has had the highest growth in Europe regarding the proportion of fixed-term workers. In 2006, one year after PE entry into the capital of Zelmer, close to 30 per cent of all workers in Poland were hired on fixed-term contracts, well above the EU15 average of 16.2 per cent (Baranowska and Lewandowski 2008). This share has remained fairly stable since then, as shown by Eurostat data.

In Netia's case, the increase in staff after PE entry until the crisis was largely the result of the 'build and buy' strategy pursued by the company. The acquisition of Tele2 Polska, a subsidiary of Swedish Tele2, the purchase and integration of new Ethernet networks, and the conversion of 303 temporary positions into full-time equivalents led to a significant rise in employment between 2006 and 2008. Like Zelmer, the company hires temporary workers, mostly in the cus-tomer care and sales areas but, unlike Zelmer, it started to do so prior to PE fund involvement.

The third company, Sygnity, released around 700 permanent staff during the first two years of operation, with employment falling from 3,200 immediately after the merger to 2,500 employees by the end of 2008. As already mentioned, this drastic cut can be attributed to the PE-initiated merger, which failed to bring the expected synergy benefits in a subdued market for IT services. The headcount further fell during the crisis. While layoffs account for part of the post-merger workforce reductions, the sales of operations not directly related to the company's core activities accounted for another significant part of the decrease.

Following the reshuffling of Sygnity's management board in July 2007 and the announcement of headcount reductions, employees in one of the departments which developed products for the banking sector threatened to leave the company. These employees finally dropped this plan after negotiating with the management board. However, a few weeks later around thirty employees from the Winuel subsidiary, a company controlled by Sygnity, handed in their resignations.

Pay and Incentives

On the whole, the case study companies monitor sector-specific wage standards and fix their pay levels either close to the average or, in the case of Netia and Zelmer, slightly above it. While wage growth and bonuses were temporarily frozen in some cases during the financial crisis, salaries have been adjusted upward in others, as illustrated by the Sygnity case. In spite of financial losses during the restructuring stage, the management board of this company approved a general increase in wages in 2007. It did so to retain key employees who had threatened to leave in the aftermath of the merger. The upward adjustment of salaries continued throughout 2008 in Sygnity in an attempt to match prevailing levels in the IT sector.

A recent survey conducted among 20,000 foreign and Polish-owned companies operating in Poland showed that, in 2011, median pay was typically higher in companies with foreign ownership, regardless of sector, region, type of job, employee age, or education (Karkocha 2012). The fact that Netia and Zelmer, with capital from foreign funds, set pay levels slightly above the market average, while Sygnity, invested in by a domestic PE fund, adjusted salaries upwards to catch up with market standards, is illustrative. It suggests that differences in pay levels arise from differences in the nationality of ownership rather than from differences in types of ownership structure.

Turning to performance remuneration and appraisal in the case study companies, financial incentive mechanisms were introduced in Zelmer as part of the modernization of human resource (HR) policies initiated by the PE fund. In Sygnity, a broad incentive programme was introduced for sales and production employees as part of the restructuring process. In addition to mitigating the risk of staff departures, it aimed at facilitating the assessment and measurement of employee productivity in various jobs. In mid-2010, Sygnity's incentive programme for sales staff was further developed and intensified after the exit of the PE fund (Wolak 2010a).

Several bonus mechanisms are used in Netia, depending on employees' functions and departments. Monthly bonuses for salespersons, for example, are calculated on the basis of set targets (number of new subscribers), which is a typical performance system for sales staff. All Netia employees receive an annual bonus, the amount of which is based on individual and company performance. Unlike Zelmer and Sygnity, bonus mechanisms were already in use at Netia prior to PE involvement, and no known change occurred when the fund took over. At least one of the companies, Zelmer, introduced a variable component in the remuneration package of management board members, the value of which is linked to the company's quarterly performance. Unfortunately, detailed data on changes to variable pay for managers are not available for the other companies.

Share option schemes for senior management were introduced at Zelmer after the PE acquisition, and renewed and intensified at Netia. A share option programme already existed in ComputerLand prior to the merger with Emax and the ensuing creation of Sygnity. It had been introduced in 1995 by the fund Enterprise Investors and, remarkably, was the first management stock option plan ever set up in Poland (Tamowicz 2011). It was broadened in scope after the Sygnity merger but the structure of the programme remained the same, with share options being distributed to board members of the group and subsidiaries, and to employees holding key positions, within an overall limit of 300 people.

Work Relations

The lack of appropriate data makes it difficult to assess the influence of PE ownership on working conditions in portfolio companies.

However, in Zelmer there was some reorganization of personnel between departments, with some decrease in production workers and an increase in sales and marketing. In this connection, Klonowski stresses that, after a deal is closed, PE firms 'must provide active, hands-on assistance across many functional areas of the business, including marketing, finance and accounting. HR gaps in these departments become accentuated when the investee firm shifts its strategic focus to new market sectors, products or services, and geographic regions' (Klonowski 2011: 12). This often requires retraining of employees and the development of new HR training programmes. In fact, the introduction of workshops to develop employees' skills was a key feature of the modernization of HR policies undertaken by the PE fund Enterprise Investors. Incidentally, a by-product of training programmes was improved communication between different groups of Zelmer employees: workshops involving a mix of workers, management, and unions had a levelling effect on formal hierarchical relations.

Training programmes were also set up in Netia and Sygnity, but it is not clear if the PE fund managers had any influence in shaping them. In 2008 Netia established a training and development team within its HR department. The position of Organizational Effectiveness Manager was created the same year with the task of improving the effectiveness of organizational structures.

Considered in the broader national context, the fact that all three companies implemented training schemes should not be overstated, as it is consistent with the general trend in Polish firms. Employee training has become increasingly popular among mid-size and large organizations in recent years. This is reflected in figures from the European Working Conditions surveys (Eurofound 2010a). The proportion of Polish workers receiving training provided by employers rose from 23.4 per cent in 2000 to 26.3 per cent in 2005 and then to 32.8 per cent in 2010.

Industrial Relations

Private equity involvement in Polish companies has not been the subject of any negotiations or social dialogue at the national or industry level. The modest size of industries and services with PE funding relative to the rest of the economy, together with the limited coverage of collective bargaining and low union membership, explains why PE financing has not become a major industrial relations topic. The main Polish trade unions (Solidarność, Ogólnopolski Porozumienie

Zwiazków Zawodowych, and Forum Zwiazków Zawodowych) have not formulated any official stance on the involvement of PE and HFs, possibly because of the relatively limited scope of their activity. At company level some trade unions have welcomed PE investment in their company, although in other cases trade unions have been more critical.

Considering the cases studied, Sygnity and Netia did not have union representation prior to receiving PE funding and still do not. But where companies already had trade unions, no major changes in union structure occurred under PE involvement. This is the case at Zelmer, which still has several unions, the largest one having nearly 800 members. However, membership appears to have decreased somewhat over the last few years. This is partly explained by the implementation of Voluntary Departure Programmes, as the fall in membership caused by employees leaving the company was not compensated by the enrolment of new members.

Trade unions and employee representatives do not seem to have been consulted at the time of PE acquisition in any of the three companies. In the Zelmer case, however, the fund engaged in a dialogue with union representatives after its entry, providing information on its development strategy for the company and on the organizational changes associated with this. This move helped allay the concerns initially harboured by employees and unions. However, it did not prevent occasional disagreements from emerging during the implementation of the strategy. In particular, unions opposed a decision in 2006 to outsource to China the production of some minor components used in vacuum cleaners (*Gazeta Wyborcza* 2006). They also questioned the splitting of the group into several distinct entities (the Zelmer capital group now comprises ten subsidiaries), and at times conflict arose with the management regarding negotiations on pay increases (*Puls Biznesu* 2006).

Turning to Netia, the fact that no union was formed in the company comes as no surprise, given that union activity in the Polish telecommunication sector is limited to Telekomunikacja Polska, the former state-owned and largest telecommunication provider in the country. According to Sula (2007), other fixed-line and mobile operators created in the 1990s offered attractive pay levels to employees from the outset, thereby discouragaing union organization. Netia, whose articles of association do not contain any provision for trade unions, is no different in this respect from its competitors (other than Telekomunikacja Polska).

In Sygnity, despite the absence of unions in the company, groups of employees and sometimes whole departments occasionally took collective action to protest against decisions of the management board. These actions did not always meet with success though they did secure a pay rise a few months after the merger. In September 2009, following the decision of Sygnity's management to dismiss the president and vice-president of Winuel, a subsidiary operating in the utilities sector, a majority of Winuel employees signed an appeal to the Sygnity management board to revoke the decision. However, the petition was ineffective.

Finally, the fact that each headcount reduction in Zelmer was implemented in agreement with the unions is worthy of attention. What is more, redundancies in the group took the form of voluntary programmes with severance pay and replacement services as well as early retirement benefits for senior employees. In contrast, staff reductions at Sygnity and Netia often took the form of dismissals with the usual notice of termination as stipulated in the Labour Code. Therefore, the more favourable employment restructuring schemes enforced at Zelmer might be attributed to the moderating influence of unions.

Other Outcomes
The transfer of know-how occurring under PE investments appears to be a salient feature across the CEE region, and several authors highlight the instrumental role of PE funds in implementing modern methods of management in their investee companies, not least in the area of corporate governance (Dzierżanowski et al. 2009; Karsai 2009; Klonowski 2011). Tamowicz (2011) argues that PE funds in Poland played a prominent role in structuring and empowering supervisory boards of target companies. Although difficult to measure in practice, this may result in long-term growth of employment because the initial restructuring paves the way for sound financial and economic development of the company. The overall improvement of management quality in Zelmer for instance played an important role in company renewal under PE.

The Present Financial and Economic Crisis

As Karsai (2009) puts it, the crisis has marked an end to the 'golden age' of VC and PE investments in the CEE region. The outcome of the crisis for the Polish financial sector was an outflow of capital, and, consequently, smaller amounts invested in PE transactions. In this connection, the number of PE deals in Poland fell from twenty-seven in 2007 to eight in 2009 (CMBOR 2010). PE funds have become more cautious financially in an adverse economic environment and opportunities for profitable investments have shrunk. On the other hand, because bank loans are more difficult to obtain, more companies may have turned to PE investors for financing. Therefore, although they have more limited resources, the funds may have seen their bargaining power increase when deciding which companies to invest in (Karsai 2009).

It might be expected that target companies would have faced additional pressures to restructure because of the crisis. All three case study companies have reacted to the crisis with employment restructuring and layoffs. They have done so at different times, roughly corresponding (with a time lag of about three months) to when they were impacted by the crisis: autumn 2008 for Netia, summer 2009 for Zelmer, and autumn 2009 for Sygnity.

A Voluntary Departures Programme was introduced at Zelmer, similar to the one already implemented in 2006. It included training to enhance employees' skills and qualifications, partly financed by EU funds, as well as severance benefits. In all, 244 workers enlisted in this scheme and left the company. As part of the restructuring, some activities were separated out and moved to three newly created and financially independent companies; 500 employees were transferred to these new entities and Zelmer's headcount fell proportionally. Finally, the company shut down production facilities for a few days in February 2009 to cope with low order volumes, and sent some staff on training courses or on paid vacation (WNP 2009).

Netia, for its part, embarked on a cost-saving initiative called the 'Profit project', implemented in the second half of 2008 and throughout 2009, under which 267 employees were dismissed out of a total workforce of around 1,700 employees. Six per cent of employees who left the company did so on a voluntary basis, even though a dedicated severance programme was set up. Staff reductions were slightly offset by the addition of employees from the new Ethernet networks acquired in the meantime.

Other measures at Netia included a partial wage freeze as well as a recruitment freeze. In addition, about forty employees in management positions were forced to take lower-level posts, with lower remuneration. Decreasing wages (or reducing working time) seems to have been the most widely used measure among Polish companies to maintain workplaces during the crisis (Semenowicz 2009). Autosan, for instance, an unlisted, domestically-owned Polish manufacturer of buses not subject to PE financing lowered wages by 10 per cent over a six-month period in agreement with trade unions. No data are available on the overall number of organizations that resorted to pay reductions, but it is known that companies of all ownership types followed this path (Semenowicz 2009). Netia, in reducing wages for some employees, is not therefore an isolated example.

Sygnity first started to record losses during the merger year in 2007. It returned to profitability in the second quarter of 2008, when it began to reap the benefits of the restructuring plan completed in the summer of 2008. In the first quarter of 2009, the Polish IT market was markedly affected by the general economic slowdown and the group suffered record losses. Faced with falling revenues, the company embarked on a second restructuring programme in the fall of 2009. The plan envisaged a reduction in permanent staff as well as sub-contractors (350 employees dismissed in total), a recruitment freeze, a temporary reduction of employees' remuneration (including for board members), suspension of bonuses, stricter control of expenses, and enforced paid vacations for some staff.

In March 2010, the president of the board—one of the founders of the fund BB Investment—resigned following the announcement of weak financial results for the previous year. Four months later, the fund decreased its ownership stake to less than 2 per cent. Restructuring continued nonetheless throughout 2010. Initially 300 jobs were cut, and more redundancies followed up to early 2011 (Wolak 2011). Reductions were made amongst administrative staff, IT specialists, and middle and top management (including members of the board). Severance payments were granted to dismissed workers. Some of the employees left the company on their own initiative to set up new businesses that now compete with Sygnity in a number of IT markets (Wolak 2010b).

Judging whether companies with PE funding were more prone to layoffs and restructuring during the crisis would require a large sectoral comparison with a benchmark group of firms. Relevant data are unfortunately not available. Nonetheless, contrasting the case study companies with direct competitors is instructive. The way Netia and Zelmer navigated through the crisis is fairly similar to non-PE competitors. As for Sygnity, the company is an exception in its market environment.

To consider further the typicality of company responses to the economic crisis, we briefly outline developments at key competitors. Zelmer's main domestic competitor is Amica Wronki, a producer of large household appliances, privatized in 1994. The business operations of both companies followed a similar course during the crisis, with profits falling in 2008 and recovering only in late 2009. In February 2009, Amica cut 200 jobs to cope with the decrease in orders, a level comparable to the headcount reduction of 244 people that took place in Zelmer a few months later.

Telekomunikacja Polska, the largest telecommunication provider in the country and Netia's biggest competitor, is majority-owned by France Télécom. After recording significant profits between 2004 and 2008, the company's revenues deteriorated in 2009 as a result of the crisis. In agreement with trade unions the management implemented redundancies. From a total workforce of 27,700 in December 2009, 2,440 employees were to leave Telekomunikacja in 2010 and 2011, the vast majority benefiting from a voluntary departure scheme. Even though they are in different business sectors, Zelmer and Telekomunikacja exemplify the moderating effects of unions on company restructuring, irrespective of ownership. There was a continuity of union membership in both companies before and after privatization (Telekomunikacja was also formerly state-owned), and both companies implemented voluntary departures during the crisis, regardless of the fact that one is PE-owned but not the other.

Two of Sygnity's main competitors in the IT sector, Asseco and Comarch, are worth considering. Neither is owned by a PE. Asseco was left unaffected by the crisis, experiencing a steady growth of revenues and profits over the last years, particularly since 2007. The number of employees rose continuously from 1,140 employees in 2007, to 2,220 in 2009 and to 3,280 in mid-2011. The impact of the crisis on Comarch was real, but limited. The workforce in Poland decreased from 2,670 people in 2008 to 2,530 in 2009, but then rebounded to 2,740 in 2010. Compared with these competitors, the marked and lasting fall in employment observed at Sygnity looks to be unique. It is due mainly to the failed merger and the ensuing weak financial position of Sygnity at the time when the crisis broke out. Yet there are several examples of successful mergers in the Polish IT sector, such as Asseco (which is the product of four successive mergers).

It is difficult to estimate to what extent restructuring decisions were taken by PE funds voicing their views at supervisory board meetings or by management boards. In some cases, where the company president is directly chosen by the fund or, as in the case of Sygnity, is even a founder of the fund, it seems likely that the fund plays a major role in strategic decisions. However, other cases are more difficult to evaluate. For example, the Enterprise Investors fund, which holds a quasi-majority of shares in Zelmer, was very active in the year following the acquisition, but then progressively granted increased autonomy to company management. Because discussions in supervisory board meetings are not public, it is not possible to determine whether the voluntary redundancies implemented at Zelmer in 2009 can be attributed to the management board or to the PE fund.

Conclusions

Throughout the 1990s and the 2000s, PE funds have played an important role in financing and modernizing Polish companies, in the context of a fast-changing economic environment after the post-1989 transformations. This chapter has examined the impact of these funds, focusing in particular on the examples of Zelmer, Netia, and Sygnity. Evaluating the effects of PE in Polish portfolio companies in terms of restructuring practices and employment levels is a difficult task given the lack of aggregate data. But based on the three case studies, it can be argued that, on balance, PE funds have had a neutral—and possibly in some respects positive—influence on working conditions and labour. Two key observations help support this view: for one thing, some salient features in the case study companies were also observable in firms not subject to PE investment. For another, changes introduced during the period of fund involvement, if any, were broadly in line with general labour trends and practices observed in the Polish economy over the last two decades.

A short review of the most notable events observed in surveyed companies will help illustrate this. Starting with employment levels, employee headcount grew in Netia during the presence of the fund and in Zelmer until the onset of crisis. The new forms of work organization introduced at Zelmer—flexibility and the hiring of temporary workers—fits with the broader trend in Polish companies of increasingly using fixed-term employment contracts. In Netia hiring temporary workers was already an established practice before the PE fund's involvement. As to variations in headcount observed during the crisis, contrasting Netia with Telekomunikacja Polska in the telecommunications sector or Zelmer with Amica in the household appliances market, shows that redundancies were just as likely in non-PE-owned competitors.

With respect to pay levels, the slightly higher-than-market-average wages in Netia and Zelmer is a particular case of a larger phenomenon, which is that Polish companies with foreign capital tend to remunerate workers better than those with domestic capital. The reduction of wages for management positions observed at Netia during the economic meltdown appeared to be a common measure among Polish companies to maintain workplaces through the crisis.

Although setting up workshops to develop employees' skills was a key element in the fund's strategy in Zelmer, it remains unclear whether the funds in Sygnity and Netia shaped corporate training programmes in any way. Finally, turning to industrial relations, union structure was not subject to any change in Zelmer after the fund entry, whilst the absence of unions in the two other companies did not preclude collective action on some occasions to protest against directors' decisions, as illustrated in Sygnity.

Certainly, the case of Sygnity is not as clear-cut as those of Netia and Zelmer. The company has undoubtedly been an under-performer in the Polish IT market compared to its competitors, a situation which translated into persistent decline in employment after the merger and throughout the crisis years. Nevertheless, it is reasonable to attribute these events to particular circumstances. The companies Computerland and Asseco are prime counter-examples to Sygnity's story. The first one is a PE acquisition in the IT sector that resulted in company growth, and the second is one of a successful merger among Polish IT companies. Lastly, worthy of attention is the fact that restructuring in Sygnity continued under new management in 2010 after the fund exited the company. Since late 2011, the company has returned to profit.

In sum, the evidence summarized here suggests that PE has had a neutral influence on labour in Poland. Taking the argument a step further, one can find evidence of a positive effect of PE on labour in some respects. After all, PE funds helped transfer good corporate governance practices to their investee companies and, above all, when the strategy was successful, they strengthened the market position of portfolio companies, and therefore secured employment. This is well illustrated by Zelmer, where the financial investor helped the company adapt to market demands and become a strong competitor, and by Netia who gained market share against its main competitor Telekomunikacja Polska.[11] This claim of positive labour effects nevertheless requires caution. It may well be that improvements in governance would have occurred under other forms of ownership, or that Zelmer and Netia would have achieved similar results with sources of financing other than PE.

Finally, if identifying deals on the Polish market was relatively easy for PE firms in the 1990s, this task has become much more difficult today in the context of a maturing economy and an increasing number of PE funds operating in the country. Consequently, one may expect fiercer competition in the near future, especially since the recent economic crisis has ended the period of relatively high growth which began in the 1990s. As a result, PE funds might have less favourable impacts on employment and working conditions in portfolio companies. The strengthening of the regional presence of major Western PE houses, some of them recently opening offices in Warsaw, is a sign of this tightened competition (Karsai 2009). These developments, as well as the evolving involvement of HFs and SWFs in Poland, call for further scrutiny in the future.

NOTES

1. One of the few known examples is Orbis Travel, a longstanding tourism company which, indebted and in a fragile financial situation, was bought for a symbolic amount by the fund Enterprise Investors. After several months of either losses or meagre results, the fund exited the company amid dissension between the previous owner Orbis SA, the fund, and the managers (Gadomski 2010). The company filed for bankruptcy.
2. Public Offering Law of 29 July 2005. <http://isap.sejm.gov.pl/Detail sServlet?id=WDU20051841539>. Law on the Circulation of Financial Instruments of 29 July 2005. <http://isap.sejm.gov.pl/DetailsServlet?id=WDU20051831538>. Law on the Supervision of Capital Markets of 29 July 2005. <http://isap.sejm.gov.pl/DetailsServlet?id=WDU20051831537>.
3. Dzierżanowski and Tamowicz (2002) provide several examples where a majority shareholder was able to reject the auditor proposed by minority shareholders thanks to a loophole in the law. See also Przybyłowski and Tamowicz (2006).
4. As of the writing of this chapter the average corporate income tax rates in the EU as a whole, in the new Member States who joined after 2004, and in older Member Sates were, respectively: 22 per cent, 18.5 per cent, and 25 per cent (own calculations using the European Commission Taxes in Europe database).

5. Corporate income tax rates in Brazil, Argentina, China, and India typically range between 30 and 35 per cent.
6. Shipyards are not included in sectors requiring government authorization for acquisition by foreign owners. In 2009 the government began negotiations with the SWF Qatar Investment Authority over the sale of the state-owned shipyards of Szczecin and Gdynia but a deal was not reached.
7. Between 1990 and 1998, privatization programmes affected about 6,130 state-owned companies, of which forty-five were partially or wholly acquired by PE firms (Klonowski 2011).
8. For an earlier and detailed version of each case study, see Eurofound (2010b).
9. The survey was conducted among forty-four PE funds in which the EBRD invested between 1992 and 2005. These funds made 450 investments in 399 companies during the period, operating in Central and Eastern Europe, the Baltic states, South-eastern Europe, and the Commonwealth of Independent States.
10. Headcount reductions usually involved selected employees who were given early retirement benefits. In 2006 a Voluntary Departures Programme was introduced, under which 147 employees left the company. The same year, 133 employees were moved out of the group as a result of the spin-off of Meta-Zel Ltd, a company which took over Zelmer's casting operations. All of these changes were agreed with trade unions.
11. Groenewegen and Lemstra (2010) make an interesting case that the telecommunications sector in Europe has been subject to speculative deals by PE leveraged buy-out firms over the last years, often leading to significant amounts of debt, limited cash flow, and bankruptcy. However, their thesis does not apply to Netia where the deal was not a leveraged buy-out and where the company has experienced good financial health.

BIBLIOGRAPHY

Antkiewicz, S. (2007). 'Fundusze hedgingowe jako innowacyjne fundusze inwestycyjne dla zamożnych osób fizycznych', *Studia Gdańskie*, 4: 116–29.
Baranowska, A. and Lewandowski, P. (2008). 'Adaptability to economic changes', in Maciej Bukowski (ed.), *Employment in Poland 2007: Security on a Flexible Labour Market*. Warsaw: Ministry of Labour and Social Policy, <http://www. mpips. gov.pl/download/gfx/mpips/en/default-opisy/77/1/1/ZWP_2007_eng.pdf>.
Bernoth, K., Colavecchio, R., and Sass, M. (2010). 'Drivers of Private Equity Investment in CEE and Western European Countries', DIW Discussion Paper, 1002, Berlin: German Institute for Economic Research.

CMBOR (2010). *European Management Buy-out Review.* Nottingham: Centre for Management Buyout Research (CMBOR).

Dzierżanowski, M. and Tamowicz, P. (2002). 'Ownership and Control of Polish Listed Corporations', Gdańsk: Gdańsk Institute for Market Economics, <http://papers.ssrn.com/sol3/papers.cfm?abstract_id=386822>.

Dzierżanowski, M., Milewski, G., Przybyłowski, M., and Zagórski, M. (2009). *Dylematy regulacji polskiego rynku kapitałowego w obliczu potrzeb krajowego sektora przedsiębiorstw i procesu integracji z rynkiem europejskim.* Gdańsk: Gdańsk Institute for Market Economics.

EBRD (2006). *Transition Report 2006: Finance in Transition.* London: European Bank for Reconstruction and Development (EBRD), 70–80.

EBRD (2010). 'Commercial laws of Poland: An assessment by the EBRD', London: European Bank for Reconstruction and Development (EBRD), <http://www.ebrd.com/downloads/sector/legal/poland.pdf>.

Eurofound (2010a). *Fifth European Working Conditions Survey: 2010.* Dublin: European Foundation for the Improvement of Living and Working Conditions (Eurofund), <http://www.eurofound.europa.eu/surveys/ewcs/2010/index.htm>.

Eurofound (2010b). *The Impact of Investment Funds on Restructuring Practices and Employment Levels: Company Case Studies.* Dublin: European Foundation for the Improvement of Living and Working Conditions (Eurofund), <http://www.eurofound.europa.eu/publications/htmlfiles/ef1065.htm>.

EVCA (2006). 'Private Equity Fund Structures in Europe', Brussels: European Private Equity and Venture Capital Association (EVCA), <http://www.evca.eu/uploadedFiles/fund_structures.pdf>.

EVCA (2008). *Benchmarking European Tax and Legal Environments.* Brussels: European Private Equity and Venture Capital Association (EVCA), <http://www.evca.eu/uploadedFiles/Executive_Summary_Benchmark_2008.pdf>.

EVCA (2009a). 'Central and Eastern Europe Statistics 2008', Brussels: European Private Equity and Venture Capital Association (EVCA),

EVCA (2009b). 'Poland: Tax and legal update: January 2009', Brussels: European Private Equity and Venture Capital Association (EVCA).

EVCA (2009c). 'Poland: Tax and legal update: September 2009', Brussels: European Private Equity and Venture Capital Association (EVCA).

EVCA (2011). 'Central and Eastern Europe Statistics 2010', Brussels: European Private Equity and Venture Capital Association (EVCA).

Fulton, L. (2011). 'Poland', Brussels: Labour Research Department and European Trade Union Institute, <http://www.worker-participation.eu/National-Industrial-Relations/Countries/Poland>.

Gadomski, W. (2010). 'Dlaczego upadł Orbis Travel? Koniec turystycznej marki', *Gazeta Wyborcza*, 4 October, <http://wyborcza.biz/

biznes/1,101562,8458898,   Dlaczego_upadl_Orbis_Travel__Koniec_
turystycznej_marki.html>.

Gazeta Wyborcza (2006). 'Zelmer będzie produkował w Chinach',
  Gazeta Wyborcza, 2 November, <http://www.wnp.pl/wiadomosci/
  zelmer-bedzie-produkowal-w-chinach,16391_1_0_0_0_0.html>.

Groenewegen, J. and Lemstra, W. (2010). 'Private Equity Leveraged
  Buyout: Exposing a Flow in the Governance of the Telecommunications
  Sector?', Delft: Delft University of Technology, <http://regulation.upf.
  edu/dublin-10-papers/6J2.pdf>.

Groh, A. and Liechtenstein, H. (2009). 'How attractive is Central Eastern
  Europe for risk capital investors?,' *Journal of International Money and
  Finance*, 28 (4): 625–47.

Groh, A., Liechtenstein, H., and Lieser, K. (2011). *The Global Venture Capital
  and Private Equity Country Attractiveness Index 2011*. Barcelona: IESE
  Business School, University of Navarra, <http://www.iese.edu/research/
  pdfs/ESTUDIO-143-E.pdf>.

Grynkiewicz, T. and Makarenko, V. (2008). 'Nasza klasa, bałtycka kasa',
  Gazeta Wyborcza, 9 June, <http://gospodarka.gazeta.pl/gospodarka/
  1,33181,5295508.html>.

Karkocha, I. (2012). 'Wynagrodzenia w przedsiębiorstwach z kapitałem pol-
  skim i zagranicznym w roku 2011', Krakow: Sedlak & Sedlak, <http://
  www.wynagrodzenia.pl/artykul.php/wpis.2414>.

Karsai, J. (2009). 'The End of the Golden Age: The Developments of the
  Venture Capital and Private Equity Industry in Central and Eastern
  Europe', Discussion paper MT-DP-2009/1, Budapest: Hungarian Academy
  of Sciences.

Klonowski, D. (2011). *Private Equity in Poland: Winning Leadership in
  Emerging Markets.* New York: Palgrave Macmillan.

Kornasiewicz, A. (2004). *Venture Capital w Krajach Rozwiniętych i w Polsce.*
  Warsaw: Wydawnictwo CeDeWu.

Kucharczyk, K. (2010). 'E Fructu Arbor Cognoscitur: European Private
  Equity Country Attractiveness & Market Segmentation', Master's thesis,
  Maastricht: Maastricht University School of Business and Economics

Leibrecht, M. and Scharler, J. (2009). 'How important is employment protection legislation for Foreign Direct Investment', *Economics of Transition*, 17
  (2): 275–95.

Mergermarket (2008). *Private Equity in Emerging Europe.* London:
  Mergermarket.

OECD (2004). *Employment Outlook.* Paris: OECD.

Próchnicka-Grabias, I. (2008). *Inwestycje alternatywne.* Warsaw: Wydawnictwo
  CeDeWu.

Przybyłowski, M. and Tamowicz, P. (2006). 'Still much to be done: Corporate
  governance in Poland', *International Journal of Disclosure and Governance*,
  3 (4): 306–16.

Puls Biznesu (2006). 'Związki i zarząd Zelmer SA w sporze płacowym', *Puls Biznesu*, 3 March, <http://www.pb.pl/1390557,104208,zwiazki-i-zarzad-zelmer-sa-w-sporze-placowym>.

Semenowicz, A. (2009). 'Tackling the Recession: Poland', Warsaw: Institute of Public Affairs, <http://www.eurofound.europa.eu/emcc/erm/studies/tn0907020s/pl0907029q.htm>.

Shertler, A. (2003). 'Driving Forces of Venture Capital Investments in Europe: A Dynamic Panel Data Analysis', EIFC Working Paper, No. 03-27. Maastricht: United Nations University.

Sula, P. (2007). 'Representativeness of the Social Partners: Telecommunications Sector', Warsaw: Institute of Public Affairs, <http://www.eurofound.europa.eu/eiro/2006/06/studies/tn0606017s.htm>.

Tamowicz, P. (2011). 'Corporate governance in Poland', in C. Mallin (ed.), *Handbook on International Corporate Governance.* Cheltenham: Edward Elgar Publishing, 177–91.

Towalski, R. (2009). 'Poland: Wage Flexibility and Collective Bargaining', Warsaw: Institute of Public Affairs, <http://www.eurofound.europa.eu/eiro/studies/tn0803019s/pl0803019q.htm>.

United Nations (2004). *Economic Survey of Europe 2004 No. 1.* Geneva: United Nations.

Uryniuk, J. (2011). 'Fundusze hedgingowe zdobywają rynek', *Dziennik Gazeta Prawna*, 14 February, <http://biznes.gazetaprawna.pl/artykuly/486904,fundusze_ hedgingowe_zdobywaja_rynek.html>.

Venn, D. (2009). 'Legislation, Collective Bargaining and Enforcement: Updating the OECD Employment Protection Indicators', OECD Social, Employment and Migration Working Paper, 89, Paris: OECD. <http://www.oecd.org/els/workingpapers>.

Vitols, S. (2010). 'The European Participation Index (EPI): A Tool for Cross-National Quantitative Comparison', Brussels: European Trade Union Institute, <http://www.worker-participation.eu/About-WP/European-Participation-Index-EPI>.

WBJ (2009). 'Sunk without a trace', *Warsaw Business Journal*, 7 September, <http://www.wbj.pl/article-46597-sunk-without-a-trace.html, Warsaw Business Journal (WBJ)>.

Wiśniewski, P. (2009). 'Sovereign wealth funds: Państwowe fundusze majątkowe', *Infos—Biuro Analiz Sejmowych*, 19 (66), <http://www.bas.sejm.gov.pl/infos.php>.

WNP (2009). 'Zelmer na kilka dni zawiesza produkcję', *WNP.pl*, 6 February, <http://www.praca.wnp.pl/zelmer-na-kilka-dni-zawiesza-produkcje,71834_1_0_0.php>.

Wolak, D. (2010a). 'Sygnity kończy restrukturyzację i zaczyna myśleć o rozwoju,' *Parkiet*, 25 September, <http://www.parkiet.com/artykul/971692.html>.

Wolak, D. (2010b). 'Sygnity: zwolnienia nabrały tempa', *Parkiet*, 30 August, <http://www.parkiet.com/artykul/962765.html>.

Wolak, D. (2011). 'Sygnity zapowiada poprawę wyników,' *Parkiet*, 23 March, <http://www.parkiet.com/artykul/1033327.html>.

Zasuń, R. (2010). 'Libijczycy w Enei? Nie wszędzie mile widziani', *Gazeta Wyborcza*, 5 November, <http://wyborcza.biz/biznes/1,101562,8621980, Libijczycy_w_Enei__ Nie_wszedzie_mile_widziani.html>.

10

Japan: Limits to Investment Fund Activity

KATSUYUKI KUBO

Introduction

This chapter examines the behaviour of private equity (PE), activist hedge funds (HFs), and sovereign wealth funds (SWFs) in Japan, with particular emphasis on the effect on firm performance in general and employment outcomes in particular. This is in a context where previous studies show that mergers and acquisitions (M&As), in particular hostile takeovers, are rare in Japan (Odagiri 1994). It is also commonly believed that these activities are not consistent with the Japanese business environment.

There are several characteristics of Japanese firms to which initial reference should be made. These include insider-dominated corporate governance and long-term employment. It has been argued that one of the main characteristics of large Japanese firms is that they focus on employees' interests rather than that of shareholders (Abbeglen and Stalk 1985). In other words, firms try to maximize stakeholders' interests rather than those of shareholders. While it is not easy to confirm these arguments empirically, several questionnaire surveys provide supporting evidence. For example, Yoshimori (1995) surveys managers in the USA, the UK, France, Germany, and Japan. Managers were asked under which of the following assumptions a large company in their country is managed. The two possible responses were: (1) shareholders' interest should be given first priority or (2) a firm gives equal priority to the interest of all stakeholders. Almost all the managers in Japan (97.1 per cent) stated that a firm's objective is to maximize all stakeholders' wealth, whereas most managers in the USA (75.6 per cent) and the UK (70.5 per cent) said that the shareholders' interests are the main priority.[1] In addition, Yoshimori posed the further question: 'Suppose a Chief Executive Officer (CEO) must choose either to reduce dividends or to lay off a number of employees. In your country which of these alternatives would be chosen?' Again, most managers in Japan would prefer to cut dividends, while an overwhelming proportion of managers in the USA and the UK would choose to reduce employment. These answers suggest that Japan's top managers tend to look to employees' interests over those of shareholders. This result suggests they may not merge their firm with other firms without the consent of employees, even if it would increase shareholder value.

In general, employees in all countries do not welcome reorganization. In Japan, this attitude would seem to be particularly strong. Thus, the *Nikkei* newspaper conducted a questionnaire survey of employees in Japanese firms concerning their opinions on mergers. More than 80 per cent responded that they would be concerned if the firm they worked for was subject to a takeover. Among other reasons, this is because they would expect less opportunity for promotion. In addition, employees believe that their conditions of employment would deteriorate. The same attitudes may exist in other countries, but would seem to be particularly strong in Japan and it might be argued more likely to be heeded (*Nikkei* newspaper 2006).

Another distinctive feature of large Japanese firms is long-term employment. Typically, workers enter the firm after graduating and work for the same company for the long term. Indeed, many of them continue working with the same firm until retirement. In addition to legal constraints, which make it difficult for firms to dismiss workers, the operating assumption is that there is an implicit contract between managers and employees that employment with firms will be long-term. This employment system became prevalent among large firms after the Second World War, when the economy was growing rapidly (Koike 1988). As employers found it difficult to attract enough skilled workers to meet rising demand, it was important for them to keep their incumbent employees.

A popular perception is that the effects of the long-term recession in the 1990s have made it impossible for firms to maintain this relationship. In addition, firms are finding it difficult to maintain the higher salaries of older workers as their workforces are ageing. Consequently, more and more firms are thought to be forsaking the traditional long-term employment system. However, many studies indicate that for the most part firms still maintain the relationship (Chuma 1998; Kato 2001; Ono 2010; Shimizutani and Yokoyama 2009). For example, using the Employment Trends Survey from 1991 to 2003, Ono (2010) finds that the separation rate for employees of age 25–59 has been stable over time. For regular workers on full-time contracts, there is little change in the length of service (Kubo 2008).[2]

Having stated these starting characteristics, the remainder of the chapter proceeds as follows. The next section describes the institutional framework which surrounds corporate finance and ownership and new investment funds in Japan. The following section describes the activities of these funds and their impact on firm performance. The effects of these activities on employment are considered in a subsequent section while the final section draws conclusions.

Institutional Framework

In the 1990s, there were significant changes in Japan's financial markets. These changes included the advent of more foreign shareholders, the introduction of new financial products, and increasing household investment in financial products other than bank deposits. In response to these changes, several laws were introduced or amended, such as the Financial Instruments and Exchange Law, which was further extend and revised in 2006. In this section, we examine the institutional framework of the investment funds industry in Japan. This includes regulations on capital markets, shareholder rights, company law, and regulations on foreign direct investment. It should be noted throughout that many of these changes were introduced to make it easier for firms to conduct M&As through capital markets.

Capital Regulation—Financial Instruments and Exchange Law

The Financial Instruments and Exchange Law was introduced as an amendment to the Securities and Exchange Act of 1948. The objective of the law was to enhance the development of capital markets and to protect investors. This law establishes a broad, flexible framework for a wide range of financial instruments and services by expanding the scope of regulated products and services and by introducing cross-sectional regulation on those involved in financial activities. It also aims to enhance disclosure requirements and to provide strict enforcement measures against securities violations by increasing maximum criminal penalties.

From the viewpoint of investment funds, there are three important points to be mentioned under this legislation: regulation on those involved in financial activities, disclosure of large shareholdings, and tender offer systems. According to the law, those engaged in financial business are required to register. These financial activities include sales and solicitation of securities and derivative transactions, investment advisory services, investment management, and customer asset administration services. In addition, such businesses are required to comply with the rules governing advertising and the obligation to deliver documents before a contract is signed. However, it should be noted that the law categorizes financial activities into several types and that the regulation depends on that type. In particular, if the customers of the financial instruments businesses are 'professional investors', then some regulations are not applied. Thus, PE funds, whose customers are professional investors such as other financial institutions, are exempt from many regulations.

Another important aspect of this law relates to reporting obligations for large shareholdings. Investors who acquire a large proportion of shares are required to disclose their holding so that other investors are able to obtain information. In particular, if investors' shareholdings in a listed company are above 5 per cent, they should report within five business days through EDINET, an electronic disclosure system.

Those who try to acquire shares of listed companies need to make these acquisitions through a tender offer to ensure transparency and fairness. In particular, an investor is required to disclose information including offer periods, volumes, and prices, if shareholdings exceed 5 per cent after the purchase. However, it should be noted that the objective of the tender offer system is to protect investors, not employees. Notably, the law makes no mention of employees in this respect (Ukegawa 2010). Moreover, acquirers are not required to disclose information to employees or to consult them.

The Company Act

Another important piece of legislation from the viewpoint of investment funds is the Company Act of 2005, which provides rules on the restructuring of firms. This law consolidated related laws, such as the earlier Commercial Code and the Limited Liability Company Law. In particular, the Company Act frames regulations on mergers and 'company splits', in addition to other types of restructuring. Thus, when a company is planning organizational change, such as a merger or divestment, it is required to follow certain procedures including information disclosure.

For example, when a company is planning to merge with another firm, it must complete a merger agreement which includes details of the transaction. These details are disclosed to shareholders and creditors. Shareholders who oppose the merger can demand the firm purchases their shares. Furthermore, creditors can object to the merger agreement. Again, it should be noted that there is no clause to protect employees (Ukegawa 2010). Moreover, when firms are planning to merge, they are not required to disclose information to employees; they have no duty to provide information concerning possible changes in employment conditions; or to consult employees or trade unions.

Among various types of restructuring, explicit legal protection of employees is provided only in the case of company splits, where one company is divided into several. The relevant Act on the Succession to Labour Contracts on Company Split was introduced in 2000 to promote the protection of workers by prescribing special provisions to the Company Act. Under the Act, companies are required to notify employees and labour unions before the company is to be split.

Shareholders' Rights

According to the Company Act, shareholders in Japan have significant *de jure* power over senior managers (Spamann 2010). In particular, at shareholder general meetings, they have the right to determine executive compensation. However, *de facto*, this is seldom used, and in practice shareholders have limited power over senior managers.

As stated in the introduction, top managers would seem to place less emphasis on shareholder value in Japan than in other countries. One of the main reasons is ownership structure. Traditionally, there are several distinctive characteristics of Japanese company ownership. In particular, significant proportions of shares are cross-held between companies. In this way, firms tend to own stocks of other firms in the same corporate group or of firms with which they do business. Financial institutions, such as banks and insurance companies, also own significant proportions of shares of other firms. Top managers in these firms are relatively free from shareholder pressure, because the objective of such shareholding is not to maximize returns but to reduce shareholder turnover. Moreover, because these 'insiders' trade their shareholdings infrequently, it is difficult for outside investors to acquire firms through hostile takeovers.

These traditional ownership structures were common until the financial crisis of the late 1990s (Miyajima and Kuroki 2007; Miyajima and Nitta 2011). Miyajima and Kuroki (2007) examine the change in the composition of shareholder ownership, which includes ownership by banks, insurance companies, and other companies, between 1987 and 2002. They found that banks tended to sell the shares of a firm when they are not the main or leading bank in a relationship. Miyajima and Nitta (2011) also study the change in ownership structure. They show that over time cross shareholdings are becoming smaller. Thus the proportion of cross shareholdings in total shareholdings was 15.1 per cent in 1987 and only 9.0 per cent in 2008. In particular, the proportion for banks declined from 10.4 per cent in 1987 to 4.1 per cent in 2008.

One consequence of the stable ownership structure in Japan is that there are few hostile takeovers (Odagiri 1994). Kubo and Saito (2012) examine the effect of mergers on employment conditions of listed firms between 1990 and 2003. Among the 111 merger transactions they examined, there was no merger as a consequence of a hostile takeover. As described in the introduction, one reason that hostile takeovers are uncommon might indeed be the employment relationship, since a successful merger needs the cooperation of employees. Because of long-term employment, many workers progress their career within the firm through internal promotion. However, employees are concerned that M&As will limit such opportunity for internal promotion.

The fact that hostile takeovers are rare combined with the fact that stable ownership is large, suggests it is not easy for investors to purchase other firms. In addition, stakeholders of the targeted firm are likely to strongly oppose the acquisition unless their firm is in serious trouble. As we will see, while some activist HFs have acquired a part of a firm despite the objection of management, there is only one case in which a listed firm attempted to acquire another listed firm through a hostile takeover. This was the failed acquisition by Oji Paper of Hokuetsu Paper. In 2006, Oji Paper announced a takeover attempt on Hokuetsu Paper after the senior management of Hokuetsu declined the offer of a friendly merger. The stakeholders of Hokuetsu Paper, including employees, banks, and local politicians, supported the senior management of Hokuetsu and accused Oji of attempting to take over another firm without the consent of stakeholders. The trade union of Hokuetsu Paper, which had a cooperative relationship with management, publicly announced that they supported the senior management. They also argued that consultation and agreement with the trade union of the target firm would be essential for a successful merger. The Governor of Niigata prefecture and the Mayor of Nagaoka city also supported the senior management at Hokuetsu Paper. In these circumstances, Oji Paper failed to acquire Hokuetsu Paper. This failed takeover shows how in Japan employees and other stakeholders can be a significant obstacle to a hostile takeover.

Sometimes merger plans are cancelled in response to such opposition, even after senior management have made a formal announcement, although employees do not have statutory power to cancel the plan. In April 1994, the merger of three banks, Kita-Nihon Bank, Syokusan Bank, and Tokuyo City Bank, was announced. It was reported that the merger was planned to rescue the latter, which had significant amounts of bad debt. However, from the viewpoint of the employees of the other two banks, the merger might have had a negative impact on their employment conditions. Three days after the announcement, the trade union of Syokusan Bank made a statement opposing the merger. In addition, later in May, a resolution opposing the merger was passed in a meeting of the trade union of Kita-Nihon Bank. In response to this opposition, in June the merger plans were cancelled. These and several other similar cases suggest that in Japan it is difficult for senior management to go through with merger activities without the consent of employees. In other words, senior management may not conduct M&As even when it is likely to improve shareholder value.

A further reason why senior management may not seek to maximize shareholder value is that they have little financial incentive in this respect. Kubo and Saito (2008) show that senior management receive only a small financial remuneration even when they achieve high shareholder returns. They estimate the sensitivity of Japanese company presidents' wealth to shareholders' wealth for the period 1977–2000, showing that pay sensitivity was very low compared with the USA. According to their estimation, presidents in 2000 typically received $22,100 when stock returns increased from –2.1 per cent to 14.8 per cent. This figure is significantly smaller than for CEOs in the USA (Hall and Liebman 1998). Their finding is consistent with the notion that senior management are not managing the firm in order to maximize shareholder value.

Constraints on Foreign Direct Investment
There are several regulations on foreign direct investment (FDI) in Japan, including the Foreign Exchange and Foreign Trade Act of 1997. This legislation requires foreign investors to report when

their ownership of a listed firm exceeds 10 per cent (Hirose 2007). In principle, foreign investors can report after they acquire the shares. However, a prior filing is required if foreign investors intend to invest in certain protected sectors which are considered to be important from the viewpoint of national security.

In addition, there are particular laws in certain industries which regulate foreign ownership. These include *inter alia* mining, broadcasting, aerospace, and shipping. For example, under the Japanese Broadcasting Law, foreign ownership is limited to 33 per cent in wireless/mobile telecommunications infrastructure. Similarly, foreign ownership is limited to 33 per cent for the domestic railway freight transportation sector by the Cargo Forwarding Service Act.

There are several government programmes to promote FDI. However, some foreign investors claim that the government tries to discourage certain types of foreign investors, in particular investment funds, from purchasing large proportions of Japanese firms (*New York Times* 2008). In 2008, The Children's Investment Fund, an activist HF, increased its ownership of J-Power, which generates power and operates transmission lines. The firm also had planned to construct a nuclear power plant. By 2007, the fund had purchased 9.9 per cent of the firm. It then submitted a plan to increase ownership to 20 per cent in 2008. The government 'recommended' that the fund not take this course of action. As the fund refused voluntarily to follow this recommendation, the government ordered the fund not to proceed on the grounds that the acquisition has the potential to disturb civil order. In particular, it was pointed out that the nuclear power plant which the firm planned to construct was related to Japan's then nuclear cycle programme. A major concern was that the fund might underinvest in the nuclear plant relative to the goals of the programme.

Labour Market Regulation—Abusive Use of Dismissal Rights and the Labour Contract Act

A starting point of the Japanese Civil Code is that both employers and employees can terminate an employment contract. The only condition imposed by the Code is that those who wish to terminate the contract need to provide notice in advance. However, additional regulation makes it difficult for firms to dismiss regular employees. Through case law, the courts have developed a judicial principle to restrict firms' dismissal rights, called the Principle of Abusive Dismissal. According to this understanding, dismissal is considered to be an abusive exercise of the employer's rights unless they can provide strong justification to do so.[3]

A 2003 amendment of the Labour Standards Law and later the Labour Contract Act 2007 incorporated this principle. The stated objective of the latter Act was to contribute to bringing about stability in individual labour relationships. In particular, it provides employee protection by asserting the principle of agreement under which a labour contract can be established or changed only through negotiation.

One of the most important elements of the Act is that it establishes a procedure to terminate employment. Thus, article 16 states that a dismissal is considered to be an abuse of rights and invalid, unless it is based on objectively reasonable grounds and unless it is considered to be appropriate in general societal terms.[4] In other words, taking all this into account, in Japan, it is not easy for firms to dismiss regular workers unless the firm is in severe distress. First, dismissal is only accepted when a reduction in the workforce is absolutely necessary, such as in the case of financial distress. In practice, it is indeed the case that firms dismiss employees in insolvency proceedings since this is deemed to be serious distress (Fujimoto 2007). Second, the employer must make every effort to avoid dismissing employees. In other words, the firm is required to stop hiring new employees, reduce bonuses, and dismiss non-regular workers before they start to dismiss regular workers. Third, employers are required to select workers to be dismissed using a fair and rational approach, which for example could involve the firm selecting the employees to be dismissed according to length of service along with their performance. Fourth, employers must hold discussions with their workers and unions in an attempt to reach an agreement. In conclusion, these requirements show that it is not easy for firms to dismiss employees, even when it is desirable from the viewpoint of shareholders.

Employee Protection in Company Restructurings and the Act on the Succession to Labour Contract on Company Splits

It is often the case that a company restructures its organization, through such mechanisms as mergers or the sale of parts of the business. As seen in previous sections, there is no explicit clause to protect employees in most of these types of situations. The exception is in the case of a company split, where a firm is divided into several companies. The Act on the Succession to Labour Contracts on Company Splits was introduced to provide employee protection using a special provision to the Company Act. Under the law, a firm is required to abide by several procedures when it is being split. Firms need to consult with the labour union and with workers whose labour contracts are transferred to the new companies. In addition, under certain conditions, workers can file objections regarding the transfer of their employment contract. Moreover, under the law, a company is required to try to obtain the understanding and cooperation of workers.

Employee Protection in Insolvency Proceedings

After the crash of the so-called 'bubble economy' in the early 1990s, many Japanese companies experienced financial distress and economic contraction. In response, there were several changes made to the insolvency legislation after 1999 to make it easier for firms to utilize these procedures. These changes include the introduction of the Civil Rehabilitation Law, amendment of the Corporate Reorganization Law, and the introduction of a revised Bankruptcy Law, which came into effect respectively in 2000, 2003, and 2005. The Bankruptcy Law provides a procedure for liquidation, while the Civil Rehabilitation Law and the Corporate Reorganization Law are corporate reorganization proceedings. The Corporate Reorganization Law is intended to be used by large firms and is applicable only for joint-stock companies, while the Civil Rehabilitation Law is intended to be applied to medium and small firms.

There are several mechanisms which protect employees with respect to these procedures. Thus, unpaid wages and salaries have priority over unsecured creditors. Under the Bankruptcy Law, a claim for the salary of an employee for the three months preceding the commencement of bankruptcy proceedings is repaid with high priority. Under the Corporate Reorganization Law, a claim for salary for the six months before the procedure has high priority for repayment. Similarly, the full amount of unpaid salaries before the start of the procedure is repaid with high priority in Civil Rehabilitation Law.[5]

Under both the Company Reorganization Law and the Civil Rehabilitation Law, employees must be consulted during insolvency procedures. For example, under the Civil Rehabilitation Law, the court hears the argument of the labour union or other representatives of employees when the petition for the commencement of rehabilitation proceedings is filed.[6] Then the court makes a decision whether to accept the petition to start the insolvency procedure. Under the Civil Rehabilitation Law, the firm needs to obtain the permission of the court in order to transfer the entirety or a significant part of the operation or business. In this case, the court would grant permission only when it finds it necessary. The court hears the argument of the labour union before making a decision. The Company Reorganization Law has similar mechanisms through which employees can present their case.

In this section, we have described the most important changes in financial markets and their regulation. One of the main aims of these changes has been to make it easier for firms to undertake reorganizations. Thus, it makes it more likely for firms engage in mergers, acquisitions, and other types of reorganizations. However, overall, it is important to note that there is little mention of employees in these pieces of legislation.

New Investment Funds

Private Equity

Sugiura (2010) and the Japan Buy-out Research Institute Corporation (2011) provide the best account of the behaviour of PE funds from 1997 to 2011. PE firms began operating in Japan in the late 1990s. Unison Capital, a Japanese PE firm, established their first fund in 1998 with ¥38 billion in capital. In addition, foreign funds were established in Japan. Ripplewood Holdings established an office in Japan in 1999 and the Carlyle Group in 2000. According to the Japan Buy-out Research Institute Corporation (2011), the first buy-out transaction occurred in 1998 for ¥3.8 billion. The number of transactions increased and reached a peak in 2007 with 90 such transactions. The total value of transactions peaked at ¥1.24 trillion in 2008. In that year, buy-outs of Tokyo Star Bank, Ashikaga Holdings, and Arysta LifeScience occurred. Tokyo Star Bank was acquired by Advantage Partners from Lone Star Funds for around ¥250 billion. Permira Advisors purchased Arysta LifeScience from Olympus Capital Holdings Asia for around ¥250 billion. These were among the largest transactions made by PE funds in recent years. The number of transactions decreased to 45 in 2010, with a total value of ¥293 billion.

Sugiura (2010) and Japan Buy-out Research Institute Corporation (2011) classify buy-outs into several types, such as divestiture, turnaround of distressed firms, going-private buy-outs, and secondary buy-outs.[7] Of the 588 buy-outs from 1998 to 2011, 178 transactions are classified as divestitures, 129 as turnaround of distressed firms, 104 as going-private buy-outs, and thirty-eight as secondary buy-outs. Sixteen transactions exceeded ¥100 billion. The sources also classify these transitions by type of exit. In all, 279 of the 588 PE buy-outs were exited by selling shares. Twenty-four exits were structured as initial public offerings (IPOs).

There are several studies which examine the effect of PE investment. For example, Xu (2011) examines the case of Kito, which was purchased by the Carlyle Group and delisted from the Japanese Association of Securities Dealers Automated Quotation (JASDAQ) stock market in 2003, where it had been listed since 1980. Kito operates in the manufacturing and distribution of material handling equipment and in engineering and construction management. Since 1999 the company had made losses, for example in 2001 the company's return on equity (ROE) was –19.51 per cent. Before the acquisition, the CEO came from the founding family and owned 5.8 per cent of the firm's shares. One year after the acquisition, the Carlyle Group held 88.9 per cent of the shares and three positions on the board of directors. After the acquisition, the firm conducted a restructuring, including the sale of assets and its loss-making automated warehouse system division. After this restructuring, the firm's profitability improved and it was listed on the Tokyo Stock Exchange in 2007. Its ROE exceeded 20 per cent from 2006 to 2009, demonstrating that company performance improved following the buy-out.

However, in a precautionary manner, Xu also notes that it may not be easy to generalize this case, because there are not many examples of firms acquired by PE firms which have later been listed on the stock market. Rather, in Japan, it is often the case that PE funds purchase part of a listed firm, rather than the whole firm, which is referred to as private investment in public equity (PIPES). One of the largest transactions made through PIPES was the acquisition of part of Sanyo Electronics by Daiwa Securities Capital Markets and the Goldman Sachs Group for around ¥250 billion in 2006.

Nose and Ito (2009) analyse the impact of buy-outs by PE funds on shareholder value. Their sample consists of both buy-outs and minority investments in listed firms by PE from January 2000 to March 2008. During this period, there were thirty-six transactions in which listed firms were taken into private ownership. In addition, there were 104 investments in which the target companies remained public. The authors used thirty-four and sixty-six transactions in their analysis, respectively. They stress two initial features of these investments. First, target firms, both through being taken into private ownership or PIPES, were smaller than other listed firms. On average, the total value of the assets of all listed firms was ¥405 billion compared with ¥58 billion for the target firm. The average market value of listed firms was ¥163 billion while that of target firms was ¥25 billion. There are few differences in the size of those which went private and those which were targets of PIPES. Second, as targets, PE firms chose companies whose performance was worse than average. The ROE of listed firms was 4.9 per cent, while that of the target firm was –4 per cent. In particular, the ROE of the firms which were the target of PIPES was very low at –8.2 per cent. The ROE of firms that went private was 3.7 per cent.

Nose and Ito (2009) also examined the impact of such investments on share prices using a standard event study method. They found that the cumulative abnormal return (CAR) of these investments was positive and significant. In particular, the average CAR of investments involving conversion to private ownership was 21.4 per cent while that of PIPES was 9.7 per cent, suggesting a strong positive effect of these investments. In other words, shareholders' return improved, at least in the short run. In both types of transactions, CAR increased as market value decreased. The authors therefore suggested that PE firms must have invested in under-valued firms. They also showed that investors are more likely to choose going private when the proportion of shares owned by managers is larger. In addition, they found that the cost to sales ratio decreased significantly. According to the authors, the increase in market value can be explained by cost reduction.

In a further article, Nose and Ito (2011) also examined the long-term impact of PIPES investment on firm performance. Their sample included transactions completed between January 2001 and March 2008, in which a PE fund acquired a significant proportion of a firm's shares. Of 137 such transactions they used sixty-two cases in their analysis. They show that the number of these transactions increased from eleven in 2006 to eighteen in 2008. The average market value of the target firm was ¥20.2 billion with assets of ¥51 billion. The size of the target firm increased during the sample period and peaked in 2007. They showed that the performance of target firms improved after investment. Specifically, the difference between return on assets (ROA) one year before the investment and two years after was 2.3 per cent (median) higher than in the control group. They also examined the change in shareholder value by examining CAR and the buy-and-hold abnormal return for 240, 480, and 720 days after the investment, but did not find any significant effect. In other words, in the long run, they found no significant change in shareholder wealth between the sample and control firms. The authors noted that the funds achieved positive returns because they tended to purchase the shares at a discount relative to market price.[8]

Activist Hedge Funds

Activist HFs were a focus of media attention in Japan in the 2000s. In particular, the behaviour of two HFs, M&A Consulting, also known as the Murakami Fund, and Steel Partners Japan Fund, attracted significant media attention. These funds have made a number of con-troversial acquisitions. There are several studies which examine the behaviour of activist HFs.

Inoue and Kato (2007) examine the characteristics of the firms in which activist HFs invested. They focused on six HFs, including the Murakami Fund. These funds acquired a portion of shares in a firm considered to be under-valued in order to intervene in their manage-ment. Between January 2000 and December 2005, these six funds invested in 204 firms. The authors focused on 108 acquisitions in which more than 5 per cent of shares were purchased. They showed that the target firms of these funds are smaller than comparable firms. On average, the market value of target firms was ¥69 billion while that of all firms in the first section of the Tokyo Stock Exchange was around ¥200 billion. They also examined whether these funds pro-posed a plan to the firm, finding that a proposal was made in only 12 per cent of purchases. There is a difference in the average exit rate during the sample period between the Murakami Fund and the other funds. For the Murakami Fund, the exit rate was 97 per cent while that of other funds was 25 per cent or less. They suggest that the transfer of wealth, rather than value creation, was the main source of return for the Murakami Fund, as their average investment period was significantly shorter than that of other funds. The price to book ratio and ROE were significantly lower in the target firms relative to the comparison sample, while there was no significant difference in ROA.

Inoue and Kato (2007) also examined the impact on stock prices of acquisitions by HFs. They show that stock markets reacted positively to these investments. The CAR from one day before to one day after was 3.7 per cent and significant. They also reported a 240 day CAR of 8.7 per cent, which was also significant, suggesting that the invest-ment of the fund increased the firm's value.

Xu (2006) investigated the characteristics of forty-three firms which were targets of two HFs, Murakami Fund and Steel Partners Japan. Of these, Murakami Fund invested in twenty-five firms. Xu found that there are several notable differences between target firms and firms in the control group. Target firms hold more cash and securities than firms in the counter sample—the proportion of cash, and of cash plus securities, relative to total assets in the target firms was 38.7 per cent and 16 per cent higher respectively than for firms in the com-parison group. In addition, the target firms' Tobin's Q averaged 0.526, lower than that of the counter group firms at 0.872. The target firms also had lower leverage. Buchanan et al. (2012) also summarize the characteristics of the firms which are the target of activist HFs. These characteristics include lower leverage, a high cash-to-asset ratio, high dividends, and low insider ownership.

Subsequently, Uchida and Xu (2008) extended their sample to sixty-seven firms which had been targets of these two funds. Again, they found that target firms had more cash and a lower market to book ratio. The authors also investigated the effect of investment by Murakami Fund and Steel Partners Japan. They found a positive and significant CAR for the acquisitions. For example, the two-day CAR from day –1 to day +1 is 4.6 per cent and significant. Three-day and five-day CARs were also positive and significant. The CAR was larger when the target firm had more cash, suggesting that the return is generated by the payout policy. They reported that long-term per-formance was also positive in some specifications. Buchanan et al. (2012) additionally confirm that most of Murakami Funds' activities were successful.

Sovereign Wealth Funds

Sovereign wealth funds have investments in Japan. However, these investments are difficult to observe because they invest through other financial institutions or because their investments are less than 5 per cent of total shares. For example, the investment by ADIA, the SWF of Abu Dhabi, into Japan is around US$40 billion, of which around 70 per cent is portfolio investment (Embassy of Japan in Abu Dhabi 2007). One exception in which investment is disclosed is the SWF of Singapore. As explained in the previous section, large sharehold-ers in Japan whose ownership exceeds 5 per cent of a listed firm are required to provide information on their shares. In this way it can be seen that the Singapore Government Investment Corporation (GIC) is on the list of the largest shareholders of several listed firms. There are several other cases in which Singapore's SWF invested in Japanese firms, such as the acquisition of part of Mitsui Life Insurance and E-Mobile by the SWF Temasek Holdings. According to Shu (2007), who cites the monthly report of the Japanese Chamber of Commerce in Singapore, Japan's share in Temasek's portfolio of $129 billion Singapore is around 1 per cent while that of GIC is around 8–10 per cent. In addition, GIC Real Estate, the real estate division of the Singapore government, invested in several projects in Japan, including the Westin Tokyo Hotel.

The Japanese government itself does not operate a SWF. However, it is sometimes the case that the government provides capital through the Industrial Revitalization Corporation of Japan (IRCJ) to funds that invest in distressed firms. IRCJ was established in 2003 based on the Industrial Revitalization Corporation Act. The main shareholder is the Deposit Insurance Corporation of Japan, which provides deposit insurance. IRCJ has supported forty-one corporate groups, including Daiei, a large supermarket chain, and Kanebo, a large textile, cosmetics, and food company. IRCJ dissolved its operations in 2007. In addition to IRCJ, the Japanese government provided capital to several funds, such as Phoenix Capital, through the Development Bank of Japan, a government-owned financial institution.

Funds and Labour

In this section we will cite a number of studies. In the most directly relevant, Nose and Ito (2011) examined changes in several variables related to firms in which PE funds invested. In addition to changes in financial and accounting variables such as ROA and shareholder returns, they examined the change in the number of employees and labour's share of firms' value added. They show that the number of employees decreased significantly after investment by PE. On average, the decrease in the number of employees was 29.3 per cent larger than in the control group, suggesting that there is a large reduction in employment after the investment by PE. However, they found little change in labour's share of value added. They also showed that there is no significant relationship between employment reduction and long-term shareholder returns. In other words, a decrease in the number of employees is not a source of shareholder value. Thus, they suggested that there is little transfer of wealth from employees to shareholders.

In a more tangential study, Kubo and Saito (2012) examined the change in employment conditions after mergers in large Japanese firms, using 111 mergers between listed firms from 1990 and 2003. Typically, the number of employees decreased by 4.5 per cent three years after a merger, even after controlling for changes in sales and other variables. However, they show that it takes several years for firms to reduce the number of employees. Their interpretation is that such Japanese firms try to decrease their workforce without dismissing employees. Instead, companies try to reduce the headcount after a merger in a moderate way by postponing the recruitment of new employees or by soliciting voluntary retirement. At the same time, it should be noted that, after a merger, wages increase by 5.5 per cent per employee. Their results suggest that employment conditions improve for those who stay in the firm. Workers enjoy higher wages, in particular after related and non-rescue mergers. They suggest that the main motive behind mergers is not to divest employees of their wealth.

It is sometimes the case that there is a severe conflict of interest between shareholders and employees after M&As. For example, in the case of Toptour, the dispute between the trade union and the owner, a PE fund, attracted media attention. Toptour, formerly Tokyu Kanko, is a travel agency and used to be a subsidiary of Tokyu Corporation, an owner of railways and department stores. The firm is a major travel agency in Japan with around 2,000 employees. However, during the early 2000s it performed poorly, partly because of the Iraq war and the SARS outbreak. Tokyu therefore decided in 2004 to sell it to Activ Investment Partners Ltd, a PE firm. The transaction was reported to be valued at ¥2.5 billion. After the purchase, a dispute arose between employees and top management, which was now controlled by the PE firm. According to the trade union, the firm refused to pay bonuses which it promised before the acquisition. For its part, the firm established an 'employees association' to reduce the influence of the trade union. It then paid bonuses only to employees belonging to the association in order to encourage employees to move from the union to the new association. The union argued that the fund, which owned the firm and appointed executives to the firm, should have a meeting with the trade union. However, the fund declined to enter into collective bargaining. After this case went to arbitration by the

Labour Relations Commission of Tokyo, a compromise was reached. The content of the compromise agreement has not been disclosed. In their announcement, the firm and the union stated that their future aim was to cooperate to establish good industrial relations.

Buchanan et al. (2012) show that stakeholders of the firm, in particular employees, strongly opposed the acquisition by activist HFs. They examine the impact of activism on Japanese firms. In particular, they describe the case of the Steel Partners' failed attempt to control Bull-Dog Sauce. After acquiring around 10 per cent of Bull-Dog Sauce's shares in 2007, Steel Partners made an offer to purchase all of the firm's shares. The board of directors of the firm declined the offer and obtained approval for anti-takeover measures at the Annual General Meeting of shareholders. Steel Partners filed a motion with the Tokyo District Court to block the anti-takeover defence plan, but were unsuccessful. The fund appealed to the Tokyo High Court, but this was dismissed. In particular, the Tokyo High Court's ruling stated that the fund was seeking short- or medium-term profits and that it had no particular interest in running the business. Ultimately, Steel Partners failed to acquire the firm, but nevertheless obtained a good return by selling their shares.

There are two striking features in this case. First, many stakeholders, in particular employees, strongly opposed the HF plan. Employees made an announcement that they supported the board and that the plan would undermine the relationship between the firm and its customers. Second, most shareholders supported the directors even though Steel Partners' plan may have improved shareholder value. At the Annual General Meeting, more than 80 per cent of the shareholders affirmed the anti-takeover defence plan.

Olcott (2009) examines the behaviour of Japanese firms which have been acquired by foreign investors. One firm in his sample is Shinsei Bank, which was a successor of the Long-Term Credit Bank of Japan (LTCB). After the LTCB was nationalized in 1998 owing to poor performance, a group led by Ripplewood Holdings purchased the firm in 2000. Ripplewood sold most of the shares of the bank in 2004 when the bank was listed on the Tokyo Stock Exchange. Olcott describes major changes in the employment relationships after the purchase. Many new employees were recruited as the bank attempted to change the nature of its business. In 2003, three years after the purchase, 55 per cent of the employees of the bank were ex-employees of the LTCB. Employees considered that less importance was attached to long-term employment practices. A new CEO was also recruited externally. In addition, the proportion of female managers increased from 1 per cent in 1998 to 10 per cent in 2003.

The Japan Trade Union Confederation (Rengo) argue that funds may cause damage to firm value by dismissing employees and requiring excessive dividends (Japan Trade Union Confederation 2007). In this report, the union makes several recommendations. One of their main considerations is employees' rights to communicate with large shareholders. When investment funds acquire a large proportion of a company, they can control the firm and choose the senior management. The investment funds may decide on a policy that affects employment conditions. For example, if the funds decide to sell a division of the firm, employees of the division are forced to leave the company. However, according to Rengo, the problem is that unions cannot communicate with those investors, as they are shareholders. Although unions have the right to bargain with senior management, large shareholders have no legal duty to bargain with employees of the firm in which they invest. Therefore, employees cannot discuss important matters with investors even when shareholders have power over company policy. Rengo argues that labour law should incorporate the rights of trade unions to negotiate with large shareholders when they have power over senior management through share ownership and board directorships. More broadly Rengo also argues that company law should incorporate some mechanism through which employees have a voice in M&As and similar types of transactions. In addition, they argue that disclosure rules and regulations on funds should be strengthened.

Conclusions

This chapter has examined the behaviour and effect of PE, activist HFs, and SWFs in Japan. Although these funds have been less active in Japan than some other countries, such as the USA and the UK, the number of transactions, as well as the transaction size, increased, at least up to the late 2000s. However, a *Nikkei Business* (2011) survey of investment funds, including both PE and activist HFs, shows how funds in Japan decreased their investment from ¥3.466 trillion in 2008 to ¥2.601 trillion in 2011. In addition, some funds, including Steel Partners, withdrew their capital from Japan. At the same time, other funds, such as Carlyle Group and Advantage Partners, have continued to operate and indeed have a positive attitude towards investing in firms and sectors which were damaged by the March 2011 earthquake.

Some statistical studies show that PE transactions have a positive effect on shareholder returns. However, some also suggest a negative effect on employment, wages, and employee voice arrangements. Over the years, the government has introduced several new laws with the intention of revitalizing financial markets. Through these laws, including the Company Law and the Financial Instruments and Exchange Laws, it has become easier for firms to restructure themselves through M&As. This suggests that in future the activity of investment funds is likely to increase. However, this is in a context in Japan where it is still difficult for management to make significant organizational change without the consent of employees. The fact that the number of hostile takeovers is still very low in Japan indicates the constraints on fund activity imposed by the institutional context in this country.[9]

NOTES

1. Around 78 per cent of managers in France and 82 per cent in Germany also responded that a firm exists to pursue the interest of all stakeholders.
2. It should be noted that long-term employment applies mainly to regular workers of large firms. Moreover, the proportion of workers who are covered is decreasing. According to Ono (2010), around 20 per cent of total workers were covered in 2005.
3. See Kambayashi (2010) and Hanami and Komiya (2011).
4. After the introduction of the Labour Contract Act, duplicate articles in the Labour Standard Law were removed.
5. If firms in insolvency procedures cannot meet these requirements, the government pays employees up to 80 per cent of their unpaid salary and severance pay, under the Act on Security of Wage Payment. Any unpaid bonuses are not paid. The payment limit depends on age. If the worker is over 45 years, the government pays up to 3.7 million yen.
6. If there is a labour union which represents the majority of employees, the union must be consulted. In the absence of such a union, the court hears a representative of the majority.
7. Secondary buy-outs refer to a transaction between PE funds, i.e. a PE fund purchases shares which another PE firm sells it, often in the process of exiting.

8. On average, the discount rate is −17.2 per cent while the median value is −13 per cent.
9. I acknowledge the support of a Grant-in-Aid for Scientific Research (19530292) from the Japanese Ministry of Education, Science, Sports, and Culture and a Waseda University Grant for Special Research Projects (Project number: 2009A-502).

BIBLIOGRAPHY

Abbeglen, J. and Stalk Jr, G. (1985). *Kaisha: The Japanese Corporation.* New York: Basic Books.
Buchanan, J., Chai, D., and Deakin, S. (2012). *Hedge Fund Activism in Japan: The Limits of Shareholder Primacy.* Cambridge: Cambridge University Press.
Chuma, H. (1998). 'Is Japan's long-term employment system changing?', in I. Ohashi, and T. Tachibanaki (eds), *Internal Labour Markets, Incentives and Employment.* London: Macmillan Press, 225–68.
Embassy of Japan in Abu Dhabi (2007). *Abudabitoshicho Gaiyo* (Summary Information of Abu Dhabi Investment Agency; title translated from Japanese). <http://www.dubai.uae.emb-japan.go.jp/pdf/abudhabi/abudhabi_report02.pdf>.
Fujimoto, M. (2007). *Jigyo Saisei Kateiniokeru Keieizinzi Kanrito Roshi Comyunikesyon* (Relationship between Conduct of Business, Personnel Management and Labor–Management Communications during Business Turnarounds; title translated from Japanese). JILPT Research Report, 94, Tokyo: Japan Institute of Labor Policy and Training.
Hall, B. and Liebman, J. (1998). 'Are CEOs really paid like bureaucrats?', *Quarterly Journal of Economics*, 113 (3): 653–92.
Hanami, T. and Komiya, F. (2011). *Labour Law in Japan.* Alphen aan den Rijn: Kluwer Law International.
Hirose, N. (2007). 'Gaishi Yuchi to Gaishi Kisei' (Invitation and Regulation of Foreign Capital; title translated from Japanese), National Diet Library Issue Brief, No. 600, National Diet Library.
Inoue, K. and Kato, N. (2007). 'Akutibisuto fando no kozai' (Advantages and Disadvantages of Activist Fund; title translated from Japanese), *Kezai Kenkyu*, 58, 203–16.
Japan Buy-out Research Institute Corporation (2011). 'Nihonno Baiauto Shijono Suii 2011nen6gatusue genii' (Trends in Buy-out Market in Japan until June 2011; title translated from Japanese), Tokyo: Japan Buy-out Research Institute Corporation, <http://www.jbo-research.com>.
Japan Trade Union Confederation (2007). 'Hezzifando, PEfandotonikansuru Seisakutekikadaito taiono kangaekata' (Rengo's View on HF, PE and

Other Funds; title translated from Japanese), <http://www.jtuc-rengo.or.jp/kurashi/kinyuu/hedgefund/index.html>.

Kambayashi, R. (2010). 'Dismissal Regulation in Japan', Global COE Hi-Stat Discussion Paper Series, 119, Tokyo: Hitotsubashi University.

Kato, T. (2001). 'The end of lifetime employment in Japan?: Evidence from national surveys and field research', *Journal of the Japanese and International Economies*, 15 (4): 489–514.

Koike, K. (1988). *Understanding Industrial Relations in Modern Japan*. London: Macmillan.

Kubo, K. (2008). 'Japan: The resilience of employment relationships and the changing conditions of work', in S. Lee and F. Eyraud (eds), *Globalization, Flexibilization and Working Conditions in Asia and the Pacific*. Oxford: Chandos Publishing.

Kubo, K. and Saito, T. (2008). 'The relationship between financial incentives for company presidents and firm performance in Japan', *The Japanese Economic Review*, 59: 401–18.

Kubo, K. and Saito, T. (2012). 'The effect of mergers on employment and wages: Evidence from Japan', *Journal of the Japanese and International Economies*, 26 (2): 263–84.

Miyajima, H. and Kuroki, F. (2007). 'The unwinding of cross-shareholding in Japan: Causes, effects, and implications', in M. Aoki, G. Jackson, and H. Miyajima (eds), *Corporate Governance in Japan: Institutional Change and Organizational Diversity*. Oxford: Oxford University Press.

Miyajima, H. and Nitta, K. (2011). 'Kabusiki syoyukozono tayokato sono kiketsu' (Diversification of Ownership Structure and its Effect on Performance; title translated from Japanese)', in H. Miyajima (ed.), *Nihon no Kigyo Tochi* (Corporate Governance in Japan; title translated from Japanese). Tokyo: Toyokeizai Shimposha.

New York Times (2008). 'Activist hedge funds targets J-Power in Japan test', in: *New York Times*, 5 June.

Nikkei Business (2011). 'Fukkosienni nanori' (Investing to Help Recovery from the Disaster; title translated from Japanese), *Nikkei Business*, 13 June: 38–9.

Nikkei Newspaper (2006). 'Tashakara Baishu Shainha Kangeiniwari Shafu Zinzinadoni Fuan (Employees feel insecure when the firm they work are acquired), *Nikkei Newspaper*, 7 August.

Nose, Y. and Ito, A. (2009). 'Baiauto Fandoniyoru Baisyuno Inpakutoni' (The Impact of the Buyout Fund; title translated from Japanese), *Gendai Finance*, 26: 49–66.

Nose, Y. and Ito, A. (2011). 'Kokai Izigata Biauto Zisshi Kigyo no Choki Pafomansu' (The Long-term Performance of PIPEs in Japan; title translated from Japanese), Hitotsubashi IS-FS Working Paper Series FS-2011-J-002, Tokyo: Hitotsubashi University.

Odagiri, H. (1994). *Growth through Competition, Competition through Growth: Strategic Management and the Economy in Japan.* Oxford: Oxford University Press.

Olcott, G. (2009). *Conflict and Change: Foreign Ownership and the Japanese Firm.* Cambridge: Cambridge University Press.

Ono, H. (2010). 'Lifetime employment in Japan: Concepts and measurements', *Journal of the Japanese and International Economies*, 24 (1): 1–27.

Shimizutani, S. and Yokoyama, I. (2009). 'Has Japan's long-term employment practice survived? Developments since the 1990s', *Industrial and Labor Relations Review*, 62 (3): 311–24.

Shu, E. (2007). *Asiakigyono Tainichi Toshisenryakuto Nihonno Yuchisaku* (Investment Strategy toward Japan of Asian firms; translated from Japanese). Research Report, 293, Tokyo: Fujitsu Research Institute, <http://jp.fujitsu.com/group/fri/report/ research/2007/report-293.html>.

Spamann, H. (2010). 'The "Antidirector Rights Index" revisited', *Review of Financial Studies*, 23: 467–86.

Sugiura, K. (2010). 'History of buy-out market in Japan', in K. Sugiura and J. Koshi (eds), *Praibeto Ekuitei* (Private Equity; title translated from Japanese). Tokyo: Nihon Keizai Shinbumsha, 1–26.

Uchida, K. and Xu, P. (2008). 'US Barbarians at the Japan Gate: Cross Border Hedge Fund Activism', Bank of Japan Working Paper Series, 08-E-3, February.

Ukegawa, K. (2010). 'Kigyososhikisaihento rodosya kaisyaho kinyutorihiki-hono shitenkara' (Firm Reorganization and Employees from the Viewpoint of the Company Act and Financial Instruments and Exchange Law; title translated from Japanese), in K. Kezuka (ed.), *Kigyososhiki Saihennniokeru Rodosyahogo* (Employment Protection in Firm Reorganization; title translated from Japanese). Tokyo: Chuokeizaisya.

Xu, P. (2006). 'Donokigyoga Tekitaiteki Baisyuno Targettoni Narunoka' (What are the Characteristics of Targets of Hostile Takeovers; title translated from Japanese), RIETI Discussion Paper Series, 06-L-008.

Xu, P. (2011). 'Nihonni Okeru Keieiken Shijono Keisei' (The Emergence of the Market for Corporate Control in Japan; title translated from Japanese), in H. Miyajima (ed.), *Nihonno Kigyo Tochi* (Corporate Governance in Japan; title translated from Japanese). Tokyo: Toyokeizai Shinposya.

Yoshimori, M. (1995). 'Whose company is it? The concept of the corporation in Japan and the West', *Long Range Planning*, 28: 33–44.

11

New Investment Funds and Labour Impacts: Implications for Theories of Corporate Financialization and Comparative Capitalism

SIGURT VITOLS

Introduction

This book is concerned with the relationship between three types of new investment funds (NIFs)—private equity (PE), hedge funds (HFs), and sovereign wealth funds (SWFs)—and labour, in the context of corporate financialization and comparative capitalism.

It has addressed four main sets of questions. First, what are these funds, what do they do, and how did they arise? What are the roles of regulation and national institutions in the development and spread of these funds? Overall, what is the significance of these funds in economic and financial development? Second, what is their impact on labour? Have these funds generally had adverse effects on employment, wages, work, and employee representation, as some critics have alleged, or has their impact been more mixed? Third, how much variation is there across countries? How can we explain this variation, and what implications does this have for theories of comparative capitalism? Finally, what impact has the crisis had on these NIFs? Has it hindered or helped their development, or has it perhaps fundamentally altered their strategies and functioning, including vis-à-vis labour?

Addressing these questions is complex, as beliefs about these funds and their impact vary widely and discussion has often been controversial. Systematic statistical analysis has been difficult because these funds have often been reluctant to disclose key information, and hence data are difficult or costly to obtain, particularly on labour impacts. Many studies are based on self-reported survey data or on conclusions drawn from a limited number of case studies, with the result that we cannot be confident that their results are not biased by the nature of cases selected or by the perceptions and beliefs of those participating in the research.

The book is based on a set of nine country studies. The contributors have weighed all the available evidence on these funds—case studies as well as statistical studies based on either survey or archival data— to arrive at a view on these questions. In particular, they have paid attention to archival studies, as the underlying data are less subject to bias. The authors have also supplemented this analysis with their own case studies, in order to illustrate the strategies of their funds and the potential role that institutions can play in moderating their impact on labour. A unique advantage of this book is the comparative aspect, as these same questions were posed in countries with widely varying institutions and public policies. This facilitates examination of the role of institutions and regulation in explaining national differences in NIF activities and effects.

This chapter summarizes the main conclusions which can be drawn from the individual countries. It discusses these results in the context of two main bodies of theory which provide both a developmental and comparative perspective viz. the literature on financialization and the varieties of capitalism (VoC) approach. The chapter concludes with some comments on future perspectives on these funds and on further research needs.

New Investment Funds: How Did they Arise, What Do they Do?

The question of what NIFs do, and how they arose, is the most straightforward of our four sets of questions. Although they have received quite a lot of attention, NIFs constitute a relatively small proportion of the world financial system, currently accounting for about 11 per cent of managed assets worldwide (see Figure 1.1 in Chapter 1). However, the amount of assets they control is increasing and their impact is far greater in some areas than their relative size would suggest, for example in the area of mergers and acquisitions. In addition, other financial institutions have adopted strategies typically associated with some NIFs, such as banks trading in derivatives on their own account.

An important conclusion of the book is the considerable diversity in approaches and strategies used by the different types of NIFs. It is therefore necessary to be aware of the heterogeneity of NIFs to understand their functioning and impact. Most of these funds share the characteristic of promising superior returns to those which can be achieved through passive investing in a diversified portfolio of traditional financial products. However, there are important differences in terms of strategies between the three types of funds and even within the fund types. For example, within the HF group, we have been mainly concerned with activist HFs, which account for less than 5 per cent of total HF assets under management (AUM). Whereas activist HFs attempt to bring about change in company strategy, governance, or management, and typically hold shares in companies for a year or two, other HFs follow 'passive' stock-picking or trading approaches with shorter time horizons. In the extreme case of flash trading, their holding period can be as short as a few milliseconds. Although there is somewhat less diversity in strategies used by PE than by HFs, individual PE houses tend to specialize in investments in firms in different stages of the life cycle and in different financial situations: some focus on start-ups or young firms with strong growth prospects, whilst others focus on established firms in mature markets; some specialize in companies which have strong balance sheets, whereas others are interested in firms in financial distress.

The extent and nature of restructuring which may be required differs considerably between national contexts. In Poland, for example, PE was a factor contributing to the transition to market capitalism through the transfer of capitalist company organization and management methods. In Italy, at least up to the onset of the financial and economic crisis from 2007 onwards, PE was seen as an instrument for the modernization of family firms with traditional organizational structures and management styles. In the USA, in contrast, attention has been focused on larger public-to-private deals as well as Silicon Valley-style high tech start-ups. Although less is known about SWFs, they also appear to vary in terms of the mix of strategic and financial goals pursued and in being rather more generalist than specialist. Therefore, it is important not to lump all of these funds together, especially when analysing impacts on economic systems or advancing policy prescriptions.

Another finding of the book regards the importance that state policies had for the rise of NIFs. Most obvious here are SWFs, since they are established explicitly as state-owned or -controlled vehicles, are provided with a dedicated income stream by the state, and are frequently charged with an industrial policy mission. But the chapters have also shown how public policies regarding taxation, corporate governance, and the financial system have been very important for influencing the course of development of PE and HF. As will be discussed in more detail below, this includes both policies targeted at NIFs (specifically dealing with the issues of taxation, prudential regulation, access to finance, and transparency), as well as more general measures such as the regulation of mergers and acquisitions, availability of debt finance, and the modernization of stock and derivatives exchanges. In short, NIFs have been dependent upon the willing and active assistance of the state to develop into a significant economic force.

New Investment Funds as an Aspect of Financialization

Questions regarding the overall significance of NIFs are more complex to answer and best explored in relation to theoretical perspectives on the development of financialization. This book contributes to the literature by showing that PE, HFs, and SWFs are both a result of, and a contributing force to, financialization. In particular they are a key driver of what can be called corporate financialization, that is the increasing importance of financial factors in the governance of the firm.

NIFs have relevance for all four dimensions of financialization, according to the definition offered by Dore (2008). As discussed in Chapter 1, these are (i) the increasing proportion of profits accruing to financial as opposed to non-financial activities; (ii) the increasing complexity of financial intermediation, in part due to the pursuit of speculative activities; (iii) the increasing assertiveness of owners; and (iv) increasing efforts by governments to promote an 'equity culture'.

An Increasing Proportion of Profits Accruing to Financial Activities

The financialization literature identifies the increasing proportion of profits going to financial firms as an important indicator of a relative shift in favour of finance and away from 'real' activities such as the production of goods. A frequently-cited observation is that the share of profits by financial firms of all profits by large companies increased from about 10 per cent in the 1950s to 40 per cent in 2001 (Krippner

2011). In a set of North American and European countries, finance's share of national income is higher than it has been during the last 150 years (Phillippon and Reshef 2013: 73).

Private equity and HFs contribute to this trend. In particular the 'two-and-twenty' management fee structure commonplace among these NIFs—that is, a management fee of 2 per cent of AUM and 20 per cent of the profits—is much higher than the management fees received by mutual funds and investment managers of 'traditional' financial products (which have themselves been rising as a proportion of AUM, as shown by Malkiel (2013)). This means that a greater share of profits and capital gains produced by non-financial companies gets 'captured' by the financial sector before being passed on to the ultimate investors. The use of leverage by PE, typically set against the assets of portfolio companies, also shifts resources from companies to the financial sector. The practice of 'sale and leaseback' of property, widely observed in PE activities in retail and social care (as shown in the chapters on the UK and Sweden) can intensify this. Thus, a high proportion of the financial resources extracted or value created by PE and HFs appears as profits in the financial sector (Dealbook 2010; Phalippou and Gottschalg 2009; Lack 2012). Although less is known about the fee structure of SWFs, their increasing investment in PE and HFs also contributes to this trend of a growing proportion of profits accruing to the financial sector.

The increasing importance of the financial sector within the economy can be seen in other indicators. OECD data shows an increase between 2001 and 2010 in the share of total value added accounted for by the financial/real estate/business services sector in eight of the nine countries we have examined (OECD 2013).[1] Financial services have become a leading employer and significant political force in the countries looked at here, particularly in the USA and the UK.

The Increasing Complexity of Financial Intermediation

The traditional bank-based channel for finance has a relatively simple structure and can be seen as 'relational' as opposed to 'market-based' finance. In the past, commercial banks took deposits directly from, and made loans directly to, their customers. Early stock markets were also characterized by direct ownership of stocks by individuals and companies. However, in recent decades, financial intermediation has become more complex. One development is the lengthening of the investment chain, where several financial intermediaries may stand between the original supplier and ultimate user of capital. One result of this is a move away from relational towards more market-based finance (Aoki and Dinc 2000). A related development is the increasing complexity of financial products and financial contracting. Since fees are charged at all stages of the intermediation process, this adds to the shift of resources to the financial sector mentioned above (Kay 2012).

NIFs have contributed to this development mainly through lengthening the investment chain. For example, a company may obtain capital from a PE fund, which raises a portion of its capital from a fund of funds, which in turn obtains some of its capital from an investment manager for a pension fund, which pools the retirement savings of many individuals. The debt portion of a buy-out deal may be originally provided by a bank, but then packaged together with other loans and sold off to institutional investors. An activist HF may also obtain its equity capital through a similar long channel and supplement this with leverage provided by banks. SWFs are also increasingly lengthening the investment chain by investing in PE and HFs and in fund of funds, rather than directly in stocks and bonds (Preqin 2012). Another aspect of complexity is the increasing tendency of NIFs to invest cross-border; although most large PE houses and HFs are based in the USA and the UK, they have been increasingly investing in other countries. This complexity of financial intermediation can render employees of portfolio companies vulnerable to ever-more distant and opaque financial pressures. It also increases the inter-relatedness of the components of the financial system which, as the financial crisis of 2007 onwards illustrated, can heighten systemic risk.

The Increasing Assertiveness of Owners

Of the various dimensions of financialization, this is the one where NIFs most clearly contribute. NIFs have in common the goal of providing financial returns higher than those offered by 'passive' investment strategies in traditional financial products (stocks, bonds, bank deposits, etc.). A core component of the PE business model is to intervene in companies, by exerting strong influence on corporate managers, in the interests of gaining a higher rate of return on capital. A minimum of 25 per cent return on equity per annum is a typical goal for PE investment. Activist HFs generally demand changes in management, governance, company structure, and/or dividend policies to try to cause a short-term boost in share price. Although the bulk of evidence indicates that the typical SWF is a 'patient' investor, it is increasingly investing in PE and HFs.

The ideological context to these developments has been the ascendancy of theories of shareholder value and the intellectual primacy of principal–agent perspectives. PE has been widely seen as a means to reduce the agency costs of owner–manager relationships (Jensen 1989), as the use of debt to finance PE acquisitions can be viewed as a means of putting pressure on company managers to improve performance and efficiency. Similarly, the corporate governance interventions of activist HF are designed to make company managers more responsive to shareholders and often to increase the share of profits payable to shareholders (in the form of increased dividends, special dividends, and share buy-backs).

New investment funds received widespread public attention in many of the countries examined in this volume due to the perceived aggressiveness of their tactics. In the USA, the so-called corporate raiders, for the most part PE managers, first rose to prominence in the 1980s because of their ability to execute hostile takeovers of ever larger firms. In particular the takeover of RJR Nabisco by KKR for $31 billion in 1989 caught the public eye. The takeover of the German sanitary fittings maker Grohe by the PE firm TPG, which was followed by large-scale layoffs domestically and the transfer of production to Portugal and Thailand, became the main point of reference in the 'locust' debate in Germany. PE also rose to public attention in the UK in the 2000s, particularly through the buy-out of Alliance Boots in 2007 for £12 billion (the largest PE deal so far in European history) and trade union derecognition at the Automobile Association (AA). PE also received major attention in Sweden due to buy-outs in the care sector such as Carema, which have been associated with threats to the quality of care due to savings in labour costs (Chapter 7). As discussed in Chapter 4, the attempted takeover of Qantas Airways in Australia in 2006 also spurred a parliamentary inquiry, in part due to fears of negative impacts on labour and the wider economy.

The perceived aggressiveness of activist HFs has also received widespread attention in a number of major cases discussed in the book. One of the most prominent examples of this is the Cadbury case in the UK (Chapter 3), whereby activist HFs forced the company to divest the beverage division from the core confectionary business, ultimately enabling a hostile takeover by Kraft and large-scale layoffs and plant closures. Public disquiet over this case precipitated a major review of the UK Takeover Code. In the Netherlands, pressure from the activist HF TCI on ABN Amro to embark on an unfortunate acquisition strategy was widely seen to have contributed to the bankruptcy of that financial services conglomerate (Chapter 6).

In relation to the 'increasing assertiveness' of owners, these funds have been seen by some observers as having the potential to transform national models of capitalism, particularly those based on 'patient' capital and national systems of 'cooperative' labour underlying them. Fichtner (2009) sees HFs and PE as a major factor in eroding the Rhenish model of capitalism through their pressure on companies to maximize shareholder value at the expense of labour. Huffschmid et al. (2007) see HFs and PE as spearheads of financial capital which result from neo-liberal policies. Since the onset of the financial crisis, however, critical attention regarding financial practices has largely turned to the banks rather than NIFs.

Increasing Efforts by Governments to Promote an 'Equity Culture'
The chapters in this book have shown that, in most countries examined, governments have introduced regulatory changes with the explicit goal of promoting equity finance. Some of these assisted NIFs indirectly, for example by making it easier to acquire or sell companies; other measures were specifically concerned with NIFs. Drawing on the VoC terminology, although the liberal market economies (LMEs) (particularly the USA and the UK) were leaders in this regard, the coordinated market economies (CMEs) such as Germany and Italy also introduced reforms in order to help address what they saw as structural problems in their economies: a perceived conservatism, succession problems in family firms, and a need for de-diversification in conglomerates. In the case of Poland, an equity culture was promoted in order to assist the transition from a planned to a market economy (Chapter 9).

One set of measures were aimed directly at NIFs. PE is seen as providing risk capital to firms which public equity markets do not serve. HFs are seen as fulfilling a number of functions which improve the functioning of equity markets, including the provision of liquidity and a market for equity futures and options. Although of the countries examined in this book only Australia has a significant domestic SWF, this type of fund was also seen in many countries as helping to overcome a shortage of equity capital. One important supporting measure for NIFs is the authorization of the legal structures these funds prefer. These include the following: limited partnerships for a fixed term (typically ten to twelve years) for PE and open-ended limited partnerships for HFs; light registration and licensing requirements; a lack of restrictions on the types of investment allowed by these funds; and a favourable taxation regime including freedom from double taxation. Examples of such measures in one of our countries, Australia, included the 1998 Managed Investments Act, which allowed a single entity to carry out both investment and trustee functions, and the 2001 Financial Services Reform Act, which established a single licensing regime for all financial institutions and services. In Sweden, the 1990 Act on Collective Investment Funds authorized HF to operate in that country.

A second set of measures were directed at promoting stock markets. These include the passage of laws or encouragement through government agencies and financial regulators which allowed stock exchanges to modernize through introducing electronic trading, offering derivative products, consolidating regional stock markets, and liberalizing listing requirements for initial public offerings. 'Big Bang', which took place in the UK in 1986, is perhaps the most prominent case of radical reform of the stock exchange and financial markets. However, stepwise reforms which also led to significant change were introduced in the countries studied in this volume, such as the four Financial Markets Promotion Acts passed in Germany between 1990 and 2002 and the regulatory changes introduced in Australia in the late 1990s and early 2000s designed to strengthen that country's position as a regional financial centre. Measures were also taken in many countries to 'liberalize' corporate governance along the LME model and to create a 'market for corporate control', including laws restricting the use of defences against takeovers such as differentiated voting rights for different classes of shares. In Germany, for example, a corporate governance reform in 1998 introduced the 'one share one vote' principle for listed companies and reduced the role of banks in proxy voting and representation on company boards. These measures were favourable to PE and HFs insofar as they increased the number of companies listed on exchanges (and thus potential targets), made these targets easier to acquire, and also improved exit options when PE and HFs wished to sell the shares they held.

A third set of measures, for the most part deregulatory, helped improve the environment for NIFs by increasing their access to finance. One type of measure was the lifting of prudential restrictions on the share of assets which pension funds and insurance companies could invest in PE and HFs. Whereas, prior to the 1980s, most of these institutional investors were highly restricted in the types of investments they could make, by 2007 only Germany, Italy, and Poland defined quantitative limits on the amount of money pension funds could invest in these funds (OECD 2007).[2] The lifting of restrictions on depository institutions to invest in risky forms of debt were important for enabling banks to provide leverage to PE and HF portfolio companies. Perhaps the most notorious example here is the deregulation of the savings and loan associations in the USA in the 1980s, which allowed them to invest massively in the 'junk bonds' used to finance hostile takeovers.

NIFs can therefore be seen as both a result of, and a driving force behind, financialization. Investments in NIFs are motivated by the expectation of higher returns, mainly by institutional investors. The leverage used by NIFs is also to a certain extent enabled by financial innovation and complexity. However, NIFs also contribute to financialization. The high fee structures of PE and HFs result in higher profits for the financial sector; the addition of these intermediaries lengthens the investment chain; but in particular, as will be discussed in the next section, they contribute to the dimension the 'increasing assertiveness' of owners with a direct impact on labour.

Impact of New Investment Funds on Labour

In addition to focusing on the increasing importance of finance, the financialization literature also suggests that this trend has a negative impact on the 'real' economy and labour. However, this literature has been less precise on the exact mechanisms linking financialization and these outcomes. For example, Assa (2012) finds a significant negative relationship between the relative importance of financial activities in various Organization for Economic Cooperation and Development (OECD) countries and equality, economic growth, and employment. However, this is a statistical relationship and the underlying mechanisms are not explored. Other commentators have claimed that there is an indirect link. For example, Freeman (2010) draws a causal link between deregulation, financialization (particularly the creation of perverse incentives in the financial sector), the financial crisis, and inequality, though Freeman focuses mainly on the increase in inequality through large job and income losses for employees which the financial crisis caused.

The current book helps identify a direct causal link between financialization and labour outcomes. Of the three fund types examined, PE has the greatest 'transformative' potential, not only for labour, but also for corporate structure, innovation, and strategy, since this change is typically an explicit part of the 'business plan' intended to boost the company's value before resale. Often employment levels, labour costs, and remuneration systems are variables which PE consciously tries to change through its ownership and management power. Activist HFs come second, since generally they do not try to take a controlling stake in the company, and their average holding period is much shorter than PE or SWFs. However, the changes which they try to impose, such as installing management with a different strategy, divesting parts of the company, or paying out accumulated cash to shareholders, frequently have consequences for labour, even if not explicitly pursued or considered by the activist HFs. These consequences include breaches of both implicit and in some cases explicit labour contracts (as highlighted in Chapter 2 on the USA), arising from increased financial pressures due to these HF actions. SWFs are generally seen as the most 'patient' of the three investors, with little transformative intent, although there is some evidence that this may be changing (The CityUK 2013).

Statistical studies dealing with the impact on labour only address PE funds. Good overviews of relevant studies are provided by Lutz and Achleitner (2009) and Goergen et al. (2011). The studies based on archival data suggest that the impact of PE activity on labour varies somewhat across countries. Table 11.1 provides a summary of these studies.

Of nineteen studies of the employment impact of PE based on archival data with some level of methodological sophistication, only three estimate significant employment increases in the short and/or medium term relative to a control group. Ten estimate significantly negative employment effects, and the rest estimate neutral or statistically insignificant employment changes relative to controls. In particular, the studies on the USA and the UK are negative. However, even in the cases of studies where positive average impacts are estimated, a significant proportion of the firms will have experienced turbulence via negative employment developments. The upshot is that these studies suggest considerable pressure on labour, at least in a significant proportion, if not the majority, of companies.

Although studies have not explicitly measured the increase in inequality at the firm level, a number of surveys have identified the introduction or strengthening of performance monitoring and performance-oriented pay in portfolio firms as a typical strategy of PE. For example, Malone (1989) finds that 41 per cent of US buy-outs

Table 11.1 *The impact of private equity on employment: summary of studies using archival data*

Country	Author year	Time	Journal	Sample	Peer reviewed	Average impact on employment	Findings
Belgium	Toubeau 2006	1995–2005	Doctoral Thesis	53 buy-outs	No	Positive	Significantly higher increase in number of employees in buy-outs compared to controls between t and t+2
France	Boucly et al. 2011	1994–2004	*Journal of Financial Economics*	839 buy-outs	Yes	Positive	18% higher employment growth in buy-outs compared to controls between t-4 and t+4
Spain	Marti Pellon et al. 2007	1993–2004	ASCI Research Paper	100 buy-outs	No	Positive	4% higher growth in employment in LBOs relative to controls, t to t+3
Sweden	Olsson and Tåg 2012	1998–2004	Working paper	201 buy-outs	No	Negative	6% employment decline in PE buy-outs relative to controls from t to t+4; no Greenfield job creation like in USA (Davis et al. 2008)
Sweden	Bergström et al. 2007	1998–2006	*Journal of Private Equity*	73 PE buy-out exits	Yes	Neutral (plus bias)	No significant difference between PE buy-outs and controls. Potential sample bias due to exclusion of bankruptcies
UK	Goergen et al. 2011		*Corporate Governance: An International Review*		Yes	Negative	Significantly negative impact on employment in buy-out firms relative to controls, without corresponding increase in productivity and profitability.
UK	Acharya and Kehoe 2008	1996–2004	Working paper	66 buy-outs	No	Negative (but not statistically significant)	Buy-outs grow employment at 1.6% CAGR compared to 2.7% in quoted peers, difference is statistically insignificant

UK	Amess and Wright 2007a	1993–2004	Working paper	533 buy-outs	No	Neutral	Controlling for endogeneity, no significantly different levels of employment in PE- & non-PE-backed LBOs than in controls
UK	Amess and Wright 2007b	1999–2004	International Journal of Economics in Business	1,350 buy-outs (MBI, MBO)	Yes	Neutral	Controlling for endogeneity, insignificant effect on employment growth of LBOs (MBO & MBIs combined) Controlling for endogeneity, higher average employment growth for MBOs & lower for MBIs compared to controls
UK	Amess et al. 2008	1996–2006	Working paper	232 buy-outs	No	Neutral	No evidence for significant impact of PE-backed LBOs on employment in t+1 or t+2 Non-PE-backed LBOs: 11% lower employment in t+1 M&A transactions: 16% lower employment in t+1, 22% lower employment in t+2
UK	Cressy et al. 2008	1995–2002	Working paper	57 buy-outs	Not yet	Negative	Relative to controls, 7% lower employment in buy-outs in t+1, cumulating to 23% lower employment in t+4; in t+5 increase by 2%
UK	Weir et al. 2008	1998–2004	Working paper	122 public to privates	Not yet	Negative	Relative to industry average, significant decrease in employment in PE-backed LBOs in t+1; further decreases in t+2 to t+5 but no significant differences to industry average. Significant decrease in employment in non-PE-backed LBOs in t+1, increase in employment in subsequent years relative to industry average

(Continued)

Table 11.1 (Continued)

Country	Author year	Time	Journal	Sample	Peer reviewed	Average impact on employment	Findings
USA	Chaplinsky et al. 1998	1980–1994	*Journal of Financial Economics*	180 buy-outs(EBO, MBO)	Yes	Negative	Relative to their industry, EBOs and MBOs reduce employment after the buy-out; Industry adjusted mean decrease: In t+3: −9.6% for EBOs, −1.8% for MBOs; In t+5: −10.8% for EBOs, −1.7% for MBOs
USA	Davis et al. 2008	1980–2005	Working paper	11,000 buy-outs; 300,000 plants	No	Negative	7% (4%) average cumulative decrease in targets relative to controls two years post-buy-out (two years pre-buy-out) No employment differences between targets and controls in manufacturing sector, significant decline in targets in retail, services & finance, insurance & real estate. Gross job creation equal in targets & controls; greater job destruction in targets. Greenfield job creation: 15% in buy-outs, 9% in controls; Acquisition (divestiture) rate: 7.3% (5.7%) in buy-outs, 4.7% (2.9%) in controls

USA	Kaplan 1989	1980–1986	Journal of Financial Economics	76 public to privates	Yes	Negative	Total sample: Relative to their industry, MBOs reduce employment between t−1 and t+1 at −12.0%; 30.9% of sample reduce employment. Excluding companies with divestitures & acquisitions: Relative to their industry, MBOs reduce employment between t−1 to t+1 at −6.2%, but results are not significant; 38.5% of sample reduce employment
USA	Lichtenberg and Siegel 1990	1983–1986	Journal of Financial Economics	1,132 buy-out Plants	Yes	Negative	Between t−1 & t+2, significant reductions in non-production worker employment, cumulative decline of 8.5%. Production worker employment declines, but less and not significant
USA	Liebeskind et al. 1992	1980–1984	Financial Management	33 public to privates	Yes	Negative	Mean number of employees declined in LBOs and grew in control firms, resulting in significant differences between the samples. Mean number of plants declined in LBOs and grew in control firms, resulting in significant differences between the samples

(Continued)

Table 11.1 (Continued)

Country	Author year	Time	Journal	Sample	Peer reviewed	Average impact on employment	Findings
USA	Muscarella and Vetsuypens 1990	1976–1987	*Journal of Finance*	72 public to privates	Yes	Neutral	For all LBOs: Median reduction in employment between LBO and IPO –0.6%; 92% of random sample showed higher employment growth. For LBOs with no acquisition/divestiture: Median increase in employment between LBO and IPO 17%; 15% of random sample showed higher employment growth
USA	Smith 1990	1977–1986	*Journal of Financial Economics*	58 public to privates	Yes	Negative	Relative to industry, number of employees decreases from t–1 to t+1, but insignificant. Relative to industry, asset-sale sample shows significant median reductions in employment from t–1 to t+1

Sources: Own update of Lutz and Achleitner (2009) and Goergen et al. (2011).

involve the introduction of performance-oriented pay. Bacon et al. (2004) find the widespread use of employee share ownership schemes as well as performance pay in UK buy-outs. Chapter 2 describes the introduction of an incentive bonus and profit sharing plan as a key part of the PE rescue plan for bankrupt US steel companies.

There do not appear to be any statistical studies examining the direct impact of activist HFs on labour. However, other studies suggest that an indirect effect of HF activism may be increased pressure on labour, at least for a proportion of target firms. Higher cash pay-outs or share buy-backs will increase financial pressure on the firm. Xu and Li (2010) find that the probability of insolvency increases significantly after activist HF intervention. Aslan and Maraachlian (2009) find that, in the long run, the bonds of target companies under-perform their benchmarks by 3–5 per cent per year and that there are more credit downgrades than upgrades for these bonds.

The widespread perception is that SWFs will have less direct impact on labour, and this is backed up by case studies on NIFs done for the European Foundation (Gospel et al. 2010). SWFs invested heavily in troubled companies during the financial crisis, for example US and UK banks, and have thus come to be seen as a positive force for employment by providing capital when traditional financial institutions are unwilling or unable to do so. However, there is evidence suggesting a more active role in management by SWFs, as evidenced by the Qatar Investment Authority's appointment of directors to Veolia Environment and Harrods in the UK (see discussion in Chapter 2). It should also be mentioned that they have an indirect impact, through their investments in HFs and PE.

From the case studies and surveys examined, however, it is clear that in the overwhelming majority of cases, NIFs do not consult or negotiate with labour representatives *ex ante*. There have been a few cases of 'beauty contests' in Germany, where different PE bidders are invited to meet with works councils or trade unions and present proposals for deals and their anticipated impact on employment and working conditions. However, these seem to be the exception to the rule. Furthermore, although *ex post* there are many cases of strife with trade unions over changed employment levels, production locations, and working conditions, there have been relatively few cases of outright union de-recognition. As a result, although NIFs frequently put pressure on employment and working conditions, they rarely seem fundamentally to change the nature of industrial relations institutions.

In summary, the above discussion shows that NIFs play a role in all four dimensions of financialization, but that the importance of this role varies across the dimensions and also the different types of funds vary in terms of their role. It also shows how a direct link can be drawn between financialization and labour outcomes, specifically through the attempt of NIFs to change company strategies to gain higher returns and through the financial pressures on companies caused by high levels of debt.

A Comparative Perspective on the Role of New Investment Funds

Although there is strong evidence of an overall financialization trend, the nine country studies in this book show that there is significant cross-national variation in the dynamics of change. It is therefore important to integrate country-specific factors in order to understand NIFs and their role in these dynamics. This raises the question of which comparative theories can provide helpful and illuminating explanations for these differences. An obvious candidate is the VoC perspective, as it argues that the financial system, corporate governance practices, and labour relations are important, and inter-related, variables in its classification of capitalist countries (Hall and Soskice 2001). Here we will argue that, although VoC is helpful in identifying broad categorizations of countries, additional explanatory variables are needed in order to explain cross-national differences in the role of NIFs and their consequences for labour.

According to standard VoC classifications, the USA, the UK, and Australia are LMEs, whilst Germany, the Netherlands, Sweden, Italy, Japan, are broadly CMEs, although the latter two less clearly so; the classification of Poland is more complicated, with the category of dependent market economy (DME) perhaps fitting best to this case (Nölke and Vliegenthart 2009). VoC theory would predict a higher presence and impact of NIFs in LMEs than CMEs, for two main reasons. First, in LMEs, the greater role of markets should encourage more risk-friendly forms of finance, such PE and HFs; by contrast, in CMEs, relational bank-based finance is supposed to predominate. Second, more companies are listed on the stock market in LMEs than in CMEs, as measured by the proportion of large companies that are listed; further, ownership is supposed to be more dispersed in LMEs than CMEs. This means that the number of companies exposed to the market for corporate control should be higher in LMEs. Meanwhile, VoC would see DMEs, such as Poland, as inhospitable environments for activist HFs, since many of the largest companies tend to be wholly-owned subsidiaries of multinational enterprises, rather than independent listed companies. DMEs could, however, be seen as a favourable environment for PE, since there can be great growth potential in the 'modernization' of domestic companies.

A closer look at a number of characteristics of NIFs show that the rank order of the nine countries along many dimensions largely corresponds to the VoC predictions. However, typically there are one or two significant outliers which show that at least the simple version of VoC is only partially correct. This suggests that a more specific theory addressing this aspect would have to take into account additional country-specific variables.

A further dimension of heterogeneity of funds is in the ownership structure of these funds themselves, with PE and HFs for the most part being privately owned,[3] whereas SWFs are by definition state or quasi-state entities. This has implications for the sources of finance for these funds, with SWFs being dependent upon a portion of the profits from domestically produced commodities or trading activities, whereas PE and HFs are dependent upon investments from institutional investors, foundations, and wealthy individuals. This difference can be seen in the different distribution of the three fund types across countries. Table 11.2 illustrates the variation in the relative size of the different types of NIFs, measured by AUM accounted for by domestic NIFs as a percentage of gross domestic product (GDP).

Overall, we can see that NIFs play the greatest role in the UK and the USA, with total NIF AUM amounting to almost 29 per cent and 23 per cent of GDP, respectively. Nevertheless, this is not a simple VoC story, as the third highest country is Sweden, a CME. Australia also scores high, with NIF AUM coming to 14 per cent; however, over half of this is accounted for by the Australian SWF, meaning that the composition of NIF assets is very different. As the Australian chapter shows, the level of activity of PE and HFs is lower than in typical LMEs, and this can be attributed in part to concentrated corporate ownership structures in Australia. In the other five countries, NIF AUM came to less than 5 per cent of GDP, with the Netherlands entering at the high end of this range (Table 11.3).

Examining the individual fund types in our nine countries, we can see that SWFs play a significant role only in Australia, where AUM amounts to almost 9 per cent of GDP. Although the USA has

Table 11.2 *Assets under management by new investment funds (% of GDP)*

	Germany	Italy	Netherlands	Poland	Sweden	UK	Australia	Japan	USA
SWF	0.0	0.0	0.0	0.0	0.0	0.0	8.7	0.0	0.6
HF	0.1	0.7	1.7	0.0	6.1	13.8	3.5	0.3	8.9
PE	1.3	1.3	3.0	1.2	9.9	14.8	1.9	1.0	12.0
Combined per-centage	1.3	2.0	4.7	1.2	16.0	28.6	14.0	1.3	21.5

Source: Own calculations based on data from EVCA, Preqin, TheCityUK (2013).

Table 11.3 *Assets under management by domestic hedge funds and private equity: comparison of proportions of GDP with predictions based on 'varieties of capitalism' classifications*

Country	% GDP	VoC classification
UK	28.6	LME
USA	20.9	LME
Sweden	16.0	CME
Australia	5.4	LME
Netherlands	4.7	CME
Italy	2.0	CME
Germany	1.3	CME
Japan	1.3	CME
Poland	1.2	DME

Source: Own calculations based on data from EVCA, AVCAL, Ernst&Young, and McKinsey&Company.

a number of SWFs at the state level, their total value adds up to less than 1 per cent of GDP.[4] A correlation analysis shows that there is no significant relationship between SWF AUM and either PE or HF AUM as a percentage of GDP.[5] It is apparent from this that the factors explaining the relative size of domestic SWF AUM must be different from the factors explaining PE and HF AUM. Specifically, the country in question must have a sizeable commodities industry and the responsible government must make a decision to establish a fund which captures and reinvests some of the accrued profits. Looking at PE and HFs, there is a near perfect and positive (0.96) correlation between the level of PE and HF AUM as a percentage of GDP,[6] which suggests that there are some common factors explaining their relative importance.

Although VoC correctly predicts the rank of most of the countries in our study in terms of relative importance of domestic PE and HF (i.e. LMEs high and CMEs low), this prediction is not always correct. Sweden, a CME, is ranked in third place for AUM of PE and HFs, and its domestic PE and HF industries are almost three times the size of those in Australia, which is typically seen as an LME. Furthermore, Australia is only marginally above the Netherlands (a CME) in the ranking (5.4 versus 4.7 per cent, respectively). Thus, although predictions based on VoC appear to have some plausibility, the 'outliers' (Sweden and, to a certain extent, Australia) show the need to supplement the broad categorizations provided with VoC with country-specific factors.[7]

One of these factors is public policies towards NIFs. Although the country chapters show that the LMEs were 'first movers' in this regard, CMEs have also implemented measures in the past two decades designed to encourage NIFs. One indicator of the diversity of national policies towards PE is provided by the European Private Equity and Venture Capital Association (EVCA), which has made a major effort to benchmark the regulatory and tax environment for PE in Europe. In the mid-2000s, EVCA published a series of reports entitled *Benchmarking European Tax and Legal Environments*. EVCA considers the following factors as being particularly important in creating a favourable environment: the availability of favourable legal structures (including a lack of double taxation and restrictions on types of investment allowed); a lack of restrictions on pension funds and insurance companies investing in funds; and a set of business environment variables, including tax and fiscal incentives for companies, freedom to undertake mergers, and bankruptcy law. Of the nine countries examined in our book, six are European and thus covered in the benchmarking exercise. The ranking of these six countries corresponds roughly, but far from perfectly, with the ranking for the relative weight of PE AUM. For example, Sweden receives even higher marks than the UK on the ability of pension funds to invest in PE. A similar exercise by PriceWaterhouseCoopers for HF regulation also shows considerable variation across countries which only partially corresponds to the CME/LME divide (PriceWaterhouseCoopers 2010).

An additional factor which plays a role in explaining the level of AUM is the relative importance of institutional investors in each country. As there is a strong 'home bias' in institutional investors' investment policies (Coval and Moskowitz 1999), the size of domestic institutional investment is likely to be an important determinant of funding sources available for PE and HFs. In particular, pension funds have been an important source of funding for PE and HFs (Preqin 2013a, 2013b). A statistical analysis shows a significant and strong positive correlation (0.44) between the sum of PE and HF AUM as a percentage of GDP on the one hand and pension fund AUM as a percentage of GDP on the other hand.[8] This also helps explain the 'deviant case' of Sweden. Unlike many other European CMEs, which mainly implemented pay-as-you-go public pension schemes, Sweden chose early on in the post-war period to have a funded public scheme (Pontusson 1992). These public pension funds have been an important source of finance for the domestic Swedish PE and HF industries.

Moderating Role of Institutions

A major point where VoC has relevance to the discussion on NIFs is the moderating role of institutions. Hall and Soskice (2001) define institutions broadly, including not only laws and regulations but also the characteristics of associations, structure of markets, and also norms and values. These institutions are needed to create clear expectations on actors and also to help coordinate the interaction of actors with each other. In summary, CMEs are distinguished by a greater use of 'non-market' institutions and forms of coordination than LMEs.

Thus national institutions can be seen as playing a major role in moderating the impact of NIFs. Institutions which grant worker representatives strong rights to influence company policies and strategies, such as works councils and employee representation on company boards, exist in some of the countries in our book; they play a particularly strong role in Germany, Sweden, and the Netherlands, and the country chapters provide cases showing how these institutions can influence outcomes. In the case of Japan, although it lacks these formal institutions, it has strong norms regarding implicit contracts between management and labour which have influenced the arrangements and constrained the activities of NIFs.

One suggestive study regarding the moderating role of labour is Bacon et al. (2012). This indicates substantial regional differences in the extent to which so-called 'high performance work practices' can be introduced by PE. In northern European countries, characterized by strong forms of worker representation, PE was not able to introduce a significantly higher number of these high performance work practices. This contrasts with the situation in other European countries with weaker worker representation where there was more ability and / or need to introduce such practices.

Another suggestive result regarding the moderating influence of institutions is provided by a comparison of studies of the impact of PE on employment. Most of the rigorous studies here are on the USA and the UK, and the bulk of these studies show negative results on employment. However, there is one study of PE's impact on labour in France, which estimates an average employment increase of 18 per cent following buy-outs (Boucly et al. 2011). These results suggest that this favourable employment increase may be due to a different institutional framework in France. Key institutional features are a capital market which is less developed than in some other countries and restrictive labour regulation. These imply that PE in France tends to focus on buy-outs with stronger growth prospects and less need for extensive restructuring. PE can supply capital which is not as readily available from other sources as in other countries. A study on buy-outs in Belgium, which can also be seen as a country with stronger employment protection and a less developed capital market, also finds positive impacts of PE on employment relative to controls and thus can be taken as additional evidence for this thesis (Toubeau 2006).

The moderating role of national institutions can also be seen in the variation in the role of activist HFs across countries. No study uses the same methodology and time period across all countries, but several estimates give an approximate idea of the level of activism in each country. Table 11.4 presents different estimates of the number of activist HF events per country. By far the largest number of events takes place in the USA, with the UK in second place. However, Japan is not far behind the UK. When estimating the probability that any specific listed firm will become a target, a somewhat different picture emerges. This estimate is derived by dividing the number of HF activist events by the number of listed firms. By this measure, the USA is still by far the country where companies are most 'exposed' to HF activism, with an estimated probability of 15 per cent. However, the Netherlands (a CME) comes in second, with a probability of 11 per cent. It has a relatively small number of listed firms, however, many of these are medium to large sized and have a dispersed shareholder base. The UK is third with less than 6 per cent. Although Japan has a large absolute number of events, the large number of listed firms in Japan means that the probability of being a target is fairly low. Our third LME, Australia, where ownership is relatively concentrated, is near the bottom of the list of probabilities (Judge et al. 2010). Interestingly, although Sweden has a large domestic HF industry, this is not reflected in the level of activism, as listed companies in that country have a low level of probability of being targeted. The ownership of Swedish companies is relatively concentrated and many companies use takeover defences such as dual class shares (Giannetti and Laeven 2009).

The above analysis shows that a simple version of VoC only partially predicts the rank order of countries on this dimension. Explanations of these rank orders, and of the apparently deviant

Table 11.4 *Activist hedge fund events: number of identified activist events and probability of being a target, by country*

	Australia	Germany	Italy	Japan	Netherlands	Poland	Sweden	UK	USA	Source
No. of HF events (2000–08)	—	43	29	—	21	0	11	133	—	Becht et al. (2010b)
No. of HF events(2000–10)	19	30	11	103	20	0	6	128	—	Katelouzou (2013)
No. of HF events(2001–07)	—	—	—	—	—	—	—	—	1172	Brav et al. (2008)
No. of HF events(2001–06)	—	—	—	89	—	—	—	—	—	Uchida and Xu (2008)
No. of HF events(2000–07)	—	18	5	—	10	—	6	36	—	Stokman (2008)
Number of listed firms (2010)	1822	833	292	4049	181	239	352	2260	7847	
Estimated probability of listed firms being a target	1.0%	3.6%	3.8%	2.5%	11.0%	0.0%	1.7%	5.7%	14.9%	

Note: Estimated probability derived by dividing Brav's (2008) figure for the USA and Katelouzou's (2013) figures for the other countries by the number of listed firms.

cases, have to take into account both country and sector-specific variables. For activist HFs, it is important to target companies which have a dispersed shareholder base, since they are trying to convince the majority of shareholders to go against policies which have been devised by incumbent managers together with larger shareholders. Research by Katelouzou (2013) indicates that the vast majority of activist HF events occur in companies where the largest shareholder holds less than 20 per cent of total shares in the company. Also, activist HFs tend to favour smaller and medium-sized firms, and many countries do not have a significant number of companies of this size with dispersed shareholding listed on their stock exchanges.

A further comparative feature is the apparent large variation in the size of short-term share appreciation due to HF activity in different countries. Using the same methodology across a number of countries, Becht et al. (2010a, 2010b) estimate very different effects across countries, and their findings are reported in Table 11.5. Some of the highest returns (i.e. Sweden, Korea, and Switzerland) come in countries where corporate governance standards are not particularly shareholder-friendly, whereas returns are low or not significantly different from zero in the countries where corporate governance is considered to be most shareholder-friendly (i.e. the UK and the Netherlands). This is further evidence that national institutions—in this case the degree of 'isolation' of managers from shareholder pressure through corporate governance regulations—also have a

Table 11.5 *Short-term returns from hedge fund activism, by country*

Country	Event window	
	t–10, t+10	t–20, t+20
France	4.94*	2.65
Germany	3.76	6.09*
Italy	–0.30	2.55
Japan		5.60**
Korea		23.50**
Netherlands	–0.60	–0.82
Sweden	13.71	14.89**
Switzerland	7.45**	15.83**
UK	4.17**	2.76

Note: ** = significant at 0.05 level, * = significant at 0.10 level.
Sources: Becht et al. (2010a, 2010b).

significant moderating effect, in this case on the impact of activist HFs. Opportunities for HFs to achieve superior returns through corporate governance initiatives within companies appear to be lower where the governance system is already shareholder-friendly.

Impact of the Financial Crisis

The financial crisis starting in 2007 represented a major challenge for NIFs. During the height of the crisis there was even speculation that the era of growth for NIFs, and with that an important aspect of financialization, had come to an end. First, the collapse in equity prices, which in terms of severity was approximating the stock market crash of 1929, hit HFs and SWFs hard, as many were invested heavily in stock markets. Activist HFs were particularly affected, as many were in fact 'long only'. PE was also affected by this decline, as a shift to risk aversion on financial markets made it impossible to exit their portfolio companies through IPOs. Second, as banks came under pressure, they started liquidating their loans to HFs and stopped providing leverage to PE for new buy-outs and refinancing old loans. Third, companies in which NIFs were invested came under pressure as their sales decreased. This was especially problematic for PE portfolio companies with high debt levels due to the large fixed payment obligations for interest and amortization. During the height of the crisis, one widely-cited study estimated that 50 per cent of PE portfolio companies would default on their debt (BCG-IESE 2008). Finally, widespread demands were made for stronger financial regulation which would prohibit some of the high risk strategies pursued by NIFs.

Of the three NIF types, HFs came under the greatest pressure. Investors withdrew their investments in HFs on a large scale: first because of disappointment that many funds did not fulfil their promise of returns uncorrelated with equity markets and second because some investors needed to raise funds and investments in HFs could be withdrawn fairly easily.[9] HF AUM, which had reached a total of $2.2 trillion in 2007, collapsed to $1.6 trillion in 2008. Many HFs went bankrupt and it was estimated that up to half of all funds would have to close as a result of the crisis (Reuters 2009).

Private equity was better insulated than HFs against investor withdrawals, since financial commitments are typically made on a multi-year basis, frequently for ten to twelve years. However, new fundraising came to a halt during 2009 and many portfolio companies were revalued downwards. As a result total PE AUM stagnated during the crisis. Due to investor perception of higher risk of PE, the shares of publicly-listed PE firms declined more than the market average. It was speculated that a shakeout in the industry had started and many PE houses would not be able to start new funds or would even have to shut down.

Sovereign wealth fund equity investments also suffered during the crisis, and total AUM decreased by over $100 billion between 2008 and 2009. The near collapse of Dubai World, an investment arm for the Dubai government, led to speculation that more SWFs might come under pressure due to their heavy investments in real estate. However, in practice, SWFs are the most insulated of the three fund types from the crisis, due to their dedicated income streams, and there was no speculation about a 'shakeout' among that type of NIF.

However, as financial markets bounced back after reaching lows in March 2009 the prospects for NIFs improved. PE and SWFs already set new records for AUM by 2010 of $2.5 and $4.4 trillion, respectively. The HF industry recovered much more slowly, but in 2012 a large influx of new investment came in and, with the rise in world stock markets, by the end of the year a new high in HF total AUM was achieved.

It therefore appears that the financial crisis represented just a pause in the importance of NIFs, as institutional investor appetites for the kinds of returns HFs and PE promise remain high. Investments in PE and HFs are expected to diversify risks because of the low correlation of returns with stocks and bonds and to achieve higher returns than traditional investments. In particular, pension funds with defined benefit plans are under pressure to make high returns since their obligations are fixed; however, the value of their equity investments decreased during the crisis at the same time that the size of the workforce contributing to either company or public pension funds decreased. Insurance companies, with products with fixed annuities, are also under great pressure to realize high returns. Surveys of institutional investors indicate that they would like to continue to increase their allocations to PE and HFs (Preqin 2013a, 2013b). Even though there have been questions raised regarding the extent to which PE and HFs as an investment class outperform public equities (Lack 2012; Phalippou and Gottschalg 2009), institutional investors still believe in their ability to pick the higher performing PE and HFs.

Although the funding base for SWFs is very different, there is no indication that sponsoring governments are fundamentally re-thinking the logic of using SWFs as financial vehicles. Furthermore, short of a major collapse in commodity prices, there is no indication that there will be a reduction in the streams of new funding going into SWFs.

Thus, in general, the indications are that NIFs will continue to grow in significance as financial actors in the foreseeable future.

The introduction of new regulations on PE and HFs in Europe and the USA of course represent a significant change in the regulatory environment for these industries (Ernst & Young 2012, Fairless 2010). The cost of compliance with risk management and reporting requirements are supporting a process of concentration, particularly among HFs. The amount of leverage used by PE and HFs is also considerably lower than the levels used before the crisis. As a result, these funds should become somewhat more stable than was the case in the past, when they had a higher degree of leverage. It also appears that many SWFs are slowly converging to practices of institutional investors such as pension funds. For example, SWFs have responded at least to some extent to public criticism, for example by signing the Santiago Principles, a set of twenty-four voluntary 'best practice' guidelines which include increasing transparency (IWG 2008). Thus, although the behaviour of NIFs may change somewhat in comparison to that before the crisis, the basic strategies and mechanisms for intervention will remain. Like a phoenix arising from the ashes, NIFs have more than recovered from the crisis and would seem to be back on a growth path.

Conclusion

This book has gathered and analysed a considerable amount of evidence on NIFs and their impact. It has shown that these funds have become significant actors and will in all likelihood continue to be important or to increase in importance in the foreseeable future. It has argued against simplistic views which see all of these funds as either 'angels' or 'demons', as such views do not do justice to the fund heterogeneity. It has shown that, although a portion of PE buy-outs may lead to employment increases in the long run, on balance, these funds put pressure on labour. They have also likely contributed to inequality, both through performance pay systems on the one hand and high pay for top PE and HF managers on the other.[10] Furthermore, although PE and HFs cannot bear a first order blame for the financial crisis, the leverage used directly by HFs and the high debt incurred by PE portfolio companies likely contributed to the fragility of the financial system. A looming refinancing crisis for many PE portfolio companies indicates potential dangers for the employees of these companies in the next few years, if this debt is not successfully refinanced.

However, the evidence on many of the impacts of NIFs remains limited. Most statistical studies (and the only ones dealing with employment impacts) are on PE. However, almost all the econometric studies with archival data are on the USA and the UK, and thus the evidence of the comparative impact of labour institutions remains sketchy. The country studies reported in this book provide documentary and case study based evidence on the impact of NIFs, and as such deepen our understanding of processes and effects. They show, for instance, that strong labour regulation can have a major impact on the bargaining process. Nevertheless, further cross-nationally comparative studies of a statistical nature would help to shed more light on the net impact of these institutions.

Even less is known about activist HFs and their impact. For comparative work, a big constraint is a 'small numbers' problem, as the vast bulk of activist HF interventions occur in the USA, and most of the rest in a handful of countries. However, research on a broader set of outcomes could also be done, as statistical studies of activist HFs focus mainly on short-term share price development; only a few consider long-term impacts and none specifically look at the impact on labour. The chapters in this book have to varying extents reported cases of HF activism which appear to have had some impact, albeit usually indirect, on labour. There is a need to build on the insights arising from case study investigations to develop larger-scale statistical and comparative investigations. One possible aid to researchers is the recently implemented requirements for registration and greater transparency by HFs. In the USA, under the Dodd–Frank financial reform legislation, HFs must provide the Securities and Exchange Commission with information about their assets, investments, and risk profile. Much of this information is made available to the public, and this new data should be of use to researchers in studying HFs.

The least is known about SWFs, despite the fact that they have become by far the largest type of NIF and continue to have a more rapid growth rate in AUM than PE or HFs. For example, there is no statistical study on the impact of SWF investments on labour, and the only known case studies were done by contributors to this volume. This is partially because of the low level of transparency of these funds and their strategies, but also because they have only recently emerged on the radar screen of researchers. However, data on their investments are available from other sources, for example information on large shareholdings from national securities regulators. A major research challenge is to understand the changing strategies of SWFs, for example through the signing of the Santiago Principles mentioned above.

Further research could not only help fill in some of the gaps in our understanding of NIFs and their impacts, but also inform a number of theoretical perspectives, particularly those of corporate financialization and comparative capitalisms. The financial crisis and regulatory steps taken in response to it have raised important questions. For example, it appears that the broad financialization process may have reversed on some indicators, such as the level of household debt in the USA. The research reported in this book suggests that financialization is a complex process and some of its dimensions are not highly correlated across countries, and this may also apply to trends, at least in the short run.

Regarding the comparative capitalisms perspective, a more systematic examination of NIFs in different contexts could help VoC further develop some of the weaker points in its theory, including the issue of institutional change and the role of the state. The VoC literature has also focused for the most part on the advanced industrialized countries, and the growing activity of NIFs outside of these countries offers the opportunity for VoC to expand its research to a wider variety of countries and institutional settings. The area of NIFs will thus continue to be an important area for research and public policy into the future.

NOTES

1. Sweden experienced a slight decrease in this period, from 22.5 to 21.8 per cent of total value added.
2. In 2007 pension funds in Germany and Poland were only allowed to invest up to 10 per cent of their total assets in collective investment funds; in Italy this figure was 20 per cent.

3. Some PE was originally established by the state, e.g. 3i, one of the biggest PE firms, was created by the British government after the Second World War to provide long-term finance to industry. However, for the most part, state ownership is currently restricted to the VC side of PE as a part of national innovation policy.

4. The Sovereign Wealth Fund Institute ranks the Alaska Permanent Fund, Texas Permanent School Fund, and Alabama Trust Fund, which have dedicated revenues from oil and gas, as among the world's largest SWFs (see <http://www.swfinstitute.org/fund-rankings/>).

5. The correlation coefficient between PE and SWFs as a percentage of GDP is –0.19 and between HFs and SWFs only –0.003.

6. Based on own calculations.

7. General criticisms of VoC which show the difficulty of applying it to our questions include: the lack of propositions regarding institutional change; the absence of a role for state action and public policy; and an identification of ideal firm types with countries, which obfuscates the degree of heterogenity within countries.

8. Own analysis based on the PE and HF data described above and pension fund data from the OECD pension fund project (<www.oecd.org>).

9. Investments in most HFs can typically be withdrawn with sufficient notice at the end of each financial quarter.

10. The Chief Executive Officers (CEOs) of the largest PE houses and HFs can earn billions of dollars annually. Collectively, the highest earning HF managers received $16.7 billion in 2012. The highest reported annual fee of an NIF CEO was John Paulson, who was reported to have earned $4.9 billion in 2010 (Forbes 2013). More than half of the members of Forbes' list of the 400 richest Americans in 2007 were PE and HF managers (Finfacts Team 2007).

BIBLIOGRAPHY

Acharya, V. and Kehoe, C. (2008). 'Corporate Governance and Value Creation: Evidence from Private Equity', Working Paper, London: London Business School.

Amess, K. and Wright, M. (2007a). 'Barbarians at the Gate? Leveraged Buyouts, Private Equity and Jobs', Working Paper, Nottingham: Nottingham University.

Amess, K. and Wright, M. (2007b). 'The wage and employment effects of leveraged buy-outs in the UK', *International Journal of the Economics of Business*, 14 (2): 179–95.

Amess, K., Girma, S., and Wright, M. (2008). 'What are the Wage and Employment Consequences of Leveraged Buyouts, Private Equity and Acquisitions in the UK?', NUBS Research Paper Series, 2008-01, Nottingham: Nottingham University.

Aoki, M. and Dinc, S. (2000). 'Relational financing as an institution and its viability under competition', in M. Aoki, and S. Dinc (eds), *Finance, Governance, and Competitiveness in Japan*. Oxford: Oxford University Press, 19–42.

Aslan, H. and Maraachlian, H. (2009). 'Wealth Effects of Hedge Fund Activism', <http://ssrn.com/abstract=1343403>.

Assa, J. (2012). 'Financialization and its consequences: The OECD experience', *Finance Research*, 1 (1): 35–9.

Bacon, N., Wright, M., and Demina, N. (2004). 'Management buyouts and human resource management', *British Journal of Industrial Relations*, 42 (2): 325–47.

Bacon, N., Wright, M., Meuleman, M., and Scholes, L. (2012). 'The impact of private equity on management practices in European buy-outs: Short-termism, Anglo-Saxon, or host country effects?', *Industrial Relations*, April, 51: 605–26.

Becht, M., Franks, J., and Grant, J. (2010a). 'Hedge Fund Activism in Europe', ECGI Working Paper Series in Finance, 283/2010, May, <http://papers.ssrn.com/sol3/papers.cfm?abstract_id=1616340>.

Becht, M., Franks, J., and Grant, J. (2010b). 'Unfulfilled expectations? The Returns to International Hedge Fund Activism', The tenth European Corporate Governance Conference, 6–7 December, Brussels.

Bergström, C., Grubb, M., and Jonsson, S. (2007). 'The operating impact of buyouts in Sweden: A study of value creation', *Journal of Private Equity*, 11: 22–39.

BCG and IESE (2008). 'Get ready for the Private Equity Shakeout: Will this be the next Shock to the Global Economy?', December, Boston Consultung Group (BCG) and IESE Business School.

Boucly, Q., Sraer, D., and Thesmar, D. (2011). 'Growth LBOs', *Journal of Financial Economics*, 102: 432–53.

Brav, A., Jiang, W., Partnoy, F., and Thomas, R. (2008). 'The returns to hedge fund activism', *Financial Analysts Journal*, November / December, 64 (6): 45.

Chaplinsky, S., Niehaus, G., and Van de Gucht, L. (1998). 'Employee buy-outs: Causes, Structure, and consequences', *Journal of Financial Economics*, 48: 283–332.

Coval, J. and Moskowitz, T (1999). 'Home bias at home: local equity preferences in domestic portfolios', *Journal of Finance*, 54: 2045–73.

Cressy, R., Munari, F., and Malipiero, A. (2008). 'Creative Destruction? UK Evidence that Buyouts Cut Jobs to Raise Returns', Working Paper, Birmingham, Bologna: University of Birmingham, University of Bologna.

Davis, S., Haltiwanger, J., Jarmin, R., Lerner, J., and Miranda, J. (2008). 'Private Equity and Employment', Working Paper, <http://ssrn.com/abstract=1107175?.

Dealbook (2010). 'Private equity firms reap big fees: Report says', *New York Times*, 1 November.

Dore, R. (2008). 'Financialization of the global economy', *Industrial and Corporate Change*, 17: 1097–112.

Ernst & Young (2012). *Global Hedge Fund and Investor Survey 2012*. London: Ernst & Young.

Fairless, T. (2010). 'Private equity set for consolidation', *New York Times*, 1 February.

Fichtner, J. (2009). 'Activist Hedge Funds and the Erosion of Rhenish Capitalism: The Impact of Impatient Capital', Working Paper, 17, CCGES CCEAE: York University / Université de Montréal.

Finfacts Team (2007). 'Hedge fund and private equity managers make up more than half the Forbes list of the 400 richest Americans in 2007', Finfacts, 21 September.

Forbes (2013). 'John Paulson', The World's Billionaires, <http://www.forbes.com/profile/john-paulson/>.

Freeman, R. (2010). 'It's financialization!', *International Labour Review*, 149 (2): 163–83.

Giannetti, M. and Laeven, L. (2009). 'Pension reform, ownership structure, and corporate governance: evidence from a natural experiment', *Review of Financial. Studies*, 22 (10): 4091–127.

Goergen, M., O'Sullivan, N., and Wood, G. (2011). 'Private Equity Takeovers and Employment in the UK: Some Empirical Evidence', Finance Working Paper, 310/2011, Brussels: European Corporate Governance Institute.

Gospel, H., Pendleton, A., Vitols, S., and Wilke, P. (2010). 'The Impact of Investment Funds on Restructuring Practices and Employment Levels', European Foundation for the Improvement of Living and Working Conditions, Dublin, 1–103.

Hall, P. and Soskice, D. (2001). *Varieties of Capitalism: The Institutional Foundations of Comparative Advantage*. Oxford: Oxford University Press.

Huffschmid, J., Köppen, M., and Rhode, W. (2007). *Finanzinvestoren: Retter oder Raubritter?: Neue Herausforderungen durch die internationalen Kapitalmärkte*. VSA: Hamburg.

IWG (2008). *Sovereign Wealth Funds: Generally Accepted Principles and Practices, 'Santiago Principles'*. Washington: International Working Group of Sovereign Wealth Funds (IWG).

Jensen, M. (1989). 'Eclipse of the public corporation', *Harvard Business Review*, October–September: 64–5.

Judge, W., Gaur, A., and Muller-Kahle, M. (2010). 'Antecedents of share-holder activism in target firms: evidence from a multi-country study', *Corporate Governance: An International Review*, 18 (4): 258–73.

Kaplan, S. (1989). 'The effects of management buyouts on operating performance and value', *Journal of Financial Economics*, 24: 217–54.

Katelouzou, D. (2013). 'Myths and realities of hedge fund activism: Some empirical evidence'. *Virginia Law & Business Review*, 3 April, 7 (3), forthcoming, <http://ssrn.com/abstract=2152351>.

Kay, J. (2012). *The Kay Review of UK Equity Markets and Long-Term Decision Making.* London: Department of Business, Innovation, and Skills.

Krippner, G. (2011). *Capitalizing on Crisis: The Political Origins of the Rise of Finance.* Cambridge, MA: Harvard University Press.

Lack, S. (2012). *The Hedge Fund Mirage.* New York: John Wiley & Sons.

Lichtenberg, F. and Siegel, D. (1990). 'The effects of leveraged buyouts on productivity and related aspects of firm behaviour', *Journal of Financial Economics*, 27: 164–94.

Liebeskind, J., Wiersema, M., and Hansen, G. (1992). 'LBOs, corporate restructuring, and the incentive-intensity hypothesis', *Financial Management*, 21 (1): 73–88.

Lutz, E. and Achleitner, A.-K. (2009). 'Angels or demons? Evidence on the impact of private equity firms on employment', *Zeitschrift für Betriebswirtschaft (ZfB)*, Special Issue Entrepreneurial Finance, 5: 53–81.

Malkiel, B. (2013). 'Asset management fees and the growth of finance', *Journal of Economic Perspectives*, 27 (2): 97–108.

Malone, S. (1989). 'Characteristics of smaller company leveraged buyouts' *Journal of Business Venturing*, 4: 349–59.

Marti Pellon, J., Alemany, L., Zieling, N., and Salas de la Hera, M. (2007). 'Economic and Social Impact of Venture Capital & Private Equity in Spain 2007', ASCRI Research Paper, Madrid.

Muscarella, C. and Vetsuypens, M. (1990). 'Efficiency and organizational structure: A study of reverse LBOs', *Journal of Finance*, 65 (5): 1389–413.

Nölke, A. and Vliegenthart, A. (2009). 'Enlarging the varieties of capitalism: The emergence of dependent market economies in east central Europe', *World Politics*, October, 61 (4): 670–702.

OECD (2007). *Pension Fund Investment in Hedge Funds.* Paris: Organization for Economic Co-operation and Development (OECD).

OECD (2011). *Divided we Stand: Why Inequality Keeps Rising.* Paris: Organisation for Economic Co-operation and Development (OECD).

OECD (2013). *National Accounts at a Glance 2013*, Paris: Organization for Economic Co-operation and Development (OECD).

Olsson, M. and Tåg, J. (2012). 'Private Equity and Employees', IFN Working Paper, 906, Stockholm: Institutet för Näringslivsforskning.

Phalippou, L. and Gottschalg, O. (2009). 'Performance of private equity funds', *Review of Financial Studies*, 22 (4): 1747–76.

Phillippon, T. and Reshef, A. (2013). 'An international look at the growth of modern finance', *Journal of Economic Perspectives*, 27 (2): 73–96.

Pontusson, J. (1992). *Limits of Social Democracy: Investment Politics in Sweden.* New York: Cornell University Press.

Preqin (2012). *The 2012 Prequin Sovereign Wealth Fund Review*. London, New York, Singapore, Redwood Vally: Preqin.

Preqin (2013a). *The 2013 Preqin Global Private Equity Report*. February, 9(2), London, New York, Singapore, Redwood Vally: Preqin.

Preqin (2013b). 'Hedge Fund Spotlight', Newsletter, 5(1), January, <http://www.preqin.com/docs/newsletters/HF/Hedge_Fund_Spotlight_January_2013.pdf>.

PriceWaterhouseCoopers (2010). *A Second Wind: The Regulation, Taxation and Distribution of Hedge Funds around the Globe*. London: PriceWaterhouseCoopers.

Reuters (2009). 'Hedge funds' second act'. Statements from Ken Kinsey-Quick, 18 March.

Smith, A. (1990). 'Corporate ownership structure and performance', *Journal of Financial Economics*, 27: 143–64.

Stockhammer, E. (2012). 'Financialization, income distribution and the crisis', *Investigacion Economica*, 71 (279): 39–70.

Stokman, W. A. Nick (2008). 'Influences of Hedge Fund Activism on the Medium Term Target Firm Value', Working Paper, Erasmus University Rotterdam.

The CityUK (2013). *Sovereign Wealth Funds*, London: The CityUK.

Toubeau, V. (2006). 'Private Equity Firms in Belgium: Value Creators or Locusts?', Working Paper, Unpublished Document, Brussels: Solvay Business School.

Uchida, Konari and Peng Xu (2008). 'U.S. Barbarians at the Japan Gate: Cross border Hedge Fund Activism', Working Paper, The Bank of Japan.

Weir, C., Jones, P., and Wright, M. (2008). 'Public to Private Transactions, Private Equity and Performance in the UK: An Empirical Analysis of the Impact of Going Private', Working Paper, Robert Gordon University and University of Nottingham.

Xu, J. and Li, Y. (2010). 'Hedge Fund Activism and Bank Loan Contracting', AFA 2011 Denver Meetings Paper, 18 February.

Index

Index